Visual C++ Optimization
with Assembly Code

VISUAL C++ OPTIMIZATION WITH ASSEMBLY CODE

alist

YURY MAGDA

A-LIST, LLC
295 East Swedesford Rd.
PMB #285
Wayne, PA 19087
702-977-5377 (FAX)
mail@alistpublishing.com
http://www.alistpublishing.com

This book is printed on acid-free paper.

Visual C++ Optimization with Assembly Code
By Yury Magda

ISBN 1-931769-32-X

Printed in the United States of America

04 05 7 6 5 4 3 2 1

A-LIST, LLC, titles are available for site license or bulk purchase by institutions, user groups, corporations, etc.

Contents

Preface

The evolution of software development tools during the past few decades is astonishing for anyone involved in software development. This is especially true in creating applications for the Windows operating system family. Modern tools make it possible to create an application with a few mouse clicks, and this often allows a programmer to save weeks or even months of tedious work. In fact, each development environment contains application wizards that can create an application with particular features.

As one of the most powerful development tools, the Microsoft Visual C++ .NET development environment offers the programmer a wide variety of features for the development of applications of any type and level of complexity. Nevertheless, most serious applications are written with much manual work. This is because none of the high-level language development tools can provide maximum performance. This is the truth based on the structure and semantics of high-level languages.

A possible solution to the application optimization problem is the use of assembly language. Note that it is possible to write an application without using this language. There are many programs that do not require optimization. However, with regard to real-time applications, device drivers, multimedia applications, sound processing applications, graphics applications, and any applications, for which the time of execution is important, the use of assembly language is inevitable because no other optimization method will work.

In essence, assembly language is the language of the processor, and it will disappear only when processors disappear! That is why assembly language has one basic advantage over high level languages (and it always will): It is the quickest. Most applications working in real time are either written in assembly language or use assembly modules in crucial parts of code.

Many programmers who write in high level languages are afraid of using the assembler in their work. Programmers sometimes complain that assembly language is too complicated and difficult to learn; however, this is not true. Assembly language is no more complicated than other programming languages, and both experienced programmers and novices can easily learn it.

Also, powerful tools for the development of applications in the assembler appeared recently. This allows us look at the development of applications in this language from another point of view. Among such development tools are MASM32 macro assembler, AsmStudio, and NASM. These and other tools combine the flexibility and speed of assembly language and an up-to-date graphic interface. Numerous function libraries created for assembly language made this language's properties close to those of high-level application development tools. Therefore, there are no concrete reasons for the contraposition of assembly language to high level languages on the basis of its complexity.

This book will focus on the use of assembly language in programs created with Visual C++ .NET 2003, currently the most powerful C++ development environment. The material of this book will disclose two relatively independent aspects of using it as a stand-alone tool for creating individual procedures in the form of object modules and as a built-in tool integrated in C++ .NET. Microsoft continually improves the inline assembler.

This book is not a tutorial on assembly language, nor on C++ .NET. It assumes that you have a certain knowledge of these programming areas.

To create applications in Windows successfully, you should know the basics of how applications run in this operating system. You do not have to know the Windows architecture in detail because all of the necessary information is given when discussing the code of examples.

This book is intended to be a practice aid for programmers who wish to know more about programming in assembly language. Programmers writing in Visual C++ .NET will find much useful information for their work.

The book includes many examples with subsequent dissection of their code, with the belief that every theoretical issue should be supported with an example of code. It is the most effective and fastest way to learn how to write programs. Some of the examples are unique programs that cannot be found anywhere else.

All the examples were tested and run correctly. Long and complicated programs are avoided here because it would be easy to overlook key issues when analyzing such programs. Each example is designed so that it is easy to modify for use in your projects.

Visual C++ .NET 2003 was chosen as a development tool.Regarding examples in assembly language, Microsoft MASM is used. It is recommended that you use MASM32, which includes Microsoft compiler and linker. The compiler is ML version 6.14, and the linker is LINK version 5.12.

All examples use a simplified syntax of assembly language and as few high-level constructions as possible. Only the information necessary for work is provided, rather than a comprehensive description of the MASM compiler. Readers who wish to gain a deeper knowledge of this compiler will find ample information in other sources.

The material is presented in a logical order and avoids both excessive code and unnecessary theorizing. It is difficult to look at all aspects of software optimization in Windows in one book. Nevertheless, I believe the material of this book will be useful for programmers.

The Structure of the Book

This book is intended as a practice aid on C++ .NET 2003 program optimization with assembly language. Two main aspects of using this language are considered. First, assembly language can be used as a stand-alone tool for the development of individual modules. Stand-alone compilers make it possible to create both completed applications and individual object modules and function libraries that are widely used when developing applications on C++ .NET.

Second, the C++ .NET 2003 development environment includes powerful tools for programming in the inline assembly language. This book will discuss pros and cons of using the stand-alone compiler and the inline assembler.

The book is designed so that it is possible to study the material both selectively (through individual chapters) and sequentially, starting from the first chapter. This is convenient, because different readers can choose the material, in which they are interested. Both novice and experienced users will find necessary information in this book.

The practical side of using assembly language is emphasized to increase the performance of applications. Numerous examples allow you to better understand the principles of application development and optimization, and necessary theoretical material is given in the context of the examples. The tools of the assembler and high level languages are described only to the extent necessary to understand the material. It is not necessary to provide comprehensive reference material on the compiler and linkers of the macro assembler and C++ .NET in this book, because this material is covered in numerous books and user manuals.

The examples of programs are designed so that they demonstrate key techniques of using assembly language. Generally, each example highlights one aspect of using assembly language. Therefore, the algorithms of such programs are simple, and the programs themselves are small. I did not write large applications and did not try to optimize as much as possible in one application intentionally. Each complicated application has its unique way to increase performance, and various combinations of particular methods are possible.

This book demonstrates how to use "building blocks" of optimization: assembly language of the MMX and SSE extensions, assembler analogs of C++ library functions, string primitive commands, and many others.

Practically all the examples are based on the C++ .NET 2003 sample console application. To develop object modules with assembly code, Microsoft MASM 6.14 macro assembler and C++ .NET 2003 inline assembly compiler are used.

The code of the examples is designed so that you can use it in your work. The examples provided are intended to be very practical for programmers.

The book consists of 15 chapters briefly described below.

❏ *Chapter 1: "Developing Efficient Program Code."* This chapter discusses general issues of accelerating computational algorithms with assembly language. Program code is analyzed with consideration of the architecture of up-to-date processors. The basic principles of FPU, MMX, and SSE technologies are discussed.

❏ *Chapter 2: "Optimizing Calculation Algorithms."* The material of this chapter is devoted to the most important aspects of assembly language from the point of view of increasing performance. Algorithms for processing mathematical expressions, data arrays, and strings are discussed. The capabilities of the mathematical coprocessor and the use of string-processing commands are demonstrated.

❏ *Chapter 3: "Developing and Using Procedures in Assembly Language."* This chapter discusses development and optimization of subroutines in assembly language. Different methods of data processing and the use of registers and memory are discussed. In this context, the material of the chapter complements *Chapter 2*. General issues of the interface of procedures written completely in assembly language to high-level languages are also discussed in this chapter. As in the previous chapter, numerous examples illustrate the material.

❏ *Chapter 4: "Optimizing C++ Logical Structures with Assembly Language."* In this chapter, much attention is given to optimization of the most important constructions of C++ .NET: loops and conditional statements. Practical examples illustrate different methods for implementing these constructions in assembly language.

❏ *Chapter 5: "Assembly Module Interface to C++ Programs."* This chapter looks at the use of separately compiled assembly modules in C++ programs. Building the interface of such modules to applications developed in C++ .NET 2003 is discussed. Calling standards and conventions are analyzed in detail; theoretical material is supported with examples.

❏ *Chapter 6: "Developing and Using Assembly Subroutines."* While *Chapter 5* looks at the main standards and conventions used when linking assembly modules with C++ .NET applications, this chapter gives further consideration to using parameters and choosing the methods of passing parameters to assembly functions.

❏ *Chapter 7: "Linking Assembly Modules with C++ .NET Programs."* This chapter comprehensively discusses linking C++ .NET programs with stand-alone assembly modules. It considers issues that have almost never been discussed in literature such as linking applications with assembly modules.

❏ *Chapter 8: "Dynamic Link Libraries and Their Development in Assembly Language."* Dynamic link libraries are one of the most important components of Windows. They contain many procedures and are a powerful tool for writing effective programs. The chapter discusses practical aspects of creating and using DLLs. Methods of creating DLLs in assembly language and C++ .NET are described.

❏ *Chapter 9: "Basic Structures of Visual C ++ .NET 2003 Inline Assembler."* This chapter discusses the use of the C++ .NET inline assembly language to develop high-performance applications. The inline assembly language is a powerful tool for increasing application performance, and it has many advantages over stand-alone compilers. The program architecture of the C++ .NET inline assembler and its relation to C++ main structures are examined.

☐ *Chapter 10: " Inline Assembler and Application Optimization. MMX and SSE Technologies."* Practical aspects of using the C++ .NET inline assembler are illustrated with examples of implementation of computational tasks. The issues of assembly extensions for the MMX and SSE technologies in the context of programming in C++ .NET have never been discussed in literature.

☐ *Chapter 11: "Optimizing Multimedia Applications with Assembly Language."* This chapter looks at using assembly language in multimedia applications. It describes a few methods of optimization of multimedia applications using assembly language. Theoretical material is supported with practical examples.

☐ *Chapter 12: "Optimizing Multithread Applications with Assembly Language."* The concept of multithreading in Windows is the basis for this family of operating systems. The use of threads allows a programmer to make an application simpler and use the advantages of parallel processing. Using assembly language in multi-threaded applications can provide additional increase in performance. These issues are discussed in this chapter.

☐ *Chapter 13: "C++ Inline Assembler and Windows Time Functions."* Most of applications that run in Windows use timers and time functions. Time functions are necessary when it comes to real-time operations, or when writing device drivers and multimedia applications. In this chapter, practical examples illustrate how to use the inline assembler to improve the performance of real-time applications.

☐ *Chapter 14: "Using Assembly Language for System Programming in Windows."* This chapter looks at methods for optimization of system programming tasks in the Windows family of operating systems. The chapter demonstrates a few aspects of optimizing file operations, memory management, and inter-process communication.

☐ *Chapter 15: "Optimizing Procedure-Oriented Applications and System Services."* This chapter discusses the principles of using the C++ .NET 2003 inline assembly language in procedure-oriented Windows applications and system services. The use of assembly language in each of these types of applications has peculiarities that are demonstrated in this chapter.

The material of this book is complemented with a reference on Intel processor command set. Since the complete command set includes hundreds of commands, only the most frequently used commands are listed. The CD-ROM accompanying this book will be also very useful. It contains all the examples given in the book.

I am very grateful to the staff at A-LIST Publishing for preparing this book for publication.

Special thanks to my wife Julie for invaluable help and support.

Introduction

This book covers issues of using assembler language to optimize C++ software created in the Visual Studio .NET environment. In terms of software development and debugging, "optimization" means improving some of the software product's performance characteristics. In addition, the term often implies a system of measures aimed at improving software performance.

The optimization process itself may be performed either by the developer (manual optimization) or automatically (by the compiler of the development environment, in which the application is debugged). It is also possible for the developer to use a third-party debugger to debug and optimize the program.

Most developers are aware that under the pressure of tough competition, performance issues have become a crucial factor determining the success or failure of an application in the software market. So without serious work on improving a program code's performance, it is impossible to ensure that the application will be competitive. And although everyone recognizes the necessity and importance of software optimization, it still remains a controversial issue. Disputes in this area are mainly related to the following question: Is it really necessary for a developer to choose to optimize his or her application manually when there are ready-made, dedicated hardware and software tools for this task?

Some developers consider it impossible to improve an application's performance without using the debugging functionality of the compiler itself, especially given that all modern compilers have built-in tools for optimizing program code. In part, this really is the case, as today all existing development tools presuppose the use of optimizing algorithms when generating an executable module.

It is possible to rely completely on the compiler ("everything has been done in advance"), and expect it to generate optimal code without making any effort to improve the program quality. In many cases, the code needs no further revision at all. For example, small office applications or network testing utilities usually need no optimization.

But in most cases, you cannot rely completely on the standard compiler features and skip manual optimization of the program. Whether you like it or not, you will have to face the problem of improving performance when developing more serious applications, such as databases or all sorts of client-server and network applications. In most cases of this type, your development environment's optimizing compiler will not make a big difference.

If you develop real-time applications such as hardware drivers, system services, or industrial applications, the task cannot even be completed without serious work on manual code optimization to ensure the best possible performance. Not because the development tools are not perfect and do not provide the required level of optimization, but because any complex program includes a great number of interrelated parameters, which no development tool can improve better than the developer. The optimization process is more akin to an art than to "pure" programming, and thus it is difficult to describe it in terms of a universal procedure.

The process of improving an application's performance is usually difficult and time-consuming. There is no single criterion, by which we can characterize optimization. Moreover, the optimization process itself is quite controversial: For example, when you manage to reduce the program's memory usage, you achieve this at the cost of its speed.

No program can be extremely fast, have minimum size, and provide the user with full-scale functionality at the same time. It is impossible to write such an "ideal" application, although it is possible to bring the application close to this ideal.

In good applications, these characteristics are usually combined in reasonable proportions, depending on what is more important for the particular project: speed, program size (meaning both the size of the application file and its memory usage), or, say, a convenient user interface.

For most office applications, an extremely important factor is a convenient user interface and as much functionality as possible. For example, for a person using an electronic telephone directory, a response that is 10% faster or slower does not make a big difference. The size of such an application does not generally matter much either, as hard drive capacities are now large enough to hold dozens and even hundreds of such electronic database systems. The working program may need dozens of megabytes of RAM, but this does not present a problem today either. What is crucial for such an application is to provide the user with convenient ways to manipulate the data.

For an application using the client/server model for data processing and user interaction (for example, most network applications), the optimization criteria will be different. In this case, priority will be given to issues of memory usage (in particular, for the server side of the application) and optimization of client-side interaction via the network.

With real-time applications, the crucial point is synchronization in receiving, processing, and possibly transferring data in reasonable time intervals. As a rule, in such programs you will need to optimize the level of CPU usage and synchronization with the operating system. If you are a system programmer developing drivers or services for working with an operating system such as Windows 2000, then inefficient program code will at best slow down the whole system performance, and at worst could be beyond imagination.

As you can see, improving an application's performance may be determined by different factors. In each case, the criteria are selected depending on the application's purpose.

Optimization Methods

Let's now focus on optimization methods, and compare different approaches that can help you increase application performance.

Hardware Optimization

The simplest way to make an application run faster is to upgrade your computer to a faster processor or add more memory. When you upgrade the hardware, the performance problem is resolved by itself.

Using this approach, you will most probably reach deadlock, as you will always depend on hardware solutions. Incidentally, many of the expectations of the performance of new-generation processors, and new memory types and system bus architectures have been greatly exaggerated. In practical work, their performance is not as good as the manufacturers' declarations. For instance, new memory chips usually have greater data-storage capacities, but are not faster than preceding models. The same goes for hard drives: Their performance is improving more slowly than their capacity.

If you develop commercial applications, you should take into account that users will not necessarily have the latest processor model and fast memory chips. In addition, many of them will not be willing to invest in a new computer if they are quite satisfied with what they have.

So you can hardly rely on solving software problems solely by acquiring new equipment.

For this reason, let's now turn to methods of increasing performance using only algorithmic and programming methods.

Algorithmic and Program Methods

When optimizing an application, you will need to consider the following issues:

☐ Thorough elaboration of the algorithm of the program you are developing
☐ Available computer hardware and getting the most out of it
☐ Tools provided by the high-level language of the environment in which you are developing the application

❏   Using the low-level assembler language
❏   Making use of specific processor characteristics

Let's now look at each of these issues in greater detail.

Improving the Algorithm

Developing the algorithm for your future application is the most complicated part of the whole lifecycle of the program. The depth, at which you think out all the aspects of your task, will largely influence how successfully it is implemented as program code. Generally, changes in the structure of the program itself can produce a much greater effect than fine-tuning the program code. There are no ideal solutions, so there are always some mistakes or defects that may occur when the algorithm is developed. Here, it is important to find algorithm bottlenecks that have the greatest effect upon the program's performance.

Moreover, practical experience shows that almost in all cases, you can find a way to improve the program algorithm after it is ready. It is certainly much better if you work out the algorithm thoroughly at the very beginning of the development process, as this will save you a great deal of trouble on revising program code fragments in the short term. So do not try to save time on developing the program algorithm, and this will help you spare headaches when debugging and testing the program, thus saving time later on.

You should also bear in mind that an algorithm efficient in relation to application performance will never correspond completely to the task specification, and vice versa. Many well-structured and legible algorithms are often inefficient when it comes to implementation of the program code. One reason is that the developer tries to simplify the overall structure of the program by using multiple-level nested calculation structures wherever it's possible, and in this case a simpler algorithm inevitably leads to a loss of application performance.

When you start to develop an algorithm, it is difficult to envisage what the program code will look like. To develop a program algorithm correctly, you should stick to the following simple guidelines:

1. Study the application's purpose thoroughly.
2. Determine the main requirements of the application and present them in a formalized way.
3. Decide how to represent incoming and outgoing data, as well as its structure and possible limitations.
4. Based on these parameters, work out the program version (or model) for implementing the task.
5. Choose how you will implement the task.

6. Develop an algorithm to implement the program code. Be careful not to confuse the algorithm for solving the problem and the algorithm for implementing the program code. Generally, these algorithms never coincide. This is the most responsible stage in developing a software product!

7. Develop the source code of the program according to the algorithm for implementing the program code.

8. Debug and test the program code of the application.

You should not stick to these guidelines rigidly, however. In every project, the developer is free to choose how to develop the application. Some stages may be subdivided into further steps, and some of them may be skipped. For minor tasks, you can simply work out an algorithm, then correct it slightly to implement the program code, and debug the program.

When creating large applications, you may need to develop and test several isolated fragments of program code, meaning that you will have to add more detail to the program algorithm.

There are a number of resources that can help you to create the correct algorithm. The principles for building efficient algorithms are already well explored, and there are a lot of good books that cover these issues, such as "The Art of Computer Programming" by D. Knuth.

Achieving Optimal Use of Hardware

Software developers usually want to ensure that application performance should depend as little as possible on computer hardware. Therefore, you should also consider the worst-case scenario, in which the user is working on a very old computer. In this case, "revising" the hardware operation often allows you to find resources to improve the application's performance.

The first thing you need to do is to examine the performance of the hardware components that the program is supposed to use. If you know what works faster and what is slower, this can help you in developing the program. By analyzing system performance, you can find bottlenecks and make the right decision.

Carrying capacity is different for different components of the computer. The fastest are the CPU and RAM, while hard drives and CD-ROMs are relatively slow. Slowest of all are peripherals, such as printers, plotters, or scanners.

Most Windows applications employ a graphical user interface (GUI), and therefore make active use of the computer's graphics features. In this case, when developing an application, you should consider the carrying capacity of the system bus and the computer's graphics subsystem.

Virtually all applications make use of hard disk resources. In most cases, the performance of the disk subsystem has a great effect upon application performance.

If your program uses hard-disk resources — for example, if it writes and moves files quite frequently — then a slow hard drive will inevitably be an obstacle to performance.

One more example. The prevailing use of CPU registers may help you increase performance by reducing system bus traffic when the program works with the RAM. In many cases, you can improve application performance by caching the data. The data cache may be helpful for disk operations, or when working with the mouse, a printing device, etc.

If you are developing a commercial application, you should determine the lowest hardware configuration, on which your program can run. This configuration should be taken into account when planning any optimization measures.

Using this method of optimization usually involves analyzing the program code to find any bottlenecks in the operation of the program. Finding the points at which the program slows down considerably is often a difficult task. In this case, dedicated programs called *profilers* may be helpful.

The purpose of profilers is to determine the performance of an application, help you debug the program, and find points where performance drops considerably. One of the best programs of this kind is Intel's VTune Performance Analyzer, which I recommend for debugging and optimizing your applications.

Using High-Level Language Tools

High-level languages also contain built-in debugging tools. Modern compilers help you detect errors, but give you no information as to the efficiency of a program fragment. That is why it is a good idea to have a helpful profiler at hand.

Manual Optimization

Many developers prefer to debug their programs manually. This is not the worst option if you have a clear idea of how the application works. Anyway, regardless of how you are debugging, it is worth considering the following factors that affect application performance:

❑ *The number of calculations performed by the program.* One factor improving application performance is reducing the number of calculations. When running, the program should not calculate the same value twice. Instead, it should calculate every value only once and store it in the memory for future use. You can achieve considerably better performance by replacing calculations with simply accessing pre-generated value tables.

❑ *Use of mathematical operations.* Any application uses mathematical operations in one way or another. Analyzing the efficiency of these calculations is quite a complicated task, and in different cases can depend on different factors. Better performance can be achieved by using simpler arithmetic operations. Thus, you can replace multiplication and division operations by the corresponding block of addition and subtraction commands whenever possible. If the program uses floating-point operations, then try to avoid integer commands, as they will slow down performance. There is one more nuance: If possible, try to reduce the number of division operations. Performance also drops when mathematical operations are used in loops. Instead of multiplication by 2 raised to a power, you can use the commands for left-shifting bits.

❐ *Use of loop calculations and nested structures.* This concerns the use of loops like WHILE, FOR, SWITCH, and IF. Loop calculations help you simplify the structure of the program, but at the same time reduce its performance. Take a close look at the program code to find calculations using nested structures and loops. The following rules may be helpful for optimizing loops:

● Never use a loop to do what can easily be done without a loop.

● If possible, try to avoid using the jump commands within loops.

You can achieve better performance even by bringing just one or two operators outside the loop. There are some more things you can do to increase program efficiency. For example, you can calculate invariant values outside loops. You can unroll loops, or combine separate loops with the same number of iterations into a single loop. You should also try to reduce the number of commands used in the body of the loop. Also try to reduce the number of cases when a procedure or a subroutine is called from within the loop body, as the processor may slow down when calculating their efficient addresses.

It is also useful to reduce the number of jump commands in the program. To do so, you can, for example, reconstruct the conditional blocks so that the jump condition returns a TRUE condition much less often than a negative. It is also a good idea to place more general conditions to the starting point of the program branching sequence. If your program contains calls followed by returns to the program, it is better to transform them into jumps.

In summary, it is desirable to reduce the number of jumps and calls wherever it's possible, especially at those points of the program where performance is determined only by the processor. To do this, you should organize the program so that it can be executed in a direct (linear) sequence with a minimal number of jump points.

❐ *Implementation of multithreading.* If used correctly, this technique can produce better performance, but otherwise it may slow down the program. Practical experience shows that the use of multithreading is efficient for large applications, whereas smaller programs with multithreading tend to slow down. The possibility of breaking the executed process into several threads is provided by Windows architecture.

Multithreading can be helpful for optimizing programs. You should bear in mind that every thread requires additional memory and processor resources, so this method is unlikely to be effective if hardware performance is not high enough (e.g., if the system has a slow processor or not enough memory).

❐ *Allocation of similar and frequently repeated calculations into separate subroutines (procedures).* There is a widespread opinion that the use of subroutines always increases the application performance, making it possible to reuse the same code fragment for performing similar calculations at different points of the program. This is partially true, as it makes the program easily readable and the algorithm easier to understand. But "from the point of view of the processor," an algorithm with the linear sequence is always (!) more efficient than use of procedures. Every time you use a procedure, the program makes a jump to another memory address, while at the same time storing the address where it should return to the main program on the stack. This always slows down the program. This does not imply that you should reject using subroutines or procedures completely: You should just use them within reason.

Using Assembler Language

Using assembler is one of the most efficient methods of program optimization, and optimization techniques are largely similar to those used with high-level languages. But assembler provides the programmer with a number of additional options. Without repeating those issues that are similar to optimization in high-level languages, here we shall focus on techniques characteristic only for assembler.

❐ Using assembler is in many respects a good way to eliminate the problem of redundant program code. Assembler code is more compact than its high-level analog. To see this, you can simply compare the disassembled listings of the same program written in assembler and in a high-level language. The assembler code generated by a high-level language compiler, even with optimization options applied, does not solve the problem of redundant program code. At the same time, assembler lets you develop short, efficient code.

❐ As a rule, assembler program modules perform better than programs written in a high-level language. This is due to a smaller number of commands needed to implement the code fragment. It takes the processor less time to execute a smaller set of commands, thus increasing application performance.

❐ You can develop individual modules completely in assembler, and then link them to high-level language programs. You can also make use of built-in tools in high-level languages to write assembler procedures directly into the body of your program. This feature is supported by all high-level languages. By using the built-in assembler, you can obtain greater efficiency. This is most effective when used to optimize mathematical expressions, program loops, and data-array processing blocks in the main program.

Processor-Based Optimization

For optimization based on the specific properties of the processor, you need to take into account the architectural peculiarities of every particular Intel processor. This method extends to assembler optimization.

Here, we shall only consider optimization options for Pentium processors. Every new processor model usually has some new improvements in its architecture. At the same time, all Pentium processors have some characteristics in common. So processor-level optimization may be based both on the common properties of the whole family and on the specifics of each model.

Processor-level optimization of program code lets you enhance the performance of both high-level language programs and assembler procedures. Developers who use high-level languages are often unaware of this method, so it is seldom used, even though it can provide virtually unlimited possibilities. And those who develop assembler programs and procedures sometimes make use of the properties of new processor models.

It should be noted that even earlier Intel processors included additional commands. Though rarely used by developers, these commands allow the program code to be made more efficient.

So what processor properties can be used to provide optimization? First of all, it is useful to align data and addresses with the borders of 32-bit words. Besides, all processors from 80386 onward support enhanced calculation features, which you can use for optimizing the programs. These features were added by supplementary commands and by expanding the operand-addressing options. To improve program performance, you can use the following methods:

- Transfer commands with a zero or sign extension (movzx or movsx).
- Setting the byte to TRUE or FALSE depending on the content of the CPU flags. This lets you avoid using conditional jump commands (for example, commands like setz, setc, etc.).
- Commands for bit checking, settings, resetting, and scanning (bt, btc, btr, bts, bsp, bsr).
- Extended index addressing and addressing modes with index scaling.
- Quick multiplication using the lea command with scaled index addressing.
- Multiplication of 32-bit numbers and division of a 64-bit number by a 32-bit one.
- Operations for processing multibyte data arrays and strings.

Processor commands for copying and moving multibyte data arrays require a smaller number of processor cycles than classical commands of this type. From MMX processors onward, processors add complex commands combining several functions performed by separate commands. There is now a considerably larger set of commands for bit operations. These commands are also complex, and let you perform several operations at once. The options provided by these commands will be covered in *Chapter 10*, which explores built-in tools in high-level languages.

As has already been seen, using the properties of the processor's hardware architecture has great potential for optimization. This is quite a complicated business, requiring knowledge of data-processing methods and of performing processor commands at the hardware level. I can assert in all confidence that this domain contains virtually unlimited potential for program optimization.

Naturally, processor-level optimization has its own peculiarities. For instance, if your program is meant to run on systems with processors of several different generations, then you should optimize the program based on the common features of all those devices.

In addition, there is also a lot of other options for optimizing application code. As you can see, the program itself has a great deal of optimization potential. This book focuses mainly on optimization using assembler, and considering possible solutions to this task in greater detail.

Methods of Using the Assembler Language for Program Optimization

Assembler is widely used as a tool for optimizing the performance of high-level language applications. By combining assembler and high-level language modules reasonably, you can achieve both higher performance and smaller executable code. This combination is now used so frequently that the interface of high-level language programs with assembler modules included has become a special concern for compiler producers. As a rule, modern compilers come with built-in assembler.

In practical work, there are two basic options for combining assembler with high-level languages.

The *first approach* is to use a separate object module file with one or several procedures for data processing. The procedures are called from within a program created in a high-level development environment such as Visual C++ .NET.

In the source code of the high-level language application, you need to declare the assembler procedure accordingly, and can then call it from any point of the main program. During the assembly, the external object module (written in assembler) is linked to the main program.

The file containing the source code of the procedure usually has the ASM extension. To compile it, you can resort to one of the widely used packages such as Microsoft Macro Assembler (MASM), Borland Turbo Assembler (TASM 5.0), or Netwide Assembler (NASM), which is more powerful than the first two but not as widely used.

Compiling separate assembler modules has a number of advantages. First of all, you can use this program code in applications written in different high-level languages and even in different operating environments. It is also important that you can develop and debug the program code of the procedures separately. Among possible drawbacks are certain difficulties in integrating such a module with the main high-level language program. When using this approach, you should have a clear idea of the mechanism for calling external procedures and sending the parameters to the procedure you are calling. This approach also enables you to use assembler object modules or function libraries repeatedly. In this case, you should take care of the interface for interaction between the assembler module and the high-level language program. Issues of integrating assembler modules with C++ programs will be covered in more detail in *Chapter 7*.

The *second approach* is based on the use of built-in assembler. Using built-in assembler to develop procedures is convenient, first of all, due to fast debugging. Since the procedure is developed within the body of the main program, you do not need any dedicated tools to integrate this procedure with the program that calls it. Nor do you have to worry about the order of sending the parameters into the procedure you are calling, or about restoring the stack. Possible drawbacks of this approach include certain limitations imposed by the development environment on the operation of the assembler modules. In addition, procedures developed in built-in assembler cannot be transformed into external modules for repeated use.

Like the high-level languages, all modern assembler development tools come with an integrated debugger. Although such a debugger may offer you somewhat lower service than high-level languages, its features are quite enough for analyzing program code.

It is true that many developers consider assembler to be just a supplementary tool for improving programs. But in spite of this, the role of assembler has changed considerably in recent years, and it is also regarded as an independent tool for developing highly efficient applications.

Until recently, there existed a vivid stereotype of the use of assembler for application development. Lots of programmers working with high-level languages believe that assembler is complicated, the assembler software cannot be well structured, and that assembler code is hardly portable to other platforms. Many may remember the times of developing assembler programs in MS-DOS, which really was difficult. And besides, the lack of modern development tools at that time hindered the development of complicated projects.

In recent years, this situation has changed with the appearance of completely new and highly efficient tools that let you develop assembler programs quickly. These are dedicated Rapid Application Development (RAD) systems such as MASM32,

Visual Assembler, and RADASM. The size and performance of a window-based SDI (Single-Document Interface) application written in the assembler language is really impressive!

As a rule, such development tools come with resource compilers, large libraries of ready-to-use functions, and powerful debugging tools. So it is fair to say that developing programs in assembler has become as easy as developing them in high-level languages.

Thus, the main reason that kept developers from using assembler widely — i.e., the lack of Rapid Application Development tools — has been eliminated. And what applications can be developed in the assembler language? It is much easier to say for which projects you should not use it. Small and medium-sized 32-bit Windows applications can be written completely in assembler. But if you need to develop a complicated program requiring the use of advanced technologies, then you would be better off choosing high-level languages, and then using assembler to optimize certain fragments of the program.

There is one more difficulty in using assembler: It is intended for developing *procedural* applications, and does not use the *object-oriented programming* (OOP) methodology. This causes certain limitations on its usage. Nevertheless, this in no way prevents you from using assembler for writing classical procedural Windows applications.

Modern assembler development tools enable you to create a graphical user interface (GUI) while retaining the fundamental advantage of assembler: The size of your executable module will be incredibly small. Short, fast assembler applications are useful when code size and program speed are crucial factors, for example, in real-time applications, system utilities and programs, as well as hardware drivers.

The assembler programs let you control both the peripherals of the personal computer and the non-standard devices connected to it. The minimal size of the executable program code ensures high performance of these devices. The real-time applications are widely used in industrial control systems, in scientific and laboratory research, and also in military investigations.

As to the system programs and utilities, their peculiarity is close interaction with the operating system, and so the speed of such applications may have a considerable effect upon the overall performance of the whole operating system. This is also largely applicable to the development of hardware drivers and system services.

Assembler development tools also let you create fast console (command line) utilities. By using Windows calls in such utilities, you can implement a lot of very complicated functions (copying files, searching and sorting, processing and analysis of mathematical expressions, etc.) at an extremely high level of performance.

Another important use of assembler is to develop drivers for computer-controlled non-standard and specialized devices. For these tasks, assembler may be very efficient.

The huge number of examples of this sort of usage includes computer-based data-processing systems with external devices (such as microcontroller and digital processor devices used in technological processes, as well as smart-card terminals and all kinds of analyzers), single-board computers using flash memory, and systems for diagnostics and testing all kinds of equipment.

There is one more, rather exotic aspect of using assembler, which concerns using assembler for the main program and a high-level language (say, C++) for the supplementary modules. As a rule, such a program uses the powerful library functions of the high-level language, such as mathematical or string functions. In addition, if you develop the interface by calling the WIN API (Application Programming Interface), you can obtain an extremely powerful program. But this technique demands outstanding knowledge of both assembler and the high-level language.

Apart from the techniques considered above, there are a number of other methods for improving the quality of the software. Experienced developers resort to a lot of tricks and hacks to improve an application's performance level.

As mentioned above, program optimization is a creative process, and developers may have individual preferences when choosing how to debug and optimize applications.

Chapter 1: Developing Efficient Program Code

Using assembly language is one of the most efficient methods for optimizing programs. The techniques here are quite similar to those used in high-level languages; however, assembly language provides the developer with a number of additional options. Without repeating the optimization issues that are similar to ones in high-level languages, we will focus on the techniques specific to the assembler.

Optimization Potentials

Using assembly language is, in many respects, a good way to eliminate the problem of redundant program code. The assembly code is more compact than its analog in a high-level language. This is apparent by comparing the disassembled listings of the same program written in assembly language to those written in a high-level language. The assembly code generated by a high-level language compiler, even with the optimization options applied, does not solve the problem of redundant program code, whereas assembly language lets you develop the code, which is brief and efficient.

As a rule, an assembly program module has a higher performance than a program in a high-level language, because a smaller number of commands is needed for implementing the code fragment. It takes the processor less time to execute a smaller set of commands, therefore improved is the application performance.

You can develop complete separate modules in assembly language and then link them to the high-level language programs. It is also possible to make use of the built-in tools of the high-level languages to write assembly procedures in the body of your program directly. This feature is supported in all the high-level languages. By using the built-in assembly language, you can obtain high efficiency. The maximum effect is reached when you use it to optimize mathematical expressions, program loops, and the data arrays processing blocks in the main program.

Assembly language is widely used as a tool for optimizing the performance of high-level language applications. By combining the assembly and the high-level language modules in a logical way, you can achieve a high performance and reduce the size of the executable code. Such a combination is now used so frequently that the interface of the high-level language programs with included assembly modules has become a special concern for compiler producers. As a rule, the modern compilers come with the built-in assembly language.

Despite the evident optimization advantages offered by assembly language, there are indeed very few developers who apply it widely in practical work. One of the main reasons is that it seems somewhat complicated and requires a thorough understanding of the processor architecture. Assembly language is certainly more complicated than the high-level languages. However, it is well worth your time to learn assembly language, since it will greatly improve performance of the programs you create.

Two Approaches to Using Assembly Language

We will consider the possible ways of optimizing the programs by using assembly language.

The *first approach* is to include a separate assembly module into a C++ program code. This assembly module may include a function or a group of functions that perform some calculations. You can develop such modules separately from the main program, and compile them by using a stand-alone assembler compiler such as Microsoft Macro Assembler (MASM) or Borland Turbo Assembler (TASM). The result is an object module file that has the OBJ extension. You can include it into the project of a C++ application (in the Visual Studio .NET environment) and use the functions of this module according to the calling conventions. As compared to other options, this offers you certain advantages:

❐ Once developed, the object module can be used in different applications.
❐ There is no need to develop specific function interface (as is the case with DLL libraries) to call these functions from within other programs.
❐ It is easier to debug an assembly module separately, using its own development environment.

Note that the separate assembly modules may also contain several interrelated functions making up a larger calculation block.

The *second approach* to combining assembly language with high-level languages is based on the use of the built-in assembler. Using the built-in assembly language for developing procedures is convenient, primarily due to fast debugging. As a procedure is developed in the body of the main program, you do not need any specialized tools to integrate this procedure with the program that calls it. Neither do you have to concern yourself with the order of sending the parameters into the procedure you call, or with restoring the stack. To implement the functions in the built-in assembly language, you do not need to write the prologue and the epilogue, as it is needed in case of developing the assembly modules separately.

One disadvantage of this optimization approach pertains to certain limitations of the operation of the assembly modules, imposed by the development environment. Also note that the procedures developed in the built-in assembly language cannot be transformed into external modules for reuse.

Main Optimization Points

So, what parts of the program code, created in the C++ .NET environment, can be optimized with the help of assembly language?

Loops and Conditional Jumps

Loops and conditional jumps are structures such as WHILE, DO...WHILE, IF...ELSE, SWITCH...CASE. You can replace them easily with their equivalents in assembly language. It is often necessary to do so, especially if you have a set of similar calculations repeated many times. By sparing several instructions in each of such calculation loops, you can achieve considerable gain in application performance. This is equally applicable to both the independently compiled modules and the assembly blocks and functions used in the C++ .NET environment.

Assembly language also allows you to optimize the calculation algorithms inside the WHILE and DO...WHILE loops. If it takes only several assembly commands to implement such a calculation block, then the best way is to use the built-in assembler language. In this case, the use of separate modules will not produce the required effect, and it can even slow down the program. It is important to note that a separate assembler module must contain the completed functions that require performing the prologue and the epilogue every time you call them. This means that every time the program calls a function from a separate module, you need to save certain registers in the stack and then restore them. For small programs, the delay will be tolerable, but for more serious applications it can be considerable.

The IF..ELSE structures are not easy to optimize, but there are certain techniques that can be helpful. For example, instead of calculating two jump conditions, you can use one condition and one assignment operator.

Later in this chapter, these issues will be addressed in more detail with practical examples: see the sections *"Optimizing Loop Calculations"* and *"Optimizing Conditional Jumps."*

Mathematical Calculations

The large optimization potentials for C++ .NET applications lie in improving the mathematical operations. In loop calculations, the frequently repeated fragment of the program code can be implemented in assembly language, and there are often several ways to do this. The integer operations are usually easy to translate into assembly language, while for the floating-point operations, this task is much more complicated. In optimizing mathematical operations, an important role belongs to the mathematical coprocessor, or FPU (Floating-Point Unit) that performs operations over the floating-point numbers.

The FPU provides the system with additional mathematical calculation power, but does not replace any of the CPU commands. Commands such as add, sub, mul, and div are still performed by the CPU, while the FPU takes over the additional, more efficient arithmetic commands. The developer may view a system with a coprocessor as a single processor with a larger set of commands.

For more detail and practical examples on using the FPU, see the section for *"Optimizing Mathematical Calculations"* in this chapter.

Processor-Level Optimization
(Using the SIMD Technologies)

A special role in the optimization process belongs to the SIMD (Single Instruction — Multiple Data) technologies. These are implemented in such extensions as MMX (MultiMedia eXtensions) for integers and SSE (Streaming SIMD Extensions) for floating-point numbers. They facilitate the processing of several operands simultaneously. These technologies appeared quite recently, in the latest generations of the processors. To use them successfully, the developer should know the processor architecture and the system of commands, and also have a clear understanding of how to use certain functional units of the processor (registers, the cache, the command pipeline, the arithmetic logic unit, the floating-point unit, etc.). For more detail on main aspects of use of the MMX and SSE, see the *"Using SIMD Technologies (MMX, SSE)"* section in this chapter.

The early processor models used to have a rather simple architecture. They included a small set of assembly commands and operated a limited set of registers. These limitations were serious obstacles for using assembly language in developing serious applications. They were mostly used for accessing computer hardware resources and for creating hardware drivers.

The processor-level optimization of the program code lets you improve the performance of both the high-level language applications and the assembly procedures themselves. Developers working with high-level languages are often unaware of this optimization method; however, it can provide virtually unlimited possibilities. Those who develop assembly programs and procedures do sometimes make use of the features of the new processor models.

Also note that even the earlier models of the Intel processors include some additional commands. Though rarely used by developers, these commands can help you increase the efficiency of your program code.

The processor commands that perform copying and moving the multibyte data arrays require a smaller number of processor cycles than the classical commands of this type. Beginning with the MMX type, the processors add complex commands combining several functions performed by separate commands. There is now a considerably larger set of commands for bit operations. These commands are complex, as well, allowing you to perform several operations simultaneously. The options provided by these commands will be covered in *Chapter 10*, where we will explore built-in tools of the high-level languages.

As already explained, great optimization potentials depend upon correct use of the features of the processor's hardware architecture. These are quite complicated matters, requiring you to know the methods of data processing and performing the processor commands on the hardware level. This area contains virtually unlimited potential for program optimization.

Naturally, the processor-level optimization has its own peculiarities. For instance, if your program should run on systems with the processors of several generations, then you should optimize the program based on the common features of all those devices.

Like the high-level languages, all modern assembly development tools come with an integrated debugger. Although such a debugger can offer you a somewhat lower level of service as compared to the high-level languages, its features are satisfactory for analyzing the program code. Since assembly language is the closest to the machine language, the advantages of the new generations of processors bring their immediate results to assembly programming.

Optimizing High-Level Language Applications

Optimizing high-level language programs by using assembly language is somewhat labor-intensive. However, according to various estimations, it has been shown to increase application performance by 3–4 to 14–17 per cent.

To improve the high-level language programs, you can either use the assembly code in certain fragments of the program or implement the calculation algorithms in assembly language completely.

In practical work, the assembly optimization is efficient for the following tasks:

❐ Optimizing the loop calculations.

❐ Optimizing the processing of large amounts of data by using special string commands which actually let you process both character and numeric data.

❐ Optimizing the mathematical calculations. It is important to note that an increase in performance is achieved by using both the common mathematical operations and the Floating-Point Unit (FPU) commands. A special place belongs to the SIMD technology that lets you increase the application performance by a multiple.

In addition to the options noted above, it is also extremely important to combine assembly and high-level languages correctly. This largely depends on the developer's experience and background. Even in such a complicated field as assembly optimization, there are certain empirical rules that can be applied more or less successfully.

And yet, by simply replacing, say, the WHILE loop in a C++ program, you can sometimes achieve no increase in performance. This concerns other assembly analogs of the high-level language operators, too. In most cases, an increase in performance can be achieved only if you analyze a certain code fragment thoroughly. For example, assembly language gives you several different ways to implement the WHILE loop. The implementations you choose for your projects may differ from the classical calculation patterns covered in assembly language manuals. To optimize a C++ code fragment using assembly language, it is not enough to know the assembly commands and their syntax. The most important thing is to have a clear idea of how these commands work in different combinations; otherwise, the use of assembly language may give you no gain at all!

Later in this chapter, we will analyze ways to build highly efficient calculation programs in assembly language. Here, we will not concern ourselves with optimizing the C++ .NET 2003 high-level structures; this is a separate field that will be covered in *Chapter 4*. Here, we will focus on the basic principles of optimal assembly programming.

Optimizing Loop Calculations

Decrementing the Loop Counter

To begin, we will consider how you can use assembly language to program loop calculations. In the most general form, a loop presents a sequence of commands starting with a label, and returning to this label after this sequence is performed. In assembly language, the loop usually looks like this:

```
label:
    <commands>
    jmp label
```

For example, consider the following sequence of commands:

```
        mov EDX, 0
Label:
        <assembly code >
        inc EDX
        cmp EDX, 1000000
        je OutLoop
        jmp Label
OutLoop:
```

This is a simple loop. It increases the value of the EDX register from 0 to 1000000, and upon reaching this value, jumps to the OutLoop label.

This code fragment cannot be considered optimal, as it uses several commands for analyzing the loop exit condition, and for exiting the loop itself. You can improve the program code further if you analyze how the loop sequence of operators works. For a loop with a fixed number of iterations, the optimization solution in assembly language is simple (see Listing 1.1).

Listing 1.1. An assembly loop with a decremented counter

```
  . . .
  mov EDX, 1000000
label:
  . . .
  <assembly code>
  . . .
  dec EDX
  jnz label
  . . .
```

As you can see from this listing, the loop counter is placed into the EDX register. This fragment is more efficient than the previous one. The decrementing command sets the ZF flag when the counter value turns into 0. In this case, you exit the loop; otherwise, the loop takes a new iteration. As you can see, this fragment contains a smaller number of operations, and therefore will be performed faster.

Finally, you can develop an even more efficient version of the decremented loop. In this case, you can use the assembly command that is written as cmovcc in the pseudocode, with the last two letters standing for one of the conditions (eq, le, ge, etc.). The decremented loop shown in Listing 1.1 is easy to modify in the following way (Listing 1.2).

Listing 1.2. An assembly loop with the cmovz command

```
    . . .
    lea     EAX,   L1
    lea     ECX,   L2
    mov     EDX, 1000000
L1:
    . . .
    <assembly code>
    . . .
    dec     EDX
    cmovz   EAX, ECX
    jmp     EAX
L2:
    . . .
```

In this code fragment, the cmovz command performs two functions: it analyzes the ZF flag and sends the data to the EAX register if ZF is set. The cmovz command is followed by the jmp command that uses the EAX register value for jumping to the needed branch of the program.

Unrolling the Loop

The previous program code fragments demonstrate that the optimization of assembly loops largely depends on the particular task, so there is no universal technique. For example, suppose the program performs some conversion of 1-byte data stored in an array, and you need to increment the byte address in every iteration of the loop. Suppose the source address is contained in the ESI register, the destination address is stored in the EDI register, and the byte counter is placed in the ECX register. In this case, the loop algorithm for data processing can be implemented as follows (see Listing 1.3). The comments in the source code are separated with a semicolon (;).

Listing 1.3. Optimizing the byte processing loop

```
    . . .
; Places the source address to ESI

        mov ESI, src

; Places the destination address to EDI

        mov EDI, dst

; Places the byte counter to ECX

        mov ECX, count

; Adds the ESI address to ECX
; to get the loop exit condition

        add ECX, ESI

label:
        mov AL, [ESI]
        inc ESI

; Processes the byte

    <byte processing commands>

; Writes the result to the destination

        mov [EDI], AL
        inc EDI

; Checks the loop exit condition

        cmp ECX, ESI

; If the condition is not satisfied, repeats the loop

        jne label
    . . .
```

It should be noted that even a well-optimized loop might not appear as fast as the developer might expect. To further improve efficiency, you can use the method of *unrolling* the loop. This term actually means that you need to reduce the number of iterations by performing more operations during one loop. This method lets you achieve good results. Now, we are going to consider two code fragments, which use unrolling the loops.

For the initial (non-optimized) code fragment, we will take the code that copies the double-word data from one memory buffer to another. In Listing 1.4, you can see the source code of the fragment.

Listing 1.4. Copying double words (before optimization)

```
    . . .
; Places the source and destination addresses
; to the ESI and EDI registers

    mov ESI, src
    mov EDI, dst

; Places the byte counter value to ECX

    mov ECX, count

; Counts double words,
; so the ECX value is divided by 4

    shr ECX, 2
label:
    mov EAX, [ESI]
    add ESI, 4
    mov [EDI], EAX
    add EDI, 4
    dec ECX
    jnz label

    . . .
```

To unroll the loop, we will copy two double words simultaneously. In Listing 1.5, you can see the source code of the optimized fragment (with the changes shown in bold).

Listing 1.5. Unrolling the loop by copying two double words instead of one

---

```
. . .
mov ESI, src
mov EDI, dst

; Places the counter value to the ECX register

mov ECX, count

; Divides the counter value by 8
; (as we are using double words)

shr ECX, 3
label:

; Reads the first double word to the EAX register

mov EAX, [ESI]

; Reads the second double word to the EBX register

mov EBX, [ESI + 4]

; Writes the first double word to the EDI register

mov [EDI], EAX

; Writes the second double word
; to the EDI+4 address

mov [EDI + 4], EBX

; Shifts the source and destination addresses
; to point to the next double word

add ESI, 8
add EDI, 8

; Analyzes loop exit condition

dec ECX
jnz label
. . .
```

This technique allows you to *halve* the delay brought about by the loop. You can continue unrolling the loop further if you process four double words instead of two.

Here is one more example of unrolling the loops. Suppose you have an array of 20 integers. You task is to assign 0 to the elements with even numbers (0, 2, 4, etc.), and 1 to those with odd numbers.

The "straightforward" solution is shown in Listing 1.6.

Listing 1.6. Initializing the array (before optimization)

```
    . . .

; Places the array size to the ECX register

  mov   ECX, 20

; Places the first element address to the ESI register

  lea   ESI, i1

; Places the 2 divisor to the EBX register
; for finding out if the element is even or odd

  mov   EBX, 2
next:

; Placing the element counter to EAX register

  mov   EAX, ECX

; Finds out if the array element number is even or odd

  div   EBX
  cmp   EDX, 0

; If it is odd, sets the element to 1

  jne   set_1

; If it is even, sets the element to 0

  mov   DWORD PTR [ESI], 0
  jmp   L1
set_1:
```

```
    mov  DWORD PTR [ESI], 1
L1:

; Moves to the address of the next element in array
    add  ESI, 4
    loop next
    . . .
```

You can optimize this code fragment by processing two elements in one iteration. Listing 1.7 shows the source code of the modified version (the assembly commands that are left out are shown in italics).

Listing 1.7. Initializing the array (optimized)

```
    . . .
    mov  EDX, 0
;   mov  ECX, 20
    lea  ESI, i1
;   mov  EBX, 2
next:
;   mov  EAX, ECX
;   div  EBX
;   cmp  EDX, 0

    mov  DWORD PTR [ESI], 0
    mov  DWORD PTR [ESI+4], 1
    add  EDX, 2
;   jmp  L1
; set_1:
;   mov  DWORD PTR [ESI], 1
; L1:
    cmp  EDX, 19
    jae  ex
    add  ESI, 8
    jmp  next
ex:
    . . .
```

The source code of this fragment is essentially different from the code in Listing 1.6. We discarded the division commands, and at the same time, halved the number of iterations (see the add EDX, 2 command that is shown in bold). Every iteration now handles two array elements simultaneously (see the mov DWORD PTR [ESI], 0 and mov DWORD PTR [ESI+4], 1 commands that are shown in bold). In the end of each iteration, the value of the ESI register is incremented by 8 by the add ESI, 8 command, so that it points to the next pair of elements.

Now, we will use C++ .NET 2003 to develop a simple console application that implements the optimized algorithm. This application calls the initarr function (the one processing the array) from a separate assembly module.

The interface between the assembly functions and the C++ program will not be analyzed here, since these issues are covered in the following chapters. So now we will focus on our main task and consider the technique for optimizing the assembly code.

In Listing 1.8, you can see the source code of the optimized assembly module containing the initarr function. This module is adapted for compiling in the macroassembler environment MASM 6.14.

Listing 1.8. Array initialization (version for MASM 6.14)

```
.686
.model flat
  public _initarr
.code
 _initarr PROC

    ; Function prologue
    push EBP
    mov  EBP, ESP

    ; Places array size to the ECX register,
    ; and the first element address to the ESI register

    mov  ECX, DWORD PTR [EBP+12]
    mov  ESI, DWORD PTR [EBP+8]

    mov  EDX, 0
    dec  ECX
next:
    mov  DWORD PTR [ESI], 0
    mov  DWORD PTR [ESI+4], 1
    add  EDX, 2
    cmp  EDX, ECX
```

```
        jae   ex
        add   ESI, 8
        jmp   next
ex:

        ; Function epilogue

        pop   EBP
        ret
_initarr ENDP
end
```

The source code of the console application created in C++ .NET is shown in Listing 1.9.

Listing 1.9. Initializing and displaying an array of integers

```
// UNROLL_LOOP_OPT.cpp : Defines the entry point for the console
// application

#include "stdafx.h"

extern "C" void initarr(int* pil, int isize);

int _tmain(int argc, _TCHAR* argv[])
{
int i1[20];
printf ("UNROLLING LOOP DEMO\n\n");
printf("i1[20] = ");
initarr(i1, 20);
for (int cnt = 0; cnt < 20; cnt++)
    printf("%d ", i1[cnt]);
getchar();
return 0;
}
```

The application window (see Fig. 1.1) displays the contents of the array after initialization.

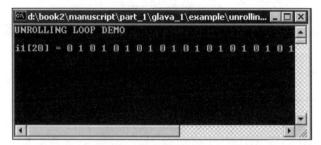

Fig. 1.1. Application window displays the outcome
of the assembly function with the optimized loop

We have covered the most general methods for optimizing loop calculations in assembly language. Although there are many other techniques as well, they are processor-specific. A detailed analysis of loop optimizing methods for particular processor types (Pentium Pro, Pentium II, Pentium III, and Pentium IV) is beyond the scope of this book.

Optimizing Conditional Jumps

Another factor that has a considerable influence upon application performance is the use of conditional jumps. In general, our recommendation (applicable to all processor types) is to avoid using conditional jumps that involve flags.

Why is that so? It is because the latest generations of Pentium processors include microprogram tools for predicting program branching, and they operate in a specific way. Sometimes, you can achieve the necessary result even without using conditional jumps: In some cases, you can do with certain bit manipulations.

Eliminating Conditional Jumps

As an example, we will consider the task of finding the absolute value of a signed number. We will consider two variants of the program code — one using conditional jumps and one not. The number is stored in the EAX register.

Here, you can see a code fragment that finds the absolute value of a number in a traditional way, by using the conditional jump commands (Listing 1.10).

Listing 1.10. Finding the absolute value of a number by using conditional jumps

---

```
. . .
    cmp   EAX, 0
    jge   ex
    neg   EAX
ex:
. . .
```

The following fragment performs the same operation without using the `jge` command (Listing 1.11).

Listing 1.11. Finding the absolute value of a number without using conditional jumps

---

```
. . .
 cdq
 xor EAX, EDX
 sub EAX, EDX
. . .
```

For calculations of this kind, the CF carrying flag is extremely helpful. We will consider one more example, which contains conditional jump operators in its traditional implementation. Suppose you need to compare two integers (i1 and i2) and set i1 equal to i2 if i2 < i1. To make it clear, we will represent it by the corresponding C++ operator:

```
if (b < a) a = b
```

The classical variant of the assembly code for implementing this task is shown in Listing 1.12.

Listing 1.12. A fragment of assembly code that evaluates the `if (b < a) a = b` expression by using conditional jumps

---

```
    . . .
; Stores the value of the i1 variable in the EAX register

    mov   EAX, DWORD PTR I1

; Compares the contents of the EAX register with the i2 value

    cmp   EAX, DWORD PTR I2

; if i1 > i2, makes i1 equal to i2

    jae   set_i2_to_i1
    jmp   ex
  set_i2_to_i1:

; Swaps the contents of EAX and i2
```

```
    xchg EAX, DWORD PTR I2

; Stores the contents of EAX in the i1 variable

    mov  DWORD PTR I1, EAX
  ex:
    . . .
```

The implementation of the same algorithm without using conditional jumps looks more elegant and appears faster in performance (Listing 1.13).

Listing 1.13. A fragment of assembly code that evaluates the if (b < a) a = b
expression without using conditional jumps

```
    . . .
mov   EAX, DWORD PTR I1
mov   EDX, DWORD PTR I2
sub   EDX, EAX
sbb   ECX, ECX
and   ECX, EDX
add   EAX, ECX
mov   DWORD PTR I1, EAX
    . . .
```

In the next example, we select one of the two numbers according to the following pseudo-code:

```
    if (i1!= 0) i1 = i2;
    else i1 = i3;
```

The classical solution using conditional jump commands can look like this (Listing 1.14).

Listing 1.14. An implementation of the if (i1 != 0) i1 = i2; else i1 = i3
algorithm with using the conditional jump commands

```
    . . .
; Stores the contents of the i1 — i3 variables
; in the EAX, EDX, ECX registers respectively

    mov EAX, DWORD PTR I1
```

```
   mov EDX, DWORD PTR I2
   mov ECX, DWORD PTR I3

; i1 = 0?

   cmp EAX, 0

; No, i1 = i2

   jne set_i2_to_i1

; Yes, i1 = i3

   mov EAX, ECX
   jmp ex
set_i2_to_i1:
   mov EAX, EDX
ex:
   mov DWORD PTR I3, EAX
. . .
```

Now, you can see a fragment of the source code that does not use the conditional jump operators (Listing 1.15).

Listing 1.15. An implementation of the `if (i1 != 0) i1 = i2; else i1 = i3`
algorithm without using the conditional jump commands

```
. . .
mov EAX, DWORD PTR I1
mov EDX, DWORD PTR I2
mov ECX, DWORD PTR I3

cmp EAX, 1
sbb EAX, EAX
xor ECX, EDX
and EAX, ECX
xor EAX, EDX

mov DWORD PTR I3, EAX
. . .
```

It is important to note that the overall performance of the application also depends on the way in which such a code fragment interacts with the rest of the program.

Optimizing Program Branching

If you cannot do without using conditional jumps, you can try optimizing the code fragment by establishing the proper program branching. To see what this means, we will consider the following example. Suppose you have a fragment performing the following sequence of commands:

```
    . . .
    test  EAX,EAX
    jz    label_A
    . . .
       <branch 1 commands>
    . . .
    jmp  label_B
label_A:
    . . .
       <branch 2 commands>
    . . .
label_B:
    . . .
```

Suppose the commands of Branch 1 are executed much more frequently than those of Branch 2. In this case, the performance will be hindered by the delays caused by resetting and reinitializing the processor branching block. This is because the jump to another branch of the code is often unpredictable. We will try organizing the loop in another way:

```
      . . .
    test EAX, EAX
    jnz    label_A
      . . .
        <branch 2 commands>
      . . .
    jmp label_B
label_A:
      . . .
        <branch 1 commands>
      . . .
label_B:
      . . .
```

In this case, the branching block will have a much greater number of "right hits," and this will increase the performance on this code fragment. The optimization of loop calculations cannot be reduced to the examples given above. To solve problems of this kind, it is necessary to have a clear idea of the principles of processor operation and its main functional units.

Optimizing Unconditional Jumps and Function Calls

The commands of unconditional jumps and function calls produce a certain impact on performance as well. That is why you should reduce the number of these commands if possible. How can these commands slow down the application performance?

The commands of unconditional jumps and function calls have a complex nature and require a large number of processor microoperations. These are needed for forming the executable addresses, rearranging the command pipeline, especially if the code contains a chain of such commands.

What affects performance greatly is that the unconditional jump commands may "force out" other jump commands from the special processor memory buffer that stores the jump addresses available. This buffer, called Branch Target Buffer (BTB), has an extremely important role in organizing the branches and jumps in the program. The algorithm for replacing the unused buffer commands is based on random selection, and this may cause a considerable delay in programs containing a lot of branches.

Reducing Unconditional Jumps and Branches

To reduce the number of unconditional jumps and branches, you can rearrange the structure of the program code. Each specific case will have an individual solution, but still, there are some general guidelines:

☐ If one `jump` command is followed by another, you can replace such a sequence by a single jump to the last label.

☐ A jump to the return command (`ret`) can be replaced by the return command itself.

As an example, we will optimize the code for a function (we will call it `myproc`), containing the following sequence of commands:

```
myproc PROC
    . . .
    <assembly code>
    . . .
```

```
    jmp    ex
    . . .
ex:
    ret
    myproc ENDP
```

This code fragment may be replaced by a more efficient one (with the changes shown in bold):

```
myproc PROC
    . . .
    <assembly code>
    . . .
    ret
    . . .
    ret
myproc ENDP
```

The `jmp ex` command, performing a jump to the label where the program exits the `myproc` function, is replaced by the `ret` command. The use of the other `ret` commands is determined by the function algorithm.

Avoiding Double Returns

If you need to call a function (or procedure) from within another one, it is highly recommended that you avoid the so-called *double return*. This would eliminate the need for manipulations with the stack pointer, which present an obstacle to the processor prediction mechanism. For instance, it is a good idea to replace such function call command as

```
    call myproc
    . . .
    ret
```

by the unconditional jump command: `jmp myproc`. In this case, the return from the main function would be performed by the `ret` command of the `myproc` procedure. Such manipulations may seem difficult to understand, so we will use an example to explain these matters in more detail.

We will now use C++ .NET to develop a simple console application that will contain a call of an assembly function (say, `fcall`). The `fcall` function calculates the difference between the two integers (the `i1` and `i2` variables in the main program), and then calls the `mul3` function that multiplies this difference by 3. This result is returned to the main program and displayed on the screen.

Listing 1.16 shows the source code of the non-optimized assembly module intended for compiling in the macroassembler environment MASM 6.14.

Listing 1.16. An assembly module containing two functions (before optimization)

```
.686
.model flat
  public _fcall
.code
_fcall PROC
  push EBP
  mov   EBP, ESP

  ; Stores the contents of the i1 variable in the EAX register

  mov   EAX, DWORD PTR [EBP+8]
  sub   EAX, DWORD PTR [EBP+12]
  call _mul3
  pop   EBP
  ret
_fcall ENDP

_mul3  PROC
  mov   EBX, 3
  imul  EBX
  ret
_mul3  ENDP
end
```

The i1 and i2 variables are transferred through the stack. We find the difference between them and place it to the EAX register. These operations are performed by the following commands:

```
mov   EAX, DWORD PTR [EBP+8]
sub   EAX, DWORD PTR [EBP+12]
```

Then we call the mul3 function that multiplies the result in EAX by 3. Note that we use the call command to call the mul3 function. To return to the main C++ program, the two ret commands are used. Now, we will optimize the assembly code as shown in Listing 1.17 (the changes are marked in bold).

Listing 1.17. The optimized variant of the assembly code with two functions

```
.686
.model flat
 public _fcall
.code
_fcall PROC
  push EBP
  mov   EBP, ESP
  mov   EAX, DWORD PTR [EBP+8]    ; i1
  sub   EAX, DWORD PTR [EBP+12]   ; i2
  pop   EBP
  jmp   _mul3
_fcall ENDP

_mul3  PROC
  mov   EBX, 3
  imul  EBX
  ret
_mul3  ENDP
end
```

As you can see from the listing, the call _mul3 command has been removed, and the pop EBP command is now placed before the jump to the procedure label. Before the jmp _mul3 command is performed, the stack contains the address for returning to the main program. After multiplying the contents of the EAX register by 3, there is a return, performed by the ret command of the mul3 function.

Listing 1.8 shows the source code of the console application created in C++ .NET 2003. This console application uses the result of the calculations programmed in the previous listing.

Listing 1.18. A console application that displays the results of the fcall function

```
// REPLACE_CALL_WITH_JMP_DEMO.cpp : Defines the entry point
// for the console application

#include "stdafx.h"

extern "C" int fcall(int i1, int i2);

int _tmain(int argc, _TCHAR* argv[])
```

```
{
 int i1, i2;
 printf("AVOIDING DOUBLE RETURN IN ASM FUNCTIONS\n");
 while (true)
 {
  printf("\nEnter i1: ");
  scanf("%d", &i1);
  printf("Enter i2: ");
  scanf("%d", &i2);
  printf("(i1 - i2)*3 = %d\n", fcall(i1, i2));
  }
 return 0;
}
```

Fig. 1.2 illustrates the window with this application running.

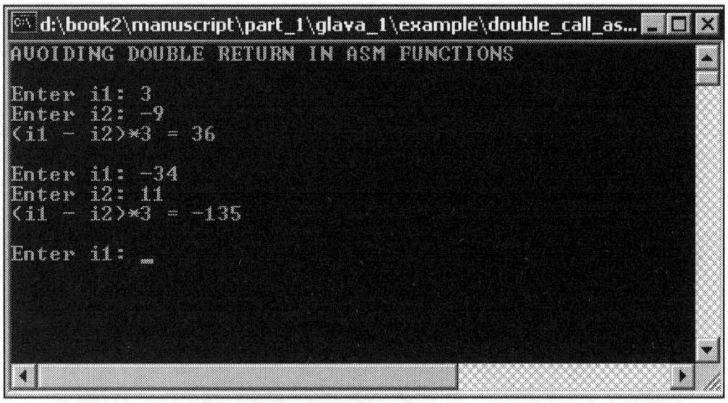

Fig. 1.2. Application that calls assembly functions
and uses a single return command

Repeating the Code Fragment

Another method for eliminating redundant unconditional jumps is to repeat the needed code fragment at the point where you run into the `jmp` command. We will consider a practical example.

Suppose you have an array of integers. The task is to select all its positive numbers and save them in one array, and also to select all the negative numbers and save them in another array. Suppose the original array contains 8 elements. To simplify the task, suppose that half of the numbers are positive, and half are negative. So, the two supplementary arrays have the dimension of 4. In Listing 1.19, you can see the source code of the assembly function that performs the required manipulations.

Listing 1.19. Selecting the positive and negative numbers out of the array (non-optimized version)

```
     . . .
    push EBX

; Places the address of the original array to the ESI register,
; the address of the array for negative numbers — to the EDI register,
; and the address of the array for positive numbers — to EBX

    lea  ESI, i1
    lea  EDI, ineg
    lea  EBX, ipos

; Places the size of the original array (i1) to the EDX register

    mov  EDX, 8
next_int:

; Checks if the element of the i1 array is equal to 0

    cmp  DWORD PTR [ESI], 0

; If the element is equal or greater than 0,
; writes it to the ipos array

    jge  store_pos

; Otherwise, writes it to the ineg array for negative numbers:

    mov  EAX, DWORD PTR [ESI]
    mov  DWORD PTR [EDI], EAX
    add  EDI, 4

; Jumps to the common branch of the program

    jmp  next
store_pos:
    mov  EAX, DWORD PTR [ESI]
    mov  DWORD PTR [EBX], EAX
```

```
      add   EBX, 4
next:
      dec   EDX
      jz    ex
      add   ESI, 4
      jmp   next_int
ex:
      pop   EBX
      . . .
```

In this code fragment, the optimization can be achieved by eliminating the unconditional jump command — `jmp next` (shown in bold). Instead of this command, you can repeat the needed code fragment. The source code of the modified version of the program is shown in Listing 1.20.

Listing 1.20. Selecting the positive and negative numbers out of the array (optimized version)

```
      . . .
   push EBX
   lea  ESI, i1
   lea  EDI, ineg
   lea  EBX, ipos

   mov  EDX, 8
next_int:
   cmp  DWORD PTR [ESI], 0
   jge  store_pos
   mov  EAX, DWORD PTR [ESI]
   mov  DWORD PTR [EDI], EAX
   add  EDI, 4
   dec  EDX
   jz   ex
   add  ESI, 4
   jmp  next_int

store_pos:
   mov  EAX, DWORD PTR [ESI]
   mov  DWORD PTR [EBX], EAX
   add  EBX, 4
```

```
dec  EDX
jz   ex
add  ESI, 4
jmp  next_int
ex:
 pop  EBX
 . . .
```

The changes made to the original program are shown in bold. As you can see from the original listing, removing the `jmp next` command required us to insert several commands from the common branch, which is marked as `next` in Listing 1.19.

Replacing Loop Commands by Jumps and Comparisons

There is another important note concerning loop calculations. The existing `loop` commands and their modifications (`loope`, `loopne`, `loopz`, `loopnz`) slow down the overall performance of the program and are indeed an anachronism to the modern processor models. To create fast applications, it is better to replace them with the combination of `cmp` / `jmp` commands.

For example, the loop that uses the `ECX` register as a counter and contains the `loop` command (one of the most frequently used) is the least efficient:

```
   . . .
     mov  ECX, counter
     . . .
 label_1:
     . . .
      <assembly commands>
     . . .
     loop  label_1
     . . .
```

There are two drawbacks to this loop. First, the `loop` command cannot be optimized by the processor well enough, and further, only the `ECX` register can be used as the loop counter. The second disadvantage is that the `ECX` register is decremented by 1, making it difficult to unroll the loop by expanding to the next step.

You can replace the `loop` command with the following sequence:

```
    . . .
    mov   ECX, counter
    . . .
```

```
label_1:
    . . .
    <assembly commands>
    . . .
    dec    ECX
    jnz    label_1
    . . .
```

In this code fragment, you can decrement the ECX counter by a value other than 1, which provides you with certain options for optimizing the code.

A somewhat worse variant, yet faster than the one with the loop, may look like this:

```
    . . .
    xor    EDX, EDX
    . . .
label_1:
    . . .
    <assembly commands>
    . . .
    inc    EDX
    cmp    EDX, counter
    jb     label_1
    . . .
```

In this case, you need to use the cmp command to check the loop exit condition, and this requires additional processor cycles. This loop is easy to unroll, too.

Using String Commands for Data Transfer

Many programs spend quite a lot of time on operations that involve copying and moving large amounts of data. For these purposes, the Intel processors have a number of commands that allow you to speed up the operations over multibyte arrays and strings. There are a number of processor instructions, called *string commands*, which have been developed for these tasks.

The group of string commands includes commands such as movs, lods, cmps, scas. When these commands are used without the repetition prefix (rep), they will hinder the application performance. Since these commands are complex, they require a fairly large number of processor cycles, and therefore cannot be optimized by the processor well enough. A good alternative to such instructions is the program code using the ordinary commands.

But if you use the string commands with the repetition prefix (rep), you can achieve high performance levels in copying and moving the data. In this case, the most efficient commands are those containing a mnemonic indication of the size of the operands (such as lodsb, lodsw, lodsd, movsb, movsw, etc.). For instance, if you need to copy 100 double words from the src memory buffer to the dst buffer, you can use the following sequence of commands:

```
. . .
mov    ECX, 100
lea    ESI, src
lea    EDI, dst
cld
rep    movsd
. . .
```

The following sequence of commands may be a good alternative to the code fragment considered above:

```
   . . .
   mov  ECX, 100
   lea  ESI, src
   lea  EDI, dst
next:
   mov  EAX, [ESI]
   mov  [EDI], EAX
   add  ESI, 4
   add  EDI, 4
   dec  ECX
   jnz  next
   . . .
```

If you proceed even further, unrolling the loop as to copy two double words simultaneously in one iteration, you will obtain a much more efficient code than the variant using the rep movsd command:

```
   . . .
   mov  ECX, 100
   lea  ESI, src
   lea  EDI, dst
next:
   mov  EAX, [ESI]
   mov  [EDI], EAX
   mov  EAX, [ESI+4]
```

```
mov  [EDI+4], EAX
add  ESI, 8
add  EDI, 8
sub  ECX, 2
jnz  next
 . . .
```

Optimizing Mathematical Calculations

Assembly language presents an efficient way for optimizing mathematical operations, and also the operations for data array processing and hardware interaction. Most of the applications make intensive use of mathematical calculations, and assembly language is often a good way to optimize the performance of these calculations. For creating highly efficient applications, the crucial factor is expertise in the Floating-Point Unit (FPU) hardware and program architecture, as well as in the SIMD technology.

In this chapter, we will focus on the principles of the FPU operation and the options for application optimization. Practical examples of how to make use of the FPU features will be considered in *Chapter 2*.

Using the Floating-Point Unit (FPU)

The earliest models of Intel processors did not have hardware support for the floating-point operations. All operations of this kind were implemented as procedures made up of the ordinary mathematical commands. For early models, a special additional chip was developed, which got the name of *mathematical coprocessor*. It included the commands enabling the computer to perform the floating-point operations much faster than was done by the procedures containing ordinary mathematical commands.

Starting from the 486DX processors, the mathematical coprocessor no longer exists as a separate device. Instead, the processors contain the FPU, but it is programmed as a separate module. The FPU program model can be described as a combination of the following registers:

❑ *FPU stack registers.* There are 8 of them, and their names are ST(0), ST(1), ST(2) ... ST(7). The floating-point numbers are stored as 80-bit numbers of the extended format. The ST(0) register always points to the top of the stack. As the numbers are received by the FPU, they are added on top of the stack.

❑ *Control/status registers.* These include the status register reflecting the information on the processor status, the control register (for controlling the FPU operation modes), and the tag status register that reflects the status of the ST(0) ... ST(7) registers.

❑ *Data point register and instruction point register.* These are intended for processing the exceptions.

Any of the registers listed above can be accessed by the program either directly or indirectly. In FPU programming, the most frequently used elements are the ST(0) ... ST(7) registers and the C0, C1, C2, and C3 bits of the status register.

The FPU registers operate as an ordinary stack of the CPU. But this stack has a limited number of positions — only 8 of them. The FPU has one more register, which is difficult for the programmer to access. This is a word containing the "labels" of each of the stack positions. This register enables the FPU to trace, which of the stack positions are currently in use and which are not engaged. Any attempt to place an object into a stack position that is already engaged creates an exception.

To place the data into the FPU stack, the program uses the load command that places the data on top of the stack. If a number stored in memory has a format other than the temporary float format, then (during the loading) the FPU converts this number to the 80-bit form.

The write commands extract the values from the FPU stack and place them into memory. If data format conversion is needed, it is performed as part of the write operation. Some forms of the write operation leave the top of the stack intact for further operations.

After being placed into the FPU stack, the data can be accessed and used by any command. The processor instructions allow both the operations between the registers and the operations between the memory and the registers. In the same way as in the CPU, between any two operands, one should be stored in a register. For the FPU, one of the operands should always be a top element of the stack, and another operand may be taken either from the memory or from the stack of registers.

Any arithmetic operation should always have the stack of registers as the destination. The FPU, being a processor unit for numeric operations, cannot write the result into memory by using the same command that performed the calculations. To send the operand back to the memory, it is necessary to use either a separate write command or a command that extracts data from the stack and then writes it into memory.

FPU Commands

All FPU commands start with the F letter to be distinguished from the CPU commands. The FPU commands can be conventionally arranged into several groups:

- ❏ Data transfer commands
- ❏ Addition and subtraction commands
- ❏ Multiplication and division commands
- ❏ Comparison commands
- ❏ Transcendental functions commands
- ❏ Control flow commands

The FPU provides the developer with hardware-level support for the algorithms that calculate trigonometric functions, logarithms, and powers. Such calculations are entirely transparent for the software developer and do not require writing any additional algorithms.

The FPU makes it possible to perform mathematical calculations with very high precision level (up to 18 digits). If you perform such calculations without using the FPU functions, the result will be less precise.

The use of assembly language for FPU programming can give you considerable gain in application performance. This is because the system of FPU instructions contains different groups of commands, providing the developer with virtually all the tools for implementing most calculation algorithms. Even if some of the needed commands are missing, you can easily find an equivalent operation made up of several assembly instructions. It should be noted that by programming the FPU with assembly commands, you could implement even the operations that are difficult or even impossible to write in C++.

With regard to mathematical functions in the C++ standard libraries, we need to note that their assembly analogs often let you obtain an even higher performance, as well as a smaller program size. Assembly language also lets developers create custom functions, which often appear more efficient than their analogs from the mathematical library in Visual C++ .NET.

Using the SIMD Technologies (MMX, SSE)

The operation of the Intel processors up to the Pentium model is governed by the following scheme: every instruction performs the actions over one or two operands. The operands can be stored both in the registers and in the memory. To perform repeated or similar operations over several operands, you must use either loops or recursive calls of certain code fragments.

MultiMedia eXtensions (MMX)

In multimedia applications, 2D/3D graphics, communications, and in a number of other tasks, the need for performing large numbers of similar operations is common. To optimize the solutions to such tasks, the SIMD technology was developed. Implementation uses the FPU registers, on which the MMX calculation block was built. The traditional FPU contains eight 80-bit registers for storing and processing the numbers in the floating-point format.

These registers form an FPU stack. In the instructions, they are addressed through the special stack pointer. Physically, the MMX block uses 64 lower bits of these registers, and these registers are addressed directly (MMX0...MMX7). The MMX uses new types of packed data placed in the 64-bit registers:

❒ Packed bytes — eight bytes
❒ Packed words — four words
❒ Packed doublewords — two double words
❒ Quadword — one 64-bit word

The MMX technology presents a considerable improvement to the architecture of the Intel microprocessors. It was developed to speed up the performance of multimedia and communication programs. The amount of data and the complexity of its processing by modern computers is increasing exponentially, demanding efficient processor performance.

MMX Instructions

Every MMX instruction performs an operation over the a whole set of operands (8, 4, 2, or 1), placed in the registers addressed. Another peculiarity of the MMX technology is the support for *saturation arithmetic.* It differs from the ordinary wraparound arithmetic with the regard to the following: If the resulting value exceeds the upper limit for the given data type, then the result is captured at the maximum possible value, with the carry ignored. If the result of the operation appears beyond the lower limit for the given data type, the result is captured at the minimal possible value. The limits are determined by the variable type (signed or unsigned) and precision. Such a calculation mode is convenient, for instance, when you need to determine the colors. The new instructions (57 of them in total) can be subdivided into the following groups:

❒ Commands for arithmetic, including addition and subtraction in different modes, multiplication, and a combination of multiplication and addition
❒ Comparison of data elements: checking the equality or comparing their value
❒ Commands for format conversion
❒ Logical commands ("AND", "AND NOT", "OR", and "XOR") over the 64-bit operands
❒ Commands for logical and arithmetic shifts
❒ Commands for data transfer between the MMX registers and the integer registers or memory
❒ MMX clearance commands that set the signs of empty registers in the tag word

FPU and MMX

There are some nuances that form an obstacle to combining the FPU and MMX instructions by using them in turn. Some of these reasons are the differences in the methods of register addressing, and also the discrepancy between the MMX and FPU data formats. So, an FPU/MMX block can operate in either of these two modes, but not in both simultaneously. For example, suppose you have to insert some MMX instructions into a chain of FPU instructions, and then continue the FPU calculations. In this case, prior to the first MMX instruction, you need to save the FPU context (the status of registers) in the memory, and after those instructions, load the context again.

These saving and loading operations take up the processor time. As a result, you may even lose the advantages of the SIMD concept. The coincidence of the MMX and FPU registers is sometimes justified by the fact that it allowed saving the MMX context in the same way as the FPU, so this demanded no additional changes in the operating system for saving the MMX context in cases of task switching. This means that the type of the processor installed (the one with MMX or without it) does not affect the operating systems. To make use of the SIMD advantages, the applications need to "know" how to use them (and not to lose performance on task switching).

Optimizing MMX Intrinsic Functions

In the Visual C++ .NET environment, the MMX support is implemented through *intrinsic* functions. All declarations of intrinsics are contained in the `mmintrin.h` header file. The developer can make use of the intrinsics in his or her own programs. The MMX intrinsics fall into several groups:

- General-purpose functions (those for packing and unpacking, MMX register clearance, data transfer)
- Comparison operations
- Arithmetic operations
- Shift operations
- Logical operations

Any intrinsic function can be represented by an equivalent in the form of assembly code. For manipulating the 64-bit variables, C++ .NET offers the `__m64` variable type. All intrinsics make use of such variables to a certain degree, though the `mm0...mm7` registers are never mentioned. The disassembled code of any of the intrinsics is redundant. It can be replaced by the assembly commands. The C++ .NET debugger supports MMX instructions, and the corresponding assembly code is generated automatically. In *Chapter 10*, you will find detailed examples on using the MMX technology.

Streaming SIMD Extensions (SSE)

Starting from the Pentium III processor, there appears the so-called SSE stream extension. This technology is intended for enhancing the performance of multimedia and communication applications. This extension (which includes new registers, data types, and instructions) has to speed up the applications for mobile video, graphics combined with video, image processing, sound synthesis, speech synthesis and compression, telephony, video communications, 2D and 3D graphics.

The applications of these types usually involve algorithms with a large amount of calculations and perform repeating operations on large sets of simple data elements. These applications have the following characteristics in common:

- ❏ They involve large amounts of data.
- ❏ Most of the operations are performed over the integers of small length.
- ❏ Graphical applications use the operations over the 8-bit pixel color values.
- ❏ Audio applications use the operations over the 16-bit audio samples of sound.
- ❏ They involve the use of parallel calculations.

The new processor types have an additional hardware-implemented block of eight 128-bit registers called XMM. Each of the XMM registers can operate four 32-bit float numbers simultaneously. The block enables a single instruction to control four 32-bit operands at once. Such a way of executing the processor instructions is called *parallel*.

The instructions with the XMM registers can also operate in the so-called *scalar* mode. In this case, the operations are applied to the lower 32-bit word. Since SSE is a hardware-implemented extension, the system does not use the FPU/MMX block when executing the new instructions.

This separate execution of the FPU/MMX commands and the SSE instructions allows you to gain more efficiency by combining the MMX instructions for integers and the SSE instructions for the float operands. In this case, the FPU registers are used for the MMX integer calculations, and the SSE block performs float calculations.

SSE Instructions

To support the SSE extension, the instruction set of the integer MMX extension adds twelve new commands:

- ❏ Commands for finding the average value, the minimum, the maximum, and the special arithmetic commands
- ❏ Unsigned multiplication, as well as several instructions connected with rearrangement of terms

The SSE extension includes the instructions of the following types:

❑ Arithmetic operations (addition, subtraction, multiplication, division, extraction of square root, finding the minimum and the maximum).
❑ Comparison operations.
❑ Conversion operations (these establish the relation between the MMX integer formats and the XMM float formats).
❑ Logical operations (including the "AND", "OR", "AND NOT", and "XOR" operations over the XMM operands).
❑ Operations for data moving and rearranging (these ensure data exchange between the XMM block and the memory or the processor integer registers, and also rearrange the terms in packed operands).
❑ Status control operations (these serve for saving and loading the additional XMM status register). This group also includes instructions for quick saving/restoring the MMX/FPU and SSE status.

The SSE also adds some new instructions for cache contents management: these instructions write the contents of the MMX and XMM registers to the memory directly, bypassing the cache. Therefore, the purpose of these functions is to eliminate stuffing the cache memory excessively. They also allow you to load the needed data to cache before calling the instructions that process these data.

For an application intended to use more than only the basic 32-bit processor resources, you will have to determine the processor type. This is easy to do by using the cpuid instruction. For the processors with SSE, the cpuid instruction also allows you to obtain the processor's unique 64-bit identifier.

SSE Intrinsic Functions

The SSE extension of the Pentium processors, in the same way as MMX, is supported by the C++ .NET intrinsics. All the declarations of the intrinsics for the SSE extension are stored in the xmmintrin.h file. To facilitate working with 128-bit variables, the _ _m128 type can be used. In *Chapter 10*, you will find practical examples of how to use the SSE extension for application programming.

Conclusion

In this chapter, we have considered different options for optimizing the assembly code. They are based on the peculiarities of operation of the Intel Pentium processors. The examples of program code given here enable you to make the most of the hardware possibilities of these processors.

Chapter 2: Optimizing Calculation Algorithms

In this chapter, we will consider aspects of assembly programming that make assembly language helpful and efficient for the purpose of optimization. We assume that readers are familiar with the system of commands of this language. In this chapter, we will explore the fundamentals of building efficient data processing algorithms in assembly language.

Assembly language is most often used for implementing mathematical algorithms, for searching in the arrays and sorting them quickly, and for optimizing repeated calculations. Tasks of this kind are very common in developing C++ programs, and it is usually time consuming to implement them.

In analyzing and building algorithms, we will use the assembly commands up to those for Pentium IV processors. The latest processor models include commands for processing data arrays quickly, as well as complex commands, which enable you to optimize the calculation algorithm itself.

Before plunging into the assembly programming, we will clarify the development tools. For illustrating calculation algorithms, we will use console applications created in C++ .NET, and the algorithms themselves will be written in the built-in assembly language of the C++ .NET 2003 programming environment. The program code fragments in the built-in assembly language enable you to analyze the calculation algorithms without having to study in-depth aspects of this C++ tool (these issues will be covered in the following chapters).

Mathematical Functions

To begin, we will focus on mathematical calculations. Virtually all applications use some operations connected with mathematical calculations, ranging from the simplest ones (such as addition and subtraction), to solving the systems of equations. The mathematical operations may use both the ordinary CPU commands such as ADD, SUB, MUL, DIV, and the specialized commands of the Floating-Point Unit (FPU).

Arithmetic commands of any microprocessor are a thing of special concern. Arithmetic calculations using these types of commands can be found in virtually any application. This group of commands, though not very numerous, performs most of the data conversion operations in the processor. In practice, arithmetic commands make up only a fraction of all executable commands, but their performance is specific.

The Visual C++ .NET 2003 programming environment is noted for its varied powerful mathematical functions. But the C++ mathematical libraries are based on a relatively simple set of the CPU and FPU commands. Assembly language does not contain such ready-made complex functions and libraries, but it allows you to develop your own, some of which may be even better than those in C++.

Here, we will consider aspects of using assembly language for optimizing calculation algorithms. The greatest optimization possibilities lie in the correct use of the floating-point operations. Developers may often create their own assembly functions that have greater calculation power and higher efficiency than the similar C++ library functions. As a rule, such functions are needed for real-time data processing solutions, and also in creating device drivers and system services.

In order to implement these tasks successfully, it is necessary to have a fairly good background in the system of commands and FPU operation peculiarities in the Intel processors.

Floating-Point Unit

The earliest models of Intel processors did not have hardware support for floating point operations. All of these operations were implemented as procedures made up of ordinary mathematical commands. In early models, a special additional chip was developed, which was called *mathematical coprocessor*. It included commands that enable the computer to perform floating-point operations much faster than was done by procedures containing ordinary mathematical commands.

Beginning with 486DX processors, the mathematical coprocessor no longer existed as a separate device. Instead, the processors contain a FPU, but it is programmed as a separate module.

The FPU provides the system with additional arithmetic calculation power, but does not replace any of the CPU commands. For example, commands such as ADD,

SUB, MUL, and DIV are performed by the CPU, while the FPU takes over the additional, more efficient arithmetic commands.

The developer may view a system with a coprocessor as a single processor with a larger set of commands.

The FPU Program Model

The FPU program model can be described as a combination of registers, which fall into the following three groups:

❏ *FPU stack registers.* There are 8 of them, and they are called ST(0), ST(1), ST(2) ... ST(7). The floating-point numbers are stored as 80-bit numbers of the extended format. The stack of registers operates according to the "Last In, First Out" (LIFO) principle. The ST(0) register always points to the top of the stack. As the numbers are received by the FPU, they are added on top of the stack. The numbers stored in the stack move to the bottom, leaving space for other numeric values.

❏ *Control/status registers.* These include the status register reflecting the information on the processor status, the controlling register (for controlling the FPU operation modes), and the tag status register that reflects the status of the ST(0) ... ST(7) registers.

❏ *The data point register and the instruction point register.* These are intended for processing exceptions.

Any of the registers listed above can be accessed by the program either directly or indirectly. In FPU programming, the most frequently used elements are the ST(0) ... ST(7) registers and the C0, C1, C2, and C3 bits of the status register.

FPU registers operate as an ordinary stack of the CPU. But this stack has a limited number of positions — only 8 of them. The FPU has one more register, which is difficult for the programmer to access. This is a word containing the "labels" of each of the stack positions. This register enables the FPU to trace, which of the stack positions are currently in use and which are not engaged. Any attempt to place an object into a stack position that is already engaged causes an exception (invalid operation).

To place the data into the FPU stack, the program uses the load command that places the data on top of the stack. If a number stored in memory has a format other than the temporary float format the FPU converts this number to the 80-bit form during its loading.

Similarly, the write commands extract values from the FPU stack and place them into memory. If the data format conversion is needed, it is performed as part of the write operation. Some forms of the write operation leave the top of the stack intact for further operations.

After being placed into the FPU stack, the data can be accessed and used by any command. The processor instructions allow both the operations between the registers and the operations between the memory and the registers. In the same way as in the CPU, between any two operands, one should be stored in a register. For the FPU, one of the operands should always be a top element of the stack, and another operand may be taken either from the memory or from the stack of registers.

Any arithmetic operation should always have the stack of registers as the destination. The FPU, being a processor unit for numeric operations, cannot write the result into memory by using the same command that performed the calculations. To send the operand back to the memory, use either a separate write command, or a command that extracts data from the stack and then writes them into the memory.

FPU Commands and Algorithm Optimization

All the FPU commands start with the F letter to be distinguished from the CPU commands. The FPU commands can be arranged conventionally into several groups:

❑ Data transfer (read/write) commands
❑ Addition and subtraction commands
❑ Multiplication and division commands
❑ Comparison commands
❑ Transcendental functions commands
❑ Control flow commands

Now, we will focus on these groups of commands in more detail.

Data Transfer Commands

Write
There are two types of *write* commands.

One of them extracts the number from the top of the stack and writes it into a memory cell. When performing such commands, the FPU converts the data from the temporary float format to the desired external form. The commands of this type are fst and fist. These commands enable you to place the value from the top of the stack automatically into the register inside the stack.

Regarding the second type of write commands, they write the data together with shifting the stack pointer. Performing the same operation of writing the data from the CPU to the memory, the fstp commands (as well as the fistp and fbstp commands) extract the number from the stack. These commands support all the external data types.

Exchange

The next data transfer command is the *exchange* command: fxch. It exchanges the contents between the top of the stack and any other register of the stack. As an operand for this command, you can use only another element of the stack. This command cannot exchange the values between the top register of the stack and a memory location. To do this, you need to use a combination of several commands. Within a single command, the FPU can perform either reading from the memory or writing to the memory, but not both simultaneously.

Read (Load)

The *read*, or *load*, commands load the data to the top of the processor stack. To load the integer data, use the fild modification.

Addition and Subtraction

Now, we continue on to the next group of commands: those for *addition* and *subtraction*. Each of these commands finds the sum or difference between the ST(0) register value and another operand. The result of this operation is always placed in an FPU register. The mnemonic representation of these commands is as follows:

```
fadd    ST(0), ST(1)
fadd    ST(0), ST(2)
fadd    ST(2), ST(0)
fiadd   WORD_INTEGER
fiadd   SHORT_INTEGER
fadd    SHORT_REAL
fadd    LONG_REAL
faddp   ST(2), ST(0)
fsub    ST(0), ST(2)
fisub   WORD_INTEGER
fsubp   ST(2), ST(0)
fsubr   ST(2), ST(0)
fisubr  SHORT_INTEGER
fsubrp  ST(2), ST(0)
```

The operands for these commands may be either the FPU stack registers or one stack register and one memory cell.

The following program code fragment (Listing 2.1) demonstrates the use of the FPU commands for finding the sum of two floating-point numbers.

Listing 2.1. Adding two floating-point numbers

```cpp
// FIADD_EXM.cpp : Defines the entry point for the console application

#include "stdafx.h"

int _tmain(int argc, _TCHAR* argv[])
{
float f1, f2, fsum;
while (true)
{
  printf("\nEnter float 1: ");
  scanf("%f", &f1);
  printf("Enter float 2: ");
  scanf("%f", &f2);
  _asm {
    finit
    fld     DWORD PTR f1
    fadd    DWORD PTR f2
    fstp    DWORD PTR fsum
    fwait
      };
 printf("f1 + f2 = %6.3f\n", fsum);
}
 return 0;
}
```

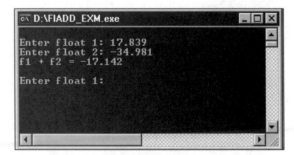

Fig. 2.1. Application adds two floating-point numbers by using the FPU commands

In the _asm {...} block, the first `fld` command loads the `f1` floating-point number from the memory to the top register of the FPU stack. The `fadd` command calculates the sum of the values of the top stack register `ST(0)` and the `f2` variable in the
memory. The result of the operation is stored on top of the FPU stack. Finally,
the `fstp` command saves the resulting sum to the `fsum` variable, at the same time
clearing the top stack register `ST(0)`. In Fig. 2.1, you can see the application window
with the output of this program.

In the next example, we will consider the use of the loading, addition, and saving
commands for summing up the elements of an array of seven integers. Tasks of
this kind are common in practice. You will see both the C++ .NET source code and
the code using assembly language. This example, like the previous one, also demonstrates the technique for using the assembly commands for performing mathematical
calculations. Listing 2.2 shows the source code of the C++ console application without
using the assembly language commands.

**Listing 2.2. Summing up the elements of an integer array by using
the C++ operators only**

```cpp
// FSUM.cpp : Defines the entry point for the console application

#include "stdafx.h"

int _tmain(int argc, _TCHAR* argv[])
{
 int iarray[6] = {1, -7, 0, 5, 3, 9};
 int *piarray = iarray;
 int isum = 0;
 int sf = sizeof(iarray)/4;
 for (int cnt = 0; cnt < sf; cnt++)
  {
    isum += *piarray;
    piarray++;
  }
 printf("Sum of integers = %d\n", isum);
 getchar();
 return 0;
}
```

In order to sum up the elements, we use a classical algorithm with the `for` loop
and the `piarray` pointer to the `iarray` array:

```cpp
    for (int cnt = 0; cnt < sf; cnt++)
      {
```

```
    isum += *piarray;
    piarray++;
  }
```

Now, we will modify the source code of the program, using the assembly commands. The new version of such a program is shown in Listing 2.3.

Listing 2.3. The assembly-language version of the program for summing up array elements

---

```
// FSUM.cpp : Defines the entry point for the console application

#include "stdafx.h"

int _tmain(int argc, _TCHAR* argv[])
{
 int iarray[6] = {-3, -7, 0, 5, 3, 9};
 int *piarray = iarray;
 int isum;
 int sf = sizeof(iarray)/4;
 _asm {
         mov       ECX, sf
         dec       ECX
         mov       ESI, DWORD PTR piarray
         finit
         fild      DWORD PTR [ESI]
  next:
         add       ESI, 4
         fiadd     DWORD PTR [ESI]
         loop      next
         fistp     DWORD PTR isum
         fwait
 }
  printf("Sum of integers = %d\n", isum);
  getchar();
  return 0;
}
```

To sum up the array elements, we use the following simple algorithm: first, we use the `fild DWORD PTR [ESI]` command to load the first array element on top of the stack, and then, in every next iteration, we will add the next array element to this value. The address of the first element is placed in the ESI register, and the number of iterations (i.e., the array size minus 1) — in the ECX register. After finding the sum, we save it to the isum variable by using the fist command.

The assembly code shown in Listing 2.3 is more efficient in terms of application performance than the addition algorithm in Listing 2.2.

Fig. 2.2 shows the application window with this program running.

Fig. 2.2. Application that calculates
the sum of elements of an integer array

Multiplication and Division

Now, we will consider the next group of commands — the *multiplication* and *division* commands for integers and floating-point numbers. They are listed as follows:

```
WORD_INTEGER          LABEL  WORD
SHORT_INTEGER         LABEL  DWORD
SHORT_REAL    LABEL  DWORD
LONG_REAL     LABEL  QWORD


fmul    SHORT_REAL
fimul   WORD_INTEGER
fmulp   ST(2), ST(0)
fdiv    ST(0), ST(2)
fidiv   SHORT_INTEGER
fdivp   ST(2), ST(0)
fdivr   ST(0), ST(2)
fidivr  WORD_INTEGER
fdivrp  ST(2), ST(0)
```

As with the addition and subtraction commands, the operands for these commands may be either the FPU registers or a combination of a stack register and a memory operand. The use of these commands is best illustrated in the following example, which has a more complicated program code and demonstrates the techniques for using different FPU commands. The task is to calculate the z variable (of the floating-point type) according to the formula: `(X - Y)/(X + Y)`. Listing 2.4 shows the source code performing the C++ console application with the assembly code included.

Listing 2.4. Evaluating a formula by using the FPU assembler commands

---

```
// FORMULA.cpp : Defines the entry point for the console application

#include "stdafx.h"

int _tmain(int argc, _TCHAR* argv[])
{
float X, Y, Z;
while (true)
{
 printf("\nEnter X: ");
 scanf("%f", &X);
 printf("Enter Y: ");
 scanf("%f", &Y);
 _asm  {
                finit
                fld    DWORD PTR X
                fadd   DWORD PTR Y
                fld    DWORD PTR X
                fsub   DWORD PTR Y
                fxch   st(1)
                fdiv   st(1), st(0)
                fxch   st(1)
                fstp   DWORD PTR Z
                fwait
        };
printf("(X - Y)/(X + Y) = %7.3f\n", Z);
 };
 return 0;
}
```

Now, we will analyze this example. To calculate the `(X - Y) / (X + Y)` expression, we will perform three steps, the first of which is to find the denominator by using the following commands:

```
fld    DWORD PTR X
fadd   DWORD PTR Y
```

To the top of the stack (the ST(0) register), we load the value of the X variable. Then, we add the Y value to this register. As a result of these two commands, the top of the stack will contain the sum of X and Y.

The next two commands calculate the difference between X and Y. To do this, we load the X value to the top of the stack, and then subtract the Y value:

```
fld    DWORD PTR X
fsub   DWORD PTR Y
```

At this moment, the ST(0) register contains the difference between X and Y. As the FPU stack is organized as a cyclic buffer, the previously calculated X + Y value has moved to the ST(1) register of the stack. So, to divide X – Y by X + Y, we need to exchange the values between the ST(0) and ST(1) registers, and then divide the contents of the ST(1) register by the ST(0) value:

```
fxch   st(1)
fdiv   st(1), st(0)
```

As a result of these commands, the ST(1) register contains the required value that needs to be written to the Z variable in the memory. To do this, use the following commands:

```
fxch   st(1)
fstp   DWORD PTR Z
```

Fig. 2.3 shows the window with this application running.

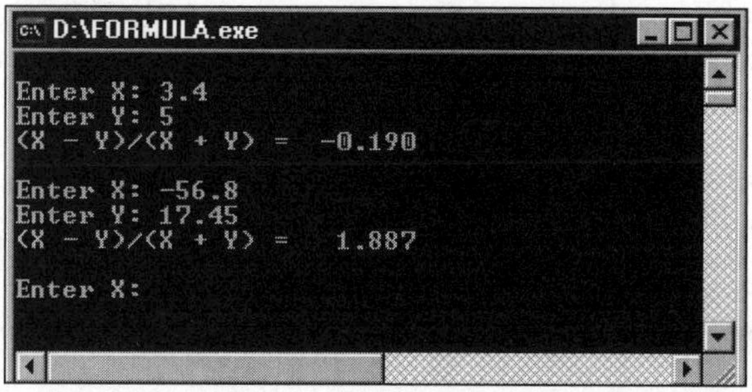

Fig. 2.3. Application that evaluates the formula by using the FPU commands

Comparison

Like in the CPU commands set, the FPU also has commands for comparing two numbers. The *comparison* commands have the following mnemonic representation:

```
WORD_INT       LABEL WORD
SHORT_INT      LABEL DWORD
```

```
SHORT_REAL     LABEL   DWORD
LONG_REAL      LABEL   QWORD

fcom
fcom    ST(2)
ficom   WORD_INT
fcom    SHORT_REAL
fcomp
ficomp  SHORT_INT
fcomp   LONG_REAL
fcompp
ftst
fxam
```

The FPU discards the comparison result itself, but sets the status flags according to this result. Before checking the status flags, the program must read the status word to the memory. The easiest way to do this is to load the status flags into the AH register, and then to the processor flags register (to facilitate checking the condition).

The comparison operation always involves the top register of the stack, so you need to specify only one operand for this command. This may be a register or a memory operand. The result of the comparison is stored in the processor status word. Here, the C0 bit is placed in the position of the CF carrying flag, C2 — in the position of the PF parity bit, and C3 — in the position of ZF.

Reflecting the result of comparison requires only two status bits: C3 and C0. Table 2.1 shows the correspondence between the operands under comparison and the values of the status bits.

Table 2.1. The correspondence between the operands under comparison and the status bits

C3	C0	Result
0	0	ST > source
0	1	ST < source
1	0	ST = source
1	1	ST and the source are incomparable

Comparing Floating-Point Numbers

The following program (Listing 2.5) compares two floating-point numbers and displays the result on the screen.

Listing 2.5. A C++ program comparing two floating-point numbers

```
// COMPARE_REAL.cpp : Defines the entry point
// for the console application

#include "stdafx.h"

int _tmain(int argc, _TCHAR* argv[])
{
float X, Y;
int   Flag = 0;
X = 0;
Y = 0;

while (true)
{
 printf("\nEnter X: ");
 scanf("%f", &X);
 printf("Enter Y: ");
 scanf("%f", &Y);

 _asm {
            finit
            fldz
            fld     DWORD PTR X
            fcomp   DWORD PTR Y
            fstsw   AX
            fwait
            sahf
            jb      xly
            je      xeqy
            mov     Flag, 2
            jmp     ex
        xly:
            mov     Flag, 0
            jmp     ex
        xeqy:
            mov     Flag, 1
        ex:
        };
    switch (Flag)
{
case 0:
    printf("X < Y\n");
```

```
   break;
case 1:
   printf("X = Y\n");
   break;
case 2:
   printf("X > Y\n");
   break;
default:
   break;
}
  }
return 0;
}
```

After initializing the FPU with the `finit` command, the X variable is placed on top of the stack. The `fcomp` command compares the number on top of the stack with the variable in the memory, and depending on the result, sets the bits in the processor's status word. The status bits are then written to the CPU status register, where they are analyzed. Depending on the bits set, there is a jump to a corresponding branch of the program. The code fragment performing these actions looks like this:

```
finit
fld      DWORD PTR X
fcomp    DWORD PTR Y
fstsw    AX
sahf
```

Fig. 2.4 shows the window with this application running.

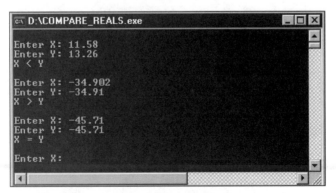

Fig. 2.4. Application that implements the algorithm
for comparing two floating-point numbers

Comparing Integers

Besides the `fcomp` command, there are also other modifications of the `fcom` comparison command. One of these is the `ficomp` modification intended for comparing integers. Below, you can see the program code for comparing two integers (Listing 2.6).

Listing 2.6. Comparing two integers

```cpp
// COMPARE_INTS.cpp : Defines the entry point
// for the console application

#include "stdafx.h"

int _tmain(int argc, _TCHAR* argv[])
{
 int X, Y;
 int   Flag = 0;
 X = 0;
 Y = 0;
 while (true)
 {
  printf("\nEnter X: ");
  scanf("%d", &X);
  printf("Enter Y: ");
  scanf("%d", &Y);
  _asm {
        finit
        fild      DWORD PTR X
        ficomp    DWORD PTR Y
        fstsw     AX
        fwait
        sahf
        jb        xly

        je        xeqy
        mov       Flag, 2
        jmp       ex
    xly:
        mov       Flag, 0
        jmp       ex
    xeqy:
        mov       Flag, 1
      ex:
        };
```

```
   switch (Flag)
{
 case 0:
   printf("X < Y\n");
   break;
 case 1:
   printf("X = Y\n");
   break;
 case 2:
   printf("X > Y\n");
   break;
default:
   break;
 }
  }


   return 0;
}
```

In general, the program code for comparing integers is almost the same as that for comparing floating-point numbers. The only difference is that the floating-point arithmetic commands (fld, fcomp) are replaced with those of the integer arithmetic (fild, ficomp).

Counting the Number of Occurrences

We will consider one more example illustrating the technique of using the FPU commands in the assembly code. Suppose you need to count the number of occurrences of the given number in an array of integers. In Listing 2.7, you can see the source code of the corresponding console application created in C++ .NET.

Listing 2.7. The application that counts the number of occurrences of the given number in the array

```
// COUNT_NUMBER.cpp : Defines the entry point for the console
// application
#include "stdafx.h"

int _tmain(int argc, _TCHAR* argv[])
{
   int iarray[10] = {-13, -7, 10, -5, 3, -7, -5, 4, -7, -3};
   int *piarray = iarray;
```

```
      int num;
      printf("Array: ");
      for (int cnt = 0; cnt < sizeof(iarray)/4; cnt++)
        {
printf("%d  ", *piarray++);
        }
      while (true)
        {
          printf("\nEnter number to find: ");
          scanf("%d", &num);
          cnt = 0;
          int sf = sizeof(iarray)/4;

          _asm {
                mov     ESI, DWORD PTR piarray
                mov     ECX, DWORD PTR sf
                finit
                fild    DWORD PTR num

             next_cmp:
                ficom   DWORD PTR [ESI]
                fstsw   AX
                sahf
                jne     skip
                inc     cnt
             skip:
                sub     ESI, 4
                loop    next_cmp
                fwait
        }
            printf("\nThe number %d occures = %d times\n", num, cnt);
        }
            return 0;
        }
```

The first commands of the assembly block initialize the ESI and ECX processor reg-isters with the address of the last array and its size, respectively. After that, the needed number is loaded from the num variable to the top of the FPU stack with the following command:

```
fild    DWORD PTR num
```

The value on top of the stack is compared in turn with each element of the array:

```
ficom   DWORD PTR [ESI]
```

This command sets the corresponding bits in the status word. To extract and analyze this data, use the following commands:

```
fstsw   AX
sahf
jne     skip
inc     cnt
```

Every time the elements appear identical, the `cnt` counter is incremented.
To continue on to the next element of the array, use the following command:

```
sub     ESI, 4
```

When the loop is completed, the `cnt` counter contains the number of times the given number occurs in the array. If this number is not found in the array, then `cnt = 0`.
Fig. 2.5 shows the application window.

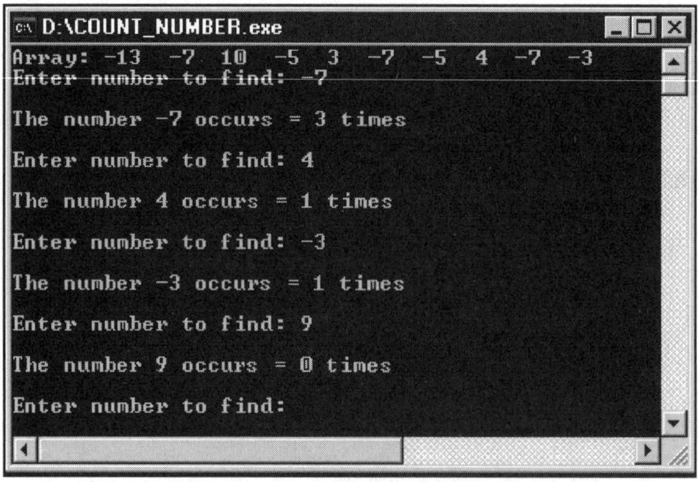

Fig. 2.5. Application that counts the number of occurrences
of the given integer in the array

The comparison commands that extract the value from the stack present a convenient way for clearing the stack. The FPU has no command that would extract an operand from the stack in a convenient way. Instead, you can use the comparison commands with the extraction. These commands also alter the status register, so you should not use them if you need the status bits for further operations. But in most cases, these commands give you a quick way for extracting one or two operands from the stack. As the FPU issues an error on stack overflow, you need to remove all the operands from the stack after completing the calculations.

Specialized Comparison Commands

There are two specialized comparison commands. One of these is the command that allows you to compare the contents of the top register of the stack with zero (0). It is a quick way for finding the sign of the number stored on top of the stack.

The other specialized command is `fxam`. It sets all four status register flags (c_3 ... c_0), reflecting the type of the number contained in the top register of the stack. The FPU can process numbers represented in any form (not only the formalized floating-point numbers). The `fxam` command allows you to determine what type number is stored on top of the stack.

If the arithmetic processing does not demand anything special, and the results of operations do not reach the limits of the FPU registers, then it is not logical to use the `fxam` command. Here, we will not explore the FPU's reaction to the exceptions that may sometimes occur in the calculations. There are many issues related to this and they are addressed in detail in Intel's official manual on Processor 387.

Power Functions and Trigonometric Functions

The next group of functions we are going to consider is that containing *power* functions and *trigonometric* functions.

These commands enable the FPU to calculate mathematical expressions involving logarithms, exponents, and trigonometric functions. These are the commands:

```
fsqrt
fscale
fprem
frndint
fxtract

fabs
fchs
fsin
fcos
fsincos

fptan
fpatan
f2xm1
fyl2x
fyl2xp1
```

The commands for transcendental functions are a great contribution to the calculation power of the processors. These functions calculate the results with high precision.

Note here that the angle arguments for the trigonometric functions should be specified in radian measure. For example, if you need to calculate *sin A*, the *A* angle should be given in radians. To convert angle values between degrees and radians, use the following formula:

$$A\_RAD = A * PI / 180,$$

A_RAD being the radian value, and A being the angle measured in degrees.

Now, we will consider an example that calculates the sine and the cosine of an angle. The source code of this simple program is shown in Listing 2.8.

Listing 2.8. A program for calculating the sine and the cosine of an angle

```
// SinCos.cpp : Defines the entry point for the console application

#include "stdafx.h"

int _tmain(int argc, _TCHAR* argv[])
{
 float angle, angleRad, Sine, Cosine;
 while (true)
 {
  printf("\nEnter degrees: ");
  scanf("%f", &angle);
  angleRad = angle*3.14/180;

 _asm {
      finit
      fld DWORD PTR angleRad
      fld DWORD PTR angleRad
      fsin
      fstp DWORD PTR Sine
      fcos
      fstp DWORD PTR Cosine
      fwait
     }

  printf("The angle in degrees = %7.3f\n", angle);
  printf("Sine of angle = %7.3f\n", Sine);
  printf("Cosine of angle = %7.3f\n", Cosine);
  getchar();

 }
return 0;
}
```

The `fsin` and `fcos` commands calculate the sine and the cosine of the angle value stored in the top register of the stack: `ST(0)`. These commands take no operands, and return the result to the `ST(0)` register.

This means that the previous value of this register (the angle value) is no longer stored in `ST(0)` after the sine has been calculated. That is why we had to use the `fld` command twice in our procedure! Fig. 2.6 shows the application window with this program running.

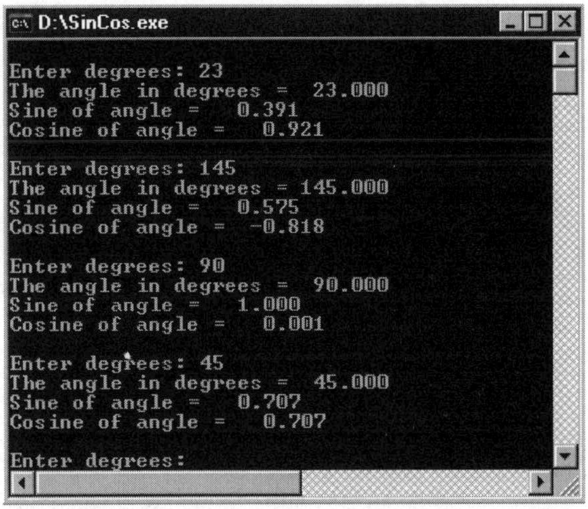

Fig. 2.6. Application calculating the sine and the cosine of an angle

Among assembly language commands for calculating trigonometric functions, there is also the `fsincos` command. It calculates both the sine and the cosine of the angle value stored in `ST(0)`, the top register of the FPU stack. This command does not take any operands. The result of this function is returned in the `ST(0)` and `ST(1)` registers, with the sine value placed in `ST(0)` and the cosine in `ST(1)`. Now, we will modify the previous example, using the `fsincos` command.

In Listing 2.9, note the modified version of the program code.

Listing 2.9. The modified program calculating the sine and the cosine of an angle

```
// SinCos_mod.cpp : Defines the entry point for the console application

#include "stdafx.h"

int _tmain(int argc, _TCHAR* argv[])
{
```

```
float angle, angleRad, Sine, Cosine;
while (true)
{
 printf("\nEnter degrees: ");
 scanf("%f", &angle);
 angleRad = angle*3.14/180;

_asm {
    finit
    fld DWORD PTR angleRad
    fsincos
    fxch st(1)
    fstp DWORD PTR Sine
    fstp DWORD PTR Cosine
    fwait
    }
 printf("The angle in degrees = %7.3f\n", angle);
 printf("Sine of angle = %7.3f\n", Sine);
 printf("Cosine of angle = %7.3f\n", Cosine);
 getchar();
 }
return 0;
}
```

The examples considered here illustrate just few of the powerful mathematical options provided by assembly language. A remarkable feature of this language is that it is fairly easy to optimize even the code written in assembly language itself!

Main Methods of Optimizing Mathematical Calculations

In the C++ .NET programming environment, as well as in other high-level languages, you can use assembly language to develop efficient solutions for optimizing crucial fragments of a program. The results may be varied in terms of performance and program code size. Below, we will consider several examples that are used successfully in practice. They use assembly language to improve the quality of the program code. We will examine how mathematical operations can be optimized. There are several methods for doing so.

Method 1. Using Integer Instructions

Instead of the FPU commands, you can use integer instructions. The data transfer operations can be replaced by more efficient integer commands. For example, commands such as

```
fld  QWORD PTR [ESI]
fstp QWORD PTR [EDI]
```

can be replaced by these:

```
mov EAX, [ESI]
mov EBX, [ESI+4]
mov [EDI], EAX
mov [EDI+4], EBX
```

Method 2. Optimizing Zero Test for Floating-Point Numbers

To check if a floating-point number is equal to zero (0), you can use the integer instructions as well. Note the code that implements the zero test by using a sequence of the FPU commands. Here is the source code of a simple C++ .NET console application using this test (Listing 2.10).

Listing 2.10. Testing if the floating-point number is equal to zero (0)

```cpp
// CHANGE_FPU_INT.cpp : Defines the entry point for the console
// application

#include "stdafx.h"

int _tmain(int argc, _TCHAR* argv[])
{
  float f1 = 0;
  float *pf1 = &f1;
  bool  isZero;
  while (true)
    {
    printf("\nEnter float value: ");
    scanf("%f", pf1);
    _asm {
        mov     ECX, 1
        mov     EBX, DWORD PTR pf1
        finit
        fld     DWORD PTR [EBX]
```

```
        ftst
        fstsw     AX
        sahf
        jz        ex
        mov       ECX, 0
    ex:
        mov       DWORD PTR isZero, ECX
        fwait
  }
   if (isZero)
printf("Entered value is equal to 0\n");
   else
       printf("Entered value is not equal to 0\n");
   }
  return 0;
}
```

An equivalent variant of the program using the ordinary assembly commands may look like this (here, only the assembly code fragment is shown):

```
 . . .
_asm {
        mov       ECX, 1
        mov       EBX, DWORD PTR pf1
        mov       EAX, DWORD PTR [EBX]
        add       EAX, EAX
        jz        ex
        mov       ECX, 0
    ex:
        mov       DWORD PTR isZero, ECX
        }
 . . .
```

For further optimization to the zero test algorithm, try to eliminate the branching of the program code. To do this, find an equivalent for the `jz ex` conditional jump command. For example, you can use the `cmov` command with the corresponding condition. With these changes, the assembly code fragment will look like this:

```
 . . .
_asm {
        mov       ECX, 1
        mov       EBX, DWORD PTR pf1
        mov       EAX, DWORD PTR [EBX]
        add       EAX, EAX
        cmovz     EAX, ECX
```

```
    mov     ECX, 0
    cmovnz  EAX, ECX
    mov     DWORD PTR isZero, EAX
}
. . .
```

Take into account that the latter two code fragments work with the operands in double-word format. For float numbers with double precision (QWORD), you need to test only the bits numbered 32–64. If these bits are equal to 0, then the number is equal to 0.

Fig. 2.7 shows the application window for all three modifications of the program code.

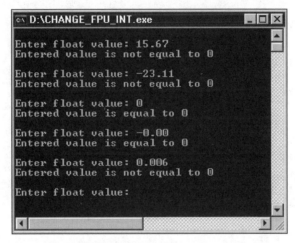

Fig. 2.7. Application that tests whether
the given floating-point number is equal to zero (0)

Method 3. Using the LEA *Commands for Optimization*

To optimize mathematical calculations, you can also use the `lea` commands to load the address. For example, a command such as

```
lea EAX, 3[-100][EDX+ECX]
```

can replace a whole group of the following commands:

```
mov EAX, ECX
add EAX, EDX
add EAX, 100
sub EAX, 3
```

In Listing 2.11, note the source code of a small console application using this command.

Listing 2.11. The use of the LEA instruction as an arithmetic command

---

```cpp
// LEAEX.cpp : Defines the entry point for the console application

#include "stdafx.h"

int _tmain(int argc, _TCHAR* argv[])
{
    int i1, i2, ires;
    while (true)
     {
printf("\nEnter i1 -> ECX: ");
        scanf("%d", &i1);
        printf("\nEnter i2 -> EDX: ");
        scanf("%d", &i2);
  _asm {
        mov EDX, DWORD PTR i1
        mov ECX, DWORD PTR i2
        lea EAX, 3[-100][EDX+ECX]
        mov DWORD PTR ires, EAX
        }
  printf("Calculated result = %d\n", ires);
 }
 return 0;
}
```

The source code of the program is simple and does not require further explanation. Fig. 2.8 shows the window with this application running.

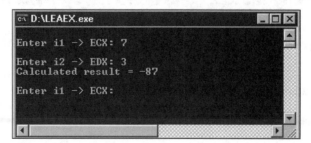

Fig. 2.8. Using the LEA (address loading) command
for performing mathematical operations

We have considered only a part of the whole set of assembly mathematical functions. This consideration encourages you to use the full range of FPU features in your programs in assembly language. If necessary, you can use assembly language to modify existing mathematical algorithms, or even write your own, which are not found in high-level languages.

Working with Strings and Data Arrays

Assembly language also has many advantages concerning processing strings and data arrays. To perform such operations, a whole group of commands has been developed. In the Intel terminology, they are referred to as *string commands*. While discussing the issues of string processing, we will apply the following operations:

- ❐ Comparing two strings
- ❐ Copying the source string to the destination string
- ❐ Reading a string from a device or a file
- ❐ Writing a string to a device or a file
- ❐ Determining the length of the string
- ❐ Finding a substring in the given string
- ❐ Merging two strings (concatenation)

The string operations are widely used in high-level languages. By implementing these operations in assembly language, you can achieve considerable gain in performance of high-level language applications, especially for those processing a great number of operating system strings or arrays.

First, we will consider the main assembly language commands for manipulating the strings.

String Operations in Assembly Language

A string of characters or a set of numbers, which is treated by the program as a group, is a common data type. The program may send the string from one location to another, compare it with other strings, or find the given value within the string.

The program presents every word, sentence, or another structure through the use of a sequence of characters in the memory. For example, the text editors mainly use the search and transfer operations. The processor's string commands can perform these operations with minimal overhead, and within minimal time intervals.

First, we will address the main principles of working with strings.

The program may perform string operations over bytes, words, and double words.

The string commands do not use the addressing methods used by other commands. They address the operands with combinations of the ESI or EDI registers. For the source operands, the ESI register is used, and for the resulting operands, the EDI register is used. All string commands correct the address after performing the operation.

The string may consist of several elements, but the string commands can process only one element at a time. The automatic incrementing (increasing) or decrementing (decreasing) of the address of the operand makes it possible to process the string data quickly. The Direct Flag in the status register determines the direction of string processing.

If the Direct Flag is set to 1, the address will be decremented, and if it is set to 0, the address is incremented. The increment or decrement value itself is determined by the size of the operand. For example, for character strings with 1-byte operands, the string processing commands change the address by 1 after each operation. If you process an array of integers with each operand having the size of 4 bytes, the string commands will change the address by 4. When the operation is completed, the address pointer in the ESI or EDI register points to the next element of the string.

Now, we will explore the representation of strings in various programming languages. The most frequent are the *null-terminated strings*. They are used in the C language and in the Windows operating systems. In assembly language, such a string looks like this:

```
String_0  DB "NULL-TERMINATED STRING",  0
```

We will deal mainly with the null-terminated strings.

Basic String Commands

There are five basic commands for processing the strings, which are often referred to as *string commands*:

❑ movs — the command for moving a data string from one memory location to another.

❑ lods — for the string with the address stored in the ESI register. This command loads it to the EAX (AX, AL) accumulator.

❑ stos — this command saves the contents of the EAX (AX, AL) memory register to the address specified in the EDI register.

❑ cmps — the command for comparing the strings allocated at the addresses stored in the ESI and EDI registers.

❑ scas — the string scanning command which compares the contents of the EAX (AX, AL) register to the memory value determined by the EDI register.

Each of the string processing commands has three possible formats. For example, the `movs` command is represented in the following ways: `movsb`, `movsw`, `movsd`. The `movsb` command can be used for processing 1-byte operands only, the `movsw` command deals with words, and `movsd` is intended for processing double words. The `b`, `w`, and `d` suffixes determine the value of increment or decrement for the `ESI` and `EDI` index registers. If the command is used in the general format, the type of operands should be defined explicitly.

Before performing string commands, make sure to load the addresses of the needed memory areas to the `ESI` and/or `EDI` registers.

To perform repeated operations over strings, the repetition prefix (`rep`) is used in virtually all cases. The number of repetitions for the string operation is determined by the `ECX` register.

To move data from one location to another, you may find it convenient to combine the `lods` and `stos` command. But indeed, there is a designated command for this purpose — the `movs` command for string transfer. It reads the data at the given memory address specified in the `ESI` register, and places it at the address indicated by the `EDI` register. At the same time, the values of the `ESI` and `EDI` registers change so that they point to the next elements of the strings. The `movs` command does not load the accumulator while transferring the data.

The `movs` command takes several operands. Except `movs`, there is only one more string command (`cmps`) that can work with two operands from the memory. All the other commands demand one or both operands to be stored in one of the microprocessor registers. The `movs` command, as well as the `lods` and `stos` commands, can work both with bytes and with words.

Since the string commands deal with fixed addresses, it is the developer who should control what type of operands are sent to this command. Both operands of the command should be of the same type. You can also add suffixes to the command to specify the transfer type: the `movsb` command is used for byte strings, and `movsw` for strings consisting of words. If the program uses the command in its basic form (`movs`), the assembler verifies the variables, checking whether the segment addressing is correct and the operands are of the same type.

The `movs` command with the `rep` prefix is an efficient way to transfer a block. With the character counter in the `ECX` register, and the `DF` flag specifying the transfer direction, the `rep movs` command is a very quick way to transfer data from one memory location to another.

With regard to the scanning operation (`scas`), the last scanning iteration also resets the zero flag (`ZF`) when the `ECX` register reaches the zero value (0). This indicates that there is no corresponding element in the array.

The Use of String Commands

Copying the Strings

The following program illustrates the process of copying one string to another, with both strings having the Cstring type. Now, we will use the C++ .NET Application Wizard to develop a dialog box application. In the main application form, place two Edit Control controls. These will be linked to the variables for the source string (cSrc) and the destination string (cDst), both of the Cstring type. In the cSrc editing field, enter the string that you need to copy to cDst and display on the screen. We will also add two Static Text controls and a Button control to the form. When the button is clicked, the contents of the cSrc string are copied to the cDst string. To clarify further, we will use the interim variables (s1 and s2) of the Cstring type. The source code for the button click handler is shown in Listing 2.12.

Listing 2.12. Using the assembly-language commands for copying a string in a button click handler in a C++ .NET program

```
. . .
 void CCP_STRINGDlg::OnBnClickedButton1()
{
// TODO: Add your control notification handler code here.

UpdateData(TRUE);
CString s1, s2;
LPCTSTR lps1, lps2;

s1 = cSrc;
s2 = cDst;


    lps1 = s1.GetBuffer(32);
    int lsrc = s1.GetLength();

 _asm {
        lea     ESI, DWORD PTR lps1
        lea     EDI, DWORD PTR lps2
        mov     ECX, lsrc
        cld
    next:

        lodsb
```

```
        stosb
        loop      next
    };

  s2 = (CString)lps2;
  cDst = s2;
  UpdateData(FALSE);
  }
```

. . .

Now, we will analyze the code of the handler. The contents of the cSrc variable are placed to the s1 string. Then, the s1 string is copied to s2. And finally, the contents of the s2 string are displayed in the editing field corresponding to the cDst variable. When working with strings of the CString type, it is convenient to refer to them as null-terminated strings. To do this, you need to know the address of the string buffer and the length of the string. To obtain these parameters, use the following operators:

```
CString s1, s2;
LPCTSTR lps1, lps2;

s1 = cSrc;
s2 = cDst;
lps1 = s1.GetBuffer(32);
int lsrc = s1.GetLength();
```

The string buffer size has been made equal to 32 for convenience only.

After that, we copy the string with the lps1 pointer to the string determined by the lps2 pointer. To do this, use the following assembly-language commands:

```
      . . .
  _asm {
        lea       ESI, DWORD PTR lps1
        lea       EDI, DWORD PTR lps2
        mov       ECX, lsrc
        cld

    next:
        lodsb
        stosb
        loop      next
    }

      . . .
```

Before starting the copying operation, you need to set the Direct Flag so that the source and destination addresses can be incremented after each operation. To do this, set the flag to 0 with the `cld` command. The length of the `lsrc` string is placed to the `ECX` register.

There are two commands that perform the copying operation: `lodsb` and `stosb`. The `lodsb` command loads the byte from the memory location determined by the `ESI` register (the `lps1` string) to the `AL` accumulator. And the `stosb` command writes the resulting byte from the accumulator to the memory address stored in `EDI` (the `lps2` string).

After the data transfer operation, the values of the `ESI` and `EDI` registers are incremented by 1 automatically. In this case, the increment value is determined by the type of string command. Our program performs the copying operations over bytes; that is why the addresses will be incremented by 1.

For this code fragment to operate properly, the memory space allocated for the destination string (`lps2`) must be not less than the size of the source string.

Fig. 2.9 shows the results of the copying operation.

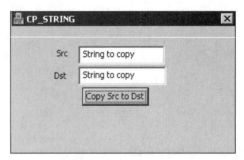

Fig. 2.9. Application that copies one string to another

To simplify the previous program, you can replace the two `lodsb` and `stosb` commands with a single `movsb` command for copying the strings (Listing 2.13).

Listing 2.13. Using the `movsb` command for copying the strings

```
. . .
_asm {
        lea     ESI, DWORD PTR lps1
        lea     EDI, DWORD PTR lps2
        mov     ECX, lsrc
        cld
    next:
        movsb
```

```
        loop    next
    }
    . . .
```

To further simplify the source code of the program, you can use the `movsb` command with the repetition prefix (`rep`). The `rep` prefix uses the contents of the ECX register as a parameter:

```
_asm {
        lea     ESI, DWORD PTR lps1
        lea     EDI, DWORD PTR lps2
        mov     ECX, lsrc
        cld
        rep     movsb
    }
```

Copying the Arrays

The copying operations can also be applied to the arrays of integers or floating-point numbers. The following console program (Listing 2.14) uses the assembly commands to copy the contents of one the integer array (SARRAY) to another (DARRAY).

Listing 2.14. Using assembly language for copying an array of integers

```cpp
// COPY_INT_ARRAYS.cpp : Defines the entry point
// for the console application

#include "stdafx.h"

int _tmain(int argc, _TCHAR* argv[])
{
 int sarray[6] = {245, 11, -34, 56, 7, 19};
 int darray[8] = {0, 0, 14, 45, 56, 7, 21, -56};
 int lenarray = sizeof(sarray) / 4;

printf("sarray: ");
for (int cnt = 0; cnt < sizeof(sarray)/4; cnt++)
    printf("%d\t", sarray[cnt]);
printf("\ndarray: ");
for (int cnt = 0; cnt < sizeof(darray)/4; cnt++)
```

```
    printf("%d\t", darray[cnt]);

_asm {
      cld
      mov  ECX, DWORD PTR lenarray
      lea  ESI, DWORD PTR sarray
      lea  EDI, DWORD PTR darray
      rep  movsd
    };
printf("\ndarray after copy: ");
for (int cnt = 0; cnt < sizeof(darray)/4; cnt++)
    printf("%d\t", darray[cnt]);
getchar();
return 0;
}
```

The source code of the program is easy to analyze. Note the use of the `rep movsd`
command for copying double words. Fig. 2.10 shows the application window.

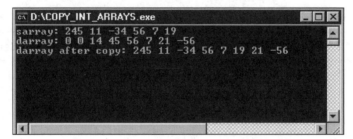

Fig. 2.10. Application copying the elements of one array to another

Concatenation of Strings

The `movs` command can also be used for another useful operation called *concatenation*.
This operation adds the elements of the source string to the destination string. In this
case, make sure that the size of the destination buffer is large enough to hold the
merged string. The following technique is often used: place space characters at the end
of the destination string, and then replace them with the elements of the source string.
The size of the destination buffer must be at least equal to the sum of the lengths of the
strings concatenated. You can see this technique illustrated in the source code of
a C++ .NET console application (Listing 2.15).

Listing 2.15. Using assembly language for string concatenation in a C++ .NET program

```
// STRINGS_CONCAT.cpp : Defines the entry point
// for the console application


#include "stdafx.h"

int _tmain(int argc, _TCHAR* argv[])
   {
   char s1[] = "Visual            ";
   char s2[] = " C++ .NET";
   printf("String-destination: %s\n", s1);
   printf("String-source: %s\n", s2);

   int ls2 = strlen(s2);
   _asm {
          lea    ESI, DWORD PTR s2
          lea    EDI, DWORD PTR s1
          cld
          mov    AL, ' '
     again:
          scasb
          je     next
          jmp    again
      next:
          dec    EDI
          mov    ECX, ls2
          rep    movsb
        };

   printf("Result of concatenation : %s\n", s1);
   getchar();
   return 0;
}
```

Look carefully at the following assembly commands:

```
lea    ESI, DWORD PTR s2
lea    EDI, DWORD PTR s1
cld
mov    AL, ' '
```

They load the addresses of the s1 and s2 strings to the ESI and EDI registers, and also set the direct flag for incrementing the address. In the AL register, we place the space character to determine the address in the buffer of the s1 string, after which we will place the elements of the s2 string.

To copy the s2 string to replace the space characters in s1, use the rep movsb command. At the same time, the ECX register stores the length of the s2 string.

Fig. 2.11 illustrates the window with this application running.

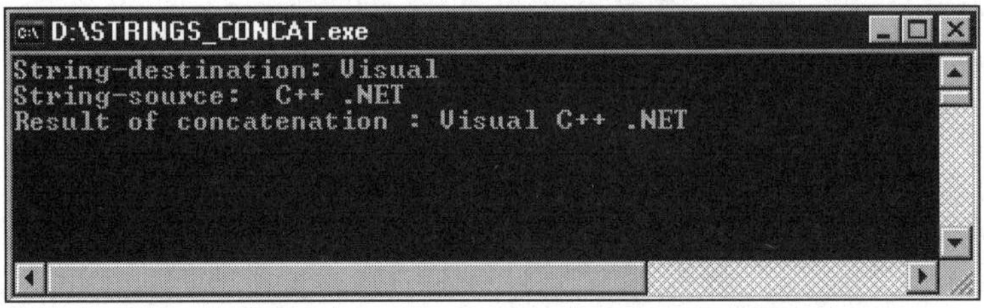

Fig. 2.11. Application that performs concatenation of two strings

Concatenation of Arrays

The concatenation of arrays of integers or floating-point numbers is slightly different from the corresponding operation over character strings, although they have much in common. The destination array should be large enough to hold the new elements from the source array. When re-counting the needed shift for the destination array, consider the byte size of the array element.

In Listing 2.16, note the source code of a console application that performs concatenation of two integer arrays.

Listing 2.16. Concatenation of two integer arrays

```
// CONCAT_INT_AARAYS.cpp : Defines the entry point
// for the console application

#include "stdafx.h"

int _tmain(int argc, _TCHAR* argv[])
{
 int i1[] = {23, 44, 8, 0, 0, 0, 0};
 int i2[] = {-56, 7, -3, 7};
 int ilen = sizeof(i2)/4;

 printf("Source array i2:\t ");
```

```
for (int cnt = 0; cnt < sizeof(i2)/4; cnt++)
    printf("%d\t", i2[cnt]);
printf("\nDest array i2:\t\t ");
for (int cnt = 0; cnt < sizeof(i1)/4; cnt++)
    printf("%d\t", i1[cnt]);

_asm {
        lea    ESI, DWORD PTR i2
        lea    EDI, DWORD PTR i1
        cld
        mov    EAX, 0
    again:
        scasd
        je     next
        jmp    again
    next:
        sub    EDI, 4
        mov    ECX, ilen
        rep    movsd
};
printf("\nConcatenated arrays:\t ");
for (int cnt = 0; cnt < sizeof(i1)/4; cnt++)
    printf("%d\t", i1[cnt]);
getchar();
return 0;
}
```

This code fragment writes the elements of the source array (i2) to the destination array (i1), beginning with the fourth element. The first elements of these arrays automation event placed to the ESI and EDI registers, and the ECX register holds the number of the elements to be written (it is equal to the size of the i2 array).

Fig. 2.12 shows the application window.

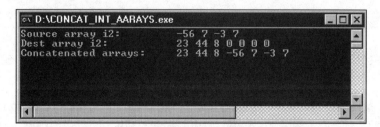

Fig. 2.12. Application that performs concatenation of arrays

Comparing Two Strings

Another frequently used array operation is comparison. To compare the elements of strings and arrays, you can use the cmps command and its modifications. The following program code fragment in the MASM assembly language (Listing 2.17) compares two character strings.

Listing 2.17. Using the assembly commands for comparing two strings

```
   . . .
 SRC     DB "STRING 1 "
 LSRC    EQU $-SRC
 DST     DB "STRING 1"
 LDST    EQU $-DST
 FLAG    DD 0

   . . .

 cld
 lea     ESI, SRC
 lea     EDI, DST
 mov     ECX, LSRC
 mov     EDX, LDST
 cmp     ECX, EDX
 je      next_check
 jmp     continue
next_check:
 repe    CMPSB
 je      equal
 mov     EAX, FLAG
 jmp     continue
equal:
 mov     FLAG, 1
continue:

   . . .
```

As the strings are compared by bytes, this code fragment uses the cmpsb command with the repe prefix for repetition. If the strings are identical, then the FLAG variable is set to 1; otherwise, it is set to 0. In our example, the strings do not coincide, so the FLAG variable will be set to 0. The result will be the same if the strings contain the same number of elements but are different in at least one of them. If the strings differ in length, then the FLAG variable will be set to 0, too.

Comparing Two Arrays

Now, we can modify the previous code fragment, adjusting it to compare the arrays of integers. The resulting program code is shown in Listing 2.18.

Listing 2.18. Comparing the arrays of integers

```
    . . .
ISRC    DD   3, 16, 89, 11
LISRC   EQU ($-ISRC)/4
IDST    DD   3, 16, 89, 11, 9
LIDST   EQU ($-IDST)/4
FLAG    DD
    . . .
cld
lea     ESI, ISRC
lea     EDI, IDST
mov     ECX, LISRC
mov     EDX, LIDST
cmp     ECX, EDX
je      next_check
jmp     continue
next_check:
repe    cmpsd
je      equal
mov     EAX, FLAG
jmp     continue
equal:
mov     FLAG, 1
continue:
    . . .
```

The difference between the program code for processing integer arrays and that for processing bytes is mainly related to the size of the operands. Since an integer takes up 4 bytes in the memory, you should replace the cmpsb command with the cmpsd command to compare double words. As before, we write the size of the original array to the ECX register, but this size is now measured as the number of double words. That is why we need to divide the resulting values by 4:

```
ISRC    DD   3, 16, 89, 11
LISRC   EQU ($-ISRC)/4
IDST    DD   3, 16, 89, 11, 9
LIDST   EQU ($-IDST)/4
```

Filling a String or Array

One more example that is often useful is the task of filling a certain memory location with the given character or number. For example, if you need to fill a character string with space characters, you can use the following code (Listing 2.19).

Listing 2.19. Using the assembly-language commands to fill a string with space characters

```
. . .
SRC   DB  "This string will be filled with space characters"
LSRC    EQU $-SRC

    . . .
cld
mov   AL, ' '
mov   ECX, LSRC
lea   EDI, SRC
rep   stosb
    . . .
```

To fill an integer array with zeroes, you can use the code fragment presented in Listing 2.20.

Listing 2.20. Filling an integer array with zeroes

```
    . . .
ISRC   DD  3, 16, 89, 11, -99, 4
LISRC   EQU ($-ISRC)/4

    . . .
cld
lea     EDI, ISRC
mov     ECX, LISRC
mov     EAX, 0
rep     stosd
    . . .
```

The string commands of assembly language are extremely useful for optimizing the programs created in Visual C++ .NET. Any high-level language has its own commands for copying the strings, concatenation, searching for elements, and filling a memory location with certain values. But when implemented in assembly language, such operations require a much smaller program code and are performed faster.

Conversion between Lowercase and Uppercase Characters

Now, we will consider one more example dealing with string operations. You may often need to convert lowercase characters to the corresponding uppercase ones. In the code fragment implementing this task, the use of string commands may make the program too complicated where it is hardly justified. So, we will use ordinary operators. Listing 2.21 shows the full source code of the corresponding C++ console application.

Listing 2.21. Converting lowercase characters to uppercase ones

```
// CONVERT_TO_UPPER.cpp : Defines the entry point
// for the console application

#include "stdafx.h"

int _tmain(int argc, _TCHAR* argv[])
{
  char s1[] = "this string must be converted to uppercase";
  int ls1 = strlen(s1);

  printf("Before: %s\n", s1);
  _asm {
      lea    ESI, DWORD PTR s1
      mov    ECX, DWORD PTR ls1
next:
      mov    AL, BYTE PTR [ESI]
      cmp    AL, 'a'
      jb     next_addr
      cmp    AL, 'z'
      ja     next_addr
      and    AL, 0dfh
      mov    BYTE PTR [ESI], AL
next_addr:
      inc    ESI
      loop   next
    }
  printf("After: %s\n", s1);
  getchar();
  return 0;
}
```

To convert the characters to uppercase, we use a block of commands in assembly language. Before the conversion, the address of the `s1string` is loaded to the `ESI` register, and its length (`ls1`) — to the `ECX` register. As we deal with letters here, we need to analyze the elements in the `'a'-'z'` range only. The conversion algorithm is implemented in the following code fragment:

```
   . . .
next:
   mov  AL, BYTE PTR [ESI]
   cmp  AL, 'a'
   jb   next_addr
   cmp  AL, 'z'
   ja   next_addr
   and  AL, 0dfh
   mov  BYTE PTR [ESI], AL
next_addr:
   inc  ESI
   loop next
   . . .
```

Fig. 2.13 illustrates the window with this application running.

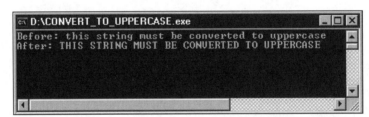

Fig. 2.13. Application converting lowercase characters to uppercase ones

Optimizing String Operations without Using String Commands

You may have the impression that string operations are efficient only if implemented through string commands. But now, we will consider an example that contains no string commands at all. You will see that the string operations can be implemented efficiently by using the ordinary assembly commands as well. This approach is illustrated in the following console application that compares two strings (Listing 2.22).

Listing 2.22. An implementation of string operations without using the string commands

```
// CMP_STRINGS_WITHOUT_PRIMITIVES.cpp : Defines the entry point
// for the console application

#include "stdafx.h"

int _tmain(int argc, _TCHAR* argv[])
{
char s1[] = "string 1";
char s2[] = "stRing 1";

bool result;
printf("String 1: %s\n", s1);
printf("String 2: %s\n", s2);

_asm {
        lea  ESI, DWORD PTR s1  // The address of the s1 string
        lea  EDI, DWORD PTR s2  // The address of the s2 string
  again:
        mov  AL, BYTE PTR [ESI]
        mov  DL, BYTE PTR [EDI]
        push EAX
        push EDX
        xor  AL, DL
        pop  EDX
        pop  EAX
        jz   streq
        jmp  strnot_eq
  streq:
        test AL, DL
        jz   succ
        inc  ESI
        inc  EDI
        jmp  again
  strnot_eq:
        mov  EAX, 0
        jmp  quit
  succ:
        mov  EAX, 1
  quit:
        mov  DWORD PTR result, EAX
```

```
};
if (result)
    printf("Equal\n");
else
    printf("Not equal\n");
getchar();
return 0;
}
```

In the assembly block, the address of the source string is placed into the ESI register, and the address of the destination string is placed to EDI. The string elements are placed to the AL and DL registers, where their values are compared:

```
    . . .
mov  AL, BYTE PTR [ESI]
mov  DL, BYTE PTR [EDI]
push EAX
push EDX
xor  AL, DL
pop  EDX
pop  EAX
jz   streq
jmp  strnot_eq
    . . .
```

If the characters are not equal, quit the procedure and return 0 to the main program. If the characters are found equal, the program checks if they are equal to 0 (see the jz streq jump command):

```
    . . .
streq:
  test AL, DL
  jz   succ
  inc  ESI
  inc  EDI
  jmp  again
    . . .
```

If the elements appear to be equal to 0, the end of string has been reached, and the comparison is completed successfully (the strings are found equal). In this case, the result variable returns 1. However, if the elements are not equal to 0 (though they are equal to each other), the program continues on to the next address in the settings and repeats the comparison loop.

In our example, the strings are not equal, so the application window displays the corresponding message (Fig. 2.14).

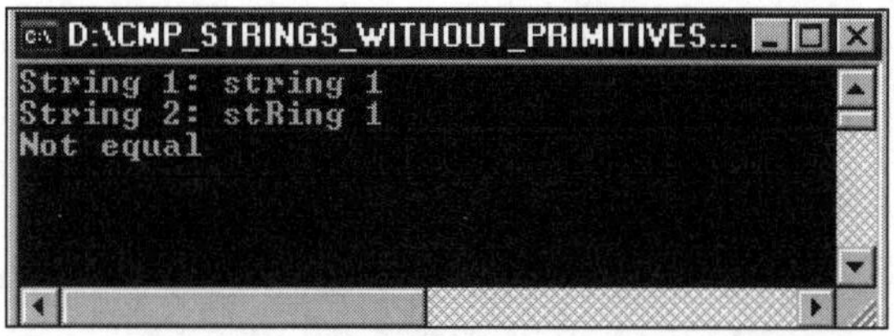

Fig. 2.14. Application for comparing two strings

As you can see, you can perform string manipulations even without using the specialized string commands, but the resulting code appears somewhat bulky because of the additional operations for incrementing or decrementing the addresses, as well as the additional commands comparing the characters and analyzing the end of strings. The highest performance for string operations is usually achieved in copying one string to another or in moving the string elements from one memory location to another. This is especially evident when you have to move large amounts of data.

A smaller gain in performance (as compared to ordinary commands) can also be achieved by search and scanning commands. In particular, the performance of these string operations is influenced by the size of the operands.

Conclusion

We have considered only few of the data optimization options offered by assembly language. In the following chapters, we will introduce additional ways to improve the quality of software products.

Chapter 3: Developing and Using Procedures in Assembly Language

In programs, especially large ones, it is often required to repeatedly implement the same task and, therefore, to write the same group of commands many times. In order to avoid this repetition, a programmer usually develops it once according to certain rules. In appropriate points of the program, he or she simply passes control to these commands, which return control after their execution. Such a group of commands, which implements a task and is designed so that it can be used any number of times at any places of code, is called a subroutine or a procedure. In contrast to a subroutine, the rest of the program is usually called the main program. This chapter discusses the principles of building procedures in assembler. These procedures are saved in files with the ASM extension and compiled to individual object module files with the OBJ extension. To use a procedure in an object module, it is necessary to add the OBJ file to the C++ project and to call the procedure in accordance with calling conventions adopted in C++ .NET.

An assembly subroutine corresponds to a C++ function, and a call to the subroutine corresponds to a function call. Implementing subroutines in assembly language is a more complicated process than declaring functions in C++ .NET. From now on, we will use the terms "subroutine", "procedure", and "function" synonymously.

In C++, many aspects of work with subroutines are hidden from a programmer, and their implementation is the compiler's job. In the assembler, a programmer has to do much work on his or her own. Although it is more difficult to write programs in assembler than in C++, the use of assembler gives full control over the program code and makes it possible to achieve a higher optimization of the application as a whole. What follows is a discussion regarding the development of procedures in the context of conventions adopted for Microsoft MASM 6.14 assembler, though the main principles are valid for any other assembler on the Intel platform.

How should you declare a procedure in the assembler? Its declaration looks like this:

```
<procedure name> proc <parameter>
   <procedure body>
<procedure name> endp
```

The body of the procedure (its commands) is preceded by the `proc` (procedure) directive and followed by the `endp` (end of procedure) directive. For example, a piece of code that declares the `AsmSub` procedure could look as follows:

```
AsmSub proc
   . . .
     ret
AsmSub endp
```

The procedure must be terminated with the `ret` command. One ASM file can contain several procedures. Here is an example of combining two procedures named `AsmSub1` and `AsmSub2` in one module:

```
      . . .
   .code
     AsmSub1 proc
        . . .
          ret
     AsmSub1  endp

     AsmSub2  proc
        . . .
          ret
     AsmSub2 endp
   end
```

The `proc` directive is considered the entry point to the procedure. Note that there is no colon after the name in the `proc` directive. Nevertheless, this name is considered a label and points to the first command of the procedure. The name of the procedure can be specified in a jump command. Then control will be passed to the first command of the procedure.

The proc directive has a parameter. It is either near or far. If the parameter is missing, it is considered near (this is why the near parameter is usually omitted). When the near parameter is used or the parameter is missing, the procedure is called "near," and with the far parameter, it is called "far." A near procedure can be called only from that command segment, in which it was declared, while a far procedure can be called from any command segment (including the segment, in which it was declared). This is the difference between near and far procedures. For 32-bit applications considered in this book, all procedure calls are near.

It should be mentioned that the names and labels declared in an assembly procedure are not local. This is why they must be unique relative to the other names used in the program. In assembler, it is possible to declare a procedure inside another procedure. However, this does not provide any advantages, so programmers rarely use nested procedures.

Now, we will discuss how procedures are called, and how they return. When programming in C++, it is enough for you to specify the name and actual parameters of a procedure in order to execute it. The work of the procedure and return to the main program are hidden from you by the compiler. However, if you write a procedure in assembler, you will have to implement all interaction between the main program and the procedure by yourself. Here are instructions on how to do this.

Two problems arise: How can you make the procedure work from the main program, and how can you return from the procedure to the main program? The first problem is easily solved. Simply execute a jump command to the first command of the procedure. In other words, specify the name of the procedure in a jump command. The other problem is more complicated. The procedure can be called from different places within the main program, therefore, it should return to different places. The procedure itself does not know where to return, but the main program does. Therefore, when calling a procedure, the main program must tell it a so-called return address. This is the address of the command in the main program, to which the procedure must return control after it completes. Usually, it is the address of the command next to the call command. The main program tells this address to the procedure, and the procedure returns control to this address. Since different calls to a procedure tell it different return addresses, the procedure returns control to different places in the main program.

How can you tell a procedure the return address? This can be done in different ways. First, you can pass it via a register. The main program writes the return address to a register, and the procedure reads it and jumps accordingly. Second, you can use the stack. Before the main program calls a procedure, it pushes the return address on the stack, and the procedure pops it and uses to jump. It is a common practice to pass the return address via the stack, so we will use only this method.

Passing the return address via the stack and returning to this address can be implemented with the commands that are already familiar to you. However, procedures

are used in actual programs very often, so the processor's command set includes special commands that make it simpler to implement jumps between the main program
and procedures. These are the `call` command and the `ret` command, which are
familiar to you. The main variants of these commands are:

```
call <procedure name>
ret
```

The `call` command pushes the address of the next command on the stack and
jumps to the first command of the specified procedure. The `ret` command pops the
address from the top of the stack and jumps to this address.

Here is an example. Suppose you want to display an integer computed by the formula `i1 - i2 - 100`, where `i1` and `i2` are integers. To compute this, write two functions in assembler and save them in an ASM file. The source code in this file is shown
in Listing 3.1.

Listing 3.1. Functions for computing the formula `i1-i2-100`

```
. . .
asmsub proc
  mov    EAX, i1
  sub    EAX, i2
  call   sub100
  ret
asmsub endp

sub100 proc
  sub    EAX, 100
  ret
sub100 endp
. . .
```

The `asmsub` procedure begins by computing the difference `i1 - i2` and puts the
intermediate result to the EAX register. The `call sub100` command pushes the address
of the next command on the stack and passes control to the beginning of the `sub100`
procedure, i.e., to the `sub EAX, 100` command. This procedure returns the final value
(equal to `i1 - i2 - 100`) via the EAX register. After that, the `ret` command pops the
address from the stack and jumps to this address. Thus the `asmsub` procedure resumes
execution from the command that follows the `call sub100` command.

There are a few versions of the `call` command. We demonstrated the main variant
where the name of a procedure is specified as a parameter of the command. However,

you can use a register as a parameter. In this case, the address of the called procedure is put in the register. Modify the previous example as shown in Listing 3.2.

Listing 3.2. A call to a procedure using a register

```
. . .
asmsub proc
  mov    EAX, i1
  sub    EAX, i2
  push   EBX
  lea    EBX, sub100
  call   EBX
  pop    EBX
  ret
asmsub endp

sub100 proc
  sub    EAX, 100
  ret
sub100 endp
. . .
```

The following four lines are most important for understanding the working principles of the procedures in this example:

```
  push   EBX
  lea    EBX, sub100
  call   EBX
  pop    EBX
```

The first command pushes the EBX register to the stack before modifying it. There are not very many registers in the PC, but almost every command uses one or another register. Therefore, it is likely that the main program and the procedure need the same registers, which would complicate using them. You could develop your application so that the main program and the procedure use different registers, but this would be rather difficult because of the limited number of processor registers. This is why the code of a procedure does not make any assumptions on what registers are used in the main program and simply saves the values of all registers.

The EBX register is one of the most frequently used in the main application, so it is important to save it and return its unchanged value to the caller. This is done with the commands push EBX and pop EBX.

After the EBX register is saved, the address of the sub100 procedure is loaded to it. Finally, the call EBX command calls the procedure, i.e., pushes the return address on the stack and passes control to the procedure.

Now, we will consider another modified variant of the code fragment. To call a procedure, you can use the jmp command (Listing 3.3).

Listing 3.3. Using the jmp command to call a procedure

```
    .  .  .
asmsub proc
   mov    EAX, i1
   sub    EAX, i2
   lea    EDX, ex
   push   EDX
   jmp    sub100
ex:
   ret
asmsub endp

sub100 proc
   sub    EAX, 100
   ret
sub100 endp
    .  .  .
```

Using the jmp command is based on the understanding that the address of the command that follows jmp in the main program is pushed on the stack first. The sub100 procedure subtracts 100 from the value in the EAX register and passes control to the calling procedure asmsub with the ret command. The ret command "does not know" that the stack stores the address of the command that follows the call command. After ret is executed, the address of the ex label is put to the program counter. This address was earlier pushed on the stack with the commands:

```
   lea    EDX, ex
   push   EDX
```

In these examples, the EAX register was used to pass parameters and return the result. This is one of the simplest variants. Generally, the problem of passing parameters and returning the result cannot be solved so simply. Therefore, it is worth more detailed consideration.

There are different ways of passing actual parameters to a procedure. The simplest one, which was demonstrated in the previous examples, is to pass the parameters via registers: The main program writes the actual parameters to registers, and the procedure reads and uses them. You can deal with the result (if any) in the same manner: The procedure writes its result to a register, and the main program extracts it. Which registers can be used to pass parameters and return the result? You may choose them at will, although there are a few rules.

To pass parameters, the EAX, EBX, ECX, and EDX registers are used most frequently, and the EBP, ESI, and EDI are used less frequently. Usually, the EBP register is used with the stack pointer register (ESP) to access parameters in the stack. We will address this topic later. It is convenient to use the ESI and EDI registers as index registers for operations over arrays. However, nothing can prevent you from using them at your discretion.

Here, we will consider an example. Suppose you need to find the maximum of two integers and compute its absolute value. Develop two procedures in the assembler (name them maxint and maxabs) that find the maximum and its absolute value.

The maxint procedure takes two integer parameters (i1 and i2) and can be declared as maxint(i1, i2). The maxabs procedure takes an integer as a parameter. Let it be intval, and its declaration can be maxabs(intval).

We will assume that the first parameter i1 is passed via the EAX register, while i2 is passed via the EBX register. The procedures will return the results in the EAX register. The result of the maxint procedure is an input parameter for the maxabs procedure. The source code of a fragment of the program that uses these procedures is shown in Listing 3.4.

Listing 3.4. Passing parameters via registers in assembly procedures

```
;the main program
    . . .
mov  EAX, i1
mov  EBX, i2
call maxint

; The maximum is in the EAX register

mov  intval, EAX
call maxabs

; The absolute value of the maximum

    . . .

; The procedures are declared here
```

```
; maxint(i1, i2)

        maxint  proc
        cmp     EAX,EBX
        jge     ex
        mov     EAX,EBX
ex:
        ret
        maxint  endp

; maxabs(intval)

        maxabs  proc
        mov     EAX, intval
        cmp     EAX, 0
        jge     quit
        neg     EAX
quit:
        ret
        maxabs  endp
    . . .
```

When passing parameters via registers, you must keep in mind one important point. The registers that the procedure uses can be exploited in other parts of the program, so destroying their contents by the procedure can cause the program to crash. It is important to save the contents of the registers before entering a procedure if you are not completely sure that their contents are not used by other procedures or by the program. To save registers, the stack is normally used. Thus, if the main program in the previous example uses the EBX register, you should modify the source code (Listing 3.5). The additional commands are in bold.

Listing 3.5. Saving registers when working with procedures

```
;the main program
    . . .
 mov  EAX, i1
 push EBX
 mov  EBX, i2
 call maxint
 pop  EBX
```

```
; The maximum is in the EAX register

mov  intval, EAX
call maxabs

; The procedures are declared here
       . . .
; maxint(i1, i2)

     maxint  proc
     . . .
     maxint  endp

; maxabs(intval)

     maxabs  proc
     . . .
     maxabs  endp
. . .
```

Another approach is often used. Both the main program and the procedure are allowed to use the same registers, but the procedure is obliged to save the values of the registers used by the main program. This is simple: The procedure must first push the values of the registers it needs on the stack, and then it can use them as it likes. Before it returns, it must restore the original values of the registers by popping them from the stack.

It is strongly recommended that you do this in every procedure, even if it is obvious that the main program and the procedure use different registers. The source code of the program might change later (in fact, this is very likely), and the main program might need the registers after the changes are made.

Therefore, it is important to save registers by using two special commands: pusha and popa. They push the values of the general-purpose registers on the stack and pop them from it.

Note that you do not have to save the register used by a procedure to return the result. Changing this register is the goal of the procedure.

It is convenient to pass parameters via registers, and this method is used frequently. It is effective when there are few parameters. However, if you have many parameters, you might be short of registers for them. In this case, another method of passing parameters is used: via the stack. The main program pushes actual parameters (their values or addresses) on the stack, and the procedure pops them from the stack.

Suppose a procedure (named myproc) has n parameters and is declared as myproc(x1,x2,...,xn). We will assume that the main program pushes the parameters on the stack in a certain order before calling the procedure. Options of arrangement of the parameters within the stack are limited; in fact, there are only two variants. The first one involves pushing the parameters on the stack from left to right: First, the first parameter is pushed; then the second, etc. In 32-bit applications, each parameter has the size of a double word, so the main program's commands that implement a procedure call are as follows:

```
push    x1
push    x2
  . . .
push    xn
call    myproc
```

According to the second variant, the parameters are pushed on the stack from right to left: The nth parameter is pushed first, then the (n - 1)th parameter, etc. In this case, you should execute the following commands before you call the function:

```
push    xn
  . . .
push    x1
call    myproc
  . . .
```

How does a procedure access its parameters? A commonly used method involves accessing the parameters by using the EBP register. You should put the address of the top of the stack (the contents of the ESP register) to the EBP register and then use an expression like [EBP+i] to access the parameters of the procedure. It is advisable to save the EBP register because it might be used in the main program. Therefore, first save the contents of this register and only then move the contents of the ESP register to it.

We will illustrate this with an example. Modify the previous example so that the stack is used for passing the parameters. Assume the parameters are passed to the maxint procedure from right to left, i.e., the i2 variable is pushed on the stack first, and then the i1 variable. The fragments of the source code of the main program and the procedures where the parameters are passed via the stack are shown in Listing 3.6.

Listing 3.6. Passing parameters to a procedure via the stack

```
; Main program
  . . .
push  i2
push  i1
call maxint
```

```
; The maximum is in the EAX register

mov  intval, EAX
push intval
call maxabs

; The absolute value of the maximum

   . . .

; The procedures are declared here

; maxint(i1, i2)

     maxint    proc
     push      EBP
     mov       EBP, ESP

; Loading the i1 parameter to the EAX register

     mov       EAX, DWORD PTR [EBP+8]

; Saving the EBX register

     push      EBX

; Loading the i2 parameter to the EBX register

     mov       EBX, DWORD PTR [EBP+12]

     cmp       EAX, EBX
     jge       ex
     mov       EAX, EBX
ex:
     pop       EBP
     ret       8
     maxint    endp

; maxabs(intval)

     maxabs    proc
     push      EBP
     mov       EBP, ESP
```

```
; Loading a parameter to the EAX register

        push      EBP
        mov       EBP, ESP
        mov       EAX, DWORD PTR [EBP+8] ; intval
        cmp       EAX, 0
        jge       quit
        neg       EAX
quit:
        pop       EBP
        ret       4
        maxabs    endp
    . . .
```

When a procedure completes, it must perform certain actions, which we will describe. Note that by the moment of exiting the procedure, the stack should have the same state as before the procedure call.

When the procedure completes, the top of the stack will contain the old value of the EBP register. Pop it and restore EBP with the pop EBP command. Now, the top of the stack contains the return address. You might think that you can exit the procedure with the ret command, but this is not the case. You should clear the stack from the parameters that you no longer need. This can be done either in the calling program or in the procedure. Of course, the main program can do this by executing the add SP, n command (where n is the number of bytes to clear) after the call mysub command.

However, it is best to clear the stack in the procedure. There can be many calls to the procedure; therefore, you will have to write the add command in the main program many times. In the procedure, you will write this command only once. Here is a useful rule for program optimization: If an action can be done either in the main program or in the procedure, it is best to do it in the procedure. In this case, you will need fewer commands.

Thus, the procedure should first clear the stack from the parameters and only then pass control to the return address. To make it simpler to implement these two actions, an extended version of the ret command was introduced to the command set. It has a direct operand that is treated as an unsigned integer:

```
ret n
```

This command pops the return address from the stack first, then it clears n bytes in the stack, and finally it jumps to the return address.

A few additional notes: First, the ret command is actually the ret 0 command, i.e., it returns without clearing the stack. Second, the operand of this command tells how many bytes in the stack should be cleared. Finally, the operand should not take into account the return address because the `ret` command pops it before clearing the stack.

After the procedure returns control in such a manner, the stack will have the same state as before the call to the procedure, i.e., before the parameters were pushed on it. Thus, all traces of the call are covered up, and this is what you want.

This is a rough design of passing parameters via the stack. Remember that this method for passing parameters is universal, and it can be used with any number of parameters. On the other hand, it is more complicated than passing parameters via registers, so you should prefer passing parameters via registers because it is simpler and shorter. As for the result, it is very seldom passed via the stack and usually via a register. It is common that the result of a procedure is returned in the EAX register.

Many procedures do not have problems with storing local data (variables necessary only for procedure execution) because registers will do for this purpose. However, when there are many local variables in a procedure, the question arises: Where should they be stored? You can store the data in the data segment, the code segment, or the stack.

The MASM macro assembler allows you to use any of these options. To store data in the data segment, you should initialize it. This is done with the `.data` directive. The data type can be specified as DB (byte), DW (word), or DD (double word). If a sequence of elements is stored in the data segment, you can define its size with the $ operator.

For example, we will examine how the data segment can be used for processing a character string. Suppose the calling procedure, or main program requires the seventh element of a string stored in a called procedure. The parameter passed to the called procedure is the position of the element within the string (in this case — six, because the first element index is zero). The procedure developed in the MASM macro assembler (we will name it `findchar`) returns the result in the EAX register. The result is a character or a zero if the specified position number is greater than the string length. The source code of the procedure is shown in Listing 3.7.

Listing 3.7. Using the data segment in an assembly procedure

```
. . .
.data
  s1   DB   'STRING1!!!'
  ls   EQU  $-s1
.code
  findchar proc
    push   EBP
    mov    EBP, ESP
    mov    EDX, DWORD PTR [EBP+8]
    cmp    EDX, ls
    jbe    next
    mov    EAX, 0
```

```
    jmp     ex
next:
    lea     ESI, s1
    add     ESI, EDX
    xor     EAX, EAX
    mov     AL, BYTE PTR [ESI]
ex:
    pop     EBP
    ret
findchar  endp
end
```

The position number is passed via the stack at the address of [EBP+8]. It is saved in the EDX register and compared to the ls1 string length. If the string length is less than the passed position number, the procedure writes zero to EAX and returns.

If the position number is within the string, the corresponding element is put to the AL register. The address of this element is computed by adding the initial offset to the position number with the following commands:

```
lea     ESI, s1
add     ESI, EDX
```

In this case, the stack should be cleared either in the caller program or in the procedure.

To work with local data, you also can use the procedure's code segment.

Often, it is quite convenient because no data segment initialization is required, and performance increases. It is very easy to modify the source code of the previous example for work with local data directly in the code segment (Listing 3.8).

Listing 3.8. Using the code segment for work with local data

```
. . .
.code
    findchar proc
    jmp     strt
    s1      DB    'STRING1!!!!!'
    ls1     EQU   $-s1
strt:
    push    EBP
    mov     EBP, ESP
    mov     EDX, DWORD PTR [EBP+8]
    cmp     EDX, ls1
```

```
    jbe    next
    mov    EAX, 0
    jmp    ex
next:
    lea    ESI, s1
    add    ESI, EDX
    xor    EAX, EAX
    mov    AL, BYTE PTR [ESI]
ex:
    pop    EBP
    ret
  findchar   endp
end
```

Here, we used a simple trick with the `jmp strt` command to jump to the main branch of the procedure. The local data are stored in the code segment. The stack memory can be allocated with a standard method.

Push the current value of the `EBP` register on the stack and then set this register to the address of the top of the stack. After that, decrease the value of the `ESP` stack counter by the number of the bytes you need. For example, if the `mysub` procedure requires three double words, write the following commands:

```
mysub proc
  push  EBP
  mov   EBP, ESP
  sub   ESP, 12
  . . .
  mysub endp
```

Now, the local data can be accessed with expressions like `[EBP-i]`, where `i` is the position of the element. After the procedure completes, you should execute the following commands:

```
  . . .
  mov  ESP, EBP
  pop  EBP
  ret
  . . .
```

Allocating the stack memory is used in high-level programming languages when calling procedures (functions). For procedures in assembler, this method is less effective than, for example, using the data segment.

In most cases, especially when developing large programs, it is required to process the same data with several procedures or even individual programs. It would be very convenient to make these data available to several procedures. You might be wondering what point there is to use specific techniques for procedure interaction if data can be passed from one procedure to another as parameters. The examples above demonstrate this. However, when parameters are used for interaction between procedures, certain problems arise. Here are just a couple of them:

❐ When the number of procedures that process the same data is relatively large, the performance of a procedure decreases. Suppose a procedure contains an array of numbers that is processed with a few procedures. Every time the procedure is called, the other programs have to compute the addresses of the elements of the array. If the stack is used, which is the case in most instances, it is necessary to access the stack to obtain the memory addresses of the array elements. When the procedure is called relatively seldom, this may present no problems. However, the performance of the application can decrease by increasing the complexity of the program structure and the data-processing algorithms.
❐ When the same data is processed with different procedures, the structurability of the program that uses the assembly procedures becomes worse.

Using common, or global, variables allows you to work with them with the minimum use of the stack, which economizes the processor time. In addition, the fixed links to the common variables established at the link stage speed up access to them.

From now on, we will use the terms "common variable" and "global variable" synonymously. To work with common variables in assembly language, the `public` and `extern` directives are used. The `public` directive declares a variable or function accessible to other modules, and the `extern` directive indicates that the variable or procedure is external relative to the procedure being executed. Both directives are used for assembling the main program or a procedure from several object modules and are very convenient when building large programs.

Global variables are declared as follows:

❐ In the object module that contains such a variable, specify the accessibility of the variable with the `public` directive.
❐ In the object modules that access the common variable, declare it with the `extern` directive.

The following example demonstrates the technique of using common data in the work of two procedures. The first one (we will name it `sub2`) subtracts three integers. The first two numbers are its input parameters, and the third number (named add2res) is external to the sub2 procedure and is located in another object module. The source code of the sub2 procedure is shown in Listing 3.9.

Listing 3.9. The sub2 procedure

```
     . . .
     extern add2res: DWORD
.code
  sub2     proc
    push   EBP
    mov    EBP, ESP
    mov    EAX, DWORD PTR [EBP+8]
    sub    EAX, DWORD PTR [EBP+12]
    sub    EAX, add2res
    pop    EBP
    ret
  sub2     endp
  end
```

Note the line:

```
     extern add2res: DWORD
```

The extern directive declares the add2res variable as an external double word which corresponds to an integer.

As usual, the result is put to the EAX register.

Where should you take the add2res variable? Its value is the result of the second procedure, a2, which computes the sum of two integers being its input parameters. The add2res is declared as a double word in the data segment and contains the sum of two integers. Since add2res should be available to the sub2 procedure from another object module, it should be declared as public. The source code of the a2 procedure is shown in Listing 3.10.

Listing 3.10. The a2 procedure that adds up two integers

```
     . . .
     public add2res
.data
     add2res DD 0
.code
  a2       proc
```

```
    push   EBP
    mov    EBP, ESP
    mov    EAX, DWORD PTR [EBP+8]
    add    EAX, DWORD PTR [EBP+12]
    mov    add2res, EAX
    pop    EBP
    ret
  a2       endp
end
```

To work correctly, the main program should first call the a2 procedure and then the sub2 procedure.

This example is very simple. It demonstrates the key aspects of using common variables. If you want to pass a procedure, a string, or array by using common variables, the task becomes complicated.

For example, suppose you want to display a particular symbol of a string in your main program. Develop two procedures interacting with the main program. The first one (name it rets) contains a null-terminated character string. Its only purpose is to pass the string to the other procedure (name it fchar). The fchar procedure uses this string to search for an element whose ordinal number is passed to it from the main program as a parameter. Below is a more detailed description of this procedure. Consider the rets procedure first. Its source code is shown in Listing 3.11.

Listing 3.11. The rets procedure

```
    public as1
.data
    s1     DB 'STRING TO SEND'
           DB 0
    as1    DD 0
.code
  rets     proc
    lea    EAX, s1
    mov    as1, EAX
    ret
  rets     endp
end
```

The s1 string is declared as a null-terminated string. As you know, a string can be passed by passing its address. Since the address is 32-bit, it is convenient to store it in the as1 double-word variable with the commands:

```
lea    EAX, s1
mov    as1, EAX
```

In addition, you should declare as1 with the public directive. The source code of the fchar procedure is shown in Listing 3.12.

Listing 3.12. The fchar procedure

```
   . . .
   extern as1:DWORD
   public fchar
.code
  fchar  proc
    push  EBP
    mov   EBP, ESP
    mov   EDX, DWORD PTR [EBP+8]
    mov   ESI, DWORD PTR as1
    add   ESI, EDX
    xor   EAX, EAX
    mov   AL, BYTE PTR [ESI]
    pop   EBP
    ret
  fchar  endp
end
```

To access the string from the fchar procedure, declare the variable that contains the string address with the extern directive:

```
extern as1:DWORD
```

Then the procedure searches for the element with the given number, and the result is returned in the EAX register, as usual.

In addition to common variables, assembly language allows you to use common (global) procedures shared by several modules. As with common variables, such procedures are declared as follows:

❏ In the object module that contains a common procedure, specify the accessibility of the variable with the public directive.

❏ In the object modules that access the common procedure, declare it with the extern directive.

Here is an example. Suppose the main program displays the absolute value of the difference between two integers. The difference is computed with the subcom procedure, and the absolute value is computed with the abs procedure. The subcom procedure is used in the main program and is declared as public. The abs procedure is called from subcom and is declared as extern. The source code of the subcom procedure is shown in Listing 3.13.

Listing 3.13. The subcom procedure

```
. . .
.model flat, C
  public subcom
  extern abs:proc
.code
  subcom   proc
     push  EBP
     mov   EBP, ESP
     mov   EAX, DWORD PTR [EBP+8]
     sub   EAX, DWORD PTR [EBP+12]
     push  EAX
     call  abs
     add   ESP, 4
     pop   EBP
     ret
  subcom endp
end
```

This source code is simple. Note the following lines:

```
push  EAX
call  abs
add   ESP, 4
```

The difference of two numbers is passed to the abs procedure via the stack, with the EAX register used. After the called procedure completes, the stack is reset by the calling one, subcom in this case. The source code of the abs procedure is shown in Listing 3.14.

Listing 3.14. The abs procedure

```
. . .
  public abs
.code
  abs proc
    push  EBP
    mov   EBP, ESP
    mov   EAX, DWORD PTR [EBP+8]
    cmp   EAX, 0
    jge   no_change
    neg   EAX
no_change:
    pop   EBP
    ret
  abs endp
end
```

The abs procedure is declared as public, which makes it accessible in other modules.

This completes the discussion of the use of procedures written in the MASM 6.14 assembly language. As you see from the given examples, the assembler has many possibilities for development of separate modules, and we will use them in the consequent chapters.

Chapter 4: Optimizing C++ Logical Structures with Assembly Language

Programmers who write in high-level languages use assembly blocks and separately compiled modules to decrease the sizes and improve the performance of their applications. In this section, we will look at how the most frequently used constructions of high-level programming languages are implemented in the assembler. Constructions such as `if ... else`, `do ... while`, etc. carry certain redundancy. Therefore, by using their assembly analogs, you will be able to increase the performance of your applications. It should be mentioned that all high-level languages usually have inline assemblers, but we will postpone a discussion of the C++ .NET inline assembler until *Part 3*.

Analysis of programs written in high-level programming languages reveals their weak points, especially the unpractical use of selection instructions and loop computations. Processing large arrays and strings and mathematical calculations significantly decreases performance of programs. These is no high-level languages compiler that could completely remove redundancy and non-optimality from the code, no matter how hard it would try to optimize the size and performance of an executable module. This is also true for Intel compiler, which, we believe, has good optimization characteristics at the processor command level.

Loop computation and constructions such as `if ... else`, `while`, `do ... while`, and `switch ... case` can be optimized most easily. As a rule, optimization of selection instructions and loops is based on using comparison commands and conditional jumps depending on the result of comparison. Generally, this can be presented as follows:

```
    . . .
    cmp      operand1, operand2
    Jcond    label1
    <commands 1>
    jmp      label2
label1:
    <commands 2>
label2:
    . . .
```

Here, `operand1` and `operand2` are variables and/or expressions, and `Jcond` is a conditional jump command (such as `je`, `jl`, `jge`, `jz`, or other).

Any high-level language construction, no matter how complicated it might be, can be represented as a combination of conditional jumps and comparison commands. In this chapter, we will look at variants of implementation of high-level language constructions for practical purposes. We will begin with the `if` statement.

The *if* Statement

A single `if` statement is used for execution of a statement or a block of statements depending on whether the specified condition is true. In a general form, this statement looks like this:

```
if (condition)
    statements
```

In C++, it can be written as follows:

```
if (condition)
{
  <statements>
}
```

A more complex variant of the statement, `if ... else`, makes it possible to selectively execute one of two actions depending on the condition. Here is its syntax in C++:

```
if (condition)
  {
  <statements 1>
  }
```

```
else
 {
  <statements 2>
 }
```

There are no such constructions in assembly language, but they can be implemented easily with certain sequences of commands.

For example, we will consider an algorithm that checks two operands for equality and jumps to one or the other branch depending on the result.

In Visual C++ .NET, the expression will look like this:

```
if (operand1 = operand2)
{
    ...
}
else
{
    ...
}
```

Assembly language allows you to implement the if ... else construction quite simply:

```
    cmp     operand1, operand2
    je      YES
    <commands 1>
    jmp     EXIT
YES:
  <commands 2>
EXIT:
    ...
```

Another variant is also possible:

```
    cmp     operand1, operand2
    jne     NO
    <commands 2>
EXIT:
    ...
NO:
  <commands 1>
    jmp     EXIT
```

Develop a code fragment that compares two integers, x and y. Depending on the result of comparison, the x variable takes the value of y if x is greater than y, and remains unchanged if x is less or equal to y.

In C++, this code fragment looks like this:

```
if (X > Y)
    X = Y;
```

Here is its implementation in the assembler:

```
    mov     EAX, DWORD PTR Y
    cmp     EAX, DWORD PTR X
    jge     EXIT
    mov     DWORD PTR X, EAX
EXIT:
```

Since 32-bit operands are used, all variables and registers are declared appropriately. The cmp comparison command cannot be executed if both its operands are located in the memory, so one of them (Y in this case) is put to the EAX register. The result is stored in the X variable.

The following fragment of code computes the sum of two integers, X and Y, if both are within the range from 1 to 100.

In Visual C++, this fragment of code looks like this:

```
if ((X <= 100 && X >= 1) && (Y <= 100 && Y >= 1))
    X = X + Y
```

The code in the assembler is shown in Listing 4.1.

**Listing 4.1. A fragment of an assembly program, with an analog
of the if statement, that adds up two integers**

```
    . . .
    cmp     DWORD PTR X, 1
    jge     check_x100
    jmp     EXIT
check_x100:
    cmp     DWORD PTR X, 100
    jle     check_y1
    jmp     EXIT
check_y1:
    cmp     DWORD PTR Y, 1
    jge     check_y100
    jmp     EXIT
check_y100:
    cmp     DWORD PTR Y, 100
    jg      EXIT
```

```
mov     EAX, DWORD PTR Y
add     DWORD PTR X, EAX
EXIT:
  . . .
```

As you can see from the algorithm, in order to find the sum of X and Y, you need to check at least four conditions:

- ☐ X is greater or equal to 1
- ☐ X is less or equal to 100
- ☐ Y is greater or equal to 1
- ☐ Y is less or equal to 100

Only if these four conditions are true simultaneously can you assign the X variable the value of the X + Y expression. To implement such a task, you should break the condition

```
(X <= 100 && X >= 1) && (Y <= 100 && Y >= 1)
```

into the following four simpler constructions:

```
X <= 100, X >= 1, Y <= 100, Y >= 1
```

The task is simpler now. Each of the four conditions can be checked easily with the cmp command. For example, checking the X <= 100 condition and the subsequent jump is done as follows:

```
cmp     DWORD PTR X, 100
jle     check_y1
```

The other checks can be done with similar combinations of commands.

It is important to note that an assembly analog of a high-level language construction is not necessarily obvious, and this is illustrated in the following example.

Develop some code to compute the absolute value of the X integer. A possible variant of implementing such a task involves the if … else construction.

In Visual C++, it will look like this:

```
if (X >= 0)
    AbsX = X
else
    AbsX = -X
```

where AbsX is a variable that stores the absolute value of X. Here is an implementation of this construction in the assembler:

```
cmp     DWORD PTR X, 0
jl      NOT_X
jmp     EXIT
```

```
NOT_X:
    neg        DWORD PTR X
EXIT:
    mov        EAX, DWORD PTR X
    mov        DWORD PTR AbsX, EAX
```

An assignment statement is executed in both the `if` and `else` branch. These two assignments can be combined and put at the end of the fragment of code:

```
mov        EAX, DWORD PTR X
mov        DWORD PTR AbsX, EAX
```

The `else` branch is implemented in the assembler with the command:

```
NOT_X:
    neg        DWORD PTR X
```

The result is stored in the `AbsX` variable.

Now, we will solve a simple problem. Find the maximum of two integers and assign it to a third variable. An appropriate C++ .NET console application would consist of a few lines of code, and its code is shown in Listing 4.2.

Listing 4.2. Computing the maximum of two numbers and displaying it

---

```cpp
// IF_ELSE_SETCC.cpp : Defines the entry point
// for the console application

#include "stdafx.h"

int _tmain(int argc, _TCHAR* argv[])
{
 int i1, i2, ires;
 while (true)
   {
   printf("\n");
   printf("Enter first number (i1): ");
   scanf("%d", &i1);
   printf("Enter second number (i2): ");
   scanf("%d", &i2);
   if (i1 >= i2) ires = i1;
   else ires = i2;
   printf("Maximum = %d\n", ires);
 }
return 0;
}
```

As you can see from the listing, a comparison is made with the following statements:

```
if (i1 >= i2) ires = i1;
else ires = i2;
```

Now, we will try to optimize the code fragment that contains the if ... else statement. It will be convenient to use the Visual C++ .NET inline assembler for this purpose. An assembly language analog of a conditional statement will look like this:

```
_asm {
        mov   EAX, i1
        mov   EBX, i2
        cmp   EAX, EBX
        jge   set_ires
        xchg  EAX, EBX
set_ires:
        mov   ires, EAX
    }
```

This fragment of code is simple and does not require additional explanation. You can create even more effective code if you get rid of branches and jumps in the program or at least minimize their number. Processors such as Pentium II and higher include a number of commands that allow you to effectively implement branches in a program. Among these commands are setcc (set conditionally) and the cmov and fcmov commands. By combining these, you can achieve significant results, while improving the performance of your applications.

An assembly analog of the if ... else statement that uses the setge and cmovl commands looks like this:

```
_asm {
        xor    EBX, EBX
        mov    EAX, i1
        mov    EDX, i2
        cmp    EAX, EDX
        setge  BL
        mov    ires, EAX
        cmp    BL, 1
        cmovl  EAX, EDX
        mov    ires, EAX
    }
```

First, the EBX register is zeroed because it will be used as a "greater than or less than" indicator. The first number (i1) is put to the EAX register, and the second number (i2) to the EDX register. If the contents of the EAX register are greater than or equal to those of the EDX register, the setge BL command writes a one to the low order part of EBX; otherwise, zero will remain in EBX. If BL = 0, the contents of EDX are put to the EAX register. Before the last command, the EAX register contains the maximum, which is stored in the ires variable. As you can see from this fragment of code, there are no branches and jumps. Before you use the cmov command, you should make sure that your processor supports it. The check can be done with the cpuid command.

The complete code of the console application is shown in Listing 4.3.

Listing 4.3. A modified variant of the program that includes the if ... else statement

```
// IF_ELSE_SETCC.cpp : Defines the entry point
// for the console application

#include "stdafx.h"

int _tmain(int argc, _TCHAR* argv[])
{
int i1, i2, ires;
 while (true)
  {
   printf("\n");
   printf("Enter first number (i1): ");
   scanf("%d", &i1);
   printf("Enter second number (i2): ");
   scanf("%d", &i2);

   _asm {
           xor    EBX, EBX
           mov    EAX, i1
           mov    EDX, i2
           cmp    EAX, EDX
           setge BL
           mov    ires, EAX
           cmp    BL, 1
           cmovl EAX, EDX
           mov    ires, EAX
       }
   printf("Maximum = %d\n", ires);
  }
return 0;
}
```

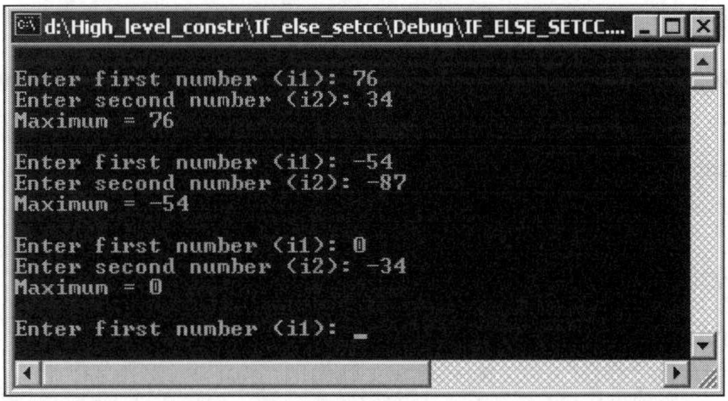

Fig. 4.1. Window of an application that uses optimized code for computing the maximum of two integers

The window of the application is shown in Fig. 4.1.

The *while* Loop

This loop is used when the number of iterations is not known beforehand. The `while` loop is a pretest loop, and its execution depends on the initial condition. Its general syntax can be presented as follows:

```
while (condition)
    <statements>
```

The loop exits if the condition is false. Since the condition is checked at the beginning of each iteration, it may happen that the body of the loop is not executed even once.

In C++, a `while` loop looks like this:

```
while (condition)
{
  <statements>
}
```

The following fragment of code demonstrates the use of the `while` loop. Suppose you have an array of ten integers and want to find the number of elements that precede the first zero element (if there is any). A fragment of the program should return the number of elements that precede the first zero element or a zero if such an element is not found. This code could be used to search for and extract null-terminated strings. This task is easily implemented with a `for` loop, but here we will do this with a `while` loop.

The following variables will be used:

- ❏ X1 — an integer array
- ❏ IX1 — the current array index
- ❏ SX1 — the array size
- ❏ Counter — the counter of elements

This fragment of code will be executed as follows:

- ❏ After initialization of the variables, the program checks the element of the X1 array for being not equal to zero at the beginning of each iteration in the while loop. If the element is equal to zero, the loop intermediately interrupts.
- ❏ If the condition is true, i.e., the array element is not equal to zero, the loop body is executed. The Counter and the IX1 index are incremented. If the last element of the array is encountered, the loop exits (the if statement).
- ❏ In any case, the Counter contains the number of elements that precede the first zero element or a zero if such an element is not found.

The Visual C++ code for this task is shown in Listing 4.4.

Listing 4.4. A fragment of code that uses a while loop

```
...
int    X1[10] = {12, 90, -6, 30, 22, 10, 22, 89, -0, 47};
int    Counter = 0;
int    IX1 = 0;
int    SX1 = sizeof (X1) / 4;
while (X1[IX1] != 0)
{
  Counter++;
  if (IX1 == SX1) break;
  IX1++;
};
if (Counter == SX1+1)
  Counter = 0;
...
```

At first glance, the implementation of this task in the assembler (Listing 4.5) would seem more complicated than in the previous examples.

Listing 4.5. An assembly-language implementation of the task that uses a `while` loop

```
.686
.model flat, stdcall
.data
  X1       DD 2, -23, 5, 9, -1, 0, 9, 3
  SX1      DD $-X1
  Counter DD 0
.code
 start:
  push    EBX
  mov     ECX, 0
  mov     EBX, offset X1
  mov     EDX, DWORD PTR SX1
  shr     EDX, 2
  mov     ESI, EDX
AGAIN:
  mov     EAX, DWORD PTR [EBX]
  cmp     EAX, 0
  je      RUNOUT
  inc     ECX
  dec     EDX
  jz      RUNOUT
  add     EBX, 4
  jmp     AGAIN
RUNOUT:
  cmp     ECX, ESI
  jne     SET_CNT
  xor     ECX, ECX
SET_CNT:
  mov     DWORD PTR Counter, ECX
  pop     EBX
  ...
end start
```

A few important notes should be made. The first one relates to the use of registers. When working with external programs and modules in high-level languages, it is recommended that you save the EBX, EBP, ESI, and EDI registers by pushing them on the stack. With regard to the other registers (EAX, ECX, and EDX), you can use them as you like.

The second note relates to work with arrays and strings in the assembler. To access such data in Windows, 32-bit variables that store the addresses of the arrays and strings are always used. To access the elements of the X1 array, you can use the EBX register by putting the address of the first array element to it:

```
mov      EBX, offset X1
```

To work with an array, you should know its size. It can be stored in the EDX register:

```
mov      EDX, DWORD PTR SX1
```

The counter of non-zero elements is stored in the ECX register. Since each element of the array is four bytes long (a double word), the following command is used to access the next element:

```
add      EBX, 4
```

This example includes two high-level constructions: a while loop and an if conditional statement. The while loop is implemented with three commands:

```
mov      EAX, DWORD PTR [EBX]
cmp      EAX, 0
je       RUNOUT,
```

and the if statement is implemented with the following commands:

```
cmp      ECX, EDX
je       RUNOUT
```

If no zero element is found, zero is written to the counter according to the condition of the task:

```
cmp      ECX, EDX
jne      SET_CNT
xor      ECX, ECX
```

We provide such a detailed analysis of the assembly version of the program so that you understand that there is no unique solution for the task of optimization of logical structures in high-level languages! In many cases, a building block of such an optimization is the following pair of assembly commands:

```
cmp      operand1, operand2
Jcond    label
```

In principle, the assembler allows you to implement any logical expressions and branches, no matter how complicated they are. The only limitation is your imagination and experience.

A while loop can be implemented in the assembler by using commands of string primitives. These commands are widely used for processing arrays and strings in loops and often simplify the algorithm of a task. A variant of implementing a while loop with the scasd command is shown in Listing 4.6.

Listing 4.6. An implementation of a while loop with the scasd command

---

```
.686
.model flat, stdcall
.data
  X1       DD 2, -23, 5, 9, -1, 0, 9, 3
  SX1      DD $-X1
  IX1      DD 1
  Counter DD 0
.code
 start:
   mov    EDI, offset X1
   xor    ECX, ECX
   mov    EDX, DWORD PTR SX1
   shr    EDX, 2
   cld
   xor    EAX, EAX
next:
   scasd
   je     ex
   inc    ECX
   dec    EDX
   jz     ex
   jmp    next
ex:
   cmp    ECX, 10
   jne    write_cnt
   mov    Counter, 0
   jmp    quit
write_cnt:
   mov    Counter, ECX
quit:
   . . .
end start
```

The *do ... while* Loop

do ... while loops arrange execution of a loop consisting of any number of statements when the number of iterations is not known beforehand. The body of the loop will be executed at least once. The loop exits when a certain logical condition becomes false.

In C++, the do ... while loop has the following form:

```
do
{
   <statements>
}
while <condition>
```

Write some code for computing the sum of the first four elements of an integer array. Let the number of its elements be seven. To implement this task, use the following variables:

- ❐ X1 — an integer array of seven elements
- ❐ IX1 — the index of the current element of the array
- ❐ SumX1 — the current total value

A fragment of the C++ code shown in Listing 4.7 is quite simple.

Listing 4.7. A fragment of the C++ code that finds the sum of the first four elements of an array

```
   . . .
 int X1[7] = {2, -4, 5, 1, -1, 9, 3};
 int IX1 = 0;
 int sumX1 = 0;
 do
 {
    sumX1 = sumX1 + X1[IX1];
    IX1++;
 }
 while (IX1 <= 3);
   . . .
```

An assembly variant of the do ... while loop is shown in Listing 4.8.

Listing 4.8. The `do … while` loop implemented in the assembler

```
.686
.model flat
.data
  X1    DD  2, -23, 5, 9, -1, 9, 3
  SX1   DD  $-X1
  IX1   DD  1
  CNT   EQU 3
  SUMX1 DD  0

.code
  start:
  push    EBX
  mov     EBX, offset X1
  mov     EAX, 0
  mov     EDX, DWORD PTR SX1
  shr     EDX, 2
  cmp     EDX, CNT
  jl      EXIT

NEXT:
  add     EAX, [EBX]
  cmp     DWORD PTR IX1, CNT
  jg      EXIT
  inc     DWORD PTR IX1
  add     EBX, 4
  jmp     NEXT
EXIT:
  mov     DWORD PTR SUMX1, EAX
  pop     EBX
  . . .

end start
```

First, all necessary variables are initialized. To access the elements of the array, its address is put to the EBX register:

```
mov     EBX, offset X1
```

The initial total value equal to zero is put to the EAX register:

```
mov    EAX, 0
```

The condition of the do ... while loop is checked in the assembly code with the following command:

```
cmp    DWORD PTR IX1, CNT
```

where IX1 is the current array index.

Since an integer value of an array element takes a double word in the memory, to access the next element, you should increase the address value by four, just like in the previous example:

```
add    EBX, 4
```

The result is put to the SUMX1 variable for later use.

The *for* Loop

A for loop arranges execution of a statement or a group of statements for a particular number of times.

In its general form, the loop looks like this:

```
For (initialization expression; condition; modifier expression)
    <statements>
```

When a program encounters the loop, it executes the initialization expression, which sets the loop counter to the initial value. Then the so-called terminating condition is evaluated. The loop executes while this expression is true. Every time the loop body is executed, the modifier expression changes the loop counter. When the condition is false, the for loop terminates, and the statements that immediately follow it are executed.

In Visual C++, a for loop has a uniform syntax regardless of the direction of the modifier:

```
for (initialization expression; condition; modifier)
```

Most often, a for loop is used for iterative mathematical calculations with a constant increment and a known number of iterations, or it is used to search for elements in arrays or strings. Here, we will look at an example of using a for loop. Suppose you want to find the sum of the first seven elements of an array of 10 integers.

In C++ .NET, a fragment of the code could appear as shown in Listing 4.9.

Listing 4.9. A fragment of C++ code that uses a `for` loop

```
...
int i1[10] = {3, -5, 2, 7, -9, 1, -3, -7, -11, 15};
int isum = 0;
for (int cnt = 0; cnt < 7; cnt++)
{
    isum = isum + i1[cnt];
}
...
```

In assembler, it is convenient to implement a `for` loop with the `loop` command. In this case, the loop counter is put to the ECX register, and the current total is put to the EAX register. The address of the `i1` integer array is put to the ESI register.

Before jumping to the next iteration, the address in ESI is increased by 4. After the loop terminates, the sum is stored in the `isum` variable.

The code fragment is shown in Listing 4.10.

Listing 4.10. An assembly variant of a program that finds the sum of the first seven elements of an array with the `for` loop

```
.686
.model flat
.data
  i1      DD 3, -5, 2, 7, -9, 1, -3, -7, -11, 15
  isum    DD 0
.code
 start:
  mov     ECX, 7
  xor     EAX, EAX
  lea     ESI, DWORD PTR i1
next:
  add     EAX, [ESI]
  add     ESI, 4
  loop    next
  mov     DWORD PTR isum, EAX
  ...
end start
```

The *switch* Conditional Statement

A switch conditional statement makes it possible to select one of the branches of execution, depending on the value of the control expression. The value of the control expression is compared to an integer or character constant in a list. If a coincidence is detected, the statements associated with the constant are executed.

The form of this statement can be represented as follows:

```
switch (expression) {
      case constant 1:
        <statements>
        break;
      case constant 2:
        <statements>
        break;

      ...

      default:
  }
```

To implement a switch statement in the assembler, you can use a comparison command for each case and a jump to an appropriate label in the program (Listing 4.11).

Listing 4.11. A fragment of assembly code that implements a switch statement

```
  ...
  mov     EAX, DWORD PTR N
  cmp     EAX, VALUE_1
  je      BRANCH_1
  cmp     EAX, VALUE_2
  je      BRANCH_2
  cmp     EAX, VALUE_3
  je      BRANCH_3
  ...
  cmp     EAX, VALUE_N
  je      BRANCH_N
  ...

BRANCH_1:
  <statements>
BRANCH_2:
  <statements>
BRANCH_N:
  <statements>
  ...
```

It is often convenient to call subroutines processing the condition rather than make conditional jumps (Listing 4.12).

Listing 4.12. A fragment of assembly code that uses condition-processing subroutines

```
    . . .
    mov     EAX, DWORD PTR N
    cmp     EAX, VALUE_1
    jne     BRANCH_1
    call    PROC_1
    jmp     EXIT

BRANCH_1:
    cmp     EAX, VALUE_2
    jne     BRANCH_2
    call    PROC_2
    jmp     EXIT

BRANCH_2:
    cmp     EAX, VALUE_3
    jne     BRANCH_3
    call    PROC_3
    jmp     EXIT

BRANCH_3:
    cmp     EAX, VALUE_4
    jne     EXIT
    call    PROC_4
    . . .
EXIT:
    cmp     EAX, VALUE_2
    je      BRANCH_2
    cmp     EAX, VALUE_3
    je      BRANCH_3
    . . .
    cmp     EAX, VALUE_N
    je      BRANCH_N
    . . .
```

Now, we will consider a C++ program that adds, subtracts, or multiplies two integers depending on the selection of one of three cases. The source code of the console application is shown in Listing 4.13.

Listing 4.13. A C++ program that demonstrates the use of the `switch` statement

```cpp
// SWITCH_EXM.cpp : Defines the entry point for the console application

#include "stdafx.h"

int _tmain(int argc, _TCHAR* argv[])
{
 int i1, i2, isw, ires;
 while (true)
   {
    printf("\nEnter first number (i1): ");
    scanf("%d", &i1);
    printf("Enter second number (i2): ");
    scanf("%d", &i2);
    printf ("Choice: 1 - i1+i2, 2 - i1-i2, 3 - i1*i2\n");
    scanf("%d", &isw);
    switch (isw) {
        case 1:
          ires = i1+i2;
          break;
        case 2:
          ires = i1-i2;
          break;
        case 3:
          ires = i1*i2;
          break;
        default:
          break;
        }
    printf("Result = %d\n", ires);
    }
 return 0;
}
```

It would be useful to write some effective assembly code for this task. If you got rid of the `switch` ... `case` branching, the program performance would increase significantly. As noted earlier, the command set of Pentium II and higher includes the `cmov` and `fcmov` commands that make it possible to implement the switch ... case algorithm. Modify the previous listing so that the cmov command can be used. Use the C++ .NET inline assembler for this purpose. The source code of the program is shown in Listing 4.14.

Listing 4.14. Eliminating the switch ... case branching by using the inline assembler in a C++ program

```cpp
// SWITCH_EXM.cpp : Defines the entry point for the console application

#include "stdafx.h"

int _tmain(int argc, _TCHAR* argv[])
{
 int i1, i2, isw, ires;
 int iadd, isub, im;
 while (true)
  {
   printf("\n");
   printf("Enter first number (i1): ");
   scanf("%d", &i1);
   printf("Enter second number (i2): ");
   scanf("%d", &i2);
   printf ("Choice: 1 - i1+i2, 2 - i1-i2, 3 - i1*i2\n");
   scanf("%d", &isw);
   iadd = i1+i2;
   isub = i1-i2;
   im = i1*i2;
   _asm {
         xor    EDX, EDX
         mov    EAX, isw
         cmp    EAX, 1
         cmove EDX, iadd
         cmp    EAX, 2
         cmove EDX, isub
         cmp    EAX, 3
         cmove EDX, im
         mov    ires, EDX
        }
  printf("Result = %d\n", ires);
  }
return 0;
}
```

As you can see from Listing 4.14, the `switch` statement is replaced with its assembly analog, a group of commands in the `_asm {...}` block. To implement an assembly version, you should declare a few auxiliary variables in the source code:

```
int iadd, isub, im;
```

Write the following statements just before the assembly block:

```
iadd = i1+i2;
isub = i1-i2;
im = i1*i2;
```

These statements are necessary for the `cmove` command. Depending on flags set with the previous command, this command moves the contents of a register or a memory cell to another register. Before you use the `cmov` command, make sure it is supported by the processor. This is done with the `cpuid` command.

The window of the application is shown in Fig. 4.2.

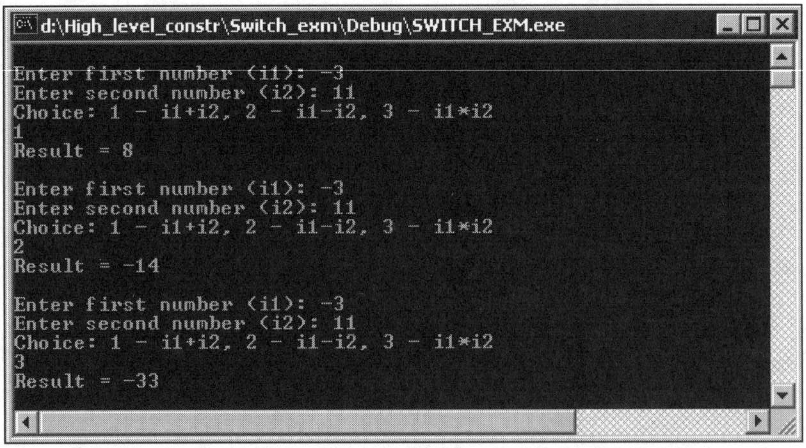

Fig. 4.2. Window of an application that demonstrates
the use of assembly commands for replacing the `switch` statement

This completes the discussion of C++ .NET logical structures and their optimization with the assembler. You can easily modify any example from this chapter and use it in your own applications.

Chapter 5: Assembly Module Interface to C++ Programs

The Visual C++ .NET 2003 development environment is very powerful and has inline assembly language development tools. The main advantage of the inline assembly code is the simplicity, because you do not have to create an additional code for linking and you do not have problems naming and passing parameters.

On the other hand, the inline assembler has certain disadvantages. Limitations laid by the compiler affect the code of assembly blocks and functions, especially when it comes to optimizing the application. Problems with inline assembly code can arise when compiling an application for different platforms.

The use of stand-alone assembly modules in C++ .NET programs gives you many more options for optimization of your applications. Also, modules that are compiled separately can be reused in other applications, something that is hardly possible with the inline assembler.

This chapter will focus on the development of stand-alone assembly module interfaces to C++ programs.

General Principles of Developing Interfaces to High-Level Languages

In this section, we will discuss general issues of developing interfaces when calling assembly procedures from C++ .NET programs. To illustrate the material, we will use numerous original examples that cannot be found elsewhere. When necessary, detailed comments are included.

The assembly modules were developed with Microsoft MASM 6.14 compiler. When developing the modules, we used a simplified syntax of assembly language. This means we used the `.data` and `.code` directives everywhere in the source code. We will not describe all features of the MASM compiler here, since only a few of them are used, and all explanations are given in the text.

Compiled assembly modules have the OBJ extension, and the command line for the MASM compiler appears as follows:

```
ml /c /Fo <file_name.obj> <file_name.asm>
```

The obtained OBJ file should be linked to the C++ main program. When developing the assembly module interface to the main program, you should take into account the following points:

- ❏ The rules of name treatment for variables and functions in object files. The high level language compiler may or may not change the original names in the object module, and you should be aware of whether it does this and how.
- ❏ The memory model used by the assembly module (`tiny`, `small`, `compact`, `medium`, `huge`, `large`, or `flat`).
- ❏ The parameters of the call to the assembly function. The parameters of a call is a broad notion that includes the following important aspects:
  - Whether registers should be saved in the function; if yes, which ones
  - Order of passing the parameters to the function
  - Method of passing the parameters to the function (whether registers, the stack, or the shared memory is used)
  - Whether the parameters are passed to the function by value or by reference
  - If the parameters are passed via the stack, where the stack pointer is restored: in the calling or the called program of function
  - Method of returning the result to the calling program (via the stack, registers, or shared memory)

Now, we will look at the principles of developing interfaces more closely, beginning with the identifier name agreement. The C++ compiler does not change the case of letters, so the identifiers remain case-sensitive. However, the C++ compiler adds an underline character as a prefix to every external name.

You should also take into account the memory models used by external functions. For 32-bit applications, only one memory model, flat, is used. Regarding the parameters, things are quite simple, although their descriptions in some books are complicated and confusing. For those readers who want to understand these directives and conventions, we will highlight the main points of calling external functions from a C++ program:

❑ In 32-bit applications, parameters are passed to a called function in either of two manners: by value or by reference. When a parameter is passed by value, the function directly gets the 32-bit operand; when the parameter is passed by reference, the function gets the address (also 32-bit) of this operand.

❑ Parameters are passed via the stack, registers, or shared memory. Passing parameters via the shared memory in 32-bit applications is very difficult to implement and is normally used in system programming and developing device drivers. It is an isolated topic that will be addressed in greater detail in *Chapter 7*. All variants of passing parameters to a function via the stack or registers are shown in Table 5.1.

Table 5.1. Passing parameters

Directive	Order of parameters	Stack reset by...	Passing parameters via registers
_fastcall	From left to right	Procedure	ECX, EDX, the stack; from right to left
_cdecl	From right to left	Caller	No
_stdcall	From right to left	Procedure	No

Please note the following details related to Table 5.1. The order of passing parameters for each directive tells the compiler how parameters are passed to a called function. For the _cdecl and _stdcall directives, the parameters are passed via the stack. When the _fastcall directive is used, the parameters are passed via the registers (the first two parameters) and the stack (the others).

Before you return to the main program, you should restore the stack pointer. This is true for all the directives. There are no strict recommendations concerning the use of particular methods of calling external functions.. If you are using Windows API, _stdcall is the standard way of calling them. It is best to use the _cdecl directive for calls to procedures and functions from C++ programs.

The quickest way of passing parameters in Visual C++ .NET is _fastcall. The stack is not used for passing the first two parameters, so you can obtain a gain in performance.

All functions return the result either in the EAX register or on the top of the mathematical coprocessor stack ST(0).

We will illustrate this with a simple assembly function that adds together two numbers. A C++ program passes to the function two integer parameters and takes their sum as the result. We will name the function AddInts, its first parameter X1, and its second parameter X2. In this case, a call to the function will appear as AddInts(X1, X2).

The source code of the function when _stdcall is used for passing parameters is shown in Listing 5.1.

Listing 5.1. A function that adds together two numbers. The _stdcall convention is used

```
;---------------------- addints.asm--------------------
.686
.model flat
  public _AddInts@8
.data
.code
_AddInts@8 proc
  push    EBP
  mov     EBP, ESP
  mov     EAX, DWORD PTR [EBP+8]
  add     EAX, DWORD PTR [EBP+12]
  pop     EBP
  ret     8
_AddInts@8 endp
end
```

For a correct call to the function, an underline character should be put at the beginning of its name and a @n suffix should be added at its end. Here, n is the number of bytes required for passing parameters. In this example, n is equal to eight. Such a form of a function's name is required by the C++ .NET compiler.

The function receives its parameters in the stack and returns the result in the EAX register.

Since the AddInts function should be available to external program modules, it should be declared with the public directive. The first two lines of the body of the procedure are:

```
push    EBP
mov     EBP, ESP
```

They are necessary for accessing the parameters in the stack with the EBP register. The parameters are in the stack at the addresses [EBP+8] and [EBP+12]. Which of them is the first, and which is the second? To answer this question, you should specify the order of the parameters in the calling program.

The _stdcall directive (see Table 5.1) indicates that the X1 and X2 parameters of the AddInts procedure are passed via the stack from right to left. That is, X2 is pushed on the stack first, and then X1. Since the stack grows from larger addresses to lesser, X2 will have a larger address than X1.

After the AddInts procedure is called and the EBP register is saved, the X1 and X2 parameters will be located on the stack as shown in Fig. 5.1.

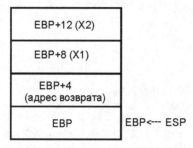

Fig. 5.1. The location of the parameters in the stack

To find the sum of two integers, the following commands are used:

```
mov     EAX, DWORD PTR [EBP+8]
add     EAX, DWORD PTR [EBP+12]
```

After these commands are executed, the sum is in the EAX register. When returning control to the calling program, the AddInts function restores the stack in accordance with the _stdcall directive. Before the ret command is executed, there are two double words, i.e., eight bytes, on the stack. To clear the stack, you should specify the 8 parameter in the ret 8 command. You can use the following sequence of commands:

```
add     ESP, 8
ret
```

Save the source code of the function in the AddInts.asm file and compile it:

```
ml /c AddInts.asm
```

The /c option tells the compiler that the source module should be only compiled. If there are no errors, you will obtain the AddInts.obj object module file that will be used in the main program.

A C++ .NET program that calls the AddInts function should declare it in the variables and functions declaration section:

```
extern "C" int _stdcall AddInts(int i1, int i2);
```

It is important to concentrate on the directives and specifiers in the declaration of the `AddInts` function, because understanding them is necessary in order to correctly develop the interfaces to any external functions.

The `extern` directive indicates that the function is external to the module that uses it.

The `"C"` specifier prohibits the C++ compiler to decorate (modify) the name of the external identifier. The decorated name of a function used in C++ holds the following information:

❑ Function name
❑ Class whose member the function is
❑ Namespace (the scope) of the function
❑ Types of the function's parameters
❑ Calling convention
❑ Return type

Decorated names are meaningful only to the C++ .NET compiler and linker. Examples of original and decorated names are given in Table 5.2.

Table 5.2. Examples of original and decorated names

Original name	Decorated name
`int a(char)`	?a@@YAHD@Z
`{`	
`  int i=3;`	
`  return i;`	
`};`	
`void __stdcallb::c(float){};`	?c@b@@AAGXM@Z

In most cases, you do not need to know the decorated name of a function. It can be necessary, for example, when you call C++ functions from assembly programs.

The function declaration uses the `_stdcall` calling convention. In general, a calling convention in the C++ .NET development environment can be set on the project properties page. The compiler can work with the following options:

❑ `/Gd` is set by default; it defines the `_cdecl` convention for all functions except member functions and functions explicitly declared as `_stdcall` or `_fastcall`.
❑ `/Gr` defines the `_fastcall` convention for all functions except member functions and functions explicitly declared as `_cdecl` or `_stdcall`. All `_fastcall` functions should have prototypes.

❏ /Gz defines the _stdcall convention for all functions except those with a variable number of arguments and functions explicitly declared as _cdecl or __fastcall. All _stdcall functions should have prototypes.

To set these options in the Visual C++ .NET compiler, proceed as follows.

1. Open the project property page (the **Property Pages** dialog box).

2. Select the **C/C++** folder.

3. Select the **Advanced** page.

4. Change the **Calling Convention** property.

Now, we will return to our program. Before compiling a C++ program, you should add to the project the object module file containing your function. The simplest way is to copy this to the project work directory.

A fragment of a C++ program that uses the AddInts external function could look like this:

```
   ...
int Int1 = 74;
int Int2 = -56;
int ires;
   ...
ires = AddInts(Int1, Int2);
   ...
```

One more note: The Visual C++ linker works with object module files in the COFF (Common Object File Format) format. When compiling a source module with MASM, you can obtain object file either in the COFF format or in the OMF (Object Module Format) format. This is why, when linking a project, the C++ .NET linker can display the following warning:

```
Warning: Converting object format from OMF to COFF.
```

Generally speaking, this does not matter, because the C++ compiler converts the OMF format to COFF in any case. You can specify the /coff option in the MASM compiler to obtain a COFF file:

```
ml /c /coff AddInts.asm
```

Now, we will discuss how this interface will work when the _cdecl calling convention is used (Listing 5.2). This method of passing parameters differs from _stdcall in that the calling program must restore the stack on its own. Parameters are passed from right to left, like in _stdcall.

Listing 5.2. An assembly function with the _cdecl calling convention

---

```
;------------------- addints.asm-----------------
.686
.model flat
  public _AddInts
.data
.code
_AddInts proc
  push    EBP
  mov     EBP, ESP
  mov     EAX, DWORD PTR [EBP+8]
  add     EAX, DWORD PTR [EBP+12]
  pop     EBP
  ret
_AddInts endp
end
```

As you can see from the source code, you should add an underscore character at the beginning of the function to work with the _cdecl directive. The ret command that exits the function is used here without parameters.

With regard to the source code of the Visual C++ program, the changes are minimal and should be done in the declaration section, in which you should replace the _stdcall directive with _cdecl:

```
extern "C" int _cdecl AddInts(int i1, int i2);
```

Finally, we will consider a widely used register method of passing parameters to a called function. It is specified with the _fastcall directive. The arguments are passed via the ECX and EDX registers from left to right. If there are three or more arguments, the third and others are passed via the stack. We will consider a function (named AddSubFc) that computes I1 - I2 − I3 + I4, where I1, I2, I3, and I4 are integers. The source code of this function is shown in Listing 5.3.

Listing 5.3. A function with the _fastcall calling convention

```
;----------------- addsubfc.asm -------------------
.686
.model flat
  public @AddSubFc@16
.code
@AddSubFc@16 proc
  push    EBP
  mov     EBP, ESP
  sub     ECX, EDX
  sub     ECX, DWORD PTR [EBP+8]
  add     ECX, DWORD PTR [EBP+12]
  mov     EAX, ECX
  pop     EBP
  ret     8
@AddSubFc@16 endp
end
```

When the number of parameters is not greater than two, the _fastcall method makes it possible to significantly speed up the application as a whole because stack initialization and restoration are not required, unlike the other methods of passing parameters. However, you should not abuse this method, because intensive use of processor registers in functions will hamper optimization done by the compiler. As you know, many high-level language compilers use the processor registers for program optimization.

Note the @16 suffix in the function's name. It specifies the total number of bytes taken by the parameters (two double words in the ECX and EDX registers and two double words in the stack).

In the main Visual C++ program, the _fastcall should be specified to call this procedure:

```
extern "C" int _fastcall AddInts(int i1, int i2, int i3, int i4);
```

In practice, you often deal with more than one assembly modules, so now we will discuss a more complex variant of the interface between a C++ .NET program and assembly procedures. Suppose the main program must compute the sum of two integers and decrease it by 20. Use two separately compiled assembly functions. Let the first one (name it AddTwo) add together two integers, Int1 and Int2, taken as parameters. The second function (named Sub20) will subtract 20 from the result obtained by AddTwo. Let the final result be returned to the main program by the AddTwo function.

Save the source code of the AddTwo function in the AddTwo.asm file, and the source code of the Sub20 function in the Sub20.asm file.

Also, let the AddTwo function process the parameters in accordance with the _stdcall directive, and the Sub20 function process its parameters in accordance with the _cdecl directive. The source code of the AddTwo function is shown in Listing 5.4.

Listing 5.4. The AddTwo function (a modified variant)

```
;------------------ AddTwo.asm --------------------
.686
.model flat
  public _AddTwo@8
  extern _Sub20:proc
.code
_AddTwo@8 proc
  push EBP
  mov   EBP, ESP
  mov   EAX, DWORD PTR [EBP+8]
  add   EAX, DWORD PTR [EBP+12]
  push EAX
  call _Sub20
  add   ESP, 4
  pop   EBP
  ret   8
_AddTwo@8 endp
  end
```

Now, we will discuss the difference between the modified variant of the AddTwo function and the original. First, there is the line:

```
extern _Sub20:proc
```

in the directives section. This line makes the MASM compiler treat the Sub20 function as external to the module that contains AddTwo. Also, when the application is built, the Visual C++ .NET compiler assumes that the parameters are passed to the Sub20 function in accordance with the _cdecl directive (because the function's identifier begins with an underscore character).

Second, there are the commands:

```
push      EAX
call      _Sub20
add       ESP, 4
```

At the moment of execution of these lines, the EAX register contains the sum of two integers. This value is a parameter of the Sub20 function. It is pushed on the stack with the push EAX command. After the Sub20 function completes, the result is stored in the EAX register. Since the main program should restore the stack when a _cdecl call is made, the presence of the add ESP, 4 command is explicable.

Consider the source code of the Sub20 function (Listing 5.5).

Listing 5.5. The Sub20 assembly function

```
;--------------- Sub20.asm ---------------
.686
.model flat
  public _Sub20
.code
_Sub20 proc
  push EBP
  mov   EBP, ESP
  mov   EAX, DWORD PTR [EBP+8]
  sub   EAX, 20
  pop   EBP
  ret
_Sub20 endp
end
```

The Sub20 function takes the sum of two integers as a parameter. It returns the result in the EAX register and does not restore the stack before returning, because this must be done by a caller, the AddTwo function in this case. The directive

```
public _Sub20
```

makes the Sub20 function available to other modules.

After you compile the AddTwo.asm and Sub20.asm files, you should add the obtained object modules AddTwo.obj and Sub20.obj to your Visual C++ .NET project. Use the Visual Studio .NET 2003 Application Wizard to develop a Windows console application that will use the AddTwo and Sub20 functions. The source code of the main project file is shown in Listing 5.6.

Listing 5.6. A project file that uses the AddTwo and Sub20 functions

---

```
// This is the main project file for VC++ application project
// generated using an Application Wizard.

#include "stdafx.h"
extern "C" int _stdcall AddTwo(int i1, int i2);
extern "C" int _cdecl Sub20(int i3);
#using <mscorlib.dll>

using namespace System;

int _tmain()
{
// TODO: Please replace the sample code below with your own.

    String  *SInt1, *SInt2, *SIres;
    int Int1, Int2, ires;

    Console::Write("Enter Int1: ");
    SInt1 = Console::ReadLine();
    Console::Write("Enter Int2: ");
    SInt2 = Console::ReadLine ();
    Int1 = Convert::ToInt32 (SInt1);
    Int2 = Convert::ToInt32 (SInt2);

    ires = AddTwo(Int1, Int2);
    SIres = Convert::ToString(ires);
    Console::Write("Result:[Int1 + Int2 - 20] = ");
    Console::WriteLine(ires);
    Console::WriteLine("Press any key to exit...");
    Console::ReadLine ();
    return 0;
}
```

As you can see from this source code, the declaration section should contain the following lines:

```
extern "C" int _stdcall AddTwo(int i1, int i2);
extern "C" int _cdecl Sub20(int i3);
```

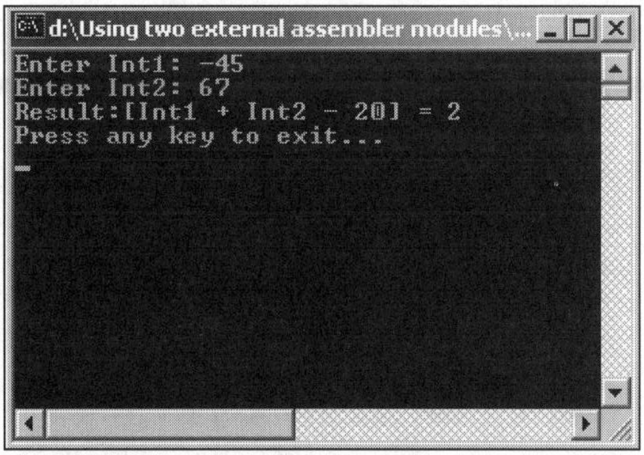

Fig. 5.2. Window of an application that demonstrates the use of two stand-alone assembly procedures from two object files

The rest of the code is simple and does not require further explanation. The window of the application is shown in Fig. 5.2.

Linking and debugging this application can be made simpler by using one file with the source codes of the functions rather than two. Save the source codes of the AddTwo and Sub20 assembly functions in the AddSub.asm file. Change the source code of the Sub20 function a little by replacing the sub EAX, 20 command with sub EAX, 100. Name the modified function Sub100. The source code of the functions in the AddSub.asm file is shown in Listing 5.7.

Listing 5.7. The AddTwo and Sub100 functions

```
;------------ AddSub.asm --------------
.686
.model flat
  public _AddTwo@8      ;_stdcall convention
  public _Sub100        ;_cdecl convention
.code
_AddTwo@8 proc
  push EBP
  mov  EBP, ESP
  mov  EAX, DWORD PTR [EBP+8]
  add  EAX, DWORD PTR [EBP+12]
  push EAX
  call _Sub100
  add  ESP, 4
  pop  EBP
```

```
  ret  8
_AddTwo@8 endp

_Sub100 proc
  push EBP
  mov  EBP, ESP
  mov  EAX, DWORD PTR [EBP+8]
  sub  EAX, 100
  pop  EBP
  ret
_Sub100 endp
end
```

As you can see from the listing, the line

```
extern _Sub20:proc
```

disappeared from the declaration section because both procedures are in the same module now. If the MASM compile does not detect any errors, you will obtain the AddSub.obj object module file. In the C++ project source file, change the line:

```
extern "C" int _cdecl Sub20(int i3);
```

to

```
extern "C" int _cdecl Sub100(int i3);
```

Also, delete the files AddTwo.obj and Sub20.obj from the project and add the AddSub.obj file to the project. The window of the application is shown in Fig. 5.3.

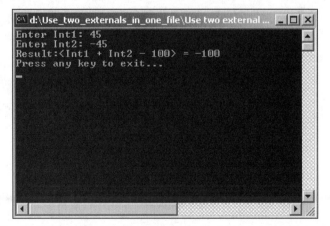

Fig. 5.3. Window of an application that demonstrates the use of two stand-alone assembly procedures from one object file

From these examples, you can see that every time you call functions written according to the _stdcall or _cdecl convention, you have to save and restore the stack. With intensive computation when such functions are called many times, these operations may decrease the performance of your application. If you use the _fastcall convention when developing your functions, this will allow you to increase the performance of your application. You should use this method with care because the C++ .NET compiler uses the registers intensively.

The next example computes the formula Int1-Int2-Int3+Int4-100, where Int1, Int2, Int3, and Int4 are integers, and displays the result. Develop a dialog-based C++ .NET application. Put five edit controls, a button, and five static text controls on the main form. Associate the edit controls with the integer variables i1 to i4 that correspond to the numbers from Int1 to Int4 and with the ires variable that will hold the result. The result is displayed after clicking the button.

The computation is done with two assembly functions, AddSubFc and Sub100, which use the _fastcall and _cdecl calling conventions, respectively. Their source code is shown in Listing 5.8.

Listing 5.8. Functions that use the _fastcall and _cdecl calling conventions

```
.686
.model flat
  public @AddSubFc@16, _Sub100
.code
@AddSubFc@16 proc
  push    EBP
  mov     EBP, ESP
  sub     ECX, EDX                 ; ECX -> Int1-Int2
  sub     ECX, DWORD PTR [EBP+8]   ; ECX -> ECX-Int3
  add     ECX, DWORD PTR [EBP+12]  ; ECX -> ECX+Int4
  mov     EAX, ECX
  push    EAX
  call    _Sub100
  add     ESP, 4
  pop     EBP
  ret     8
@AddSubFc@16 endp
_Sub100 proc
  push    EBP
```

```
    mov      EBP, ESP
    mov      EAX, DWORD PTR [EBP+8]
    sub      EAX, 100
    pop      EBP
    ret
_Sub100 endp
end
```

The first parameter of the AddSubFc function (i.e., Int1) is passed via the ECX register. The second parameter, Int2, is in the EDX register. The third parameter, Int3, is on the stack at the [EBP+8] address, and the fourth is at the [EBP+12] address. Before the call to the Sub100 function, the intermediate result is moved from the ECX register to EAX with the mov EAX, ECX command. The sequence of commands:

```
    push     EAX
    call     _Sub100
    add      ESP, 4
```

is standard for a procedure that conforms to the _cdecl convention and takes one parameter. Save the source code of the function in the AddSubFc.asm file and compile it. If there are no errors, you will obtain the AddSubFc.obj file. Add it to your C++ .NET project.

Add the following lines to the declaration section in the C++ project source file:

```
extern "C" int _fastcall AddSubFc(int i1, int i2, int i3, int i4);
extern "C" int _cdecl Sub100(int i3);
```

The OnBnClicked handler in the C++ calling program is shown in Listing 5.9.

Listing 5.9. The OnBnClicked handler

```
void CCdecl_FastCall_MFCDlg::OnBnClickedButton1()
{
// TODO: Add your control notification handler code here
    UpdateData(TRUE);
    ires = AddSubFc(i1, i2, i3, i4);
    UpdateData(FALSE);
}
```

After you successfully build the project and start the application, its window will appear as shown in Fig. 5.4.

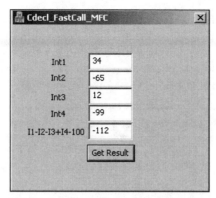

Fig. 5.4. Window of an application that demonstrates the use
of functions with `_cdecl` and `_fastcall` convention

The final example in this chapter demonstrates how the result of a mathematical operation can be returned via the stack of the mathematical coprocessor. Suppose a function (named `nfp`) takes a floating-point number as a parameter and inverts it. The result is returned on the top of the stack `ST(0)`. The source code of the `nfp` function is shown in Listing 5.10.

Listing 5.10. The nfp function that returns the result on the coprocessor's stack

```
;------------------ nfp.asm ------------------
.686
.model flat
  public _nfp@4
.code
_nfp@4 proc
  push   EBP
  mov    EBP, ESP
  finit
  fld    DWORD PTR [EBP+8]
  fchs
  fwait
  pop    EBP
  ret    4
_nfp@4 endp
end
```

The parameter, which is a floating-point number, is pushed on the top of the co-processor stack with the `fld DWORD PTR [EBP+8]` command. The sign is changed with the `fchs` command, and the result remains on the top of the coprocessor stack.

A C++ .NET console application uses the result of the `nfp` function to display it. The source code of this application is shown in Listing 5.11.

Listing 5.11. An application that uses the nfp function

```cpp
// This is the main project file for VC++ application project
// generated using an Application Wizard.

#include "stdafx.h"
extern "C" float _stdcall nfp(float f1);
#using <mscorlib.dll>

using namespace System;

int _tmain()
{
// TODO: Please replace the sample code below with your own.
    String *s1;
    float f1;
    Console::Write("Enter float value: ");
    s1 = Console::ReadLine();
    f1 = Convert::ToSingle(s1);
    f1 = nfp(f1);
    s1 = Convert::ToString(f1);
    Console::Write("Changed value: ");
    Console::WriteLine(s1);
    Console::Write("Press any key to exit...");
    Console::ReadLine();
    return 0;
}
```

The called function is declares as follows:

```cpp
extern "C" float _stdcall nfp(float f1);
```

Its result is stored in the `f1` variable:

```cpp
f1 = nfp(f1);
```

In this case, the number on the top of the coprocessor stack is copied to the f1 variable without using the EAX register. The window of the application is shown in Fig. 5.5.

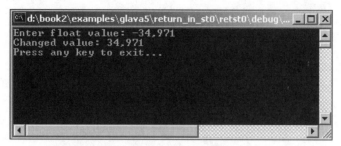

Fig. 5.5. Window of an application that displays
an inverted floating-point number

This chapter concentrated on the interfaces of external assembly modules to C++ .NET programs and did not focus on various types of parameters. This will be addressed in the next chapter, in which the method of passing parameters and checking the returned results will be comprehensively discussed for various data types.

Chapter 6: Developing and Using Assembly Subroutines

The previous chapter looked at general principles of creating assembly module interfaces with a C++ .NET program and the main standards and conventions used in programs. Now, we will look at using parameters in calls to assembly functions more closely. There are two main methods for passing data to a function for further processing: by value and by reference. First, we will consider passing parameters by value.

In this case, the called function receives a copy of the variable, and the copy is lost when the function returns control. The variable in the calling program does not change. Consider a simple example of a console application, in which the called function multiplies an integer parameter by five and returns the result to the main program via the EAX register. We will assume that the main program and the called function in the examples in this and the following chapters use the stdcall convention.

The assembly function that multiplies numbers is shown in Listing 6.1.

Listing 6.1. A function that multiplies an integer by 5

```
.686
.model flat
  public _mul5@4
.code
_mul5@4   proc
```

```
    push    EBP
    mov     EBP, ESP
    mov     EAX, DWORD PTR [EBP+8]
    mov     ECX, 5
    mul     ECX
    pop     EBP
    ret
_mul5@4  endp
end
```

The source code of the function is straightforward. The Visual C++ .NET main program is written as a console application, and its source code is shown in Listing 6.2.

Listing 6.2. A C++ program that uses the mul5 procedure

```
// This is the main project file for VC++ application project
// generated by using an Application Wizard.

#include "stdafx.h"

#using <mscorlib.dll>

extern "C" int _stdcall mul5(int i1);

using namespace System;

int _tmain()
{
    // TODO: Please replace the sample code below with your own.

 int i1, i5;
 String *Si1, *Si5;
 Console::Write("Enter integer value: ");
 Si1 = Console::ReadLine();
 i1 = Convert::ToInt32 (Si1);

 i5 = mul5(i1);
 Si1 = Convert::ToString(i1);
 Si5 = Convert::ToString (i5);

 Console::Write("Entered integer = ");
```

```
Console::WriteLine (Si1);
Console::Write("Multiplying i1 x 5 = ");
Console::WriteLine (Si5);
Console::ReadLine();
return 0;
}
```

After `mul5` procedure is called with the statement `i5 = mul5(i1)`, the value of the `i1` variable does not change. This is evident in Fig. 6.1, which shows the application window.

Fig. 6.1. Window of an application that multiplies an integer by a constant

Passing parameters by value in function calls is inconvenient when processing arrays of numeric and character data.

To process such data, pointers are usually used in function calls, and passing parameters in such a manner is called passing by reference.

Now we will look at using pointer parameters for processing strings and arrays in C++ .NET with assembly functions more closely. It is well known that a pointer is a variable that contains the memory address of another variable. The address of a string or array is the address of its first element. The addresses of subsequent elements are computed by adding the value equal to the size of the element of the string or array. For ASCII strings, which we will consider, the address of the next element is one greater than the address of the previous element. For an integer array, the address of the next element is four greater than the address of the previous item.

Another important note: In all the examples in this chapter, null-terminated strings are used in string operations.

The following example illustrates how a character string can be passed to the main program from an assembly module and displayed in the program's window. The source code of the assembly function is shown in Listing 6.3.

Listing 6.3. An assembly function that passes a character string to the main program

```
;----------------- strshow.asm -----------------
 .686
.model flat
  public _strshow@0
.data
  TESTSTR DB "THIS STRING GOES FROM ASM PROCEDURE !", 0
.code
_strshow@0 proc
  mov     EAX, offset TESTSTR
  ret
_strshow@0 endp
end
```

The function is very simple. It does not take any parameters and returns the address of the TESTSTR string in the EAX register. The source code of the C++ .NET console application that calls the strshow function is also easy to analyze (Listing 6.4).

Listing 6.4. A console application that calls the strshow function

```
// This is the main project file for VC++ application project
// generated by using an Application Wizard.

#include "stdafx.h"
extern "C" char* _stdcall strshow(void);
#using <mscorlib.dll>

using namespace System;

int _tmain()
{
      Console::Write (strshow());
      Console::ReadLine();
      return 0;
}
```

The string is output to the application window with the `Console::Write` statement. The `Write` method of the `System::Console` class takes the pointer to the string buffer returned by the `strshow` function as an argument.

The window of the application is shown in Fig. 6.2.

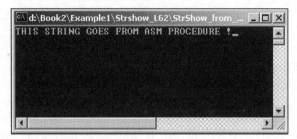

Fig. 6.2. Window of an application that displays a string received
from an assembly function

Another method for passing a string or array to the main program involves copying the string to the main program's memory buffer. The source code of an assembly function that does this is shown in Listing 6.5.

Listing 6.5. An assembly function that copies a string to the main application

```
;---------------- copystr.asm -------------

.686
.model flat
  public _copystr@4
.data
  TESTSTR   DB  "TEST STRING IS COPIED FROM ASM PROCEDURE !", 0
  LENSTR    EQU $-TESTSTR
.code
_copystr@4 proc
  push      ESI
  push      EDI
  push      EBP
  mov       EBP, ESP
  cld
  mov       ECX, LENSTR
  mov       ESI, offset TESTSTR
  mov       EDI, DWORD PTR [EBP+16]
  rep       movsb
```

```
    pop      EBP
    pop      EDI
    pop      ESI
    ret      4
_copystr@4 endp
end
```

The parameter of this function is the address of the memory buffer of the calling program, to which the string must be copied. The buffer is assumed to be large enough to hold the whole string. The string length in bytes is put to the ECX register. The ESI register contains the address of the TESTSTR source string, and the EDI register contains the address of the target string in the main program. Copying is done with the rep movsb command.

The C++ .NET console application that displays a copy of a string can be coded as follows (Listing 6.6).

The window of the application is shown in Fig. 6.3.

Listing 6.6. A console application that displays a copy of a string

```cpp
// This is the main project file for VC++ application project
// generated by using an Application Wizard.

#include "stdafx.h"
extern "C" void _stdcall copystr(char* s1);
#using <mscorlib.dll>

using namespace System;

int _tmain()
{
    // TODO: Please replace the sample code below with your own.

    char buf[64];
    copystr(buf);
    Console::WriteLine(buf);
    Console::ReadLine();
    return 0;
}
```

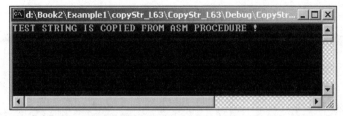

Fig. 6.3. Window of an application that displays a copy of a string

When linking the application in Visual C++ .NET, always include the file of the object module written in the assembler into your project.

We will continue by considering a few more examples that demonstrate techniques of passing parameters and processing data in assembly functions.

It is often necessary to pass to the main program a part of a string (a substring) starting from a certain position, rather than the whole string. The next example illustrates how this can be done.

Suppose an assembly module contains a character string, and you want to pass to the main program a substring starting from a certain position. In this case, the assembly function takes the offset from the beginning of the string as a parameter and returns the address of the first element of the extracted substring.

The source code of the assembly function (named strpart) is shown in Listing 6.7.

Listing 6.7. A function that returns a substring to the C++ program

---

```
;-------------------- strpart.asm --------------------
.686
.model flat
  public _strpart@8
.data
.code
_strpart@8 proc
  push    EBP
  mov     EBP, ESP
  mov     ECX, DWORD PTR [EBP+12]
  mov     EAX, DWORD PTR [EBP+8]
  add     EAX, ECX
  pop     EBP
  ret     8
_strpart@8 endp
end
```

Choose a standard variant of a procedure-oriented Windows application as a template for the C++ .NET main program. After the Application Wizard generates the frame, make necessary changes and additions to the source text and add the **Return Part of String** item to the menu. Bind the ID_PartStr identifier to it. When this menu item is selected, the source string, substring, and offset in the initial string will be displayed in the application window.

In the declaration section of the WinMain main program, create a reference to the external procedure:

```
extern "C" char* _stdcall strpart(char *ps, int off);
```

The parameters of the strpart function are the address of the source string (ps) and the offset from its beginning (off).

The application uses a few more variables, which are shown below:

```
char src[] = "STRING1 STRING2 STRING3 STRING4 STRING5";
char *dst;
int  off, ioff;
char buf[4];
```

where

☐ src string is a source string for processing.
☐ dst string is the destination string.
☐ off integer is the offset from the beginning of the source string.
☐ buf string and the ioff integer are used by the sprintf function to format the output.

In the WndProc callback function, create a menu item selection handler ID_PartStr (Listing 6.8).

Listing 6.8. The ID_PartStr menu item selection handler

```
case ID_PartStr:
  hdc = GetDC(hWnd);
  GetClientRect(hWnd, &rect);
  off = 10;
  dst = strpart(src, off);
  ioff = sprintf(buf, "%d", off);
  TextOut(hdc,(rect.right - rect.left)/4, (rect.bottom - rect.top)/4,
        "Source:", 7);
  TextOut(hdc, (rect.right - rect.left)/3, (rect.bottom - rect.top)/4,
        src, strlen(src));
```

```
TextOut(hdc, (rect.right - rect.left)/4, (rect.bottom - rect.top)/3,
        "Dest:", 5);
TextOut(hdc, (rect.right - rect.left)/3, (rect.bottom - rect.top)/3,
        dst, strlen(dst));
TextOut(hdc, (rect.right - rect.left)/4,
            (rect.bottom - rect.top)/3 + 30, "Offset:", 7);
TextOut(hdc, (rect.right - rect.left)/3,
            (rect.bottom - rect.top)/3 + 30, buf, ioff);
ReleaseDC(hWnd, hdc);
break;
```

The `TextOut` function outputs text to the client area. Its first parameter is the device context descriptor of the display. The device context descriptor is returned by the `GetDC` function.

To output the text to the client area of the window, access the coordinates of this area with the `GetClientRect` function.

The `sprintf` function is used to format the `off` integer when displaying it. The prototype of this function is described in the `stdio.h` file, so it is necessary to add the following line to the declaration section of the `WinMain` function:

```
#include <stdio.h>
```

The application window will look better if you change the standard white background to gray:

```
wcex.hbrBackground = (HBRUSH)GetStockObject(GRAY_BRUSH);
```

The full source code of the application is shown in Listing 6.9.

Listing 6.9. A C++ program that displays a substring

```
#include "stdafx.h"
#include "Return Part of String in C.NET.h"
#define  MAX_LOADSTRING 100
#include <stdio.h>

HINSTANCE hInst;
TCHAR     szTitle[MAX_LOADSTRING];
TCHAR     szWindowClass[MAX_LOADSTRING];

// References to the functions declared in this module

ATOM   MyRegisterClass(HINSTANCE hInstance);
```

```
BOOL    InitInstance(HINSTANCE, int);
LRESULT CALLBACK  WndProc(HWND, UINT, WPARAM, LPARAM);
LRESULT CALLBACK  About(HWND, UINT, WPARAM, LPARAM);


extern "C" char* _stdcall strpart(char *ps, int off);

int APIENTRY _tWinMain(HINSTANCE hInstance,
                       HINSTANCE hPrevInstance,
                       LPTSTR    lpCmdLine,
                       int       nCmdShow)
{
  MSG msg;
  HACCEL hAccelTable;

  LoadString(hInstance, IDS_APP_TITLE, szTitle, MAX_LOADSTRING);
  LoadString(hInstance, IDC_RETURNPARTOFSTRINGINCNET,
             szWindowClass, MAX_LOADSTRING);
  MyRegisterClass(hInstance);
  if (!InitInstance(hInstance, nCmdShow))
  {
    return FALSE;
  }

  hAccelTable = LoadAccelerators(hInstance,
                (LPCTSTR)IDC_RETURNPARTOFSTRINGINCNET);

  while (GetMessage(&msg, NULL, 0, 0))
  {
    if (!TranslateAccelerator(msg.hwnd, hAccelTable, &msg))
    {
      TranslateMessage(&msg);
      DispatchMessage(&msg);
    }
  }
  return (int)msg.wParam;
}

ATOM MyRegisterClass(HINSTANCE hInstance)
{
  WNDCLASSEX wcex;
  wcex.cbSize         = sizeof(WNDCLASSEX);
  wcex.style          = CS_HREDRAW | CS_VREDRAW;
```

```
    wcex.lpfnWndProc      = (WNDPROC)WndProc;
    wcex.cbClsExtra       = 0;
    wcex.cbWndExtra       = 0;
    wcex.hInstance        = hInstance;
    wcex.hIcon            = LoadIcon(hInstance,
                                 (LPCTSTR)IDI_RETURNPARTOFSTRINGINCNET);
    wcex.hCursor          = LoadCursor(NULL, IDC_ARROW);
    wcex.hbrBackground    = (HBRUSH)GetStockObject(GRAY_BRUSH);

    wcex.lpszMenuName     = (LPCTSTR)IDC_RETURNPARTOFSTRINGINCNET;
    wcex.lpszClassName    = szWindowClass;
    wcex.hIconSm          = LoadIcon(wcex.hInstance,
                                 (LPCTSTR)IDI_SMALL);
    return RegisterClassEx(&wcex);
}


BOOL InitInstance(HINSTANCE hInstance, int nCmdShow)
{
  HWND hWnd;
  hInst = hInstance;
  hWnd = CreateWindow(szWindowClass, szTitle, WS_OVERLAPPEDWINDOW,
                      CW_USEDEFAULT, 0, CW_USEDEFAULT, 0, NULL, NULL,
                      hInstance, NULL);
  if (!hWnd)
  {
     return FALSE;
  }
  ShowWindow(hWnd, nCmdShow);
  UpdateWindow(hWnd);
  return TRUE;
}


LRESULT CALLBACK WndProc(HWND hWnd, UINT message, WPARAM wParam,
                         LPARAM lParam)
{
  int   wmId, wmEvent;
  PAINTSTRUCT ps;
  HDC   hdc;
  RECT  rect;
  char src[] = "STRING1 STRING2 STRING3 STRING4 STRING5";

  char *dst;
  int  off, ioff;
```

```
char buf[4];

switch (message)
{
  case WM_COMMAND:
        wmId    = LOWORD(wParam);
        wmEvent = HIWORD(wParam);
        switch (wmId)
        {
          case IDM_ABOUT:
                DialogBox(hInst, (LPCTSTR)IDD_ABOUTBOX,
                          hWnd, (DLGPROC)About);
                break;
          case IDM_EXIT:
                DestroyWindow(hWnd);
                break;
          case ID_PartStr:
                hdc  = GetDC(hWnd);
                GetClientRect(hWnd, &rect);
                off  = 10;
                dst  = strpart(src, off);
                ioff = sprintf(buf,"%d",off);
                TextOut(hdc, (rect.right - rect.left)/4,
                        (rect.bottom - rect.top)/4, "Source:", 7);
                TextOut(hdc, (rect.right - rect.left)/3,
                        (rect.bottom - rect.top)/4, src, strlen(src));
                TextOut(hdc, (rect.right - rect.left)/4,
                        (rect.bottom - rect.top)/3, "Dest:", 5);
                TextOut(hdc, (rect.right - rect.left)/3,
                        (rect.bottom - rect.top)/3, dst, strlen(dst));
                TextOut(hdc, (rect.right - rect.left)/4,
                        (rect.bottom - rect.top)/3 + 30, "Offset:", 7);
                TextOut(hdc, (rect.right - rect.left)/3,
                        (rect.bottom - rect.top)/3 + 30, buf, ioff);

                ReleaseDC(hWnd, hdc);
                break;
          default:
                return DefWindowProc(hWnd, message, wParam, lParam);
        }
        break;
  case WM_PAINT:
        hdc = BeginPaint(hWnd, &ps);
```

```
            EndPaint(hWnd, &ps);
            break;
        case WM_DESTROY:
            PostQuitMessage(0);
            break;
        default:
            return DefWindowProc(hWnd, message, wParam, lParam);
    }
    return 0;
}

LRESULT CALLBACK About(HWND hDlg, UINT message, WPARAM wParam,
                       LPARAM lParam)
{
    switch (message)
    {
        case WM_INITDIALOG:
            return TRUE;
        case WM_COMMAND:
            if (LOWORD(wParam) == IDOK || LOWORD(wParam) == IDCANCEL)
            {
                EndDialog(hDlg, LOWORD(wParam));
                return TRUE;
            }
            break;
    }
    return FALSE;
}
```

The window of this application is shown in Fig. 6.4.

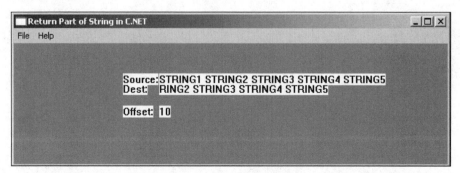

Fig. 6.4. Window of an application that displays a part of a string
from a C++ .NET program

The next example demonstrates how a string element can be found. An assembly function passes the main program the position of the first occurence of the sought element in the string (if it finds any) or zero otherwise. The function's parameters are the string address and a character to search for.

The source code of the assembly function (named charpos) is shown in Listing 6.10.

Listing 6.10. A function that searches for a character in a string

```
;-------------------- charpos.asm--------------------
.686
.model flat
  public _charpos@8
.data
.code
_charpos@8 proc
  push    EBX
  push    EBP
  mov     EBP, ESP
  mov     EBX, DWORD PTR [EBP+12]
  xor     EAX, EAX
  mov     AL,  BYTE PTR [EBP+16]
  mov     ECX, 1
next_check:
  cmp     AL, [EBX]
  je      quit
  cmp     BYTE PTR [EBX], 0
  jne     inc_cnt
  jmp     not_found
quit:
  mov     EAX, ECX
  pop     EBP
  pop     EBX
  ret     8
inc_cnt:
  inc     ECX
  inc     EBX
  jmp     next_check
not_found:
  xor     ECX, ECX
  jmp     quit
_charpos@8 endp
  end
```

Parameters of the charpos function are the string address located in the address stored in [EBP+12] and the character to search for in [EBP+16]. The first element of the string has the number 1. Therefore, the counter is initialized to this value:

```
mov    ECX, 1
```

The string address is put to the EBX register, and the character to search for is put to the AL register. Then the character whose address is in the EBX register is compared with the contents of the AL register. Depending on the result, the function jumps to an appropriate branch:

```
cmp    AL, [EBX]
je     quit
cmp    BYTE PTR [EBX], 0
jne    inc_cnt
jmp    not_found
```

If the sought character is found, its number is written to the ECX register. If the last element is null, i.e., the end-of-string character is found, the contents of the ECX register is reset to zero. If the sought character is not found, but the end of the string has not been encountered yet, the registers EBX and ECX are incremented, and the loop resumes from the next_check label:

```
jmp    next_check
```

As usual, the procedure returns the result in the EAX register and frees up the stack with the ret 8 command.

Select the dialog-based application template for the C++ program. Put three edit controls, three static text controls, and a button onto the main form. Bind the src and cSrc variables of the CString type to the **Source** and **Character** edit controls and the iPos integer variable to the **Number** edit control. Write an event handler for clicking the Button button (Listing 6.11).

Listing 6.11. An on-button-clicked event handler in a C++ application

---

```
void GetNumberOfCharinStringforCNETDlg::OnBnClickedButton1()
{
    // TODO: Add your control notification handler code here.

    CString s1;
    CString c1;
    char *pc1;
    UpdateData(TRUE);
    s1 = src;
```

```
  c1 = cSrc;
  pc1 = c1.GetBuffer(8);
  iPos = charpos(s1.GetBuffer(16), *pc1);
  UpdateData(FALSE);
}
```

If the character is found, the **Number** edit control will contain the number of the character; otherwise, it will contain zero.

The application window is shown in Fig. 6.5.

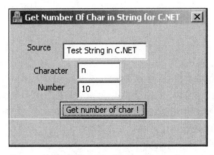

Fig. 6.5. Window of an application that searches for a character in a string

The next example demonstrates how to search for the maximum element in a floating-point array and display it on the screen. Let the array size be equal to nine. Develop a classic procedure-oriented application in Visual C++ .NET. In such an application, there are usually two interrelated pieces of code: the WinMain main procedure, which registers the window class and initializes an application window instance, and a callback function (a window procedure).

The search for the maximum element in a floating-point array is done with the maxreal assembly function (Listing 6.12).

Listing 6.12. A function that searches for the maximum element in a floating-point array

```
;------------------------ maxreal.asm --------------------
.686
.model flat
  public _maxreal@8
.data
  MAXREAL DD 0
.code
```

```
_maxreal@8 proc
   push    EBX
   push    EBP
   mov     EBP, ESP
   mov     EBX, DWORD PTR [EBP+12]
   mov     EDX, DWORD PTR [EBP+16]
   mov     ECX, 1
   finit
   fld     DWORD PTR [EBX]
NEXT_CMP:
   add     EBX, 4
   fcom    DWORD PTR [EBX]
   fstsw   AX
   sahf
   jnc     CHECK_INDEX
   fld     DWORD PTR [EBX]
CHECK_INDEX:
   cmp     ECX, EDX
   je      FIN
   inc     ECX
   jmp     NEXT_CMP
FIN:
   fwait
   fstp    DWORD PTR MAXREAL
   mov     EAX, offset MAXREAL
   pop     EBP
   pop     EBX
   ret     8
_maxreal@8 endp
end
```

This function uses mathematical coprocessor commands. To extract parameters, the EBP register is used. The array address is passed via [EBP+12], and the array size is passed via [EBP+16]. The current maximum value is stored in the local variable MAXREAL.

After processing the array, the address of the maximum element is put to the EAX register:

```
fstp    DWORD PTR MAXREAL
mov     EAX, offset MAXREAL
```

Use the Application Wizard to develop a common 32-bit Windows application that uses the result of the assembly function. The source code of the `WinMain` procedure and the callback function is shown in Listing 6.13.

Listing 6.13. A C++ program that displays the maximum value

```cpp
#include "stdafx.h"
#include "Find Max Value in Array of Reals.h"
#define  MAX_LOADSTRING 100

// Global variables

HINSTANCE hInst;
TCHAR     szTitle[MAX_LOADSTRING];
TCHAR     szWindowClass[MAX_LOADSTRING];

// Declarations of this module's functions

ATOM      MyRegisterClass(HINSTANCE hInstance);
BOOL      InitInstance(HINSTANCE, int);
LRESULT CALLBACK WndProc(HWND, UINT, WPARAM, LPARAM);
LRESULT CALLBACK About(HWND, UINT, WPARAM, LPARAM);
extern "C" float* _stdcall maxreal(float *px, int sx);

int APIENTRY _tWinMain(HINSTANCE hInstance,
                       HINSTANCE hPrevInstance,
                       LPTSTR    lpCmdLine,
                       int       nCmdShow)
{
  MSG msg;
  HACCEL hAccelTable;

  LoadString(hInstance, IDS_APP_TITLE, szTitle, MAX_LOADSTRING);
  LoadString(hInstance, IDC_FINDMAXVALUEINARRAYOFREALS,
             szWindowClass, MAX_LOADSTRING);
  MyRegisterClass(hInstance);

  // Initializing the application

  if (!InitInstance (hInstance, nCmdShow))
  {
    return FALSE;
  }
}
```

```
   hAccelTable = LoadAccelerators(hInstance,
                            (LPCTSTR)IDC_FINDMAXVALUEINARRAYOFREALS);

   // A message processing loop

   while (GetMessage(&msg, NULL, 0, 0))
   {
     if (!TranslateAccelerator(msg.hwnd, hAccelTable, &msg))
     {
       TranslateMessage(&msg);
       DispatchMessage(&msg);
     }
   }
   return (int) msg.wParam;
}

// A window class registration function

ATOM MyRegisterClass(HINSTANCE hInstance)
{
   WNDCLASSEX wcex;
   wcex.cbSize         = sizeof(WNDCLASSEX);
   wcex.style          = CS_HREDRAW | CS_VREDRAW;
   wcex.lpfnWndProc    = (WNDPROC)WndProc;
   wcex.cbClsExtra     = 0;
   wcex.cbWndExtra     = 0;
   wcex.hInstance      = hInstance;
   wcex.hIcon          = LoadIcon(hInstance,
                         (LPCTSTR)IDI_FINDMAXVALUEINARRAYOFREALS);
   wcex.hCursor        = LoadCursor(NULL, IDC_ARROW);

   wcex.hbrBackground  = (HBRUSH)GetStockObject(GRAY_BRUSH);

   wcex.lpszMenuName   = (LPCTSTR)IDC_FINDMAXVALUEINARRAYOFREALS;
   wcex.lpszClassName  = szWindowClass;
   wcex.hIconSm        = LoadIcon(wcex.hInstance, (LPCTSTR)IDI_SMALL);

   return RegisterClassEx(&wcex);

}

BOOL InitInstance(HINSTANCE hInstance, int nCmdShow)
{
   HWND hWnd;
```

```
hInst = hInstance;
hWnd = CreateWindow(szWindowClass, szTitle,
                    WS_OVERLAPPEDWINDOW, CW_USEDEFAULT, 0,
                    CW_USEDEFAULT, 0, NULL, NULL, hInstance, NULL);

if (!hWnd)
{
  return FALSE;
}

ShowWindow(hWnd, nCmdShow);
UpdateWindow(hWnd);
return TRUE;
}
LRESULT CALLBACK WndProc(HWND hWnd, UINT message, WPARAM wParam,
                         LPARAM lParam)
{
  int wmId, wmEvent;
  PAINTSTRUCT ps;
  HDC hdc;
  char buf[16];
  float xarray[9] = {12.43, 93.54, -23.1, 23.59, 16.09,
                     10.67, -54.7, 11.49, 98.06};
  float *xres;
  int cnt;
  switch (message)
  {
    case WM_COMMAND:
        wmId    = LOWORD(wParam);
        wmEvent = HIWORD(wParam);
        switch (wmId)
        {
          case IDM_ABOUT:
              DialogBox(hInst, (LPCTSTR)IDD_ABOUTBOX,
                        hWnd, (DLGPROC)About);
              break;
          case IDM_EXIT:
              DestroyWindow(hWnd);
              break;
          default:
              return DefWindowProc(hWnd, message, wParam, lParam);

        }
        break;
```

```
      case WM_PAINT:
           hdc = BeginPaint(hWnd, &ps);

           // Our handler's code is here

           TextOut(hdc, 30, 80, "ARRAY: ", 7);
           for (cnt = 0; cnt < 9; cnt++)
           {
             gcvt(xarray[cnt], 6, buf);
             TextOut(hdc, 100 + cnt*50, 80, buf, 5);
           }
           TextOut(hdc, 30, 100, "MAXIMUM: ", 9);
           xres = maxreal(xarray, 9);
           gcvt(*xres, 5, buf);
           TextOut(hdc, 220, 100, (LPCTSTR)buf, 5);
           EndPaint(hWnd, &ps);
           break;
      case WM_DESTROY:
           PostQuitMessage(0);
           break;
      default:
           return DefWindowProc(hWnd, message, wParam, lParam);
  }

  return 0;
}


LRESULT CALLBACK About(HWND hDlg, UINT message, WPARAM wParam,
                       LPARAM lParam)
{
  switch (message)
  {
    case WM_INITDIALOG:
         return TRUE;
    case WM_COMMAND:
         if (LOWORD(wParam) == IDOK || LOWORD(wParam) == IDCANCEL)
         {
           EndDialog(hDlg, LOWORD(wParam));
           return TRUE;
         }
         break;
  }
  return FALSE;
}
```

The program outputs two lines to the application window work area. One of them contains all elements of the array, and the other shown below contains the maximum element. Displaying is done with the WM_PAINT handler using the TextOut function.

Declare the following variables in the WndProc callback function:

```
char buf[16];
float xarray[9] = {12.43, 93.54, -23.1, 23.59, 16.09,
                   10.67, -54.7, 11.49, 98.06};

float *xres;
int cnt;
```

The buf string is used to store the result of conversion of a floating-point number to text, and the xarray floating-point array contains nine elements. Also, xres is a pointer to a floating-point number, and cnt is a counter for displaying the nine elements of the array.

Displaying the lines is implemented with the following code in the WM_PAINT handler (Listing 6.14).

Listing 6.14. Displaying the lines

```
TextOut(hdc, 30, 80, "ARRAY: ", 7);
for (cnt = 0; cnt < 9; cnt++)
{
  gcvt(xarray[cnt], 6, buf);
  TextOut(hdc, 100 + cnt*50, 80, buf, 5);
}
TextOut(hdc, 30, 100, "MAXIMUM: ", 9);
xres = maxreal(xarray, 9);
gcvt(*xres, 5, buf);
TextOut(hdc, 220, 100, (LPCTSTR)buf, 5);
```

The first line of this code is a call to the TextOut function whose parameters are the device context (hdc), the horizontal and vertical coordinates in the client rectangle, the pointer to the text string, and the number of items to output.

To display numbers, you must convert the array to a sequence of strings. Conversion of a floating-point number to a string can be done with the gcvt function whose parameters are a floating-point number, a number of characters to output, and the pointer to a buffer for storing the result of conversion. The for statement is used to display all nine elements of the array.

Displaying the maximum element is done in a similar manner. However, you should first call the maxreal function:

```
xres = maxreal(xarray, 9);
```

Since `xres` is a pointer, the correct call to the `gcvt` function is the following:

```
gcvt(*xres, 5, buf);
```

After this statement is executed, the maximum element is put to the `buf` variable and displayed with the `TextOut` function.

Finally, be sure to add a declaration of the assembly function to the source code of your program:

```
extern "C" float* _stdcall maxreal(float *px, int sx);
```

The window of the application is shown in Fig. 6.6.

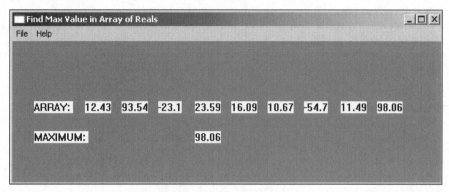

Fig. 6.6. Window of an application that looks for the maximum element
in a floating-point array

Structures and unions are very important data types in C++ .NET. Structures are arrays or vectors consisting of closely related elements, but, unlike arrays or vectors, they can contain elements of different types.

Unions are similar to structures. Using unions, it is possible to store elements of different types in a continuous fragment of the system memory. Structures and unions are used in most spreadsheet and database applications. Using assembly functions when working with such data types makes it possible to increase the speed of applications and to decrease the load on the operating system as a whole. The remainder of this chapter will demonstrate how to work with structures and unions by using functions from separately compiled assembly modules. We will begin with structures.

A structure is declared with the `struct` keyword. The next example uses the `intstr` structure that has three integer fields:

```
struct intstr {
        int i1;
        int i2;
        int i3;
    };
```

When declaring a structure, no variable is created; only the data types contained in this structure are defined. To declare a variable of the `intstr` type (we will call it `ist`), write the following line:

```
struct intstr ist
```

The `ist` variable is an example of the `intstr` structure. To manipulate with the elements of a structure, it is convenient to use a pointer to the structure. Consider an example, in which the `i2` element of the `intstr` structure will be inverted in an assembly procedure. The source code of the procedure is shown in Listing 6.15.

Listing 6.15. Inverting an integer in an assembly procedure

```
;----------------- negint.asm -----------

.686
.model flat
 public _negint@4
.code
  _negint@4 proc
   push    EBP
   mov     EBP, ESP
   mov     EAX, DWORD PTR [EBP+8]
   neg     EAX
   pop     EBP
   ret     4
  _negint@4 endp
end
```

The procedure takes one parameter, an integer, and returns its inverted value in the EAX register. The source text of a console application that uses this procedure is shown in Listing 6.16.

Listing 6.16. A console application that demonstrates processing the elements of a structure in an assembly procedure

```
// This is the main project file for VC++ application project
// generated by using an Application Wizard.

#include "stdafx.h"

#using <mscorlib.dll>
```

```
extern "C" int _stdcall negint(int i1);
using namespace System;

int _tmain()
{
    // TODO: Please replace the sample code below with your own.
    struct intstr {
                int i1;
                int i2;
                int i3;
                };

        struct intstr ist, *pist;
        pist = &ist;

        String *s;
        Console::Write("Enter i2: ");

        s = Console::ReadLine();
        pist->i2 = Convert::ToInt32(s);
        pist->i2 = negint(pist->i2);

        s = Convert::ToString(pist->i2);
        Console::WriteLine("New value of i2 = {0}", s);
        Console::WriteLine("Press any key to exit...");
        Console::ReadLine();
        return 0;
}
```

The `intstr` structure contains three integer elements: `i1`, `i2`, and `i3`. The lines

```
struct intstr ist, *pist;
pist = &ist;
```

declare the `ist` variable and the `pist` pointer to the structure. The `pist` pointer is assigned the address of the `ist` structure instance. To access a structure element, `i1`, for example, you can use one of the following expressions:

```
ist.i1
pist->i1
```

Inverting the `i2` element is done with the following statement:

```
pist->i2 = negint(pist->i2);
```

When using an external assembly module, you should declare the function it contains as external:

```
extern "C" int _stdcall negint(int i1);
```

The window of the application is shown in Fig. 6.7.

Fig. 6.7. Window of an application that demonstrates the work
with an element of a structure

Now, we will consider using assembly functions for manipulations with the elements of unions. I will use the union

```
union test_union {
        int i;
        char c;
        };
```

that consists of two elements. Declaring a union does not create any variables, so to create an instance of a union variable, use, for example, the following statement:

```
union test_union tu, *ptu;
```

The compiler allocates for a union as much memory as the largest element takes. In our case, four bytes are allocated. A union allows you to treat the same sequence of bits in various ways. Consider an example in which an assembly function first processes a character and then an integer. The source code of the function (named uex) is shown in Listing 6.17.

Listing 6.17. A function processing the elements of a union

```
;---------------- uex.asm------------

.686
.model flat
  public _uex@8
.code
```

```
_uex@8 proc
   push  EBP
   mov   EBP, ESP
   mov   EDX, DWORD PTR [EBP+12]    ; Load the indicator parameter to EDX.
   cmp   EDX, 0                     ; Is the 1st parameter integer?
   je    int_exec                   ; If yes, invert the number.
   cmp   EDX, 1                     ; Is the 1st parameter a character?
   je    char_exec                  ; If yes, convert it to the upper case.
   xor   EAX, EAX                   ; The 2nd parameter is out of range.
                                    ; Write 0 to EAX 0 and return.

   jmp   ex
int_exec:
   mov   EAX, DWORD PTR [EBP+8]     ; Put the first parameter to EAX
   neg   EAX                        ; as integer and invert it.
   jmp   ex
char_exec:
   xor   EAX, EAX                   ; Zeroing EAX
   mov   AL, BYTE PTR [EBP+8]       ; Put the character to AL
   cmp   AL, 97                     ; and analyze it.
   jb    ex
   cmp   AL, 122
   ja    ex
   sub   AL, 32                     ; If the character is alphabetic,
ex:                                 ; convert it to the upper
   pop   EBP                        ; case.
   ret   8
_uex@8 endp
end
```

The uex function takes two integers as parameters. The second parameter located at the [EBP+12] address can be either one or zero. It is an indicator for the type of the first parameter passed via [EBP+8]. If the second parameter is equal to one, the first parameter is an integer. If the second parameter is equal to zero, the first parameter is a character.

Thus, the first parameter is processed differently, depending on its type. If it is an integer, the function returns its inversion; if it is a character, the function converts it to the upper case.

Develop a C++ .NET dialog-based application. Put two edit controls, two static text labels, and one button on the main form. Bind the iEdit integer variable to one edit control and the cEdit character variable to the other. The on-button-clicked handler should output the values of the variables to the edit controls. The C++ source code of the handler with the uex external function declaration is shown in Listing 6.18.

Listing 6.18. The main fragments of a C++ program that uses the uex function

```
// Union_in_ASM_procDlg.cpp : implementation file

#include "stdafx.h"
#include "Union_in_ASM_proc.h"
#include "Union_in_ASM_procDlg.h"
#include ".\union_in_asm_procdlg.h"
extern "C" int _stdcall uex(int i1, int id);

   . . .

void CUnion_in_ASM_procDlg::OnBnClickedButton1()
{
        // TODO: Add your control notification handler code here.

        union test_union {
                int i;
                char c;
        };

        union test_union tu, *ptu;
        ptu = &tu;

        ptu->i = -56;
        iEdit = uex(ptu->i, 0);

        ptu->c = 'r';
        cEdit = (char)uex(ptu->c, 1);

        UpdateData(FALSE);
}
```

The main program uses the test_union union. After the initialization, the elements of the union are assigned the numeric value –56 and the character 'r', respectively. The uex function processes these elements according to their types. For the numeric value –56, the following statements are executed:

```
ptu->i = -56;
iEdit = uex(ptu->i, 0);
```

If the union element is the 'r' character, the following statements are executed:

```
ptu->c = 'r';
cEdit = (char)uex(ptu->c, 1);
```

The rest of the program's code is simple and does not need additional explanation. The window of the application is shown in Fig. 6.8.

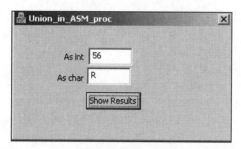

Fig. 6.8. Window of an application that demonstrates manipulations with the elements of a union

This completes the discussion of interfaces of separately compiled assembly modules and Visual C++ .NET programs. All examples in this chapter can be easily modified for use in your work.

Chapter 7: Linking Assembly Modules with C++ .NET Programs

This chapter looks at issues of building and running C++ .NET programs, including assembly modules. There are many ways to link C++ and assembly programs; here, I will try to emphasize the key aspects of this process.

A C++ application can include one or more assembly modules. Modules are either files with the OBJ extension or standard libraries (with the LIB extension). These modules can contain calls to functions in other modules. Moreover, assembly functions can in turn call C++ .NET library functions. In fact, programs normally use separately compiled object files or libraries, so building a finished application requires some effort from a developer. What are the advantages of using object files generated with separate compilers? Ready-made object files usually require a minimum of memory and other system resources, which is very useful when creating fast applications.

I will describe how to link assembly modules with a C++ .NET program, assuming the use of a stand-alone assembly compiler when creating such modules. Compilers you can use include either ML.EXE of the MASM 6.14 software package, or the ML compiler of the C++ .NET development environment, located in the \bin subdirectory of the C++ .NET working directory. Files with the ASM extension can be compiled either from a command line or at one of the stages of building an application's executable file. There are no significant differences between these compiling techniques, but you should set the assembly compiler to use the chosen technique in the development environment for the sake of debugging and tracing convenience. In either case, you'll obtain an object file that can be used.

First, a few words about the formats of the obtained object modules. The linker (LINK) operates with OBJ files of either COFF or OMF format. The Microsoft Visual C++ .NET compiler generates a COFF object file.

The linker converts OMF to COFF automatically. There are certain restrictions that sometimes hamper OMF-to-COFF conversion. More precisely, there are a few differences between the structures of files of these types. To avoid running into problems, you should set COFF-format object files as input files for the LINK linker. To obtain a COFF file, use the following command line:

```
ML /c /coff <an ASM file>
```

To use a file with useful functions in a C++ .NET application, use the following procedure:

1. Compile the source ASM file to obtain an object module in an OBJ file (the COFF format should be preferred).
2. Add the obtained OBJ files to the project and generate an application with the linker.

Step 2 can consist of several stages and can be implemented in various ways, because object files can be added to an application using various methods. Here are a few variants of integration:

❏ You can add object files to your project by specifying the appropriate functions in the declarations section.
❏ You can combine object files into static libraries of object modules. To do this, use the LIB.EXE utility of the Visual Studio C++ .NET package. The resulting LIB file can be added to your project.
❏ You can use dynamic link libraries (DLLs) that contain object files.

Of course, you can use a combination of these methods.

Now we will turn our attention to the ML.EXE compiler's options used for generating object files. For example, to obtain an object module from the myproc.asm file, execute the following command:

```
ML /c /coff myproc.asm
```

It is assumed that the source file is located in the same directory as ML.EXE.

The /c option tells the compiler to create only an object file. By default, if the compiler does not detect any errors, it will create the myproc.obj file in the COFF format. The obtained object module should be added to the C++ .NET main program and used for calling the functions it contains.

The object module file can contain several functions that can share data and call other functions of this module. With relatively small numbers of functions, variables, and their interconnections, the variant with one or more object modules is the most acceptable.

Frequently, the most convenient method of arranging and using functions of external modules involves creating a library (standard or import). In this case, the C++ .NET compiler offers many more options for application optimization. It is also very convenient to store the code of several object modules as one library. Library module files have the LIB extension. To create a library from an object file such as `myproc.obj`, use the LIB.EXE utility of the C++ .NET package:

```
LIB /OUT:myproc.lib myproc.obj
```

If there are no errors, the `myproc.lib` file will be created. You should add it to the application project.

The variant of using assembly functions from dynamic link libraries is very popular. This variant is very flexible, and it allows you to create multiple copies of a DLL easily and to use various methods of linking DLLs to your application.

We will discuss linking an application and assembly modules in more detail beginning with object modules. An assembly module is compiled with the MASM 6.14 macro assembler or the assembler of the Visual C++ .NET environment. Every assembly program in our examples begins with the following directives:

```
.686
.model flat, C
```

The `.686` directive allows the assembler to compile all commands of Pentium Pro or higher.

The `.model flat, C` directive defines the memory model used by the application, and the call convention (in this case, _cdecl).

For example, suppose you want to find the difference of two floating-point numbers and display the result. The difference will be computed with an assembly function (we will name it `subf2`). Put the source code of this function in the `sub2.asm` file.

Assume the `subf2` function is called using the _cdecl convention. The source code of the function is simple (Listing 7.1).

Listing 7.1. The source code of the sub2 function

```
;-------------- subf2.asm --------------

.686
.model flat, C
.code
```

```
subf2 proc
 push  EBP
 mov   EBP, ESP
 ;
 finit
 fld   DWORD PTR [EBP+8]  ; load f1 to ST(0)
 fsub  DWORD PTR [EBP+12] ; subtract f2 from f1
 fwait
 pop   EBP
 ret
 subf2 endp
end
```

Now, we will focus on the source code briefly. The first two directives are described earlier. The function prolog is implemented with the following assembly commands:

```
 push  EBP
 mov   EBP, ESP
```

They initialize the EBP register to the stack address to gain access to the variables. Computation is done with the mathematical coprocessor's commands, and the result is returned at the top of the coprocessor stack ST(0):

```
 fld   DWORD PTR [EBP+8]
 fsub  DWORD PTR [EBP+12]
```

The last two commands reset the stack and exit the function. Note that the ret command has no parameters according to the _cdecl convention.

Now you should obtain an object module of the main C++ .NET program and add it to the project. The object module can be generated with either of two methods: with the stand-alone compiler of the MASM 6.14 package or with the assembler of the Visual C++ .NET environment.

Here is a description of each of these two variants.

As noted earlier, when you use the MASM 6.14 stand-alone compiler, you can obtain an object module with the following command line:

```
 ML.EXE /c  /coff sub2.asm
```

Develop a C++ .NET console application that calls the subf2 function from the sub2.obj file. The source code of this application is shown in Listing 7.2.

Listing 7.2. A C++ application that uses a separate object module

```
// USING_STAND-ALONE_ASM_COMPILER.cpp : Defines the entry point for the
// console application

#include "stdafx.h"
extern "C" float subf2(float f1, float f2);
int _tmain(int argc, _TCHAR* argv[])
{
  float f1, f2;

  printf("CUSTOM BUILD WITH ASM-FILE IN PROJECT DEMO\n\n");
  printf("Enter float f1: ");
  scanf("%f", &f1);
  printf("Enter float f2: ");
  scanf("%f", &f2);

  float fsub = subf2(f1, f2);
  printf("f1 - f2 = %.2f\n", fsub);
  getchar();
  return 0;
}
```

Here is a brief analysis of the listing. Two floating-point numbers, f1 and f2, are entered in the window of the console application. Their difference is found with the subf2 function. The function is external for the executable module, so it is declared with the extern directive:

```
extern "C" float subf2(float f1, float f2)
```

By default, the _cdecl call convention is used. The subf2 function takes two floating-point variables f1 and f2 and returns their difference. The "C" specifier prohibits decorating the function name.

The statement

```
float fsub = subf2(f1, f2)
```

computes the difference between the variables f1 and f2 and writes it to the fsub variable.

The object file that contains the `subf2` function should be added to the project. To do this, select the **Add Existing Item...** option in the **Project** menu and then select the name of the module in the dialog box that will open (Fig. 7.1).

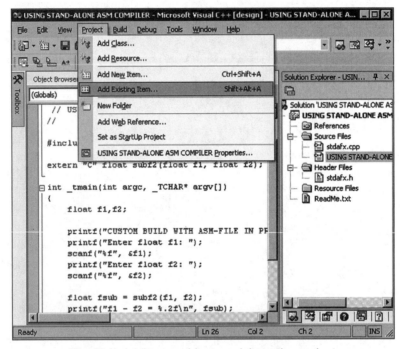

Fig. 7.1. Adding an object module to the project

After the object module is added to the project, the `sub2.obj` file name will appear in the file list in the **Solution Explorer**. Note that adding a separate module to a project does not necessarily mean that all functions of this module become visible to the application related to this project. It is important to specify the functions of the added modules with the `extern` directive.

As usual, adding a module to a project is done with the **Project** menu item. Select the **Add Existing Item...** option. In the dialog box that will open, select the object module file.

After the object module file is added to the project, the file name will appear in the project file list (Fig. 7.2).

Note that the `sub2.obj` object file is added to the project as a resource file.

Save the project and rebuild it with the **Rebuild** option of the **Build** menu item.

After you start the application and enter two floating-point numbers, the window of the program will look similar to that shown in Fig. 7.3.

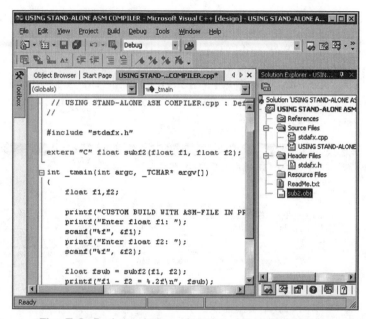

Fig. 7.2. Project window after the object file is added

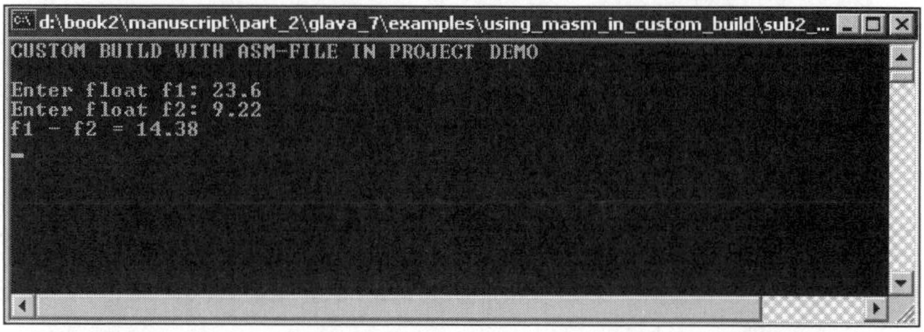

Fig. 7.3. Window of an application that computes the difference
between two numbers with a separately compiled object module

Linking an assembly function and a calling program can be done with the MASM compiler of the Visual C++ .NET development environment. Note that the C++ .NET macro assembler has features similar to those of the MASM 6.14 stand-alone compiler and supports the same directives and commands.

You will not need any other tools besides those available in C++ .NET 2003. One advantage of this method is that it is very easy to edit and debug an assembly module with the Visual C++ .NET 2003 environment interface.

At first, you might think the process is too complicated because the examples discussed here are non-trivial. Therefore, I will explain each step in detail.

As an example, we will develop a console application. Take the source code in Listing 7.2 as a sample for the source code of this application. Then add the file with the source code of the assembly function to your application. For this purpose, you must complete a few additional actions.

First, add a new text file to your project. This file will contain the source code of the assembly function. Create this file with the **Add New Item...** option of the **Project** menu item as shown in Fig. 7.4.

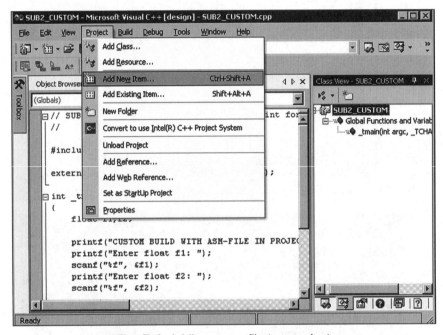

Fig. 7.4. Adding a new file to a project

Select the type of the file added to the project. There is no template for an ASM file in the Visual C++ .NET development environment. Therefore, use one of the text templates. This should be a text file. Of the available templates, select **Text File (.txt)** and specify the file name in the text box. Let it be sub2.asm.

Note that the text file does not have to have the ASM extension. Nothing prevents us from saving it as, say, sub2.txt. The C++ .NET inline assembler will process any text file you pass it.

Now we will go back to the sub2.asm file (Fig. 7.5).

Put the assembly code of the subf2 function into the empty file sub2.asm. Save the project. Next you should tell the compiler how it must process the ASM file. To do this, select the sub2.asm file in **Solution Explorer** and go to the **Properties** tab (Fig. 7.6).

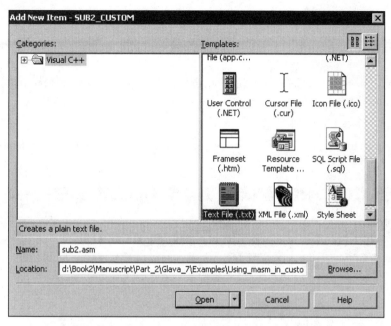

Fig. 7.5. Selecting the file type and extension

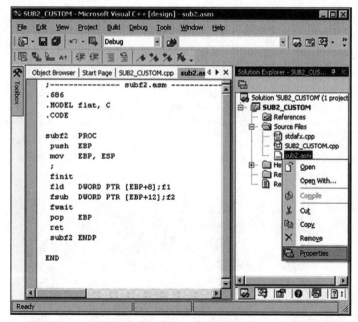

Fig. 7.6. Setting options for processing the `sub2.asm` file

In the **Property** page that will open, specify parameters for processing the sub2.asm file. The command line for the MASM inline compiler can be as follows:

```
ML /c /coff sub2.asm
```

If you saved the file as a TXT file, the only thing you should change in this command line is the file name:

```
ML /c /coff sub2.txt
```

Setting the MASM compiler options of the C++ .NET environment is shown in Fig. 7.7.

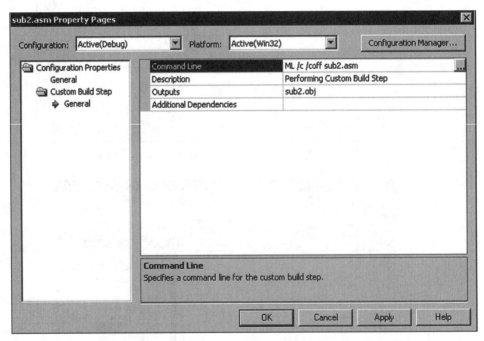

Fig. 7.7. Setting parameters for compiling the sub2.asm file

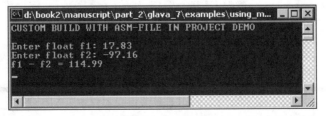

Fig. 7.8. Window of an application that demonstrates the use of an ASM file in the C++ .NET environment

The **Command Line** parameter should be the following:

```
ML.EXE /c /coff sub2.asm
```

The **Outputs** parameter should contain the object module name, `sub2.obj` in our case. Save the project again and compile it. After you start the application, its window will look like shown in Fig. 7.8.

We can draw a few conclusions concerning the use of object modules in a C++ .NET application. Although the examples above are quite simple, you can judge the advantages of a particular method of compiling and adding a module to a project from these examples.

Using the Visual C++ .NET 2003 environment for compiling ASM files and adding them to your project is very convenient. This is particularly true for the application debugging stage where you have to rebuild the application or recompile its individual modules repeatedly. Using the inline compiler saves you a lot of time in this case.

Note that object files generated with the macro assembler are external for the C++ .NET compiler regardless of the method of generating them. This means that all functions in these modules should be declared with the `extern` directive.

ASM files can contain several functions, and some of the object module's functions can be called by other functions of the same module and use their results. Change the source code of the assembly module by adding the code of a function that adds 100 to an integer parameter it takes (name the function `add100`). The modified source code is shown in Listing 7.3.

Listing 7.3. A modified version of the `subf2.asm` assembly file

```
;-------------- subf2.asm-----------
.686
.model flat, C
.code

subf2   proc ; cdecl
 push   EBP
 mov    EBP, ESP
;
 finit
 fld    DWORD PTR [EBP+8]  ; load f1 to ST(0)
 fsub   DWORD PTR [EBP+12] ; subtract f2 from f1
 fwait
 pop    EBP
 ret
```

```
subf2   endp

add100 proc
 push   EBP
  mov    EBP, ESP
  mov    EAX, DWORD PTR [EBP+8]
  add    EAX, 100
  pop    EBP
  ret
 add100 endp
end
```

Save the source code in the `subf2.asm` file. Develop a console application that uses the functions `subf2` and `add100` and add the `subf2.asm` file to your project. The source code of the console application is shown in Listing 7.4.

Listing 7.4. A console application that uses the functions `subf2` and `add100` from the added assembly module

```c
#include <stdio.h>

extern "C" float subf2(float f1, float f2);
extern "C" int add100(int i1);

void main(void)
{
 float f1, f2;

 printf("CUSTOM BUILD WITH ASM-FILE BUILT-IN\n\n");
 printf("Enter float f1: ");
 scanf("%f", &f1);
 printf("Enter float f2: ");
 scanf("%f", &f2);

 float fsub = subf2(f1, f2);
 printf("f1 - f2 = %.2f\n", fsub);
 printf("Rounded +100 = %d\n", add100((int)(fsub/10)));
 getchar();
}
```

The window of this application is shown in Fig. 7.9.

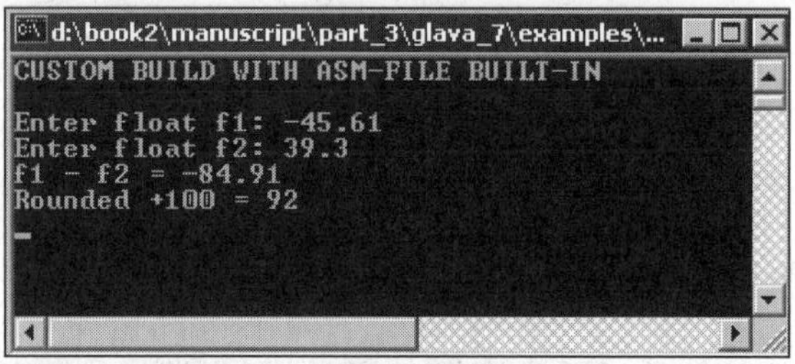

Fig. 7.9. Window of an application that demonstrates the use
of two functions from the added assembly module

So far, we assumed that the calls to the functions from the assembly module are done according to the _cdecl convention. To use another convention, such as _stdcall, you need to make some changes to the file with the source code of these functions. Suppose you want the add100 function to be called in accordance with the _stdcall convention. In this case, the source code of the subf2.asm assembly module should appear as shown in Listing 7.5 (the changes are in bold).

Listing 7.5. The source code of the functions subf2 and add100 with the conventions _cdecl and _stdcall

```
;-------------- subf2.asm (variant 3)------------

.686
.model flat
.code

_subf2  proc ; cdecl
 push   EBP
 mov    EBP, ESP
;
 finit
 fld    DWORD PTR [EBP+8]  ; Load f1 to ST(0)
 fsub   DWORD PTR [EBP+12] ; Subtract f2 from f1
 fwait
 pop    EBP
 ret
_subf2  endp
```

```
_add100@4 proc
  push   EBP
  mov    EBP, ESP
  mov    EAX, DWORD PTR [EBP+8]
  add    EAX, 100
  pop    EBP
  ret    4
_add100@4 endp
end
```

Note that if the default convention _cdecl is used for all functions of an assembly module, it will suffice to use the "C" qualifier in the model directive, and you will not need to use special notation for the function names with an underscore character at the beginning. If another convention for function calls or a mixed variant as in Listing 7.5 is used, this should be explicity specified with the function name notation.

The main program should contain the following lines corresponding to the subf2 and add100 functions:

```
extern "C" float subf2(float f1, float f2)
extern "C" int _stdcall add100(int i1)
```

The use of assembly modules is not confined to calls to functions in a C++ .NET main program. For data exchange, you can use common variables. This term is borrowed from earlier versions of Microsoft C++ compilers. It is not very precise, but it is appropriate for describing the essence of the method.

We will illustrate this with an example, taking the previous console application and the assembly module from Listing 7.5 as a model. Change the source code in the assembly file so that a common variable can be used for the result of computing. Remember that the difference of two floating-point numbers was returned by the subf2 function in the coprocessor's stack ST(0) and used in other pieces of the program code.

Now, the result of the function will be put into a double-word variable fres and then used in the main program. The modified source code of the assembly module is shown in Listing 7.6 (the changes are in bold).

Listing 7.6. The use of the fres common variable in an assembly module

```
;-------------- subf2std.asm ------------

.686
.model flat
```

```
    public _fres
.data
    _fres DD 0
.code
_subf2  proc ; cdecl
 push   EBP
 mov    EBP, ESP
;
 finit
 fld    DWORD PTR [EBP+8]   ; load f1 to ST(0)
 fsub   DWORD PTR [EBP+12] ; subtract f2 from f1
 lea    ESI, _fres
 fst    DWORD PTR [ESI]
 fwait
 pop    EBP
 ret
_subf2 endp
_add100@4 proc
 push   EBP
 mov    EBP, ESP
 mov    EAX, DWORD PTR [EBP+8]
 add    EAX, 100
 pop    EBP
 ret    4
_add100@4 endp
end
```

Now, we will explain this source code. A new section, .data, has appeared. It declares the fres variable as public. This means that the variable is accessible from other modules. Since there is no explicit call convention, you can assume the fres variable is processed in accordance with the _cdecl convention. This is why the name of the variable begins with an underscore character.

The commands

```
 lea    ESI, _fres
 fst    DWORD PTR [ESI]
```

write the result stored in the coprocessor's stack to the fres variable. Remember that the assembly module is compiled with the Visual C++ .NET macro assembler as a part of the project.

The source code of the C++ console application is shown in Listing 7.7.

Listing 7.7. The use of a common variable in a C++ .NET application

---

```
#include <stdio.h>

extern "C" void subf2(float f1, float f2);
extern "C" int _stdcall add100(int i1);
extern "C" float fres;

void main(void)
{
   float f1, f2;
   printf("CUSTOM BUILD WITH COMMON VAR IN ASM MODULE\n\n");
   printf("Enter float f1: ");
   scanf("%f", &f1);
   printf("Enter float f2: ");
   scanf("%f", &f2);
   subf2(f1, f2);
   printf("f1 - f2 = %.2f\n", fres);
   printf("Rounded +100 = %d\n", add100((int)(fres/10)));
   getchar();
}
```

Here, the subf2 function is declared as void. When subf2 terminates, the difference between f1 and f2 is written to the fres common variable. In the console application, it is necessary to declare the fres variable as extern and prohibit decorating its name: extern "C" float fres.

The Visual C++ .NET development environment allows you to use external compilers to generate object modules when developing an application. For example, to obtain an object module file from an ASM file, you can use an external assembly compiler. Note that nothing prevents you from using the macro assembler of the development environment. You can edit and compile the source assembly module in the C++ .NET development environment and add the object module to the project manually. We will illustrate this method with an example.

We will develop a console application that calls an assembly function from an object module for processing a character string. Processing the string involves the substitution of spaces with '+' characters. The original and processed strings are displayed in the application window. Name the assembly function conv and save its source code in the `convstr.asm` file on, say, disk D. The file location is chosen at will to keep the discussion general.

The source code of the `conv` function is shown in Listing 7.8.

Listing 7.8. The `conv` assembly function that processes a character string

---

```
;------------ convstr.asm -------------

.686
.model flat, C
.code
conv proc
  push  EBP
  mov   EBP, ESP
  mov   ESI, DWORD PTR [EBP+8]   ;pointer to string
  mov   ECX, DWORD PTR [EBP+12] ;length of string
  mov   AL,  ' '
next:
  cmp   AL, BYTE PTR [ESI]
  jne   next_addr
  mov   BYTE PTR [ESI], '+'
next_addr:
  inc   ESI
  dec   ECX
  jnz   next
  pop   EBP
  ret
conv   endp
end
```

The `conv` function takes the string address as the first (from left) argument and the string length as the second argument. When the function is called, both parameters are extracted with the following commands:

```
mov    ESI, DWORD PTR [EBP+8]
mov    ECX, DWORD PTR [EBP+12]
```

Here, the string address is at the address [EBP+8], and the string length is at [EBP+12]. Searching for and replacing the spaces are done in the following piece of code:

```
    . . .
next:
    cmp   AL, BYTE PTR [ESI]
```

```
    jne    next_addr
    mov    BYTE PTR [ESI], '+'
  next_addr:

      . . .
```

Passing the parameters and resetting the stack are done in accordance with the _cdecl convention, so the ret command has no parameters.

The C++ .NET console application has the following source code (Listing 7.9).

Listing 7.9. A program that uses the conv function

```
// VIRTUAL_ALLOC_AS_SHARE_MEM.cpp : Defines the entry point for the
// console application

#include "stdafx.h"
#include <windows.h>

extern "C" void conv(char* p1, int cnt);
int _tmain(int argc, _TCHAR* argv[])
{
 char* p1 = NULL;
 char* p2 = "This is a test string!!! ";
 printf("   USING EXTERNAL ASM TOOL IN C++ PROJECT\n\n");
 p1 = (char*)VirtualAlloc(NULL, 256, MEM_COMMIT, PAGE_READWRITE);
 strcpy(p1, p2);
 printf("Before conversion: %s\n\n", p1);
 conv(p1, strlen(p1));
 printf("After conversion: %s\n", p1);
 VirtualFree(p1, 0, MEM_RELEASE);
 getchar();
 return 0;
}
```

The strcpy function puts a copy of the string being processed to the memory area that is allocated with the VirtualAlloc WIN API function and addressed with the p1 pointer. After the conv(p1,strlen(p1)) statement is executed, all the found spaces are substituted with '+' characters.

Set the development environment so that the MASM compiler can be used in the project window to obtain an object module. As a compiler, you can select either a stand-alone tool such as ML.EXE of the MASM 6.14 package or the tool built into the development environment.

First, select the **External Tools...** option in the **Tools** menu item (Fig. 7.10).

Second, make settings in the **External Tools** window as shown in Fig. 7.11.

Type the compiler name in the **Title** text box. This is not important, so you can choose the name at will.

In the **Command** text box, type (or select) the name of the executable file, including the full path. In the **Arguments** text box, enter the compiler options (in this case, `/c /coff`) and the full path to the target file `$(ItemPath)`. Finally, in the **Initial directory** text box, specify that the target file (an object module) should be put to the `$(SolutionDir)` project directory.

After you set the MASM compiler as an external tool, you can open the assembly file in the project window. To compile it, it is necessary that the ASM file editing window is active.

Start the compiler with the newly-created MASM option of the **Tools** menu (Fig. 7.12).

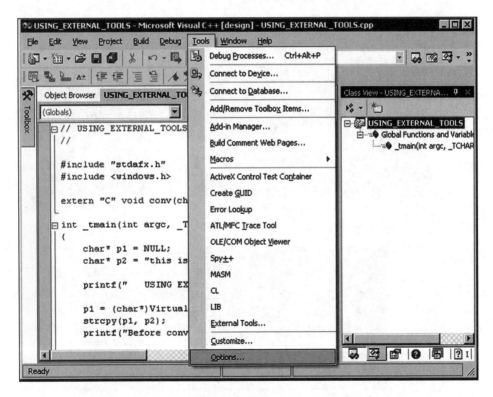

Fig. 7.10. Step 1: Selecting an external tool

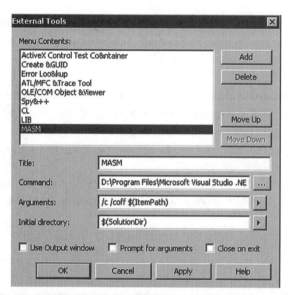

Fig. 7.11. Step 2: Selecting and setting parameters of external tools

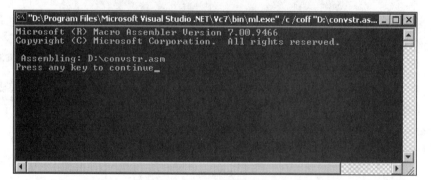

Fig. 7.12. Starting the assembly compiler from the command line

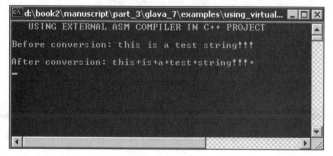

Fig. 7.13. The window of an application that demonstrates string conversion

If compiling is successful, a new OBJ file will appear in the project directory. Add it to your project with the **Add Existing Item...** option of the **Project** menu. Save the project and compile it.

After you run the application, its window will appear as shown in Fig. 7.13.

Selecting and setting an external compiler as a development tool with the **External Tools** option allows you to use unified compilation parameters for all assembly modules being components of various applications. In this case, you do not have to set compiler options individually for each assembly module.

However, this method has one disadvantage. It is pointless to add an assembly file to a project; it should be first compiled to an object module and only then added to the project.

If a C++ .NET project contains several object files, which contain several assembly functions, debugging the application becomes much more complicated. In addition, in most cases you might want to use the same modules in other applications. It would be convenient if you could combine such object modules in a library file and use it in your applications. For this purpose, use the LIB.EXE utility of the Visual C++ .NET package. In general, its syntax is

```
LIB.EXE [options] file1 file2 …
```

where `file1`, `file2`, etc. are object files.

With the LIB.EXE utility, you can fulfil the following tasks:

❑ Add object files to a library. In this case you should specify the name of an existing library and the names of the modules being added.
❑ Replace an object file in a library.
❑ Delete an object file from a library.

The LIB.EXE utility creates a library module file with the LIB extension. A LIB file can be added to any project. We will illustrate the use of the LIB.EXE utility with an example. Modify the previous project so that all lowercase letters `'t'` are substituted with uppercase letters `'T'` with the `convt` function, and all lowercase letters `'s'` are substituted with uppercase letters `'S'` with the `convs` function. Both functions are written in the assembler, and saved in the files `convt.asm` and `convs.asm`.

The source code of the `convs.asm` function is shown in Listing 7.10.

Listing 7.10. The source code of the `convs.asm` function

```
;------------- convs.asm -------------

.686
.model flat, C
```

```
.code
convs proc
  push  EBP
  mov   EBP, ESP
  mov   ESI, DWORD PTR [EBP+8]   ; pointer to string
  mov   ECX, DWORD PTR [EBP+12]  ; length of string
  mov   AL,  's'
next:
  cmp   AL, BYTE PTR [ESI]
  jne   next_addr
  mov   BYTE PTR [ESI], 'S'
next_addr:
  inc   ESI
  dec   ECX
  jnz   next
  pop   EBP
  ret
convs endp
end
```

The convt function is almost identical to the convs function except the characters being substituted. Modify the C++ console application for these functions as shown in Listing 7.11.

Listing 7.11. A console application that uses the functions convs and convt

```cpp
// VIRTUAL_ALLOC_AS_SHARE_MEM.cpp : Defines the entry point for the
// console application

#include "stdafx.h"
#include <windows.h>

extern "C" void convs(char* p1, int cnt);
extern "C" void convt(char* p1, int cnt);

int _tmain(int argc, _TCHAR* argv[])
{
 char* p1 = NULL;
 char* p2 = "This is a test string!!! ";
```

```
printf("    USING ASM LIB IN C++ PROJECT\n\n");

p1 = (char*)VirtualAlloc(NULL, 256, MEM_COMMIT, PAGE_READWRITE);
strcpy(p1, p2);
printf("Before conversion: %s\n\n", p1);

convt(p1, strlen(p1));
printf("After conversion t->T: %s\n", p1);
convs(p1, strlen(p1));
printf("After conversion s->S: %s\n", p1);

VirtualFree(p1, 0, MEM_RELEASE);
getchar();

return 0;
}
```

When finally building the application, one library file, conv.lib, will be used rather than module files convs.obj and convt.obj. To generate conv.lib, adhere to the following procedure:

1. Obtain object module files with the ML compiler of the MASM 6.14 macro assembler. For this purpose, execute the following commands from the command line:

```
ML /c /coff  convs.asm
ML /c /coff  convt.asm
```

2. Combine the obtained object files into one library file conv.lib with the LIB.EXE utility:

```
LIB /OUT:conv.lib convs.obj convt.obj
```

3. Add the library file to the project, compile the project, and run it.

The window of the application is shown in Fig. 7.14.

The main advantage of library modules is that they can contain object modules compiled both from ASM and CPP files. This allows you to create very powerful libraries. The next example demonstrates how two arithmetic functions can be combined in one library module and used in an application.

The first function, add2, is written in C++. It adds two integers, and its source code is saved in the add2.cpp file. The other (we will name it sub2) is written in the assembler. It subtracts an integer from another, and its source code is saved in the sub2.asm file. Both functions return the results in integer variables.

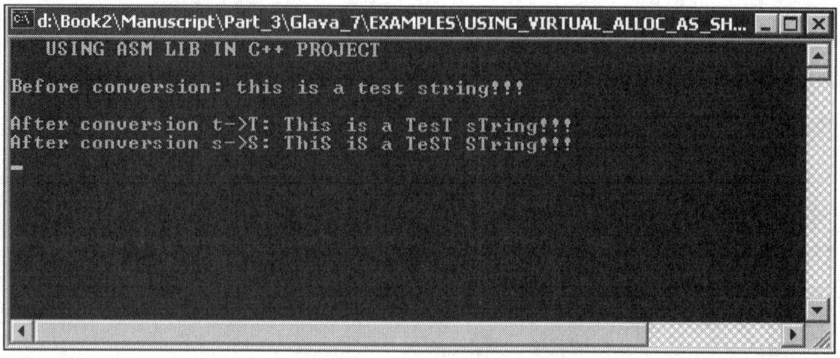

Fig. 7.14. Window of an application that demonstrates the use of a library module

The source code of the add2 function is shown in Listing 7.12.

Listing 7.12. The add2.cpp function

```
extern "C" int add2(int i1, int i2)
{
   return (i1+i2);
}
```

Note the declaration of the add2 function. In order for other modules to be able to access it, the extern directive must be used.

The source code of the sub2 function is shown in Listing 7.13.

Listing 7.13. The sub2.asm function

```
;------------ sub2.asm --------------

.686
.model flat, C
.code
  sub2     proc
    push   EBP
    mov    EBP, ESP
    mov    EAX, DWORD PTR [EBP+8]   ; i1
    sub    EAX, DWORD PTR [EBP+12]  ; i1-i2
    pop    EBP
    ret
  sub2     endp
end
```

To create a library file, it is necessary to obtain object modules from the files add2.cpp and sub2.asm first. To compile the assembly file, use the ML compiler of the MASM macro assembler from the C++ .NET 2003 environment:

```
ML /c /coff sub2.asm
```

If the compilation completes without errors, you will obtain the sub2.obj file. To compile the add2.cpp file, use the standard C++ .NET compiler:

```
CL /c add2.cpp
```

Both object modules, add2.obj and sub2.obj, can be combined in one static library file addsub.lib with the following command:

```
LIB /OUT:addsub.lib add2.obj sub2.obj
```

You can use the obtained library in a console application whose source code is shown in Listing 7.14.

Listing 7.14. An application that uses a library

```cpp
// C_n_ASM_LIB.cpp : Defines the entry point for the console application

#include "stdafx.h"

extern "C" int add2(int i1, int i2);
extern "C" int sub2(int i1, int i2);

int _tmain(int argc, _TCHAR* argv[])
{
 int i1, i2;
 printf("     USING ASM & C OBJ MODULES IN LIB-FILE\n\n");

 printf("Enter integer i1: ");
 scanf("%d", &i1);
 printf("Enter integer i2: ");
 scanf("%d", &i2);

 printf("\nResult of ADD2 call: %d\n", add2(i1, i2));
 printf("\nResult of SUB2 call: %d\n", sub2(i1, i2));
 getchar();
 return 0;
}
```

Since the functions `add2` and `sub2` are in a separate module, they must be declared as external:

```
extern "C" int add2(int i1, int i2);
extern "C" int sub2(int i1, int i2);
```

The window of the application is shown in Fig. 7.15.

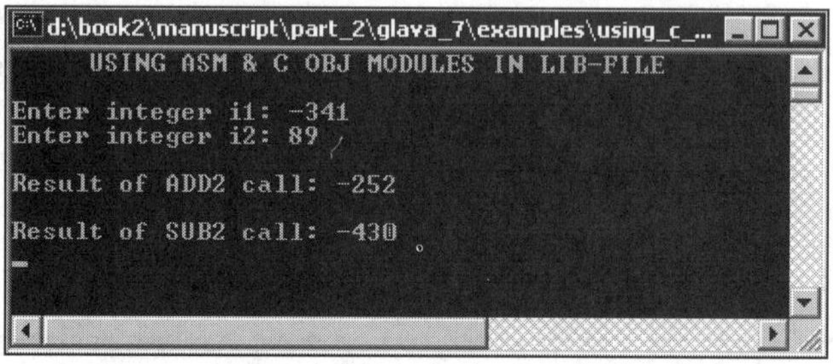

Fig. 7.15. Window of an application that demonstrates
the work of the library functions `add2` and `sub2`

It is possible to use several standard libraries in your application. The next example is a C++ .NET console application with two added libraries, `lib1asm.lib` and `lib2asm.lib`. The `lib1asm` library contains two interrelated functions `signmul` and `sub20`, and the `lib2asm` library contains the `signdiv` function.

The source code of the functions in the `lib1asm` library is shown in Listing 7.15.

Listing 7.15. The assembly functions of the `lib1asm` module

```
.686
.model flat, C
.code
  signmul proc
  push  EBP
  mov   EBP, ESP
  mov   EAX, DWORD PTR [EBP+8]
  mov   ECX, DWORD PTR [EBP+12]

  imul  ECX
  call  sub20
  pop   EBP
  ret
signmul  endp
```

```
sub20    proc
  sub    EAX, 20
  ret
sub20    endp
end
```

The `signmul` function multiplies two signed integers. The result is decreased by 20 with the `sub20` function. A distinct feature of this library is that an auxiliary function `sub20` need not be declared in the main application.

The `lib2asm.lib` library contains one function `signdiv` that returns the address of the quotient of two signed integers. The source code of the `signdiv` assembly function is shown in Listing 7.16.

Listing 7.16. The assembly function of the `lib2asm` module

```
.686
.model flat, C
.data
  fres   DD 0
.code
  signdiv proc
   push    EBP
   mov     EBP, ESP
   finit

   fild    DWORD PTR [EBP+8]
   fidiv   DWORD PTR [EBP+12]
   fistp   DWORD PTR fres
   fwait
   mov     EAX, offset fres
   pop     EBP
   ret
  signdiv  endp
end
```

For the division operation, mathematical coprocessor commands are used. The result of division is stored in the `fres` variable with the command:

```
fistp   DWORD PTR fres
```

The address of the variable is returned to the main command in the EAX register with the command:

```
mov  EAX, offset fres
```

The source code of the functions is saved in the lib1asm.asm and lib2asm.asm files. The object modules lib1asm.obj and lib2asm.obj are generated with the following commands:

```
ML /c /coff lib1asm.asm
ML /c /coff lib2asm.asm
```

The static library files can be obtained easily with the LIB.EXE utility:

```
LIB /OUT:lib1asm.lib lib1asm.obj
LIB /OUT:lib2asm.lib lib2asm.obj
```

Develop an application that uses these library files. The source code of such an application is shown in Listing 7.17.

Listing 7.17. A console application that uses the lib1asm.lib and lib2asm.lib library files

---

```cpp
// LIB1_PLUS_LIB2.cpp : Defines the entry point for the console
// application

#include "stdafx.h"

extern "C" int signmul(int i1, int i2);
extern "C" int* signdiv(int i1, int i2);

int _tmain(int argc, _TCHAR* argv[])
{
  int i1, i2;
  printf("USING SOME STANDARD LIBRARIES EXAMPLE\n\n");
  printf("Enter integer i1:");
  scanf("%d", &i1);

  printf("Enter integer i2:");
  scanf("%d", &i2);
  printf("MUL(i1, i2)-20 = %d\n", signmul(i1,i2));
  printf("DIV(i1, i2)= %d\n", *signdiv(i1,i2));

  getchar();
  return 0;
}
```

Add both files to this application's project, save, and recompile the project. The window of the application is shown in Fig. 7.16.

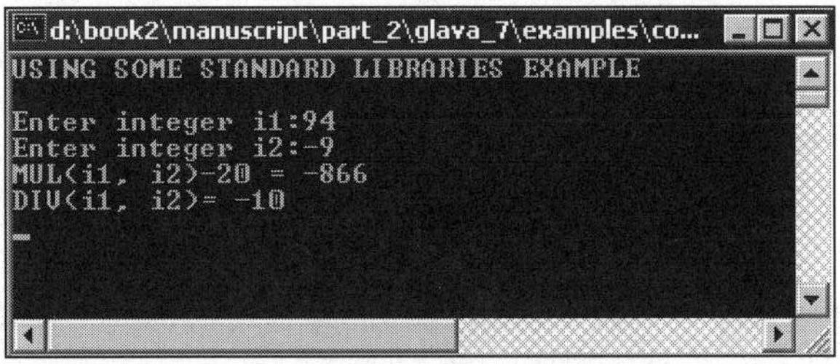

Fig. 7.16. Window of an application that uses two library files

Now, we will focus on the use of assembly functions in the dynamic link libraries (DLLs). Since theoretical issues of building DLLs are described in special literature, we will not concentrate on them here. Using assembly functions in these libraries makes it possible to improve the quality of the code, but linking an assembly module and a DLL needs a detailed explanation. We will illustrate the main points of this process with a practical example.

Suppose a console application uses the same functions as in the previous example: sub2 and add2. In addition, both functions are called from a dynamic link library (named DLL_n_ASM.dll). Develop a variant of a solution consisting of two projects. One of the projects should be a DLL, and the other should be a console application that uses functions of this library.

Develop the DLL with the C++ .NET Application Wizard. Choose a Windows console application as a template and select **DLL** in the **Application Settings** properties. Modify the source code of the CPP library file as shown in Listing 7.18 (the changes are in bold).

Listing 7.18. A modified variant of the CPP DLL file

```
// DLL_n_ASM.cpp : Defines the entry point for the DLL application

#include "stdafx.h"

extern "C" int sub2(int i1, int i2);
BOOL APIENTRY DllMain( HANDLE hModule,
                       DWORD  ul_reason_for_call,
                       LPVOID lpReserved
                     )
{
```

```
  return TRUE;
}


extern "C" __declspec(dllexport) int add2(int i1, int i2)
{
  return (i1+i2);
}


extern "C" __declspec(dllexport) int subdll2(int i1, int i2)
{
   return (sub2(i1, i2));
}
```

This DLL contains two functions. One of them, subdll2, uses the sub2 assembly function as auxiliary. The source code of the sub2 function is shown in Listing 7.19.

Listing 7.19. The sub2 function

```
;--------------- sub2.asm --------------

.686
.model flat, C
  public sub2
.code
 sub2 proc

  push EBP
  mov  EBP, ESP
  mov  EAX, DWORD PTR [EBP+8]  ; i1
  sub  EAX, DWORD PTR [EBP+12] ; i2
  pop  EBP
  ret


sub2 endp
end
```

Add the sub2.asm assembly file with the sub2 function to the DLL project and set the compiler options for this file with the **Properties** option. Save the project and compile it. If no errors are detected, you will obtain the DLL_n_ASM.dll dynamic link library with two export functions `add2` and `subdll2` and the `DLL_n_ASM.lib` import library.

To demonstrate the use of the DLL, develop a console application project related to this library. The source code of this application is shown in Listing 7.20.

Listing 7.20. A console application that uses a dynamic link library

---

```
// USE_DLL.cpp : Defines the entry point for the console application

#include "stdafx.h"

extern "C" __declspec(dllimport) int add2(int i1, int i2);
extern "C" __declspec(dllimport) int subdll2(int i1, int i2);

int _tmain(int argc, _TCHAR* argv[])
{
        int i1, i2;

        printf("USING ASM FUNC IN DLL \n\n");
        printf("Enter i1:");
        scanf("%d", &i1);
        printf("Enter i2:");

        scanf("%d", &i2);
        printf("\nResult of ADD2 call: %d\n", add2(i1, i2));
        printf("\nResult of ASM func SUB2 call: %d\n", subdll2(i1, i2));
        getchar();
        return 0;
}
```

Use static linking of the DLL to the main application. For this purpose, add the `DLL_n_ASM.lib` import library to the console application project and copy the `DLL_n_ASM.dll` file to the Windows system directory.

The window with both projects will appear as shown in Fig. 7.17.

One more note: Functions called from a DLL should be declared as imported:

```
extern "C" __declspec(dllimport) int add2(int i1, int i2)
extern "C" __declspec(dllimport) int subdll2(int i1, int i2)
```

You can compile the projects USE_DLL and DLL_n_ASM either individually or together if you select the **Rebuild Solution** option in the **Build** menu item. The window of the application is shown in Fig. 7.18.

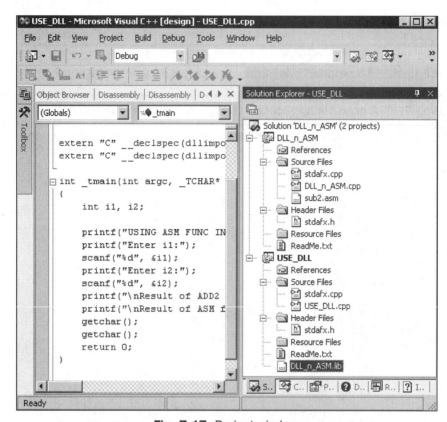

Fig. 7.17. Project window

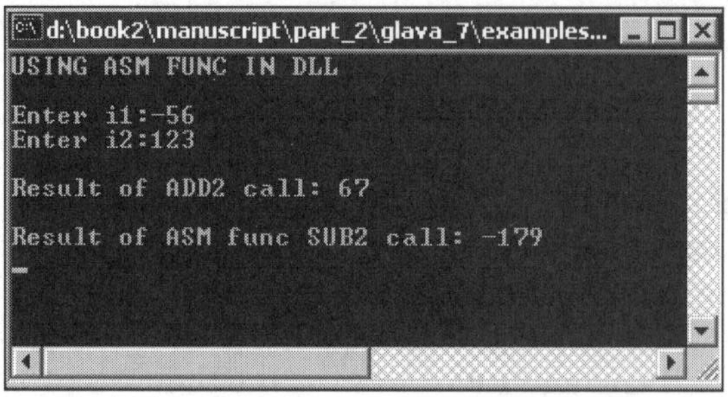

Fig. 7.18. Window of an application that demonstrates
a call to an assembly function

Using assembly functions in dynamic link libraries will be more convenient if the object modules are combined in a standard library file. Suppose you want to find the maximum of two floating-point numbers with the max function and the minimum of them with the min function. The source code of these functions is in the minmax.asm file, and it is shown in Listing 7.21.

Listing 7.21. The max and min assembly functions

```
.686
.model flat, C
.code
 fmax proc
  push  EBP
  mov   EBP, ESP
  finit
  fld   DWORD PTR [EBP+8]
  fcomp DWORD PTR [EBP+12]
  fstsw AX
  sahf
  jb    set_op
  fld   DWORD PTR [EBP+8]
  jmp   com
set_op:
  fld   DWORD PTR [EBP+12]
com:
  fwait
  pop   EBP
  ret
 fmax endp

 fmin proc
  push  EBP
  mov   EBP, ESP
  finit
  fld   DWORD PTR [EBP+8]
  fcomp DWORD PTR [EBP+12]
  fstsw AX
  sahf
  jb    set_op
  fld   DWORD PTR [EBP+12]
  jmp   com
set_op:
  fld   DWORD PTR [EBP+8]
```

```
com:
  fwait
  pop    EBP
  ret
 fmin endp
end
```

We will not dissect the source code of these functions because you encountered similar examples earlier. Put the object code of these functions to the `minimax.lib` library. To do this, execute the following commands:

```
ML /c /coff minimax.asm
LIB /OUT:minimax.lib minimax.obj
```

Create a solution consisting of two projects. The first project should be a dynamic link library (name it `USING_IMPDLL_STANDARD.dll`). Modify the source code of the library template generated by the Application Wizard as shown in Listing 7.22.

Listing 7.22. The `USING_IMPDLL_STANDARD` dynamic link library

```
// USING_IMPDLL_STANDARD.cpp : Defines the entry point for the DLL
// application

#include "stdafx.h"
extern "C" float fmax(float f1, float f2);
extern "C" float fmin(float f1, float f2);


BOOL APIENTRY DllMain( HANDLE hModule,
                       DWORD  ul_reason_for_call,
                       LPVOID lpReserved
                                     )
{
    return TRUE;
}


extern "C" float __declspec(dllexport) sub2f(float f1, float f2)
{
 return(fmax(f1,f2) - min(f1,f2));
}
```

For everything to work well, the `minimax.lib` standard library should be among the project files. The references to this library's functions are defined as follows:

```
extern "C" float fmax(float f1, float f2)
extern "C" float fmin(float f1, float f2)
```

In addition, the `sub2f` function should be declared as external with the `dllexport` attribute. After you compile the project, you will obtain a DLL and an import library. Link the DLL project to another project that will demonstrate the use of the `minimax.lib` standard library and the DLL. The source code of this application is shown in Listing 7.23.

Listing 7.23. The source code of an application that uses assembly functions of a standard library and DLL

```cpp
// USE_MINIMAX_LIB_IN_DLL.cpp : Defines the entry point for the console
// application

#include "stdafx.h"
extern "C" __declspec(dllimport) float sub2f(float f1, float f2);
extern "C" float fmax(float f1, float f2);
extern "C" float fmin(float f1, float f2);

int _tmain(int argc, _TCHAR* argv[])
{
 float f1, f2;

printf("   USING DLL WITH STANDARD LIB DEMO\n\n");
printf("Enter float f1:");
scanf("%f", &f1);
printf("Enter float f2:");
scanf("%f", &f2);
printf("\nMAX = %.2f\n", fmax(f1, f2));
printf("\nMIN - %.2f\n", fmin(f1, f2));
printf("\nMAX-MIN= %.2f\n", sub2f(f1, f2));
getchar();
return 0;
}
```

Since this application uses the `fmin` and `fmax` functions defined in another module, you should add the `minimax.lib` library to the application.

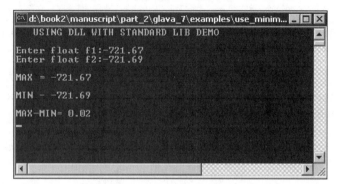

Fig. 7.19. Window of an application that demonstrates
the use of a standard library and DLL

The window of the application is shown in Fig. 7.19.

Now, we will consider another example, in which a separately compiled assembly module is used as a component of a DLL. Suppose a DLL (named COMMON_DLL.dll) contains the absfdll function that computes the absolute value of a floating-point number. In turn, absfdll uses the absf assembly function.

The computed absolute value is displayed with a C++ console application. To call the absf function from the DLL, the main application uses dynamic loading and a call to the LoadLibrary and GetProcAddress WIN API functions.

Now, we will examine the example more closely, beginning with the COMMON_DLL.dll dynamic link library. Its source code is shown in Listing 7.24.

Listing 7.24. The source code of the COMMON_DLL dynamic link library that uses the absf assembly function

---

```cpp
// COMMON_DLL.cpp : Defines the entry point for the DLL application

#include "stdafx.h"


extern "C" float absf(float f1);


BOOL APIENTRY DllMain( HANDLE hModule,
                       DWORD  ul_reason_for_call,
                       LPVOID lpReserved
                     )
{
    return TRUE;
```

```
}

extern "C" __declspec(dllexport) float absfdll(float f1)
{
        return (absf(f1));
}
```

Since the absf assembly function is located in another module, it should be declared with the extern directive. The absfdll function exported from the DLL uses absf in the return statement. Note that such a variant of calling an assembly function (with the return statement) allows you to use the assembler for work with C++ .NET manageable code, which generally is very difficult to do.

The source code of the absf assembly function is simple. It is shown in Listing 7.25.

Listing 7.25. The absf assembly function

```
;--------------absf.asm------------

.686
.model flat, C
.code

 absf proc
  push  EBP
  mov   EBP, ESP
  finit
  fld   DWORD PTR [EBP+8]
  fabs
  fwait
  pop   EBP
  ret

 absf endp
 end
```

As mentioned earlier, the main application uses dynamic loading to load the absf function from the library, and it does not require declaration of the imported DLL functions with the extern directive. Also, unlike the previous example, you do not have to add the import library file to the main application project. The source code of the C++ .NET console application is shown in Listing 7.26.

Listing 7.26. A main program that uses the DLL containing the `absfdll` function

```
// This is the main project file for VC++ application project
// generated using an Application Wizard.

#include "stdafx.h"
#include <windows.h>

int _tmain()
{

// TODO: Please replace the sample code below with your own.

typedef FLOAT (*myfunc) (FLOAT);
myfunc absfdll;

printf("   USE EXTERNAL OBJ IN DLL (DYNAMIC LOADING)\n\n");

HINSTANCE hLib = LoadLibrary("COMMON_DLL");
if (hLib == NULL)
 {
   printf("Unable to load library\n");
   getchar();
   exit (1);
 }

absfdll = (myfunc)GetProcAddress(hLib, "absfdll");
if (!absfdll)

   {
   printf("Unable to load functions!\n");
   FreeLibrary(hLib);
   getchar();
   exit (1);
 }

float f1 = -731.19;

printf("ABS of float f1 (%.3f) = %.3f", f1, absfdll(f1));
FreeLibrary(hLib);
getchar();
return 0;
}
```

The first thing you should do is to define a pointer to the function and to create an instance of this pointer to the function you are using:

```
typedef FLOAT (*myfunc) (FLOAT);
myfunc absfdll;
```

The `absfdll` function takes a `FLOAT` value as a parameter and returns also a `FLOAT` value, which is reflected in the definition of the pointer to the `myfunc` function.

If the `LoadLibrary` function completes successfully, the obtained descriptor of the loaded library module is used to get the address of the `absfdll` function:

```
absfdll = (myfunc)GetProcAddress(hLib, "absfdll")
```

After you finish the work with the DLL, you should tell the Windows operating system that the application does not need the DLL any longer. In this case, Windows will decrement the value of the DLL use counter.

The window of the application is shown in Fig. 7.20.

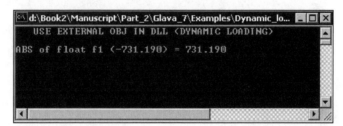

Fig. 7.20. Window of an application that demonstrates
the use of an assembly function when dynamically loading a library

Now, we will summarize the use of separately compiled assembly modules in C++ .NET 2003 applications. They can be compiled with either the stand-alone MASM compiler or the macro assembler built in the Visual C++ .NET development environment. During compilation, a standard object module file with the COFF or OMF format is generated. Further linking the application and object modules is defined by the developer and the features of the application.

Here, we described the MASM macro assembler and its features. However, any other compiler that generates an object file with the COFF format can be used for generating object files. Hopefully, the material and examples in this chapter will be helpful when implementing your tasks.

Chapter 8: Dynamic Link Libraries and Their Development in Assembly Language

Dynamic Link Libraries (DLL) are the essential and, perhaps, the most important part of Windows operating systems. They serve as a depository of procedures, including WIN API functions, and provide powerful tools for writing effective applications. We will not dwell on the principles of DLL building and functioning, because there are many publications devoted to this topic. It is much more interesting to learn how to create DLL on your own. Dynamic link libraries, regardless of the way they are created, can be used with any compiler or application.

The use of DLL provides a programmer with considerable advantages in development and replication of a program code:

❏ The size of an executable code can be reduced, because different applications can use the same library functions.

❏ Program code contained in DLL is less labor-intensive than similar functions used in several applications.

❏ Large projects can be better structured and become more manageable.

❏ The implementation of new functions to be added to the applications becomes easier: it is enough to release a new version of DLL.

Dynamic link libraries are usually written in HLL (C, Pascal, etc.), although it is possible to develop them in assembler. We will consider the key issues of development and use of DLLs in following order:

1. Initialization of DLL.
2. Export of functions and data from DLL.
3. Calling DLL with load-time dynamic linking.
4. Calling DLL with run-time dynamic linking.

Each DLL must have an entry point. In Visual C++ .NET 2003, such an entry point is the DllMain function. DLL, written in assembler MASM, has an entry point called LibMain. The operation system calls these functions in the following cases:

- ❐ When an application calls DLL for the first time
- ❐ When the process linked to this library creates a new stream
- ❐ When the process linked to this library deletes a stream
- ❐ When DLL is removed from memory

Functions and data can be exported from DLL in any of the following ways:

- ❐ Creating a DEF file whose EXPORT section contains the names of exported elements
- ❐ Creating references to exported elements defined with the keyword __declspec (dllexport)

The method using a DEF file is now considered obsolete, though it is still utilized. The handling and configuring of a DEF file can turn out to be a difficult task, especially when different compilers are used for DLL and application developments.

The __declspec method is preferable for work with 32-bit applications and can be applied in most cases. The 32-bit versions of compilers (not only C++ .NET) can export data, functions, classes, and functions — members of classes from DLL by using the __declspec(dllexport) keyword. This keyword inserts instruction to export the project to the object file, which allows manipulating it without the DEF file.

Dynamic link library can be loaded simultaneously with the application (load-time dynamic linking) or during the application executing (run-time dynamic linking).

Load-time dynamic linking requires the user to specify whether the application is DLL-dependent. For this purpose, the program project must include the import library (LIB file). Compiler C++ .NET will create the import library automatically during the DLL generation. The LIB file is not an ordinary static library. It does not contain a program code — only references to all functions exported from the DLL file, in which the code resides. Import libraries are usually smaller than DLL files.

When launching an application, Windows finds necessary DLLs and calculates addresses of each reference to the library. Searching for the library is implemented in the application working directory first, and then in the Windows system directory.

To illustrate the method of load-time dynamic linking, we will develop two programs — a dynamic link library (named impdll) and the application test_impdll, which uses the impdll. DLL includes the sub2dll function that returns the difference of two integers used as parameters. We will generate our application as a Win32 Project using the Application Wizard of C++ .NET 2003. Define the type of the application as DLL and create the project files. The DLL source code is very simple and includes only the DllMain entry point. To make the DLL workable, we have to include the sub2dll function's source code in the project. The final version of the code is shown in Listing 8.1, where the sub2dll function is in bold.

Listing 8.1. Source code for imdll.dll

```
// impdll.cpp : Defines the entry point for the DLL application.

#include "stdafx.h"
BOOL APIENTRY DllMain( HANDLE hModule,
                       DWORD  ul_reason_for_call,
                       LPVOID lpReserved
                      )
{
    return TRUE;
}


int __declspec(dllexport) sub2dll(int i1, int i2)
{
 return (i1-i2);
}
```

Function sub2dll must be accessible from other modules, so it is to be declared with a keyword __declspec(dllexport) (note that *two* underscore characters precede the declaration).

We will develop an application calling the sub2dll function from impdll.dll. As a template, we will take the Win32 Project and compile it as a console application (named as test_impdll). The source code of the application is shown in Listing 8.2.

Listing 8.2. Using `impdll` in the application `test_impdll`

```cpp
// test_impdll.cpp : Defines the entry point for the console application.

#include "stdafx.h"
int __declspec(dllimport) sub2dll(int i1, int i2);

int _tmain(int argc, _TCHAR* argv[])
{
 int isub;
 int i1 = 56;
 int i2 = -34;
 printf("i1 = %d, ", i1);
 printf("i2 = %d\n", i2);
 printf("i1 - i2 = %d", sub2dll(i1, i2));
 getchar();
 return 0;
}
```

The `sub2dll` function is to be imported from another module (in Listing 8.2, it is in bold face type). An application project also has to include the `impdll.lib` import library. Also, the `impdll.dll` file must be saved in the application-working directory or in the system directory.

A window of the running application is shown in Fig. 8.1.

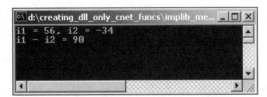

Fig. 8.1. Application window that demonstrates how to use the `impdll.dll` import library

You can create a DLL using MASM. Assembly code is very efficient for writing DLLs: this considerably improves performance and reduces the size of a code. We will develop an assembly version of `impdll.dll` in MASM. The source code of the DLL template (named as `templdll.asm`) is simple and is shown in Listing 8.3.

Listing 8.3. Template of DLL developed in MASM

```
;----------------------templdll.asm----------------

.686
.model flat, C
option casemap:none
.code
LibMain proc hInstDLL:DWORD, reason:DWORD, unused:DWORD
 mov EAX, 1
 ret
LibMain Endp
End LibMain
```

The template includes only the `LibMain` function, which is an entry point of the DLL. Listing 8.3 shows the simplest implementation of a dynamic link library.

Compilation and linking of DLL should be done by the following commands:

```
ml/c/coff templdll.asm
link/SUBSYSTEM:WINDOWS/DLL templdll.obj
```

Our `templdll.dll` library created with MASM is just a stub that cannot do anything useful. Therefore, we will change the DLL source code. Include in DLL the source code of function calculating the difference of two integers (name it `sub2`). The content of the file modified (named `assub2.asm`) is shown in Listing 8.4.

Listing 8.4. The modified variant of DLL's assembly version

```
;-----------------------sub2.asm----------------
.686
.model flat, C
option casemap:none
.code

LibMain proc hInstDLL:DWORD, reason:DWORD, unused:DWORD
 mov EAX, 1
 ret
LibMain endp

sub2 proc
 push EBP
```

```
mov  EBP, ESP
mov  EAX, [EBP+8]   ; i1
sub  EAX, [EBP+12]  ; -i2
pop  EBP
ret
sub2 endp
end LibMain
```

To use DLL with C++ .NET application, we have to specify the programming language in the `model` directive:

```
.model flat, C
```

This means that the calling convention `_cdecl` is used, which is why the last command `ret` of the `sub2` function goes without parameters and the stack is cleared by the main program in C++. The source code of the `sub2` function is simple and no additional explanation is required.

To create the import library, we need a file with a description of exported functions. Such files have a DEF extension. We will create it and name it `sub2.def`. The file should include the following lines:

```
LIBRARY sub2
EXPORTS
      sub2
```

The DEF file is needed only for creation of the import library and will not be used anymore. The following commands implement the assembly of DLL:

```
ml/c/coff sub2.asm
link/SUBSYSTEM:WINDOWS/DLL/DEF:sub2.def sub2.obj
```

If the compilation is successfully completed, we will have the files:

```
sub2.obj
sub2.lib
sub2.dll
sub2.exp
```

Now, we will test the DLL, using the method of load-time dynamic linking. To do this, we will need the `sub2.dll` and `sub2.lib` files. Develop a console application in C++ .NET using Application Wizard. It is necessary to include the `sub2.lib` file into the project and copy `sub2.dll` in an application-working directory. The source code is shown in Listing 8.5.

Listing 8.5. Calling of a function from DLL using the load-time dynamic linking

```
// test_asmdll.cpp: Defines the entry point for the console application.

#include "stdafx.h"
extern "C" int sub2 (int i1, int i2);

int _tmain (int argc, _TCHAR* argv [])
{
int i1 = -23;
int i2 = -19;
printf (" i1 = %d, ", i1);
printf (" i2 = %d\n ", i2);
printf (" i1 - i2 = %d ", sub2 (i1, i2));
getchar ();
return 0;
}
```

Pay attention to the following line:

```
extern "C" int sub2 (int i1, int i2);
```

The keyword `__declspec (dllimport)` is not necessary to use for libraries generated with the assembler: It is enough to declare function as external and forbid the name declaration. The application window is shown in Fig. 8.2.

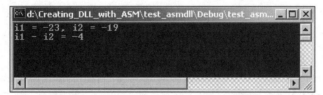

Fig. 8.2. Demonstration of using the load-time dynamic linking of DLL

You can include in DLL the functions written in assembler and stored in a separate object module. The most common way is to generate a DLL template in C++ .NET and include in it the functions written in assembler. (Macro assembler saves these as OBJ files). Such combining allows you to vary the size of a source code and operating-system resources and performance simultaneously with modest development time.

Consider an example, in which the main program in C++ calls three functions from DLL. The first function (named `add2`) returns the sum of two integers. The second function (named as sub2) returns the difference between two integers. Suppose that function sub2 is written in assembler and compiled as a separate OBJ file. The third function (named submul5) uses the result returned by sub2 for multiplying it by 5. We will use the Application Wizard of Visual C++ .NET again and develop the DLL that contains functions described above. The template of DLL created by Wizard is shown as a file addsub.cpp in Listing 8.6.

Listing 8.6. DLL template

```
// addsub.cpp: Defines the entry point for the DLL application.

#include "stdafx.h"
BOOL APIENTRY DllMain (HANDLE hModule,
                       DWORD ul_reason_for_call,
                       LPVOID lpReserved)
{
  return TRUE;
}
```

Now insert the code for calling functions into the DLL source code shown in Listing 8.6. The add2 function is defined as follows:

```
extern "C" __declspec(dllexport) int add2 (int i1, int i2)
{
 return (i1+i2);
};
```

The sub2 function is placed in a separate assembly module and declared as

```
extern "C" int sub2 (int i1, int i2);
```

The source code of the sub2 function is shown in Listing 8.7.

Listing 8.7. Function sub2

```
;------------------sub2.asm-----------
.686
.model flat, C
  public sub2
.code
sub2 proc
    push EBP
    mov  EBP, ESP
```

```
    mov   EAX, DWORD PTR [EBP+8]
    sub   EAX, DWORD PTR [EBP+12]
    pop   EBP
    ret
 sub2 endp
end
```

We will save the source code of the sub2 function in the sub2.asm file and compile it using MASM. Then we will include the OBJ module obtained in our DLL project.

The function, as mentioned above, implements the subtraction of two integers and returns their difference. This result is used by the exported function submul5:

```
    extern "C" __declspec (dllexport) int submul5 (int i1, int i2)
    {
      return (sub2 (i1, i2) *5);
    };
```

The source code of DLL with all changes is presented in Listing 8.8.

Listing 8.8. Using the object modules in DLL

```
// addsub.cpp: Defines the entry point for the DLL application.

#include "stdafx.h"
BOOL APIENTRY DllMain (HANDLE hModule,
                       DWORD ul_reason_for_call,
                       LPVOID lpReserved
)
{
    return TRUE;
}


extern "C" __declspec (dllexport) int add2 (int i1, int i2)
{
 return (i1+i2);
};


extern "C" int sub2 (int i1, int i2);


extern "C" __declspec (dllexport) int submul5 (int i1, int i2)
{
 return (sub2 (i1, i2) *5);
};
```

After compilation of the DLL project, we will get the `addsub.dll` and the `addsub.lib` import library.

Now, we will develop a test application using functions from the `addsub.dll` library. The dialog-based application will include four `Edit Control` elements, four `Static Text` controls and a `Button`. Link the `Edit Control` controls to integer variables `i1`, `i2`, `add2Edit`, and `submul5Edit`. In the editable fields that correspond to variables `i1` and `i2`, we will enter integer values, and in the editable fields boxes corresponding to output values, we will see the results of calling functions `add2` and `submul5`. All of these manipulations are implemented by the button handler — `OnBnClickedButton1`. This is a key issue; the full source code of the program is shown in Listing 8.9.

Listing 8.9. More complicated example where load-time dynamic linking is used

```cpp
// testdllDlg.cpp: implementation file
#include "stdafx.h"
#include "testdll.h"
#include "testdllDlg.h"
#include ".\testdlldlg.h"

int __declspec(dllimport) add2 (int i1, int i2);
int __declspec(dllimport) submul5 (int i1, int i2);

#ifdef _DEBUG
#define new DEBUG_NEW
#endif
// CAboutDlg dialog used for App About

class CAboutDlg: public CDialog
{
public:
      CAboutDlg ();

// Dialog Data
      enum {IDD = IDD_ABOUTBOX};
      protected:
      virtual void DoDataExchange (CDataExchange* pDX); // DDX/DDV support

// Implementation
protected:
      DECLARE_MESSAGE_MAP ()
};
```

```
CAboutDlg:: CAboutDlg (): CDialog (CAboutDlg:: IDD)
{
}

void CAboutDlg:: DoDataExchange (CDataExchange* pDX)
{
       CDialog:: DoDataExchange (pDX);
}

BEGIN_MESSAGE_MAP (CAboutDlg, CDialog)
END_MESSAGE_MAP ()

// CtestdllDlg dialog
CtestdllDlg:: CtestdllDlg (CWnd* pParent / * = NULL*/)
     : CDialog (CtestdllDlg:: IDD, pParent)
     , i1 (0)
     , i2 (0)
     , add2Edit (0)
     , submul5Edit (0)
{
       m_hIcon = AfxGetApp ()-> LoadIcon (IDR_MAINFRAME);
}

void CtestdllDlg:: DoDataExchange (CDataExchange* pDX)
{
       CDialog:: DoDataExchange (pDX);
       DDX_Text (pDX, IDC_EDIT1, i1);
       DDX_Text (pDX, IDC_EDIT2, i2);
       DDX_Text (pDX, IDC_EDIT3, add2Edit);
       DDX_Text (pDX, IDC_EDIT4, submul5Edit);
}

BEGIN_MESSAGE_MAP (CtestdllDlg, CDialog)
       ON_WM_SYSCOMMAND ()
       ON_WM_PAINT ()
       ON_WM_QUERYDRAGICON ()
       //}} AFX_MSG_MAP
       ON_BN_CLICKED (IDC_BUTTON1, OnBnClickedButton1)
END_MESSAGE_MAP ()
// CtestdllDlg message handlers
BOOL CtestdllDlg:: OnInitDialog ()
{
```

```
        CDialog:: OnInitDialog ();
        // Add " About... " menu item to the system menu.
        // IDM_ABOUTBOX must be in the system command range.
        ASSERT ((IDM_ABOUTBOX and 0xFFF0) == IDM_ABOUTBOX);
        ASSERT (IDM_ABOUTBOX <0xF000);

        CMenu* pSysMenu = GetSystemMenu (FALSE);
        if (pSysMenu! = NULL)
        {
                CString strAboutMenu;
                strAboutMenu. LoadString (IDS_ABOUTBOX);
                if (! strAboutMenu. IsEmpty ())
                {
                        pSysMenu-> AppendMenu (MF_SEPARATOR);
                        pSysMenu-> AppendMenu (MF_STRING, IDM_ABOUTBOX,
strAboutMenu);
}
}

// Set the icon for this dialog. The framework does this automatically
// when the main application window is not a dialog.
        SetIcon (m_hIcon, TRUE); // Set big icon
        SetIcon (m_hIcon, FALSE); // Set small icon
// TODO: Add extra initialization here.
        return TRUE; // Return TRUE unless you set the focus on a control.
}

void CtestdllDlg:: OnSysCommand (UINT nID, LPARAM lParam)
{
 if ((nID and 0xFFF0) == IDM_ABOUTBOX)
 {
  CAboutDlg dlgAbout;
  dlgAbout. DoModal ();
}
else
 {
CDialog:: OnSysCommand (nID, lParam);
}
}

void CtestdllDlg:: OnPaint ()
{
 if (IsIconic ())
```

```
  {
    CPaintDC dc (this); // Device context for painting
SendMessage (WM_ICONERASEBKGND, reinterpret_cast <WPARAM> (dc. GetSafeHdc ()), 0);
    // Center icon in the client rectangle
    int cxIcon = GetSystemMetrics (SM_CXICON);
    int cyIcon = GetSystemMetrics (SM_CYICON);
    CRect rect;
    GetClientRect (*rect);
    int x = (rect.Width () - cxIcon + 1) / 2;
    int y = (rect.Height () - cyIcon + 1) / 2;
    // Draw the icon
    dc. DrawIcon (x, y, m_hIcon);
  }
    else
    {
      CDialog:: OnPaint ();
  }
  }
// The system calls this function to obtain the cursor to display
// while the user drags the minimized window.
HCURSOR CtestdllDlg:: OnQueryDragIcon ()
{
 return static_cast <HCURSOR> (m_hIcon);
}

void CtestdllDlg:: OnBnClickedButton1 ()
{
 // TODO: Add your control notification handler code here.
 UpdateData (TRUE);
 add2Edit = add2 (i1, i2);
 submul5Edit = submul5 (i1, i2);
 UpdateData (FALSE);
}
```

Functions imported from DLL must be declared, which is shown on the following lines of the source code:

```
    int __declspec(dllimport) add2 (int i1, int i2);
    int __declspec(dllimport) submul5 (int i1, int i2);
```

We need to include the import library addsub.lib in the project and copy addsub.dll into the working directory.

The application window is shown in Fig. 8.3.

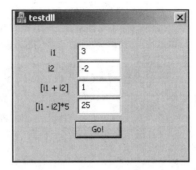

Fig. 8.3. Application window that demonstrates the use of the `addsub.dll` library

Until now, we considered load-time dynamic linking of DLL by means of import library. Another frequently used method is run-time dynamic linking of library while application runs. In this case, there is no need to link the application with an import library. For run-time dynamic linking of DLL, the `LoadLibrary` function is used. The function returns a descriptor of an instance, which refers to DLL. If an error occurs, `NULL` is returned. To use any function exported from DLL, it is necessary to call the `GetProcAddress` function with a library instance descriptor and the name of a function. The `GetProcAddress` function returns the pointer to the called function, or `NULL` if an error occurred.

After work with library is completed, remove it from memory by using the `FreeLibrary` function call.

To demonstrate the method of run-time dynamic linking, I will use the `addsub.dll` library developed before. The only thing you need is to develop the application in C++ .NET. The source code of the application is shown in Listing 8.10.

Listing 8.10. Demonstration of run-time linking of DLL

```
// testsub2.cpp: Defines the entry point for the console application.

#include "stdafx.h"
#include <windows.h>

int _tmain (int argc, _TCHAR* argv [])
{
        typedef UINT (*LPFNDLLFUNC) (UINT, UINT);
        LPFNDLLFUNC add2, submul5;
        HINSTANCE hDll = LoadLibrary ("addsub");
        if (! hDll)
        {
         printf (" Unable to load library\n ");
```

```
    getchar ();
    exit (1);
}
    add2 = (LPFNDLLFUNC) GetProcAddress (hDll, "add2");
    submul5 = (LPFNDLLFUNC) GetProcAddress (hDll, "submul5");
    if ((add2 == NULL) || (submul5 == NULL))
        {
            printf (" Unable to load functions! \n ");
            FreeLibrary (hDll);
            getchar ();
            exit (1);
}
    int i1 =  5;
    int i2 = -3;

    int ires = add2 (i1, i2);
    printf (" add2 (%d, %d) \t = %d\n ", i1, i2, ires);

    ires = submul5 (i1, i2);
    printf (" submul5 (%d, %d) = %d\n ", i1, i2, ires);
    FreeLibrary (hDll);
    getchar ();
    return 0;
}
```

Now we will analyze the source code. First of all, define the pointer to a function that takes two integer parameters, and then declare add2 and submul5 as such pointers. The declaration looks like this:

```
typedef UINT (*LPFNDLLFUNC) (UINT, UINT);
LPFNDLLFUNC add2, submul5;
```

The LoadLibrary function loads DLL into the memory, and after successful completion, returns a descriptor of the loaded module; otherwise, the result is set to 0 and the application terminates:

```
HINSTANCE hDll = LoadLibrary ("addsub");
if (! hDll)
{
  printf (" Unable to load library\n ");
  getchar ();
  exit (1);
}
```

After the library is loaded, the pointers on memory locations where the functions reside are to be stored:

```
add2 = (LPFNDLLFUNC) GetProcAddress (hDll, "add2");
submul5 = (LPFNDLLFUNC) GetProcAddress (hDll, "submul5");
if ((add2 == NULL) || (submul5 == NULL))
  {
  printf (" Unable to load functions! \n ");
  FreeLibrary (hDll);
  getchar ();
  exit (1);
}
```

In the case of successful execution of this chunk of code, variables add2 and submul5 contain the start addresses of executive images. Operators

```
int ires = add2 (i1, i2);
ires = submul5 (i1, i2);
```

call the add2 and submul5 functions. After completing the execution, the current instance of DLL must be released through the call of a WIN API function — FreeLibrary.

The working application window is shown in Fig. 8.4.

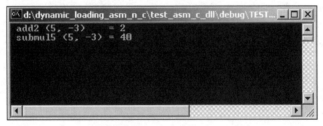

Fig. 8.4. Application window that shows dynamic loading of add2 and submul5 functions

We have considered an example of run-time dynamic linking of DLL, when the library was created using Application Wizard C++ .NET, and a separate object module with assembly functions included. However, DLLs written in MASM could be dynamically loaded at the application's run time. We'll develop in assembler a DLL that includes the add2 and sub2 functions, implementing addition and subtraction of two integers, respectively. The source code of assembly module is shown in Listing 8.11.

Listing 8.11. Source code of addsub2.dll

```
;----------------------addsub2.asm----------------
```

.686

```
.model flat, C
option casemap:none
.code

LibMain proc hInstDLL:DWORD, reason:DWORD, unused:DWORD
   mov EAX, 1
   ret
LibMain endp

add2 proc
  push EBP
  mov  EBP, ESP
  mov  EAX, [EBP+8]  ; i1
  add  EAX, [EBP+12] ; +i2
  pop  EBP
  ret
add2 endp

sub2 proc
  push EBP
  mov  EBP, ESP
  mov  EAX, [EBP+8]  ;  i1
  sub  EAX, [EBP+12] ; -i2
  pop  EBP
  ret
sub2 endp
end LibMain
```

The DEF file of exported functions (named as `addsub2.def`) contains the following lines:

```
LIBRARY addsub2
EXPORTS
  add2
  sub2
```

The library `addsub2.dll` can be created while the sequence of commands will execute:

```
@echo off
if exist addsub2.obj del addsub2.obj
if exist addsub2.dll del addsub2.dll
ml/c/coff addsub2.asm
Link/SUBSYSTEM:WINDOWS/DLL/DEF:addsub2.def addsub2.obj
dir addsub2.*
pause
```

The source code of the console application (named as `test_asmdyn`), which uses the functions from `addsub2.dll`, is shown in Listing 8.12.

Listing 8.12. The source code of application using `addsub2.dll`

```cpp
// TEST_ASMDYN.cpp: Defines the entry point for the console application.

#include "stdafx.h"
#include <windows.h>

int _tmain (int argc, _TCHAR* argv [])
{
        typedef UINT (*LPFNDLLFUNC) (UINT, UINT);
        LPFNDLLFUNC add2, sub2;
        HINSTANCE hDll = LoadLibrary ("addsub2");
        if (! hDll)
        {
          printf (" Unable to load library\n ");
          getchar ();
          exit (1);
        }
        add2 = (LPFNDLLFUNC) GetProcAddress (hDll, "add2");
        sub2 = (LPFNDLLFUNC) GetProcAddress (hDll, "sub2");
        if ((add2 == NULL) || (sub2 == NULL))
        {
         printf (" Unable to load functions! \n ");
         FreeLibrary (hDll);
         getchar ();
         exit (1);
        }
        int i1 = -5;
        int i2 = -13;

        int ires = add2 (i1, i2);
        printf (" add2 (%d, %d) \t = %d\n ", i1, i2, ires);

        ires = sub2 (i1, i2);
        printf (" sub2 (%d, %d) = %d\n ", i1, i2, ires);
        FreeLibrary (hDll);
        getchar ();
        return 0;
}
```

The last two listings illustrate the fact that run-time dynamic linking of DLL is very convenient and has two major advantages. First, when the required DLL is not available, an application using load-time dynamic linking simply terminates, while the run-time dynamic linking is able to respond to the error. Second, if the DLL code changes, an application that uses load-time dynamic linking may also terminate, while an application linked at run-time is only affected if the desired functions are absent in the DLL.

The window of the running application is shown in Fig. 8.5.

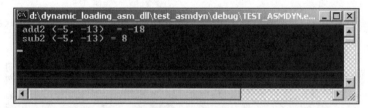

Fig. 8.5. Window of the appendix showing dynamic loading of functions from library, developed in assembly language

NOTE

Using DLL written in the assembler
(but it concerns any library written in C++)

By default, C++ .NET compiler uses the calling convention _cdecl. Keep this in mind while creating the DLL in the assembler and compile the modules with appropriate setting.

For example, if you specify the parameters of a command `ret` in the assembly module (bold font in Listing 8.13), the result can be rather unsuccessful.

Listing 8.13. Incorrect use of calling convention

```
;------------------------addsub2.asm----------------

.686
.model flat, C
option casemap:none
.code

LibMain proc hInstDLL:DWORD, reason:DWORD, unused:DWORD
    mov EAX, 1
    ret
LibMain endp

add2 proc
```

```
push EBP
mov  EBP, ESP
mov  EAX, [EBP+8]  ; i1
add  EAX, [EBP+12] ; +i2
pop  EBP
ret  8
add2 endp
```

MASM created the object module without errors, but making the call of function from the main program will lead the application to crash (Fig. 8.6).

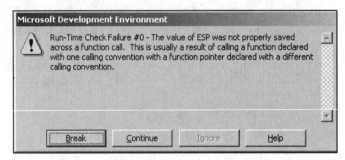

Fig. 8.6. Abnormal termination of the program
at non-observance of the calling convention

Of course, you can set the options of the C++ .NET compiler so that the use of calling conventions different from _cdecl will be possible. Keep in mind that it can make the debugging of an application more complicated. Therefore, if there are no special needs, it is easier to write a DLL code with default settings, accepted in C++ .NET.

Our overview of the use of the assembler in development of DLL is now complete. This analysis could of course be more in-depth, and some questions may inevitably arise. However, our intention is that the material in this chapter will help the reader to resolve difficult problems of development and optimization of DLL with assembler.

Chapter 9: Basic Structures of Visual C ++ .NET 2003 Inline Assembler

This chapter will focus on how to use the C ++ .NET 2003 inline assembler for optimizing applications. The inline assembler is a very effective tool for improving program performance. Microsoft has included it in the developer's environment. A review of the inline assembler concerns only Intel Pentium processors; however, the technique of using an inline assembler can be successfully applied to other types of processors as well.

In the early stages of software and hardware development, the low-level language availability in C allowed users to control a personal computer with high efficiency. The MS-DOS operating system permitted user applications to completely control a personal computer. The combination of an assembly language and C gave developers new possibilities in the writing of high-efficiency programs.

The situation has changed in the course of developments in the Windows operating system. The program still could use an assembler for controlling hardware directly, but only in Windows 95/98/Me. Advanced operating systems, such as Windows NT/2000/XP, have essentially limited user possibilities in controlling work on both an operating system and PC hardware.

The inline assembler for High-Level Languages (HLL) developed in the mid-90s was perceived more as a tribute to the past, than as a serious tool in software development. However, HLLs, despite powerful libraries, did not generate as effective a code as necessary.

A new generation of processors required new approaches to optimization. Since Windows NT/2000/XP appeared, the problem of real-time applications increased. This created a demand for leading software vendors, such as Microsoft, Borland, IBM, and Intel, to improve an inline assembler of HLLs.

An inline assembler is also a very effective tool for loop optimization, data processing, and the implementation of high-efficiency mathematical calculations. Algorithms and stand-alone functions written in an assembly language are widely used while developing Windows device drivers and system services. Note that modern compilers of HLLs (not only C ++ .NET) do not use 100 % of the latest processors capabilities. A comprehensive implementation of a processor's capabilities could be accomplished only with an assembly language.

Discussions regarding whether an assembler is useful or not for developers who write their applications in HLL have ceased. It became clear that an assembler is an integral part of all programs and one of the basic tools for improving HLL applications performance.

A comparison between an inline assembler and a separate compiler, such as MASM or IA-32, does not address the question as to which is more effective. The advantage of a separate assembler is in minimizing the use of computer resources (memory and processor time). Separately compiled modules (object files) are very useful while implementing the same algorithms for other programs.

The C ++ .NET inline assembler does not allow the user to create separate modules to be used in other applications, though a user can do this by writing dynamic link libraries (DLL) with the inline assembly functions included. The inline assembler is closely integrated with the development environment, which provides many advantages.

The inline assembler doesn't require separate assembly and link steps. This is more convenient than working with a separate assembler. An inline assembly code can use any C++ variable or function name that allows easy integration with a C++ code. Also, an assembly code can be mixed with C++ statements, which allows the user to perform tasks that otherwise could not be executed.

The main disadvantage of this tool is the strong link with the C++ .NET compiler that complicates the application debugging in achieving optimal performance.

The Visual C++ .NET development environment includes the most powerful tools for supporting assembly programming. Any assembler code included in a C++ program must begin with the _asm keyword and be enclosed in braces. The following code is a simple _asm block:

```
_asm {
        mov     EAX, val1
        sub     EAX, EBX
    }
```

You can also write _asm at the beginning of each assembly instruction:

```
_asm mov      EAX, val1
_asm sub      EAX, EBX
```

If the _asm keyword is a statement separator, you can write assembly instructions on the same line:

```
_asm mov      EAX, val1 _asm sub EAX, EBX
```

Examples above generate the same code, but the first style with the _asm block enclosed in braces has certain advantages. First, the assembly code is separated from a C++ code by braces and it avoids repetition of the _asm keyword. Braces prevent from ambiguities. Second, when you want to put a C++ statement on the same line as the _asm block, you must enclose the block in braces. Finally, because the text in braces has the same format as MASM text, it is easy to cut text from existing MASM source files and paste it into a C++ source module.

The C++ .NET development environment offers a very convenient way to use an inline assembly code with macros. You can insert macros into a program by following these steps:

1. Close the _asm block with braces.
2. Write the _asm keyword at the beginning of each assembly instruction.
3. Use the old style for comments (/* *the comment* */) instead of the assembler style (;) or the one-line variant (// *the comment*).

The following code fragment illustrates how to create a macro to output a data byte to the printer's parallel port:

```
#define PORTIO378 _ _asm
/* Port output */
{
    _ _asm mov AL,0x3
    _ _asm mov EDX, 0x378
    _ _asm out EDX, AL
}
```

This macro can be overwritten as follows:

```
#define PORTIO378 {_asm mov AL, 0x3 _asm mov EDX, 0x378 _asm out EDX, AL}
```

A macro written in assembler can accept one or several parameters as opposed to the usual macros written in C++, in which the assembly macro does not return a result. Therefore, it is impossible to use such macros in C++ expressions. Be careful while using assembly macros with parameters. For example, the function call of a macro used in other functions and declared as _fastcall can be complicated and interfere with results.

The term "function" is used in C++ definition for separate subroutines, which will be explored in further detail.

Programmers using MASM may ask: How does the C++ .NET development environment support syntax of MASM?

Many MASM constructions, such as DB, DW, DD, DQ, DF, or operators DUP and THIS, are not supported. The inline assembler also does not support instructions such as STRUC, RECORD, WIDTH, and MASK.

Assembly operators such as LENGTH, SIZE, or TYPE are limited in use with applications developed in Visual C ++ .NET. Operators cannot be applied with operator DUP, because the instructions DB, DW, DD, DQ, and DF aren't used for data definition. However, they can be used to define variable sizes as follows:

☐ LENGTH returns a number of array elements or 1 for common variables.
☐ SIZE returns the size of a C or C++ variable.
☐ TYPE returns a variable size. If the variable specifies an array, this operator returns the size of a single array element.

For example, suppose that the program uses an array of 20 integers declared like this:

```
int iarray [20],
```

The result of using these operators appears in Table 9.1.

Table 9.1. Correspondence of assembly operators to C++ operators

_asm operator	Analog in C++	Size
LENGTH iarray	sizeof(iarray) / sizeof(iarray[0])	20
SIZE iarray	sizeof(iarray)	80
TYPE iarray	sizeof(iarray[0])	4

Comments in a program and in MASM are separated from operators by a semicolon, as shown in the following example:

```
_asm {
    mov EAX, val1  ; Comment for the first line
    sub EAX, EBX   ; Comment for the second line
}
```

Since inline-assembly commands are alternated with C++ operators, they can refer to structures and variables used in C ++ .NET. That is why various C++ elements can be used in the _asm block:

☐ Symbols, including labels, variables, and function names
☐ Constants, including characters and strings

❑ Macros and preprocessor instructions

❑ Comments in the C style (/**/and //)

❑ typedef names, normally used with PTR and TYPE operators or for accessing union or structure elements

Within an assembly block, you can define integer constants accepted both in C++ and the assembly language. For example, the blank symbol can be written as 0x20 or 20h.

The use of the define instruction for constant definition also is possible. Such definition will operate both in the _asm block and in the C++ program.

Before continuing our discussion of inline assembly tools, we will illustrate the details mentioned above. We will use an assembly macro to calculate the difference between two integers (Listing 9.1).

Listing 9.1. Using a macro with the inline assembler.

```
// USE_ASM_MACRO_IN_C.cpp:  Defines the entry point for the console
// application.

#include "stdafx.h"

#define sub2(x1,x2) {_asm mov EAX, x1 _asm sub EAX, x2 _asm mov x1, EAX}

int _tmain(int argc, _TCHAR* argv[])
{
    int i1 = 357;
    int i2 = -672;
    sub2(i1, i2);
    printf("i1 - i2 = %d\n", i1);
    getchar();
    return 0;
}
```

The application window is shown in Fig. 9.1.

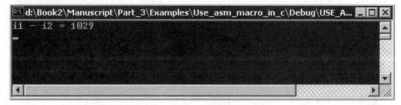

Fig. 9.1. Application window demonstrating how to use an assembly macro

There are special features of using C++ operators in assembly blocks. It is impossible to directly apply C++ operators. At the same time, some operators have a completely different meaning in the assembler and in C++. For example, the square brackets operator [] in C++ is used to define the size of an array. In the inline assembler, the same operator is applied to indexing access to variables. The misunderstanding of such operators will lead to difficult-to-locate errors in the program.

The following example shows both the correct and incorrect use of square brackets. To illustrate this tip, we will develop a C++. NET application.

We will place onto the main application form three Edit controls, Button control, and three Label controls for the static text. The main program will include the function written in the inline assembler and a handler for the buttons. The handler will be used to display the results of calculations. We have an integer array with 5 elements. We need to replace the element with index 3 with the integer value equal −115 and chosen randomly. Replacement will be implemented in two ways (in both cases, the _asm block is used).

We will use the CString variables necessary for formatting a result and displaying it in edit boxes, and then link the array elements from the edit boxes to those variables. We will assign the iOrigin variable to Edit1 (label Original); iAsmCorr to Edit2 (label Correct); and iAsmWrong to Edit3 (label Wrong). While a button is pressed, the corresponding edit boxes will be filled with the elements from the source array (Edit1), elements of correctly converted array (Edit2), and elements of incorrectly converted array (Edit3). The program source of a button handler is submitted in Listing 9.2.

Listing 9.2. Using the square brackets in the _asm block through a button handler

---

```
   . . .
#include <string.h>
#define   NUM_BYTES 4
   . . .
 void CUSING_OPERATORS_BRACKETSDlg::OnBnClickedButton1()
{
   // TODO: Add your control notification handler code here.

   int arr[5] = {4, 0, 9, -7, 50};
   int arrw[5], arrc[5];

   memcpy(arrw, arr, NUM_BYTES * 5);
   memcpy(arrc, arr, NUM_BYTES * 5);

   int* parr = arr;
   int isize = sizeof(arr) / 4;
```

```
  int cnt;
  CString stmp;

  stmp.Empty();
  for (cnt = 0; cnt < isize; cnt++)
  {
    stmp.Format("%d", *parr);
    iOrigin = iOrigin + "  " + stmp;
    parr++;
  };

  parr = arrc;
  _asm {
        mov      EAX, -115
        mov      arrc[3 * TYPE int], EAX
        };

  stmp.Empty();
  for (cnt = 0; cnt < isize; cnt++)
  {
    stmp.Format("%d", *parr);
    iAsmCorr = iAsmCorr + "  " + stmp;
    parr++;
  };

  parr = arrw;
  _asm {
        mov EAX, -115
        mov arrw[3], EAX
        };

  stmp.Empty();
  for (int cnt = 0; cnt < isize; cnt++)
  {
    stmp.Format("%d", *parr);
    iAsmWrong = iAsmWrong + "  " + stmp;
    parr++;
  };
  UpdateData(FALSE);
};
```

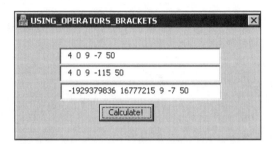

Fig. 9.2. Application window demonstrating the correct
and incorrect use of C++ operators

The application window is represented in Fig. 9.2.

We will carry out the analysis of the button handler code. During the program start-up, the functions create two copies of the source array:

```
memcpy (arrw, arr, NUM_BYTES * 5);
memcpy (arrc, arr, NUM_BYTES * 5);
```

Since here bytes are copied, the last parameter of the memcpy functions is a number of bytes of the array. The prototype of memcpy is defined in string.h, therefore, the header file is included in the declaration section:

```
#include <string.h>
```

The button-pressing handler has three for loops that prepare the buffers of iOrigin, iAsmCorr, and iAsmWrong for outputting values to the edit boxes. Consider in detail what occurs with the arrc and arrw arrays while attempting to replace their fourth element. Instructions on how to store value –115 in the arrc array are shown here:

```
parr = arrc;                    // Initialization of the index
_asm {
   mov EAX, -115               // Move a value in the EAX register
   mov arrc [3 * TYPE int], EAX // Move contents of EAX to an address
                               // An element with index 3 (it is correct!)
};
```

Now, the 4th element of the arrc array is –115. Another situation occurs while manipulating with the arrw array. The 4th element is stored if the following commands are completed:

```
parr = arrw;
_asm {
   mov EAX, -115
   mov arrw [3], EAX // THE WRONG COMMAND!
};
```

Note that after this chunk of code is completed, the four bytes in memory will be overwritten starting from the element with index 3. Obviously, the 4th byte is the last one for the first element of the array; and bytes 5 to 7 overlap the memory occupied by the second element of the array. As a result, the contents of the first two elements of the array will be destroyed (see Fig. 9.2).

Similar situations can occur while developing applications with the C++ .NET inline assembler. It is necessary to trace carefully all conversions in such programs.

As mentioned, you can use any C++ symbols inside an _asm block, but there are some limitations:

❑ Any assembly command can refer to only one symbol (variable, function, or label). To use several symbols in one command, they should be included in LENGTH, TYPE, and SIZE.

❑ Functions that refer to the commands of the _asm block should be declared in advance; otherwise, the compiler will not be able to distinguish a reference to the function from a label.

❑ It is impossible to use C++ symbols that are similar to MASM instructions in assembly blocks.

❑ Structures and unions are not distinguished in _asm blocks.

The most valuable feature of the C++ .NET inline assembler is its ability to recognize and use C++ variables. Suppose that in the C++ module, an inline assembler is used and the val1 and val2 variables are declared. In that case, the following reference in _asm block will be correct:

```
_asm {
        mov EAX, val1
        add EAX, val2
}
```

C++ functions return the result to the main program through the return operator. For example, the following function (named as MulInts) returns value i1 * i2 + 100 (Listing 9.3).

Listing 9.3. The function returning results through a return operator

---

```
int CReturnValueinregisterEAXwithinlineassemblerDlg:: MulInts (int i1,
                                                    int i2)
{
int valMul;
  _asm {
        mov EAX, i1
```

```
        mov EBX, i2
        mul EBX
        xchg EAX, EDX
        add EDX, 100
        mov valMul, EDX
};
    return valMul;
}
```

The inline assembler allows the user to avoid the return operator by using the EAX register instead. The same function MulInts with few changes is illustrated below (Listing 9.4).

Listing 9.4. The function returning result in the EAX register

```
int CReturnValueinregisterEAXwithinlineassemblerDlg:: MulInts (int i1,
                                                              int i2)
{
  _asm {
        mov EAX, i1
        mov EBX, i2
        mul EBX
        add EAX, 100
};
}
```

In spite of the fact that the function does not return a result through return, the compiler can not generate the error message and provide information about missing the return statement.

While developing the inline assembly code, there is no need to keep registers EBX, ESI, and EDI. If the program uses these registers, the compiler saves them while the function call is executing and automatically restores after it is finished. Keep in mind that numerous calls of such functions can decrease the program performance to some degree.

If your program uses the assembly command cld or std, it is necessary to restore a direction flag when you exit from the function.

Often, it is necessary to use C++ .NET library functions in _asm blocks or macros. Such a combination of assembly commands and library functions allows both to reduce the code size and to increase the application performance. To use these options effectively, you should clearly understand interfacing between the inline assembler and C++ .NET standard functions. We will introduce the steps on how such interface can be built. Take a standard C++ function, for example, printf. The main program is developed as the console application. It consists of practically a single assembly block that subtracts two integers and outputs a result on the screen using the printf function.

The application is shown in Listing 9.5.

Listing 9.5. Using the printf library function in the assembly block

```
// CALL_C_FUNC_IN_INLINEASM.cpp : Defines the entry point for the console
// application.

#include "stdafx.h"
#include <stdio.h>

int _tmain(int argc, _TCHAR* argv[])
{
        int i1, i2, ires;
        char c1[] = "Result of substraction = %d\n";
        while (true)
        {
         printf("\nEnter i1: ");
         scanf("%d", &i1);
         printf("Enter i2: ");
         scanf("%d", &i2);
         _asm {
                mov   EAX, i1
                sub   EAX, i2
                mov   ires, EAX
                push ires
                lea   EAX, c1
                push EAX
                call printf
                add   ESP, 8
            };
     };
   return 0;
}
```

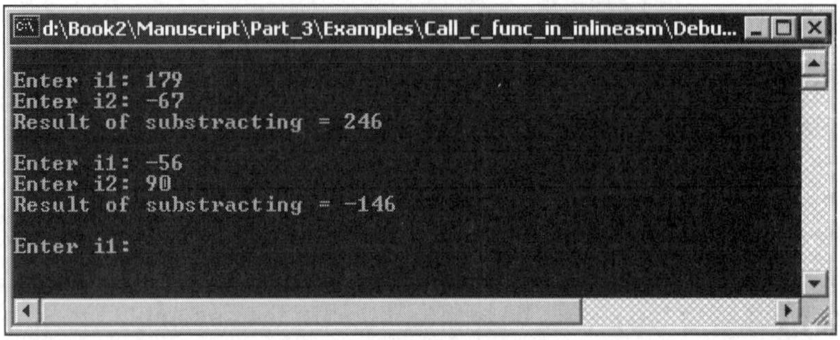

Fig. 9.3. Application window illustrating a call of C++ function
from the assembly block

A window of the working application is shown in Fig. 9.3.

The first three lines of the _asm {...} block are quite accessible. The printf call requires passing the parameters to this function. To do it correctly, the C++ function printf will look like:

```
printf (" Result of substraction = %d\n ", ires)
```

The printf function requires two parameters — an address of the string and the ires variable. Since function arguments are passed via the stack, simply push the needed arguments — a string pointer and an integer value — before calling the function. The arguments are pushed in reverse order and come off the stack in the desired order.

The chunk of a code, which implements the printf call, is realized as follows:

```
push ires
lea EAX, c1
push EAX
call printf
```

Use the _cdecl conventions for all C++ .NET projects. This means that the main program must clear the stack. The command add ESP, 8 is used for this purpose. This is very important, because if you forget to clear the stack, the application will crash immediately. The same thing will happen if the number of bytes popped from the stack differs from pushed onto it. If you mark the add ESP, 8 command as a comment (with //) and recompile the project, you will see an error message generated by a debugger after running the application (Fig. 9.4).

It is also important to note that it is not necessary to change a name of the (printf) function as in the case when you work with the separately compiled assembly procedures.

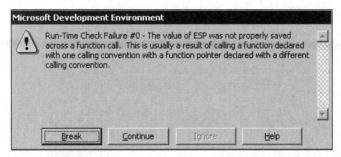

Fig. 9.4. Message from the debugger not operating with the stack

The following example is more complicated. The program takes two integers as strings, converts them to an integer format using the atoi library function (ASCII to Integer), and implements their multiplication. The results will be displayed on the screen. Strings s1[16] and s2[16] save the symbolic representation of integers i1 and i2. All operations are implemented in an assembly block. The source code is shown in Listing 9.6.

Listing 9.6. Using C++ functions atoi and printf within an assembly block

```
// ATOI_INLINE.cpp: Defines the entry point for the console application.

#include "stdafx.h"

int _tmain (int argc, _TCHAR* argv [])
{
int i1, i2, ires;
char s1 [16], s2 [16];
char c1 [] = " i1 * i2 = %d\n ";
while (true)
{
 printf (" \nEnter i1: ");
 scanf ("%s", s1);
 printf (" Enter i2: ");
 scanf ("%s", s2);
 _asm {
        lea EAX, s1
        push EAX
        call atoi
        add ESP, 4
        mov i1, EAX

        lea EAX, s2
```

```
        push EAX
        call atoi
        add ESP, 4
        mov i2, EAX

        mov EAX, i1
        mov EBX, i2
        imul EBX

        mov ires, EAX
        push ires

        lea EAX, c1
        push EAX
        call printf
        add ESP, 8
};
};
return 0;
}
```

The application window is represented in Fig. 9.5.

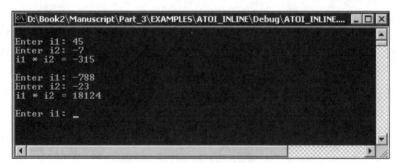

Fig. 9.5. Window of the application demonstrating
the use of the library functions `atoi` and `printf`

We will focus on the key points of this program. The `atoi` function has the following syntax:

```
int atoi (const char* str),
```

where the `str` variable is a pointer to the string. The function returns an integer value. Note that that `atoi` accepts a single parameter — an address of the string.

The assembly variant of the function call (for the `s1` string and `i1` variable) looks like this:

```
lea  EAX, s1
push EAX
call atoi
add  ESP, 4
mov  i1, EAX
```

The function passes a result in the usual way, through the EAX register. Further, the content of EAX is stored in the `i1` variable. Similar operations are implemented with variables `s2` and `i2`.

Multiplication is executed by a block of commands:

```
mov  EAX, i1
mov  EBX, i2
imul EBX
```

The `printf` function outputs results in the same way. The stack is cleared with the add ESP, n command, where n is the total number of bytes needed for storing parameters.

It is important to stress an important aspect of using the C++ .NET library functions. While developing the console applications, the Win32 framework was used with the option `Console application`. If this option is `Empty project`, you must manually include all header files needed for a project.

The next example is the most complex. It shows technique of using the inline assembler in applications. We will develop the application with a dialog window using the C++ .NET application wizard. The application should display a result of the calculation of $(X1-X2) * (X1+X2)$ on the screen. We will place on the main form of the application three Edit controls. Two edit boxes accept integers `X1` and `X2`, and the third edit box displays the result of the calculations (`X1MULX2`). Also, we will place three Static Text controls and the Button control. The final calculations will be displayed by clicking the left button of the mouse.

Now, we will link the variables `X1`, `X2` and `X1MULX2` to the Edit controls. Also we need to use two integer variables `I1` and `I2` (shown in bold in Listing 9.7). For intermediate calculations, the following functions should be developed with the inline assembler:

☐ `Add2ints` — for calculation of `X1 + X2`
☐ `Sub2ints` — for calculation of `X1 - X2`
☐ `Imul2` — for calculation of $(X1 - X2) * (X1 + X2)$

After generating the function frames, mark as a comment `return 0` (bold font in Listing 9.7), because these functions return results to the EAX register. Consider how the `Add2ints` and `Sub2ints` functions calls are implemented using the `Imul2` function.

Parameters are passed via a stack as usual, so it is not necessary to use the `add ESP, n` command for clearing the stack. The compiler automatically includes prologue-epilogue commands for functions. Therefore, including the `add ESP, n` command after the `call` command will cause an error in the stack and the crash of the program! The source code of the application is shown in Listing 9.7.

Listing 9.7. Complex example of using the inline assembler

```cpp
// CALL_FROM_INLINEASMDlg.cpp: implementation file

#include "stdafx.h"
#include "CALL_FROM_INLINEASM.h"
#include "CALL_FROM_INLINEASMDlg.h"
#include ".\call_from_inlineasmdlg.h"

#ifdef _DEBUG
#define new DEBUG_NEW
#endif

int I1, I2;

...

int CCALL_FROM_INLINEASMDlg:: Add2ints (int i1, int i2)
{
 _asm {
        mov EAX, i1
        add EAX, i2
}
 // return 0;
}

int CCALL_FROM_INLINEASMDlg:: Sub2ints (int i1, int i2)
{
  _asm {
        mov EAX, i1
        sub EAX, i2
};
  // return 0;
}

 int CCALL_FROM_INLINEASMDlg:: Imul2 (void)
 {
 _asm {
```

```
        push I2
        push I1
        call Add2ints
        mov EDX, EAX

        push I2
        push I1
        call Sub2ints
        mov EBX, EAX
        mov EAX, EDX

        imul EBX
};
// return 0;
}

void CCALL_FROM_INLINEASMDlg:: OnBnClickedButton1 ()
 {
  // TODO: Add your control notification handler code here
  UpdateData (TRUE);
  I1 = X1;
  I2 = X2;
  X1MULX2 = Imul2 ();
  UpdateData (FALSE);
}
```

A window of the working application is shown in Fig. 9.6.

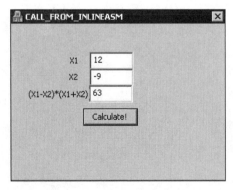

Fig. 9.6. Window of the application using the inline assembler

This concludes our consideration of the Visual C++ .NET inline-assembly capabilities. The following chapters focus on practical aspects of programming with the inline assembler.

Chapter 10: Inline Assembler and Application Optimization. MMX and SSE Technologies

This chapter will focus on practical issues related to the use of the inline assembler in C++ .NET applications. While the previous chapter described basic principles of using the inline assembler, this one will present practical examples of using this tool to implement various tasks. The inline assembler is used most frequently in computational tasks, multimedia applications, and for text processing. Certain assembler features were demonstrated in *Chapter 2*, and here we will discuss this topic in more detail.

To demonstrate specific technologies, we will use practical examples. All theoretical aspects will be considered in the context of these examples, and all necessary explanations will be given during analysis of them.

Inline Assembler and Optimizing Mathematical Operations

The first example is computing the sum of the elements of a floating-point array. In addition to demonstrating the work of the mathematical coprocessor, we will show how to use a pointer to return a result. Develop a C++ .NET dialog-based application.

On the application's main form, place two edit controls, two static text controls, and one button. The entire floating-point array will be output to the Edit1 edit control, and the Edit2 control will display the result of computation. Associate the s_Array and f_Summa variables with the Edit1 and Edit2 controls, respectively. Assign the s_Array variable the CString string type, and assign the f_Summa variable the float type.

Computing the sum of the floating-point array elements will be done with the sumReals function. This function takes two parameters: the address and size of the array. Add the function to the dialog box class and comment out the return 0 statement (marked in bold). The source code of this function and the OnBnClicked handler is shown in Listing 10.1.

Listing 10.1. Using pointers in a program that computes the sum of the floating-point array elements

```
float* CSummaofRealsDlg::sumReals(float* farray, int lf)
{
    float fsum;
    _asm {
            mov     ESI, farray
            mov     ECX, lf
            dec     ECX
            finit
            fldz
            fld     [ESI]
        next:
            add     ESI, 4
            fadd    [ESI]
            loop    next
            fstp    fsum
            fwait
            lea     EAX, fsum
    };
    // Return 0;
}


void CSummaofRealsDlg::OnBnClickedButton1()
{
    // TODO: Add your control notification handler code here

    float farray[] = {9.34, 15.05, -4.32, -173.12, -88.45};

    int fsize = sizeof(farray)/4;
```

```
CString stmp;

UpdateData(TRUE);
stmp.Empty;
for (int cnt = 0; cnt < fsize; cnt++)
{
  stmp.Format("%.2f", farray[cnt]);
  s_Array = s_Array + "   " + stmp;
};

f_Summa = *sumReals(farray, fsize);
UpdateData(FALSE);
}
```

As noted earlier, it is not necessary to save the ESI register when calling a function. This is why the sumReals function loads the address of the farray array to the ESI register and the size of the array to the ESI register at the beginning.

```
mov      ESI, farray
mov      ECX, lf
```

The address of the farray array is a pointer to its first element. The contents of the ESI register is used for organizing loop computation. The value of the first element of the array is pushed to the stack with the following coprocessor command:

```
fld      [ESI]
```

In each iteration of the loop, the pointer is moved to the next element of the array, and the value of the element is added to the top of the stack:

```
next:
  add      ESI, 4
  fadd     [ESI]
  loop     next
```

The sum is stored in the fsum local variable:

```
fstp     fsum
```

The last command of the assembly function is:

```
lea      EAX, fsum
```

It loads the address of the fsum variable to the EAX register. The function returns this address to the main program.

The `OnBnClicked` handler uses string variables for conversion of numeric values to text. We will address strings in later examples. Now look at the following statement:

```
f_Summa = *sumReals(farray, fsize);
```

Here, `f_Summa` is a variable of the `float` type, and the `sumReals` function returns an address. To get the value by the address, the dereference operator ("`*`") is used before the address expression, which is the function name in our case.

The first parameter passed to the `sumReals` function is the address of the array. It can be expressed in an alternative form. As you know, the address of an array points to the first element, so the statement being discussed can be written in the other form:

```
f_Summa = *sumReals(&farray[0], fsize);
```

where the address operator ("`&`") is used to present the first parameter in a correct form.

The window of the application is shown in Fig. 10.1.

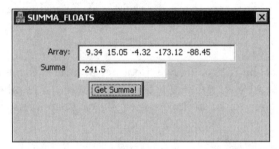

Fig. 10.1. Window of an application that computes
the sum of the floating-point array elements

Subsequent examples will illustrate the implementation of simple algorithms for sorting and searching for the maximum element. Using these examples, we will estimate the effectiveness of the inline assembler for program optimization. We will look at an algorithm for searching for the maximum element in an integer array first. Use the Visual C++ .NET Application Wizard to create a dialog-based application frame.

On the main form, place two edit controls, two static text controls, and a button. The search for the maximum element of an integer array will be done with the `findMax` function. The function takes the address and size of the array as parameters. The result of the function is the value of the maximum element of the array. The code of the `findMax` function and the `OnBnClicked` handler is shown in Listing 10.2.

Listing 10.2. Looking for the maximum element in an integer array and displaying the result

---

```
int CFIND_MAX_IN_ARRAY_OF_INTSDlg::findMax(int* pi1, int si1)
{
  int maxVal;
  _asm {
        mov     EDI, pi1
        mov     ECX, si1
        mov     EDX, [EDI]
        mov     maxVal, EDX
      next:
        add     EDI, 4
        mov     EAX, [EDI]
        cmp     EAX, maxVal
        jl      no_change
        push    EAX
        pop     maxVal
  no_change:
        loop    next
      ex:
        mov     EAX, maxVal
};
  // Return 0;
}


 void CFIND_MAX_IN_ARRAY_OF_INTSDlg::OnBnClickedButton1()
 {
// TODO: Add your control notification handler code here
  CString s1;
  int i1[] = {2, 33, -19, -7, 32, -90, 13};
  int si1 = sizeof(i1)/4;
  s1.Empty;
  for (int cnt = 0; cnt < si1; cnt++)
  {
    s1.Format("%d", i1[cnt]);
    s_Array = s_Array + " " + s1;
  };
  i_Max = findMax(i1, si1);
  UpdateData(FALSE);
}
```

Now, we will discuss the algorithm of the `findMax` function. The first element of the array is presumed maximum compared to the other elements in a loop. If one of the next elements is greater than the current maximum, it is considered maximum. The loop is repeated until the end of the array is reached. The commands

```
mov     EDI, pi1
mov     ECX, si1
```

load the pointer to the array and its size to the `EDI` and `ECX` registers, respectively. The comparison between the current maximum and the array element and the choice of a new value as the maximum is done with the following group of commands:

```
...
next:
    add     EDI, 4
    mov     EAX, [EDI]
    cmp     EAX, maxVal
    jl      no_change
    push    EAX
    pop     maxVal
    ...
```

As always, the function returns the maximum value in the `EAX` register:

```
mov     EAX, maxVal
```

The `OnBnClicked` handler does not do anything out of the way. The returned maximum value is assigned to the `i_Max` variable, which corresponds to the `Edit2` control, and is displayed.

The window of the application is shown in Fig. 10.2.

It would be interesting to compare two maximum search applications, one using the assembly function, and the other written in "pure" C++.

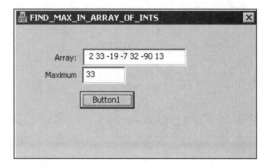

Fig. 10.2. Window of an application that searches
for the maximum element in an integer array

We already have the assembly variant, so now we will develop a similar program in C++. The code of the OnBnClicked handler is shown in Listing 10.3. The piece of code that searches for the maximum is in bold.

Listing 10.3. A fragment of a C++ program that searches for the maximum element

```
. . .
void CFindMaxIntwithCDlg::OnBnClickedButton1()
{
  // TODO: Add your control notification handler code here

  CString s1;
  int i1[] = {2, 33, -19, -7, 32, -90, 13};
  int si1 = sizeof(i1)/4;

  // Display the array

  s1.Empty;
  for (int cnt = 0; cnt < si1; cnt++)
  {
    s1.Format("%d", i1[cnt]);
    s_Array = s_Array + " " + s1;
  };

  // Look for the maximum element in an integer array

  i_Max = i1[0];
  for (int cnt = 1; cnt < si1; cnt++)
  {
    if (i_Max >= i1[cnt]) continue;
    else i_Max = i1[cnt];
  }
  UpdateData(FALSE);
};
```

The code in this fragment does not need any explanation. Look at the listing of the disassembled C++ version of the program, more precisely at its fragment that corresponds to the for loop that computes i_Max (Listing 10.4).

Listing 10.4. The code of the disassembled `for` loop

```
        i_Max = i1[0];

0041380C  mov       eax, dword ptr [this]
0041380F  mov       ecx, dword ptr [i1]
00413812  mov       dword ptr [eax+7Ch], ecx

        for (int cnt = 1;cnt < si1; cnt++)

00413815  mov       dword ptr [cnt], 1
0041381C  jmp       CFindMaxIntwithCDlg::OnBnClickedButton1+167h (413827h)
0041381E  mov       eax, dword ptr [cnt]
00413821  add       eax, 1
00413824  mov       dword ptr [cnt], eax
00413827  mov       eax, dword ptr [cnt]
0041382A  cmp       eax, dword ptr [si1]
0041382D  jge       CFindMaxIntwithCDlg::OnBnClickedButton1+18Fh (41384Fh)

        {
        if (i_Max >= i1[cnt]) continue;

0041382F  mov       eax, dword ptr [this]
00413832  mov       ecx, dword ptr [cnt]
00413835  mov       edx, dword ptr [eax+7Ch]
00413838  cmp       edx, dword ptr i1[ecx*4]
0041383C  jl        CFindMaxIntwithCDlg::OnBnClickedButton1+180h (413840h)
0041383E  jmp       CFindMaxIntwithCDlg::OnBnClickedButton1+15Eh (41381Eh)

        else i_Max = i1[cnt];

00413840  mov       eax, dword ptr [this]
00413843  mov       ecx, dword ptr [cnt]
00413846  mov       edx, dword ptr i1[ecx*4]
0041384A  mov       dword ptr [eax+7Ch], edx

        }

0041384D  jmp       CFindMaxIntwithCDlg::OnBnClickedButton1+15Eh (41381Eh)
```

Compare the disassembled code to the `findMax` function in the assembly version. A glance is enough to understand the redundancy of the C++ version. Before analyzing the disassembled code, we will consider another example — sorting the integer array in descending order.

This is a dialog-based application. On its main form, place two edit controls, two static text controls, and a button. The original (unsorted) array will be output to one of the edit controls (that corresponds to the s_Src variable), and the other edit control (corresponding to the s_Dst variable) will display the same array sorted in descending order. The array sort is done with the `sortMax` function that takes the address and size of the array as parameters. Since code of the control notification handler is similar to the code in the previous examples, we will not focus on it. The code of the `sortMax` function and the handler that calls this function is shown in Listing 10.5.

Listing 10.5. Fragment of a program that sorts an integer array and displays the result

```
void CSORT_ARRAY_BY_MAXIMUMDlg::sortMax(int* pi1, int si1)
{
int isize = si1;
_asm {
        push    EBX
        mov     EDI, DWORD PTR pi1
        mov     EBX, EDI
    big_loop:
        mov     ECX, DWORD PTR isize
        mov     EAX, [EDI]
  next:
        mov     EAX, [EDI]
        cmp     EAX, [EDI+4]
        jl      change
        jmp     cont
    change:
        xchg    EAX, [EDI+4]
        mov     [EDI], EAX
  cont:
        add     EDI, 4
        loop    next
        dec     isize
        cmp     isize, 0
        je      ex
        mov     EDI, EBX
```

```
        jmp      big_loop
    ex:
        pop      EBX
    };
}


void CSORT_ARRAY_BY_MAXIMUMDlg::OnBnClickedButton1()
{
// TODO: Add your control notification handler code here

  CString s1;
  int i1[] = {17, -9, 31, -7, 4, 76, 47, -59};
  int si1 = sizeof(i1)/4;
  s1.Empty;
  for (int cnt = 0; cnt < si1; cnt++)
  {
   s1.Format("%d", i1[cnt]);
   s_Src = s_Src + " " + s1;
  };
  sortMax(i1, si1);
  s1.Empty;
  for (int cnt = 0; cnt < si1; cnt++)
  {
   s1.Format("%d", i1[cnt]);
   s_Dst = s_Dst + " " + s1;
  };
 UpdateData(FALSE);
}
```

The window of this application is shown in Fig. 10.3.

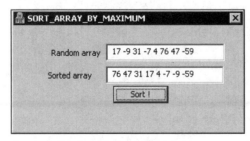

Fig. 10.3. Window of an application that sorts an integer array in descending order

Now, we will implement the same task of sorting an array with a program written in "pure" C++ and examine the disassembled code, more precisely its fragment that performs sorting. The pieces of the C++ code that sort an array and display the result are shown in Listing 10.6. The fragment, in which we are interested, is in bold.

Listing 10.6. The code that sorts an integer array only with C++ statements

---

```
void CSortbyDecreasewithCNETDlg::OnBnClickedButton1()
{

  // TODO: Add your control notification handler code here

  CString s1;
  int i1[] = {17, -9, 31, -7, 4, 76, 47, -59};
  int itmp;
  int size_i1 = sizeof(i1)/4;

  s_Src.Empty;
  s_Dst.Empty;
  UpdateData(FALSE);

  s1.Empty;

  // Display the original array in the edit control

  for (int cnt = 0; cnt < size_i1; cnt++)
  {
    s1.Format("%d", i1[cnt]);
    s_Src = s_Src + " " + s1;
  };

  // Sort the array

  int tSize_i1 = size_i1;
  while (tSize_i1 != 0)
  {
    for (int cnt = 0; cnt < tSize_i1; cnt++)
    {
      if (i1[cnt] >= i1[cnt+1]) continue;
      else
```

```
    {
      itmp = i1[cnt];
      i1[cnt] = i1[cnt+1];
      i1[cnt+1] = itmp;
    };
  };
  tSize_i1--;
};

// Display the sorted array in the edit control

for (int cnt = 0; cnt < size_i1;cnt++)
{
  s1.Format("%d", i1[cnt]);
  s_Dst = s_Dst + " " + s1;
};
UpdateData(FALSE);
}
```

We will not give a detailed analysis of the code fragment in bold because it is simple for C++ programmers. The disassembled code of this fragment is shown in Listing 10.7.

Listing 10.7. The disassembled C++ code

```
        int tSize_i1 = size_i1;

0041382D  mov      eax, dword ptr [size_i1]
00413830  mov      dword ptr [tSize_i1], eax

        while (tSize_i1 != 0)

00413833  cmp      dword ptr [tSize_i1],0
00413837  je       CSortbyDecreasewithCNETDlg::OnBnClickedButton1+1E2h  ↵
 (4138B2h)

          {
            for (int cnt = 0; cnt < tSize_i1; cnt++)

00413839  mov      dword ptr [cnt],0
```

```
00413843  jmp      CSortbyDecreasewithCNETDlg::OnBnClickedButton1+184h ↵
 (413854h)
00413845  mov      eax, dword ptr [cnt]
0041384B  add      eax, 1
0041384E  mov      dword ptr [cnt], eax
00413854  mov      eax, dword ptr [cnt]
0041385A  cmp      eax, dword ptr [tSize_i1]
0041385D  jge      CSortbyDecreasewithCNETDlg::OnBnClickedButton1+1D7h ↵
 (4138A7h)
```

```
        {
```

```
        if (i1[cnt] >= i1[cnt+1]) continue;
```

```
0041385F  mov      eax, dword ptr [cnt]
00413865  mov      ecx, dword ptr [cnt]
0041386B  mov      edx, dword ptr i1[eax*4]
0041386F  cmp      edx, dword ptr [ebp+ecx*4-44h]
00413873  jl       CSortbyDecreasewithCNETDlg::OnBnClickedButton1+1A7h ↵
 (413877h)
00413875  jmp      CSortbyDecreasewithCNETDlg::OnBnClickedButton1+175h ↵
 (413845h)
```

```
        else
        {
          itmp = i1[cnt];
```

```
00413877  mov      eax, dword ptr [cnt]
0041387D  mov      ecx, dword ptr i1[eax*4]
00413881  mov      dword ptr [itmp], ecx
```

```
        i1[cnt] = i1[cnt+1];
```

```
00413884  mov      eax, dword ptr [cnt]
0041388A  mov      ecx, dword ptr [cnt]
00413890  mov      edx, dword ptr [ebp+ecx*4-44h]
00413894  mov      dword ptr i1[eax*4], edx
```

```
        i1[cnt+1] = itmp;
```

```
00413898  mov      eax, dword ptr [cnt]
0041389E  mov      ecx, dword ptr [itmp]
```

```
004138A1  mov      dword ptr [ebp+eax*4-44h], ecx

              };
          };
```

```
004138A5  jmp      CSortbyDecreasewithCNETDlg::OnBnClickedButton1+175h ⤶
  (413845h)
```

```
          tSize_i1--;
```

```
004138A7  mov      eax, dword ptr [tSize_i1]
004138AA  sub      eax, 1
004138AD  mov      dword ptr [tSize_i1], eax

          };
```

```
004138B0  jmp      CSortbyDecreasewithCNETDlg::OnBnClickedButton1+163h ⤶
  (413833h)
```

These two disassembled fragments have common features. You might have noticed that the C++ versions of the programs intensively use the main memory for variables, while the processor registers are used much more seldom. This is not bad; however, it makes the code redundant and slows down the application in general. Such a slow-down is insignificant with little computation on small amounts of data. However, it becomes noticeable with large array sizes.

For example, swapping two elements in an array is implemented in C++ as follows:

```
itmp = i1[cnt];
i1[cnt] = i1[cnt+1];
i1[cnt+1] = itmp;
```

The equivalent assembly code is:

```
mov      eax, dword ptr [cnt]
mov      ecx, dword ptr i1[eax*4]
mov      dword ptr [itmp], ecx
mov      eax, dword ptr [cnt]
mov      ecx, dword ptr [cnt]
mov      edx, dword ptr [ebp+ecx*4-44h]
mov      dword ptr i1[eax*4], edx
mov      eax, dword ptr [cnt]
mov      ecx, dword ptr [itmp]
mov      dword ptr [ebp+eax*4-44h], ecx
```

By using these assembly commands

```
mov     EAX, [EDI]
xchg    EAX, [EDI+4]
mov     [EDI], EAX
```

you can increase the performance of the maximum search program. Here, the values of variables are stored in registers, and computation is very fast because the data exchange through the system bus is significantly decreased.

The same is true for loop optimization. It is very difficult (and often impossible) to make the C++ compiler generate code that would intensively use registers rather than the memory. Well-projected loops in assembler are executed much faster and consist of fewer commands.

We will look at the for loop in the sort program. The operator

```
for (int cnt = 0; cnt < tSize_i1; cnt++)
```

is translated into several assembly commands. The disassembled code of this statement has been modified to make it more comprehensible. For this purpose, we removed references to the physical addresses of the memory from the jump statements and put labels in appropriate places. The modified code appears as follows:

```
     mov     DWORD PTR [cnt], 0
     jmp     L2
L1:
     mov     EAX, DWORD PTR [cnt]
     add     EAX, 1
     mov     DWORD PTR [cnt], EAX
L2:
     mov     EAX, DWORD PTR [cnt]
     cmp     EAX, DWORD PTR [tSize_i1]
     jge     <address>

     < loop statements >

     jmp     L1
     ...
```

One could not say this code is not optimum. If you had only the EAX, EDX, and ECX processor registers at your disposal, you would most likely use the same algorithm for the implementation of the for loop. Because of this restriction, you would have to store the loop variables in the memory and (like in this piece of code) extract them for each iteration.

If you use the assembler, implementation of the `for` statement with the standard algorithm and the `ECX` register will be the following:

```
mov     ECX, DWORD PTR isize
 ...
loop    next
```

This is executed faster. As you see, using the assembler can solve many optimization tasks if you fully understand what should be optimized and how. This is true not only for C++ .NET, but also for other compilers.

Inline Assembler and MMX Extension

The next important topic we will address is the use of the inline assembler for optimization of applications that use Intel Single Instruction Multiple Data (SIMD) extensions. In practice, SIMD is implemented as two interrelated data processing technologies:

❒ MultiMedia eXtensions (MMX) technology used for effectively processing 64-bit integer data
❒ Streaming SIMD Extensions (SSE) technology used for effectively processing 128-bit floating-point data

Visual C++ .NET 2003 supports these technologies. *Chapter* 1 concentrated on theoretical issues of using SIMD; now, we will discuss practical aspects of using this technology. SIMD is used when developing the following types of applications:

❒ Audio signal coding, decoding, and processing
❒ Speech recognition
❒ Video signal processing and capturing
❒ Work with 3D graphics
❒ Work with 3D sound
❒ CAD/CAM
❒ Cryptography

Programming MMX and SSE requires fundamentally new approaches in comparison to developing classic programs. One of the approaches involves vectorization, or transformation, of sequentially executed code to code executed in parallel. The main advantage of the SIMD architecture is that much of computation can be done simultaneously on several operands, and this is used in code vectorization.

Using the assembler in the SIMD extensions has two advantages:

❒ Possibility of writing compact and fast code in crucial segments of an application
❒ Highly effective coding with special assembly instructions for the SIMD extensions

First, we will look at operations using MMX extension. Despite the wide use of MMX, practical examples of code with detailed explanations are scarce. Microsoft's documentation provides little information on using MMX in application development. Before demonstrating the possibilities of the C++ .NET inline assembler concerning optimization of MMX applications, it is necessary to understand how this technology is implemented.

Before developing programs supporting MMX extension, make sure that the processor supports it. For this purpose, you can use the cpuid assembly command. Before executing this command, put a one to the EAX register. After the command is executed, check the 23rd bit in the EDX register to confirm that the processor supports MMX. If this bit is equal to one, it does. The simplest console application that checks this is shown in Listing 10.8.

Listing 10.8. A check whether the processor supports MMX technology

```
// MMX_CPUID_TEST.cpp : Defines the entry point for the console
// application

#include "stdafx.h"

int _tmain(int argc, _TCHAR* argv[])
{
  bool supMMX = true;
  _asm {
        mov    supMMX, 1
        mov    EAX, 1
        cpuid
        test   EDX, 0x800000
        jnz    sup
        mov    supMMX, 0
    sup:
    };
  if (supMMX)printf("MMX is supported!\n");
  else
    printf("MMX not supported!\n");
  getchar();
  return 0;
};
```

To execute SIMD (MMX or SSE) operations, C++ .NET uses so-called intrinsics. These functions have the following syntax:

```
_mm_<operation>_<suffix>
```

where `<operation>` is the name of operation (such as `add` for addition or `sub` for subtraction). The suffix indicates data, on which the operation is done. The first two letters of the suffix indicate whether the data are packed (the letter `p`), packed with an extension (`ep`), or of a scalar type (`s`). The rest of the letters in the suffix indicate the data type:

- ❏ `s` — an ordinary-precision floating-point variable
- ❏ `d` — a double-precision floating-point variable
- ❏ `i128` — a 128-bit signed integer
- ❏ `i64` — a 64-bit signed integer
- ❏ `u64` — a 64-bit unsigned integer
- ❏ `i32` — a 32-bit signed integer
- ❏ `u32` — a 64-bit unsigned integer
- ❏ `i16` — a 16-bit signed integer
- ❏ `u16` — a 16-bit unsigned integer
- ❏ `i8` — a 8-bit signed integer
- ❏ `u8` — a 8-bit unsigned integer

The intrinsics are similar to common C++ functions. They operate with 64-bit integers. The operations can be performed on packed bytes (`8x8`), words (`16x4`), double words (`32x2`), or a quadruple word (`64x1`). Regardless of the method of processing a 64-bit value, the `_m64` notation is used in C++ .NET. The intrinsics are classified into a few main groups:

- ❏ *General support functions.* These are functions of moving, packing, and unpacking integer data.
- ❏ *Packed-arithmetic functions.* These are addition, subtraction, and multiplication of integers. It is easy to understand why division is missing from this list since the result of division is generally a real number.
- ❏ *Shift functions* that logically shift operands left or right to a certain number of positions.
- ❏ *Logical functions* (`AND`, `OR`, and `XOR`) that perform logical operations.
- ❏ *Comparison functions* that compare operands.
- ❏ *Set functions* that set bytes, words, and double words in 64-bit operands.

Intrinsics allow you to increase application performance significantly. They are all built using assembly instructions, but their code is redundant for convenience of use.

Not all intrinsics use MMX registers directly but, rather, take one or two 64-bit memory operands. On one hand, this is convenient because it saves you from learning the MMX architecture. On the other hand, it hampers optimization of computational algorithms. Now, we will examine the main idea by using an example of the int _mm_cvtsi64_si32 (__m64 m) function. It converts 32 low order bits of a 64-bit variable to an integer. Consider the following fragment of code:

```
int i1;
__m64 msres;
  ...
i1 = _mm_cvtsi64_si32 (msres);
  ...
```

The disassembled code of this fragment could be as follows:

```
00411C9D  movq      mm0, mmword ptr [msres]
00411CA4  movd      eax, mm0
00411CA7  mov       ecx, dword ptr [i1]
00411CAD  mov       dword ptr [ecx], eax
```

The last three commands of this code can be substituted with one:

```
movd DWORD PTR i1, mm0
```

Moreover, if you use the movd and movq assembly commands, which work directly with MMX registers, you will be able to avoid using intermediate 64-bit variables (in our case, msres).

Many programmers know little about using MMX extensions in practice. This is why we provide examples both in an assembly version and in a version with C++ .NET intrinsics.

As noted in *Chapter 1*, MMX extension makes it possible to operate with integer data in parallel. A threading model of data processing facilitates optimizing operations in multimedia applications, programs that process long sequences of characters and numbers, and in sort and search operations. Since operations with data are executed in MMX instructions in parallel, the commands can be executed in much less processor time.

As an example, suppose you want to substitute each byte in an 8-byte character sequence with this byte's value increased by two. The length of 8 bytes is taken for simplicity's sake. First, develop a console application that uses intrinsics. The source code of the application is shown in Listing 10.9.

Listing 10.9. Adding two 8-byte sequences

```
// MMX_2_ADD_BYTES.cpp : Defines the entry point for the console
// application

#include "stdafx.h"
```

```
#include <mmintrin.h>

int _tmain(int argc, _TCHAR* argv[])
{
 unsigned char s1[9] = "ABCDEFGH";
 unsigned char s2[9] = {0x2, 0x2, 0x2, 0x2, 0x2, 0x2, 0x2, 0x2};
 unsigned char sres[9]= "        ";
 unsigned char* psres = sres;
 __m64 ms1, ms2, msres;

ms1 = _mm_set_pi8 (s1[7], s1[6], s1[5], s1[4],
                   s1[3], s1[2], s1[1], s1[0]);
ms2 = _mm_set_pi8 (s2[7], s2[6], s2[5], s2[4],
                   s2[3], s2[2], s2[1], s2[0]);
msres = _mm_adds_pu8 (ms1, ms2);
for (int cnt = 0; cnt < 8; cnt++)
   {
     *psres = (char)_mm_cvtsi64_si32 (msres);
      psres++;
      msres = _mm_srli_si64 (msres, 8);
   };
_mm_empty();

printf("USING INTRINSICS IN MMX : PACKED ADDING OF BYTES \n\n");
printf("    Before operation: %s\n", s1);
printf("    After operation (+2): %s\n", sres);
getchar();
return 0;
 }
```

To use intrinsics of the MMX extension, be sure to include the `mmintrin.h` header file (the corresponding line is in bold) that contains declarations of intrinsics and variables. This program declares two 8-character strings (`s1` and `s2`) and the `sres` string for the result of addition of packed bytes. For intermediate results of conversions and computation, three 64-bit variables of the `__m64` type are used: `ms1`, `ms2`, and `msres`. Note that the type identifier contains two underscore characters!

To execute operations with 64-bit values, the `s1` and `s2` strings are copied to `ms1` and `ms2` with two `_mm_set_pi8` commands. Then the `_mm_adds_pu8` instruction performs bytewise addition of the `ms1` and `ms2` variables, and the result is put to the `msres` variable. The `_mm_adds_pu8` intrinsic adds 8-bit unsigned values, and this is exactly what you need.

Be very careful. Before the `for` loop is executed, the `msres` variable contains a 64-bit value. However, you want to obtain and display an 8-byte string `sres`. Therefore, you should extract eight bytes from the 64-bit variable and write them to the `sres` string. C++ .NET misses functions that could do such a conversion. To implement this task, use two intrinsics of the MMX extension:

```
int _mm_cvtsi64_si32 (__m64 m)
__m64 _mm_srli_si64 (__m64 m, int count)
```

The first of these functions converts 32 low order bits to an integer, the other shifts a 64-bit number `count` positions to the right. To increase performance, Microsoft recommends that programmers use a constant as a bit counter. To extract one byte and write it to an appropriate position in the `sres` string, use a pointer to this string declared as follows:

```
unsigned char* psres = sres
```

One byte can be easily read from the `msres` variable and written to the `sres` string with the following statement:

```
*psres = (char)_mm_cvtsi64_si32 (msres);
```

To write the next byte to the string, increment the `psres` pointer and shift the `msres` variable eight bits to the right. This sequence of operations is implemented in the `for` loop:

```
for (int cnt = 0; cnt < 8; cnt++)
  {
    *psres = (char)_mm_cvtsi64_si32 (msres);
    psres++;
    msres = _mm_srli_si64 (msres, 8);
  };
```

After the MMX operations are executed, the `_mm_empty()` function is called to reset the coprocessor.

The window of this application is shown in Fig. 10.4.

Fig. 10.4. Window of an application that demonstrates C++ intrinsics adding byte sequences

Now look at a disassembled fragment of code that adds two byte arrays (Listing 10.10). The source statements are in bold.

Listing 10.10. The disassembled fragment of code that adds two 8-byte arrays

---

```
__m64 ms1, ms2, msres;

ms1 = _mm_set_pi8 (s1[7],s1[6],s1[5],s1[4],
                   s1[3],s1[2],s1[1], s1[0]);

00411ABF  mov      al, byte ptr [s1]
00411AC2  mov      byte ptr [ebp-198h], al
00411AC8  mov      cl, byte ptr [ebp-0Fh]
00411ACB  mov      byte ptr [ebp-197h], cl
00411AD1  mov      dl, byte ptr [ebp-0Eh]
00411AD4  mov      byte ptr [ebp-196h], dl
00411ADA  mov      al, byte ptr [ebp-0Dh]
00411ADD  mov      byte ptr [ebp-195h], al
00411AE3  mov      cl, byte ptr [ebp-0Ch]
00411AE6  mov      byte ptr [ebp-194h], cl
00411AEC  mov      dl, byte ptr [ebp-0Bh]
00411AEF  mov      byte ptr [ebp-193h], dl
00411AF5  mov      al, byte ptr [ebp-0Ah]
00411AF8  mov      byte ptr [ebp-192h], al
00411AFE  mov      cl, byte ptr [ebp-9]
00411B01  mov      byte ptr [ebp-191h], cl
00411B07  movq     mm0, mmword ptr [ebp-198h]
00411B0E  movq     mmword ptr [ebp-148h], mm0
00411B15  movq     mm0, mmword ptr [ebp-148h]
00411B1C  movq     mmword ptr [ms1], mm0

ms2 = _mm_set_pi8 (s2[7], s2[6], s2[5], s2[4],
                   s2[3], s2[2], s2[1], s2[0]);

00411B20  mov      al, byte ptr [s2]
00411B23  mov      byte ptr [ebp-198h], al
00411B29  mov      cl, byte ptr [ebp-23h]
00411B2C  mov      byte ptr [ebp-197h], cl
00411B32  mov      dl, byte ptr [ebp-22h]
00411B35  mov      byte ptr [ebp-196h], dl
```

```
00411B3B   mov        al, byte ptr [ebp-21h]
00411B3E   mov        byte ptr [ebp-195h], al
00411B44   mov        cl, byte ptr [ebp-20h]
00411B47   mov        byte ptr [ebp-194h], cl
00411B4D   mov        dl, byte ptr [ebp-1Fh]
00411B50   mov        byte ptr [ebp-193h], dl
00411B56   mov        al, byte ptr [ebp-1Eh]
00411B59   mov        byte ptr [ebp-192h], al
00411B5F   mov        cl, byte ptr [ebp-1Dh]
00411B62   mov        byte ptr [ebp-191h], cl
00411B68   movq       mm0, mmword ptr [ebp-198h]
00411B6F   movq       mmword ptr [ebp-158h], mm0
00411B76   movq       mm0, mmword ptr [ebp-158h]
00411B7D   movq       mmword ptr [ms2], mm0
```

        msres = _mm_adds_pu8 (ms1, ms2);

```
00411B81   movq       mm0, mmword ptr [ms2]
00411B85   movq       mm1, mmword ptr [ms1]
00411B89   paddusb    mm1, mm0
00411B8C   movq       mmword ptr [ebp-168h], mm1
00411B93   movq       mm0, mmword ptr [ebp-168h]
00411B9A   movq       mmword ptr [msres], mm0
```

        for (int cnt = 0; cnt < 8; cnt++)

```
00411B9E   mov        dword ptr [cnt], 0
00411BA8   jmp        main+189h (411BB9h)
00411BAA   mov        eax, dword ptr [cnt]
00411BB0   add        eax, 1
00411BB3   mov        dword ptr [cnt], eax
00411BB9   cmp        dword ptr [cnt], 8
00411BC0   jge        main+1C3h (411BF3h)
```

        {
        *psres = (char)_mm_cvtsi64_si32 (msres);

```
00411BC2   movq       mm0, mmword ptr [msres]
00411BC6   movd       eax, mm0
```

```
00411BC9  mov         ecx, dword ptr [psres]
00411BCC  mov         byte ptr [ecx], al
```

psres++;

```
00411BCE  mov         eax, dword ptr [psres]
00411BD1  add         eax, 1
00411BD4  mov         dword ptr [psres], eax
```

msres = _mm_srli_si64 (msres, 8);

```
00411BD7  movq        mm0, mmword ptr [msres]
00411BDB  psrlq       mm0, 8
00411BDF  movq        mmword ptr [ebp-188h], mm0
00411BE6  movq        mm0, mmword ptr [ebp-188h]
00411BED  movq        mmword ptr [msres], mm0
```

};

```
00411BF1  jmp         main+17Ah (411BAAh)
00411BF3  emms
```

This disassembled fragment of code allows us to draw a few important conclusions. First, all the intrinsics use the MMX registers in one way or another. Second, when exchanging data between the MMX registers and 64-bit operands in the memory, the movq (more rarely, movd) command is used. Since the MMX registers are not directly available to you when working with intrinsics, the assembly version of the MMX extension operations can increase performance.

Now, we will consider the assembly version of the same task. Replace the MMX extension intrinsics with the assembly commands and slightly modify the s1 and s2 strings. The source code of the application will become much simpler (Listing 10.11).

Listing 10.11. An assembly version of the program that adds 8-byte arrays

```
// ADD_8_BYTES_MMX_ASM.cpp : Defines the entry point for the console
// application

#include "stdafx.h"

int _tmain(int argc, _TCHAR* argv[])
```

```
{
  unsigned char s1[9] = "12345678";
  unsigned char s2[9] = {0x1, 0x1, 0x1, 0x1, 0x1, 0x1, 0x1, 0x1};
  unsigned char sres[9]= "        ";
  _asm {
        movq  mm0, QWORD PTR s1
        movq  mm1, QWORD PTR s2
        paddd mm0, mm1
        movq  QWORD PTR sres, mm0
        emms
      };
  printf("USING ASSEMBLER IN MMX: PACKED ADDING OF BYTES \n\n");
  printf("    Before operation: %s\n", s1);
  printf("    After operation (+2): %s\n", sres);
  getchar();
  return 0;
}
```

Note that all computation is done in the assembly block. Listing 10.12 shows the disassembled code of the example. As you see, the code is actually optimum when assembly commands are used.

Listing 10.12. The disassembled code of the asm block

```
_asm {
          movq   mm0, qword ptr s1
00411AA7  movq          mm0, mmword ptr [s1]
          movq   mm1, qword ptr s2
00411AAB  movq          mm1, mmword ptr [s2]
          paddd  mm0, mm1
00411AAF  paddd         mm0, mm1
          movq   qword ptr sres, mm0
00411AB2  movq          mmword ptr [sres], mm0
          emms
00411AB6  emms
   };
```

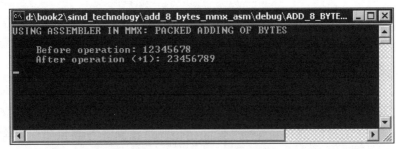

Fig. 10.5. Window of an application that adds two bytes
with MMX extension assembly commands

The window of the application is shown in Fig. 10.5.

Develop an application that adds together the elements of two integer arrays in pairs and puts the result to a third array. All three arrays have the same size. Develop three variants of such an application, each being a console application. Let the first program add the array elements with common C++ statements, the second program use MMX extension functions, and the third use MMX assembly instructions. The common variant is shown in Listing 10.13.

Listing 10.13. Pairwise addition of two integer arrays with common C++ statements

```
// MMX_2_1.cpp : Defines the entry point for the console application

#include "stdafx.h"

int _tmain(int argc, _TCHAR* argv[])
{
 int a1[] = {23, 12, -45, -9, 44, -16, -7, 19, 1, 14, -2};
 int b1[] = {12, -70, 12, 33, 12, 35, 29, -33, -99, -5, -7};
 int ires[16];

 int isize = sizeof(a1)/4;
 for (int cnt = 0; cnt < isize; cnt++)
  ires[cnt] = a1[cnt] + b1[cnt];

printf("a1: ");
for (int cnt = 0; cnt < isize; cnt++)
    printf("%d  ", a1[cnt]);
printf("\nb1: ");
for (int cnt = 0; cnt < isize; cnt++)
```

```
        printf("%d  ", b1[cnt]);
printf("\n\n");
for (int cnt = 0; cnt < isize; cnt++)
    printf("ires[%d] = %d\n", cnt, ires[cnt]);
getchar();
return 0;
};
```

You can upgrade this application with the C++ .NET intrinsics for the MMX extension. The source code of a modified program is shown in Listing 10.14.

Listing 10.14. Addition of two integer arrays with intrinsics

```
// MMX_ADD_ARRAYS_INTRINSICS.cpp : Defines the entry point for the
// console application

#include "stdafx.h"
#include <mmintrin.h>

int _tmain(int argc, _TCHAR* argv[])
{
 int a1[] = {23, 12, -45, -9, 44, -16, -7, 19, 1, 14, -2};
 int* pa1 = a1;


 int b1[] = {12, -70, 12, 33, 12, 35, 29, -33, -99, -5, -7};
 int* pb1 = b1;


 int ires[16];
 int* pires = ires;

__m64 ma1, mb1, mires;

int isize = sizeof(a1)/4;
for (int cnt = 0; cnt < isize; cnt++)
 {
   ma1 = _mm_cvtsi32_si64 (*pa1);
   mb1 = _mm_cvtsi32_si64 (*pb1);
   mires = _mm_add_pi32 (ma1, mb1);
   *pires = _mm_cvtsi64_si32 (mires);
   pa1++;
```

```
    pb1++;
    pires++;
  };

printf("a1: ");
for (int cnt = 0; cnt < isize; cnt++)
      printf("%d  ", a1[cnt]);
printf("\nb1: ");
for (int cnt = 0; cnt < isize; cnt++)
      printf("%d  ", b1[cnt]);
printf("\n\n");
for (int cnt = 0; cnt < isize; cnt++)
      printf("ires[%d] = %d\n", cnt, ires[cnt]);
getchar();
return 0;
};
```

The second version is faster despite the greater number of statements. However, it does not use the possibilities of 64-bit data processing to the full extent because one double word is processed in each iteration. The assembler can help in this situation. The third version of the program uses MMX extension assembly commands to speed up data processing even further. This is shown in Listing 10.15.

Listing 10.15. An application that adds two integer arrays with 64-bit assembly commands

```
// ADD_2_ARRAYS_MMX_ASM.cpp : Defines the entry point for the console
// application

#include "stdafx.h"

int _tmain(int argc, _TCHAR* argv[])
{
 int a1[] = {23, 12, -45, -9, 44, -16, -7, 19, 1, 14, -2};
 int b1[] = {12, -70, 12, 33, 12, 35, 29, -33, -99, -5, -7};
 int ires[16];
 bool flag = false;

 if ((sizeof(a1)%8) != 0)flag = true;
 int isize = sizeof(a1)/4;
```

```
 int qsize = sizeof(a1)/8;
_asm {
        lea    ESI, DWORD PTR a1
        lea    EDI, DWORD PTR b1
        lea    EDX, DWORD PTR ires
        sub    ESI, 8
        sub    EDI, 8
        sub    EDX, 8
        mov    ECX, DWORD PTR qsize
    next:
        add    ESI, 8
        add    EDI, 8
        add    EDX, 8

        movq   mm0, QWORD PTR [ESI]
        movq   mm1, QWORD PTR [EDI]
        paddd  mm0, mm1
        movq   DWORD PTR [EDX], mm0
        loop   next
        emms
        cmp    flag, 1
        jne    ex
        mov    EAX, DWORD PTR [ESI+8]
        add    EAX, DWORD PTR [EDI+8]
        mov    DWORD PTR [EDX+8], EAX
    ex:
    };
  printf("a1: ");
  for (int cnt = 0; cnt < isize; cnt++)
      printf("%d  ", a1[cnt]);
  printf("\nb1: ");
  for (int cnt = 0; cnt < isize; cnt++)
      printf("%d  ", b1[cnt]);
  printf("\n\n");
  for (int cnt = 0; cnt < isize; cnt++)
      printf("ires[%d] = %d\n", cnt, ires[cnt]);
  getchar();
  return 0;
};
```

This source code does not need detailed explanations. It declares the qsize variable that is equal to the size of the a1 array divided by eight. In other words, this variable determines the number of quadwords (64 bits each) contained in the array. The flag variable indicates whether there is a 32-bit variable among the 64-bit numbers. Why? The following example provides an explanation. Consider an array of eleven integers. The size of an integer variable is four bytes. For operations with MMX extension, it is desirable that a variable has a size of 64 bits. Then the performance of such operations will be very high. This can be achieved if two integers (32x2 bits) are processed as one (64x1 bits). Of eleven integers, you can make up five 64-bit numbers plus one 32-bit number, which should be processed individually.

The flag variable indicates whether there is a 32-bit variable in the array. Now, we will describe the assembly block in more detail. The commands

```
lea   ESI, DWORD PTR a1
lea   EDI, DWORD PTR b1
lea   EDX, DWORD PTR ires
sub   ESI, 8
sub   EDI, 8
sub   EDX, 8
mov   ECX, DWORD PTR qsize
```

load the addresses of the arrays a1, b1, and ires to the registers ESI, EDI, and EDX, respectively. Subtraction of an eight from the values put to the registers is done for convenience in the use of the loop loop. The number of 64-bit operands that should be processed is put to the ECX register. These operands are added with the following commands:

```
movq  mm0, QWORD PTR [ESI]
movq  mm1, QWORD PTR [EDI]
paddd mm0, mm1
```

The result is put at the address stored in the EDX register:

```
movq DWORD PTR [EDX], mm0
```

At the beginning of each iteration, the addresses of the next 64-bit variables are put to the registers ESI, EDI, and EDX by adding an eight to the addresses currently stored in the registers:

```
add   ESI, 8
add   EDI, 8
add   EDX, 8
```

Then addition is done again. After exiting the loop, the value of the flag variable is checked. If flag is equal to zero, there is no 32-bit "remainder," and the assembly block can be exited. Otherwise, the 32-bit number should be processed with the following commands:

```
mov  EAX, DWORD PTR [ESI+8]
add  EAX, DWORD PTR [EDI+8]
mov  DWORD PTR [EDX+8], EAX
```

The rest of the code is self-explanatory. The window of the application is shown in Fig. 10.6.

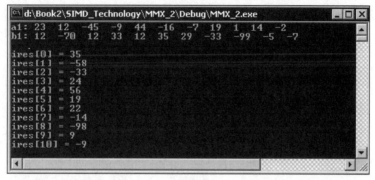

Fig. 10.6. Window of an application that demonstrates addition of the elements of two integer arrays with MMX extension assembly commands

The next group of MMX extension commands that we will discuss includes comparison commands. They can be divided into two groups: common comparison commands ("equal"/"not equal") and value comparison commands ("greater than"/"less than"). The comparison commands are executed on packed bytes, words, or double words.

The common comparison commands are pcmeqb, pcmeqw, and pcmeqd; and the value comparison commands are pcmpgtb, pcmpgtw, and pcmpgtd. The last letter in the command names denotes a byte (b), word (w), and double word (d), respectively.

The commands have the following syntax:

```
pcmpxxx <operand_1>, <operand_2>
```

As the first operand, one of the MMX registers (mm0, mm1, etc.) can be used; and as the second operand, either a MMX register or a 64-bit memory operand can be used. The result of a comparison operation is a zero or non-zero byte, word, or double word.

The common comparison operations return zero results if the bytes, words, or double words being compared are not equal. Ones are returned if the bytes, words, or double words being compared are equal. The value operations return ones if the bytes, words, or double words of the first operand are greater than those of the second.

Consider an example. Suppose you want to check two character strings for equality. For simplicity's sake, use 8-byte strings. Develop two variants: one using C++ .NET intrinsics, the other using the inline assembler.

The source code of a console application that uses intrinsics is shown in Listing 10.16.

Listing 10.16. Comparing two character strings with MMX extension intrinsics

```cpp
// CMP_8_BYTES_INTRINSICS.cpp : Defines the entry point for the console
// application

#include "stdafx.h"
#include <mmintrin.h>

int _tmain(int argc, _TCHAR* argv[])
{
  char s1[32];
  char s2[32];
  char ires[32];

  __m64 ms1, ms2, msres;

  printf("Comparison 2 strings with MMX Intrinsics\n\n");
  while(true)
    {
      memset(s1, '\0', 16);
      memset(s2, '\0', 16);
      memset(ires, '\0', 16);
      char* pires = ires;

      printf("\nEnter string s1: ");
      scanf("%s", s1);
      printf("Enter string s2: ");
      scanf("%s", s2);
      ms1 = _mm_set_pi8 (s1[7], s1[6], s1[5], s1[4],
                         s1[3], s1[2], s1[1], s1[0]);
      ms2 = _mm_set_pi8 (s2[7], s2[6], s2[5], s2[4],
                         s2[3], s2[2], s2[1], s2[0]);
      msres = _mm_cmpeq_pi8 (ms1, ms2);
```

```
*(int*)pires = _mm_cvtsi64_si32 (msres);
msres =_mm_srli_si64 (msres, 32);

pires = pires+4;
*(int*)pires = _mm_cvtsi64_si32 (msres);
_mm_empty();
for (int cnt = 0; cnt < 8; cnt++)
  {
    if (ires[cnt] == 0)
      {
      printf("s1 not equal s2 !\n");
      break;
      }
  };
  if (cnt == 8)printf("s1 = s2 !\n");
  };
return 0;
}
```

The operation of comparison of arrays (not only character arrays) involves comparing individual elements, moving the address counter to the next elements, and so on until the end of the array is encountered. MMX technology allows you to compare several bytes, words, or double words simultaneously. Comparison of eight bytes is done with the following commands:

```
ms1 = _mm_set_pi8 (s1[7], s1[6], s1[5], s1[4], s1[3], s1[2], s1[1], s1[0]);
ms2 = _mm_set_pi8 (s2[7], s2[6], s2[5], s2[4], s2[3], s2[2], s2[1], s2[0]);
msres = _mm_cmpeq_pi8 (ms1, ms2);
```

The first two statements put eight bytes from the strings s1 and s2 to 64-bit variables ms1 and ms2. The comparison proper is done with the last statement, and the result is stored in the msres variable. Then the eight bytes of this variable are written to the ires string:

```
*(int*)pires = _mm_cvtsi64_si32 (msres);
msres =_mm_srli_si64 (msres, 32);
pires = pires+4;
*(int*)pires = _mm_cvtsi64_si32 (msres);
```

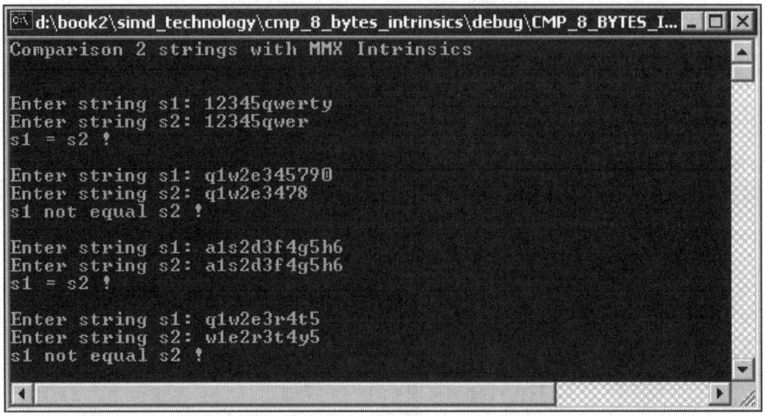

Fig. 10.7. Window of an application that compares two strings with MMX extension intrinsics

The window of the application is shown in Fig. 10.7.

The other variant of the application that uses MMX assembly instructions looks much simpler. Its source code is shown in Listing 10.17.

Listing 10.17. Comparing two 8-byte strings with MMX assembly instructions

```cpp
// CMP_8_BYTES_ASM.cpp : Defines the entry point for the console
// application

#include "stdafx.h"

int _tmain(int argc, _TCHAR* argv[])
{
 char s1[32];
 char s2[32];
 char ires[32];
 printf("Comparison 2 strings with MMX assembly instructions\n\n");
 while(true)
  {
   memset(s1, '\0', 16);
   memset(s2, '\0', 16);
   memset(ires, '\0', 16);

   printf("\nEnter string s1: ");
   scanf("%s", s1);
```

```
    printf("Enter string s2: ");
    scanf("%s", s2);

   _asm {
        movq       mm0, QWORD PTR s1
        movq       mm1, QWORD PTR s2
        pcmpeqb    mm0, mm1
        movq       QWORD PTR ires, mm0
        emms
        };

  for (int cnt = 0; cnt < 8; cnt++)
  {
   if (ires[cnt] == 0)
   {
    printf("s1 not equal s2 !\n");
    break;
   }
  };
  if (cnt == 8)printf("s1 = s2 !\n");
  };
 return 0;
};
```

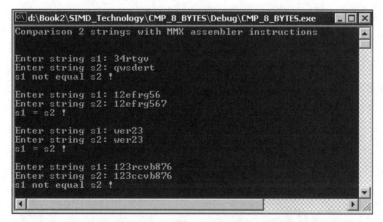

Fig. 10.8. Window of an application that compares two strings
with MMX extension assembly commands

Comparison is done in the _asm block. The contents of two strings are copied to MMX registers, and then the bytewise comparison of the contents of the registers is done with the command pcmpeqb mm0, mm1. The result is stored in the ires string with the command movq QWORD PTR ires, mm0. The obtained result is checked in the for loop.

The window of the application is shown in Fig. 10.8.

The following example compares eight bytes located on the same positions in two strings, s1 and s2. The comparison is done according to the "greater than"/"less than" principle with the pcmpgtb assembly command. If a byte of the s1 string is greater than the corresponding byte of the s2 string, ones are written to the corresponding byte of the ires string. Otherwise, zeroes are written to that byte. The result of comparison is displayed.

The source code of the application is shown in Listing 10.18.

Listing 10.18. Comparing two strings by value with MMX assembly commands

```
// CMPGT_8_ASM_MMX.cpp : Defines the entry point for the console
// application

#include "stdafx.h"

int _tmain(int argc, _TCHAR* argv[])
{
  char s1[32];
  char s2[32];
  char ires[32];

  printf("Using PCMPGTB in string comparison with assembly instructions\n\n");
  while(true)
  {
  memset(s1, '\0', 16);
  memset(s2, '\0', 16);
  memset(ires, '\0', 16);
  printf("\nEnter string s1: ");
  scanf("%s", s1);
  printf("Enter string s2: ");
  scanf("%s", s2);
  _asm {
        movq        mm0, QWORD PTR s1
        movq        mm1, QWORD PTR s2
        pcmpgtb     mm0, mm1
        movq        QWORD PTR ires, mm0
        emms
```

```
    };
for (int cnt = 0; cnt < 8; cnt++)
  {
   if (ires[cnt] != 0x0)
        printf("s1[%d] > s2[%d]\n", cnt, cnt);
   if (ires[cnt] == 0x0)
        printf("s1[%d] <= s2[%d]\n", cnt, cnt);
  };
};
return 0;
};
```

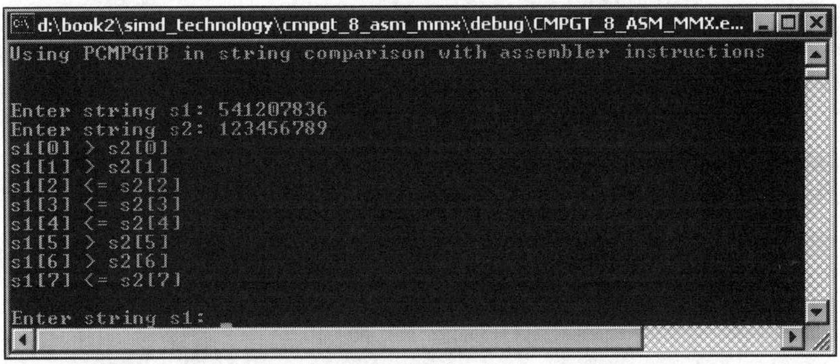

Fig. 10.9. Window of an application that does a bytewise comparison
of strings with MMX assembly commands and displays the result

The window of the application is shown in Fig. 10.9.

The assembly comparison commands make it possible to implement quick algorithms to search for elements in arrays. Consider this example. Suppose you want to find a character in a string. The search can be done with common assembly commands, but MMX instructions allow you to compare several bytes simultaneously, so the performance gain is significant. Take the program in Listing 10.17 as a sample for this application, but make a few changes in the source code. The resulting source code is shown in Listing 10.19.

Listing 10.19. Searching for a character in a string with the pcmpeqb command

```
// FIND_CHAR_PCMPEQB_ASM.cpp : Defines the entry point for the console
// application

#include "stdafx.h"
```

```
int _tmain(int argc, _TCHAR* argv[])
{
 char s1[32];
 char s2[32];
 char c1 = 'r';
 char ires[32];

 printf("Find char with PCMPEQB instruction\n\n");
 while(true)
   {
    memset(s1, '\0', 16);
    memset(s2, c1, 16);
    memset(ires, '\0', 16);

    printf("\nEnter string s1: ");
    scanf("%s", s1);
    _asm {
            movq        mm0, QWORD PTR s1
            movq        mm1, QWORD PTR s2
            pcmpeqb     mm0, mm1
            movq        QWORD PTR ires, mm0
            emms
            };

   for (int cnt = 0; cnt < 8; cnt++)
     {
      if (ires[cnt] != 0)
        {
         printf("Character %c found in s1 !\n", c1);
         break;
        }
     };
    if (cnt == 8)printf("Character %c not found in s1 !\n", c1);
   };
 return 0;
}
```

The necessary changes are in bold. Suppose you want to find the `'r'` character in the s1 string. To be able to use the `pcmeqb` command, fill the s2 string with this character:

```
memset(s2, c1, 16);
```

If there is a letter r in s1, at least one of the first eight bytes of the ires string that contains the result will be non-zero.

The window of the application that searches for an element in a string is shown in Fig. 10.10.

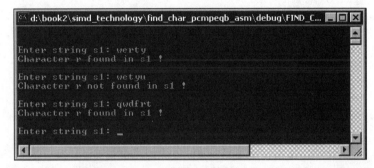

Fig. 10.10. Window of an application that searches for an element
in a character string with the MMX extension assembler

The next example, which focuses on the use of the inline assembler in MMX applications, is more complicated. In this example, we will demonstrate the use of addition, packing, and extracting commands for simultaneous pairwise addition of two integers stored in two arrays. For simplicity's sake, only positive integers are considered. Name the initial arrays a1 and b1 and the resulting array c1. The source code of the console application is shown in Listing 10.20.

Listing 10.20. Pairwise addition of positive integers stored in two arrays

```
// PACK_n_ADD_2_in_4WORD.cpp : Defines the entry point for the console
// application

#include "stdafx.h"

int _tmain(int argc, _TCHAR* argv[])
{
 int a1[4] = {12, 1, 34, 17};
 int b1[4] = {17, 7, 4, 33};
 int c1[4];
 printf(" a1: ");
```

```
for (int cnt = 0; cnt < 4; cnt++)
  printf("%d\t", a1[cnt]);
printf("\n b1: ");
for (int cnt = 0; cnt < 4; cnt++)
  printf("%d\t", b1[cnt]);
_asm {
        movq      mm0, QWORD PTR a1
        movq      mm1, QWORD PTR a1+8
        packssdw  mm0, mm1

        movq      mm1, QWORD PTR b1
        movq      mm2, QWORD PTR b1+8
        packssdw  mm1, mm2

        paddw     mm0, mm1

        lea       ESI, c1

        pextrw    EDI, mm0, 0
        mov       DWORD PTR [ESI], EDI
        add       ESI, 4

        pextrw    EDI, mm0, 1
        mov       DWORD PTR [ESI], EDI
        add       ESI, 4

        pextrw    EDI, mm0, 2
        mov       DWORD PTR [ESI], EDI
        add       ESI, 4

        pextrw    EDI, mm0, 3
        mov       DWORD PTR [ESI], EDI
        add       ESI, 4

        emms
    };
printf("\n\n          c1: \n");
for (int cnt = 0; cnt < 4; cnt++)
    printf(" a1[%d] + b1[%d] = %d\n", cnt, cnt, c1[cnt]);
getchar();
return 0;
};
```

We will analyze the source code of this example. First, look at the following commands of the assembly block:

```
movq       mm0, QWORD PTR a1
movq       mm1, QWORD PTR a1+8
packssdw mm0, mm1
```

The first two commands move two integers from the a1 array to 64-bit registers mm0 and mm1. After executing these commands, each of the registers will contain two 32-bit integers (32x2). The current task is to add simultaneously the integers in the a1 array to the integers in the a2 array. This is why the numbers in the registers mm0 and mm1 are packed, and the result is written to the mm0 register. The essence of packing is in decreasing the size of the elements by half. In our case, two 32-bit numbers from the mm0 and mm1 registers can be packed into four 16-bit numbers, and the result can be put to the mm0 register. Packing numbers allows you to perform arithmetic and logic operations simultaneously on twice as many elements as without packing. This improves the performance of an application as a whole. Keep in mind that operations on packed numbers can cause overflow, so use these commands with care.

Returning to our example, the contents of the mm0 and mm1 MMX registers are packed with the packssdw mm0, mm1 command.

The next three commands do similar operations on the first two elements of the b1 array:

```
movq       mm1, QWORD PTR b1
movq       mm2, QWORD PTR b1+8
packssdw mm1, mm2
```

Note that the mm1 and mm2 MMX registers are used for operations on the elements of the b1 array. The mm0 register cannot be used because it contains four packed 16-bit numbers from the a1 array.

After packing the array elements, four words contained in the mm0 and mm1 registers can be added with the paddw mm0, mm1 command. The result is put into the mm0 MMX register.

Now, it is necessary to extract four sums from the mm0 register and write them to the first four elements of the c1 array. For this purpose, one of additional MMX commands that appeared in Pentium III is used. The pextrw command extracts one of four packed words from the source operand into a 32-bit common register. The extracted operand is put to the low-order word of the register, and the high-order word is zeroed. The position of the extracted operand is determined by a mask containing a value from 0 to 3. A minor inconvenience of this command is that the mask must be a constant, which does not allow use of the command in loops. This command has no analogs among the Visual C++ .NET intrinsics (at least, at the time of this publication).

As a destination, the EDI register is used, into which the 16-bit sum is put. To write to the c1 array, the ESI register containing the array address is used. The lea ESI,c1 command loads the address of the first array element into the ESI register. The groups of commands that extract 16-bit numbers into an array are similar to each other, so here we will give only a code fragment for operations with the zero element of the mm0 register:

```
pextrw   EDI, mm0, 0
mov      DWORD PTR [ESI], EDI
add      ESI, 4
```

The first two commands of this fragment write a number to a particular position in the c1 array, and the add ESI, 4 command moves the pointer to the next element of the array.

The rest of the source code of the program is simple and does not require further explanation.

The window of the application is shown in Fig. 10.11.

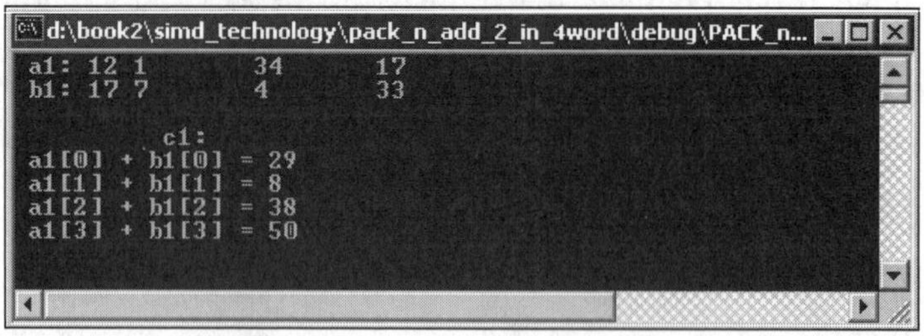

Fig. 10.11. Window of an application that demonstrates manipulations with packed data with the MMX extension assembler

In the previous example, we used the pextrw command, one of additional MMX extension commands of Pentium III and higher. Four more additional commands make it possible to increase the computational power of C++ .NET applications. These commands allow you to extract minimum or maximum values of each pair of packed elements. The elements can be unsigned bytes or signed words. These commands are very effective when implementing algorithms for sort, search, and bit fields processing in multimedia applications. We will give examples of programs that use the pmaxsw and pminsw commands.

Use the source code of the previous example and make a few changes. This application will display the maximum of two numbers located at corresponding positions in the a1 and b1 arrays. The pmaxsw command is in bold. The source code of the application is shown in Listing 10.21.

Listing 10.21. The use of the pmasw MMX command that compares elements of an integer array in pairs

```cpp
// MAX_FROM_PAIR_ARRAYS.cpp : Defines the entry point for the console
// application

#include "stdafx.h"

int _tmain(int argc, _TCHAR* argv[])
{
 int a1[4] = {9, 1, 34, 1};
 int b1[4] = {7, 5, 79, 3};
 int c1[4];
 printf(" a1: ");
 for (int cnt = 0; cnt < 4; cnt++)
   printf("%d\t", a1[cnt]);
 printf("\n b1: ");
 for (int cnt = 0; cnt < 4; cnt++)
   printf("%d\t", b1[cnt]);
 _asm {
       movq     mm0, QWORD PTR a1
       movq     mm1, QWORD PTR a1+8
       packssdw mm0, mm1

       movq     mm1, QWORD PTR b1
       movq     mm2, QWORD PTR b1+8
       packssdw mm1, mm2

       pmaxsw   mm0, mm1
       lea      ESI, c1

       pextrw   EDI, mm0, 0
       mov      DWORD PTR [ESI], EDI
       add      ESI, 4

       pextrw   EDI, mm0, 1
       mov      DWORD PTR [ESI], EDI
       add      ESI, 4

       pextrw   EDI, mm0, 2
```

```
        mov        DWORD PTR [ESI], EDI
        add        ESI, 4

        pextrw     EDI, mm0, 3
        mov        DWORD PTR [ESI], EDI
        add        ESI, 4

        emms
    };
printf("\n\n            c1: \n");
for (int cnt = 0; cnt < 4; cnt++)
    printf(" max of a1[%d] and b1[%d] = %d\n", cnt, cnt, c1[cnt]);
getchar();
return 0;
};
```

The pmaxsw command uses the mm0 and mm1 MMX registers as operands and stores the result in the mm0 register. The rest of the source code was discussed in the previous example. To find the minimum of two array elements, substitute the pmaxsw mm0, mm1 command with pminsw mm0, mm1. You can do this as an exercise.

The window of the application is shown in Fig. 10.12.

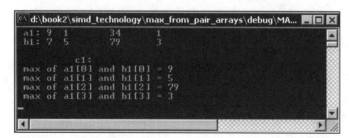

Fig. 10.12. Window of an application that demonstrates a search
for maximum elements with the MMX extension inline assembler

Another group of commands widely used in applications includes MMX logical commands. These commands implement logical operations such as AND (pand), AND-NOT (pandn), OR (por), and XOR (pxor). A distinct feature of these commands is that they perform logical operations on 64-bit values. These commands were described in *Chapter 1*. Now, we will focus on an example that uses the pxor command. With this command, you can implement an algorithm for comparing two character strings. A similar algorithm implemented with the pcmpeqb command was considered earlier, and this example uses pxor.

The source code of this console application is shown in Listing 10.22.

Listing 10.22. Comparing strings with the pxor MMX extension command

```
// COMPARE_STR_WITH_PXOR.cpp : Defines the entry point for the console
// application

#include "stdafx.h"

int _tmain(int argc, _TCHAR* argv[])
{
char s1[32];
char s2[32];
char ires[32];
printf("Comparison of strings with PXOR instruction\n\n");
while(true)
  {
   memset(s1, '\0', 16);
   memset(s2, '\0', 16);
   memset(ires, '\0', 16);

   printf("\nEnter string s1: ");
   scanf("%s", s1);
   printf("\nEnter string s2: ");
   scanf("%s", s2);

  _asm {
        movq      mm0, QWORD PTR s1
        movq      mm1, QWORD PTR s2
        pxor      mm0, mm1
        movq      QWORD PTR ires, mm0
        emms
       };
   for (int cnt = 0; cnt < 8; cnt++)
    {
     if (ires[cnt] != 0)
        {
         printf("\nString s1 not equal s2!", c1);
         break;
        }
```

```
    };
   if (cnt == 8) printf("\nString s1 = s2!", c1);
   };
  return 0;
 }
```

A distinct feature of the pxor command is that if the operands are equal, the result is zero. This feature is used when comparing two strings. The window of the application that compares two strings using this method is shown in Fig. 10.13.

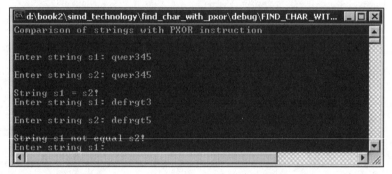

Fig. 10.13. Window of an application that compares character strings
with the pxor command

The next group of MMX extension commands we will demonstrate includes multiplication commands. The algorithm they use is different from that of common integer multiplication commands. The size of the result obtained with common multiplication commands is usually twice as large as the size of the operands. The MMX multiplication commands use another multiplication algorithm.

Multiplication is done simultaneously on four 16-bit signed operands. Integer operands can be multiplied with either the pmulhw and pmullw commands or the pmaddwd command. Here, we will demonstrate multiplication of two integers with the pmaddwd command. You can try to develop a version with the pmulhw/pmullw commands on your own.

First, develop a console application that multiplies two integers and displays the result using C++ .NET intrinsics. The source code of this application is shown in Listing 10.23.

Listing 10.23. Multiplying two integers with MMX extension intrinsics

```
// MUL_2_INTS_INTR.cpp : Defines the entry point for the console
// application

#include "stdafx.h"
```

```
#include <mmintrin.h>

int _tmain(int argc, _TCHAR* argv[])
{
 int i1, i2;
 int ires;
 __m64 mi1, mi2, mires;

 printf("MULTIPLICATION OF 2 INTS WITH INTRINSICS (MMX_EXT.)\n\n");
 while (true)
  {
   printf("\nEnter i1: ");
   scanf("%d", &i1);
   printf("Enter i2: ");
   scanf("%d", &i2);

   mi1 = _mm_cvtsi32_si64 (i1);
   mi2 = _mm_cvtsi32_si64 (i2);
   mi1 = _mm_packs_pi32 (mi1, mi1);
   mi2 = _mm_packs_pi32 (mi2, mi2);
   mires = _mm_madd_pi16 (mi1, mi2);
   ires = _mm_cvtsi64_si32 (mires);

   printf("\ni1 * i2 = %d\n", ires);
 }
return 0;
}
```

In this example, the functions _mm_cvtsi32_si64 (i1) and _mm_cvtsi32_si64 (i2) convert 32-bit integers i1 and i2 to the format of 64-bit packed variables mi1 and mi2. The i1 and i2 variables are put to 32 low-order bits of mi1 and mi2, and 32 high-order bits are padded with zeroes. The statements

```
   mi1 = _mm_packs_pi32 (mi1, mi1);
   mi2 = _mm_packs_pi32 (mi2, mi2);
```

pack four double words to four words. The source and destination in each of these functions is the same (mi1 in the first case and mi2 in the second). These functions are required to multiply the numbers with the statement:

```
   mires = _mm_madd_pi16 (mi1, mi2)
```

Finally, the statement

```
ires = _mm_cvtsi64_si32 (mires)
```

puts the product from `mires` to `ires`.

The window of the application is shown in Fig. 10.14.

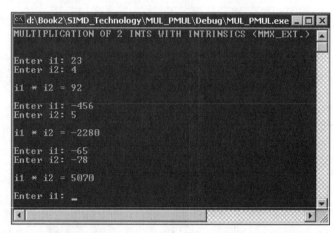

Fig. 10.14. Window of an application that demonstrates multiplication of integers with C++ .NET intrinsics

Another variant of this program that uses the inline assembler requires fewer commands. Its source code is shown in Listing 10.24.

Listing 10.24. Multiplying two integers with the MMX extension assembly commands

```cpp
// INT__MUL_ASM.cpp : Defines the entry point for the console
// application

#include "stdafx.h"

int _tmain(int argc, _TCHAR* argv[])
{
 int i1, i2;
 int ires;
 printf("MULTIPLICATION OF 2 INTS WITH ASM (MMX-EXT.)\n\n");
 while (true)
  {
   printf("\nEnter i1: ");
   scanf("%d", &i1);
```

```
    printf("Enter i2: ");
    scanf("%d", &i2);
    _asm {
            pxor        mm0, mm0
            movd        mm0, DWORD PTR i1
            packssdw    mm0, mm0
            pxor        mm1, mm1
            movd        mm1, DWORD PTR i2
            packssdw    mm1, mm1


            pmaddwd     mm0, mm1
            movd        DWORD PTR ires, mm0
            emms
        };
  printf("\ni1 * i2 = %d\n", ires);
    }
return 0;
}
```

It is easy to understand the assembly block code if you remember that movd is an assembly analog for the _mm_cvtsi32_si64 function, and packssdw and pmaddwd correspond to _mm_packs_pi32 and _mm_madd_pi16, respectively.

The window of the application is shown in Fig. 10.15.

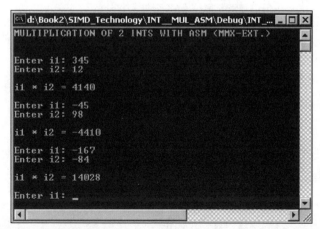

Fig. 10.15. Window of an application that multiplies integers
with the MMX extension assembly commands

The next example is a program that computes the absolute value of an integer with a few MMX operations. Here, the commands movd, pxor, and pmaxsw are used; they are already familiar to you. The result is stored in the EDI register with the pextrw command:

```
pextrw EDI, mm1, 0
```

The last operand, which is equal to zero, extracts the low order word from the mm1 register and writes it to the low order word of the EDI register. The high order word of the EDI register is zeroed.

The source code of the application is shown in Listing 10.25.

Listing 10.25. Finding the absolute value of an integer with the MMX extension assembly commands

```
// ABS_INT.cpp : Defines the entry point for the console application

#include "stdafx.h"

int _tmain(int argc, _TCHAR* argv[])
{
 int i1, modi1;
 printf(" Calculating the modulus of integer\n\n");
 while (true)
  {
   printf("\nEnter i1: ");
   scanf("%d", &i1);
   _asm {
         movd    mm0, DWORD PTR i1
         pxor    mm1, mm1
         psubw   mm1, mm0
         pmaxsw  mm1, mm0
         pextrw  EDI, mm1, 0
         mov     DWORD PTR modi1, EDI
         emms
      };
     printf("Modulus of i1 = %d\n", modi1);
      };
      return 0;
}
```

The algorithm for finding the absolute value is straightforward. The window of the application that finds the absolute value of an integer is shown in Fig. 10.16.

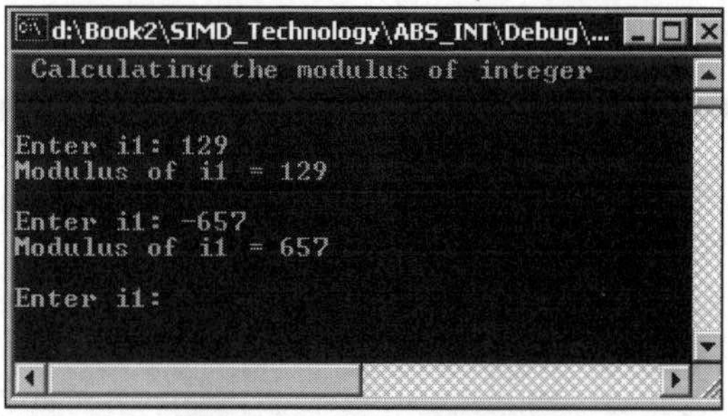

Fig. 10.16. Window of an application that finds the absolute value of an integer

These examples do not address all of the possibilities of optimizing applications with MMX extension assembly functions; however, they will be a helpful resource as you write much more complex and effective programs.

SSE Extension and Programming It in the Inline Assembler

This section discusses issues of using the inline assembler to optimize applications that use floating-point operations of SSE extension of Pentium. SSE extension includes eight additional 128-bit registers denoted as xmm0, ..., xmm7. Data in the SSE format are a sequence of four 32-bit packed numbers. For programming SSE extension, the processor's command set is extended with a number of commands.

Here, we will concentrate only on key aspects of programming the SSE extension. For a more detailed description of SSE architecture and programming these instructions in the assembler, refer to Intel's documentation.

Before you start programming SSE extension, check whether the processor and operating system support this extension. This can be easily detected with the following simple console application (Listing 10.26).

Listing 10.26. Checking the processor for the SSE extension support

---

```
// TEST_SSE_BY_PROC.cpp : Defines the entry point for the console
// application

#include "stdafx.h"

int _tmain(int argc, _TCHAR* argv[])
{
```

```
bool supSSE = true;
_asm {
      mov  EAX, 1
      cpuid
      test EDX, 0x2000000
      jnz  found
      mov  supSSE, 0
   found:
      };
  if (supSSE)printf("SSE supported by CPU!\n");
  else printf("SSE not supported by CPU!\n");
  getchar();
  return 0;
}
```

The source code of this program is almost identical to the code that checks for the MMX extension support, except that bit 25 of the EDX register is checked here.

You can check the operating system for the SSE support by running an application whose source code is shown in Listing 10.27.

Listing 10.27. Checking the operating system for the SSE extension support

```
// CHECK_SSE_SUPPORT_BY_OS.cpp : Defines the entry point for the console
// application

#include "stdafx.h"
#include <excpt.h>
#include <windows.h>

bool _tmain(int argc, _TCHAR* argv[])
{
  __try {
       _asm xorps xmm0, xmm0
       }
  __except (EXCEPTION_EXECUTE_HANDLER)
     {
     if (GetExceptionCode() == STATUS_ILLEGAL_INSTRUCTION)
      {
        printf("SSE not supported by OS!\n");
        getchar();
        return (false);
```

```
    }
  }
printf("SSE supported by OS!\n");
getchar();
return (true);
}
```

In C++ .NET, support for both SSE and MMX extension is provided with intrinsics. Like in MMX extension, each of the intrinsics that works with floating-point numbers is a pseudo code of an assembly equivalent. For example, the function

```
__m128 _mm_add_ss(__m128 a, __m128 b )
```

is an analog of the addss assembly command. Floating-point operands are represented in C++ .NET as __m128. For a more detailed description of SSE extension intrinsics, refer to the C++ .NET 2003 online help. Now we will discuss practical programming SSE extension with the inline assembler. SSE extension assembly commands can be divided into a few groups:

❑ Store commands
❑ Arithmetic commands
❑ Comparison commands
❑ Conversion commands
❑ Logical commands

There is a number of additional commands. Arithmetic commands, comparison commands, and conversion commands can be performed on either four packed double words simultaneously (parallel operations) or 32-bit numbers (scalar operations). The scalar operations process only the low order 32-bit words.

We will look at an example of scalar addition of two floating-point numbers. The source code of the application is shown in Listing 10.28.

Listing 10.28. Scalar addition of two floating-point numbers

```
// SSE_ADD_2_SCALAR.cpp : Defines the entry point for the console
// application

#include "stdafx.h"

int _tmain(int argc, _TCHAR* argv[])
{
```

```
float a1, b1, c1;
printf(" EXAMPLE OF SCALAR SUMMA IN SSE-EXT.ASM.OPERATIONS\n");
printf("\nEnter float a1: ");
scanf("%f", &a1);
printf("Enter float b1: ");
scanf("%f", &b1);
_asm {
        lea     EAX, a1
        lea     EDI, b1
        lea     EDX, c1
        movss   xmm0, DWORD PTR [EAX]
        addss   xmm0, DWORD PTR [EDI]
        movss   DWORD PTR [EDX], xmm0
    };
printf ("c1 = a1+b1 = %.3f\n", c1);
getchar();
return 0;
}
```

After the a1 and b1 floating-point numbers are entered, the assembly block adds these up as ordinary 32-bit values. The addresses of the a1 and b1 elements and the address of their sum c1 are put to the registers EAX, EDI, and EDX, respectively. Then the commands

```
movss   xmm0, DWORD PTR [EAX]
addss   xmm0, DWORD PTR [EDI]
movss   DWORD PTR [EDX], xmm0
```

add up the numbers and store the result in the c1 variable. All scalar commands have a suffix s while parallel commands have a suffix p. The window of the application is shown in Fig. 10.17.

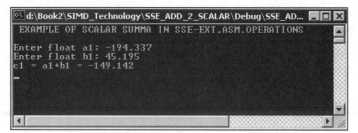

Fig. 10.17. Window of an application that performs scalar addition of two floating-point numbers with the SSE extension assembler

Adding operands in parallel significantly improves the performance of an application. Operations of this type are very convenient when processing floating-point arrays. Now, we will complicate the previous example by taking two floating-point arrays as a1 and b1 and an array containing their sum as c1. The source code of such an application is shown in Listing 10.29.

Listing 10.29. Adding elements of two arrays in parallel

```cpp
// SSE_ADD_2_FLOATS.cpp : Defines the entry point for the console
// application

#include "stdafx.h"

int _tmain(int argc, _TCHAR* argv[])
{
  float a1[4] = {34.5, -12.44, 7.53, -7.4};
  float b1[4] = {3.54, 1.23, -3.56, 7.55};
  float c1[4];

  printf("        SUMMA 2 ARRAYS in parallel\n");

  printf("\n a1: ");
  for (int cnt = 0; cnt < 4; cnt++)
  printf("%.2f\t", a1[cnt]);
  printf("\n b1: ");
  for (int cnt = 0; cnt < 4; cnt++)
      printf("%.2f\t", b1[cnt]);
_asm {
     lea     EAX, a1
     lea     EDI, b1
     lea     ECX, c1
     movups xmm0, XMMWORD PTR [EAX]
     addps  xmm0, XMMWORD PTR [EDI]
     movups  XMMWORD PTR [ECX], xmm0
    };
printf("\n\n c1: ");
for (int cnt = 0; cnt < 4; cnt++)
    printf("%.2f\t", c1[cnt]);
getchar();
return 0;
}
```

You might have noticed that the commands in the assembly block have a suffix p. In addition, the XMMWORD keyword is used to denote a 128-bit variable. The window of the application is shown in Fig. 10.18.

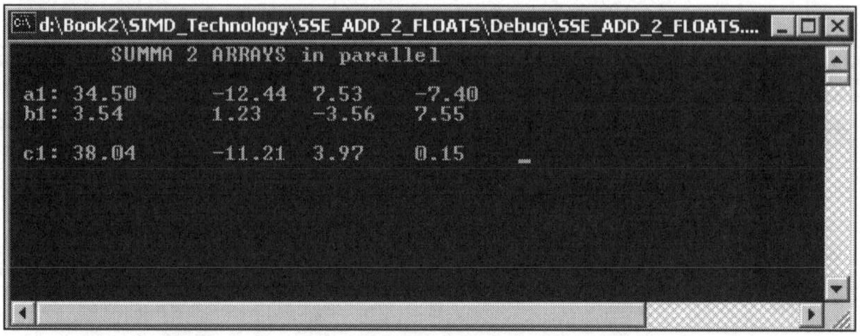

```
d:\Book2\SIMD_Technology\SSE_ADD_2_FLOATS\Debug\SSE_ADD_2_FLOATS....
        SUMMA 2 ARRAYS in parallel

a1: 34.50       -12.44  7.53     -7.40
b1: 3.54        1.23    -3.56    7.55

c1: 38.04       -11.21  3.97     0.15
```

Fig. 10.18. Window of an application that adds four floating-point numbers in parallel with the SSE extension assembler

The subps command that subtracts two 128-bit operands in parallel is useful when subtracting the elements of floating-point arrays. The next example illustrates the use of the subtraction command, as well as a few other important things related to SSE extension. Consider the source code of an application (Listing 10.30) that uses arrays of four floating-point numbers. The number of elements is chosen little for simplicity's sake.

Listing 10.30. Subtracting the elements of floating-point arrays with the subps command

```cpp
// SSE_COMBO_SUB_2.cpp : Defines the entry point for the console
// application

#include "stdafx.h"
#include <xmmintrin.h>

int _tmain(int argc, _TCHAR* argv[])
{
  __declspec (align(16)) float a1[4];
  __declspec (align(16)) float b1[4];
  __declspec (align(16)) float c1[4];

  __m128 ma1 = {12.5, 32.7, -4.8, 6};
  __m128 mb1 = {3.45, 12.67, -5.88, -23.1};
  __m128 mc1;
```

```
printf("   PARALLEL SUBSTRACTION OF  2 ALIGNED ARRAYS \n");
_asm {
        lea    EAX, a1
        lea    EDX, b1
        lea    ECX, c1

        movaps xmm0, ma1
        movaps XMMWORD PTR [EAX], xmm0
        movaps xmm1, mb1
        movaps XMMWORD PTR [EDX], xmm1

        subps  xmm0, xmm1
        movaps mc1, xmm0
        movaps XMMWORD PTR [ECX], xmm0
        };
printf("\n a1: ");
for (int cnt = 0; cnt < 4; cnt++)
    printf("%.2f\t", a1[cnt]);
printf("\n b1: ");
for (int cnt = 0; cnt < 4; cnt++)
    printf("%.2f\t", b1[cnt]);
printf("\n\n c1: ");
for (int cnt = 0; cnt < 4; cnt++)
    printf("%.2f\t", c1[cnt]);
getchar();
return 0;
};
```

A distinct feature of this example is that it demonstrates operations on variables aligned on 16-byte boundary. For this purpose, the floating-point arrays a1, b1, and c1 are declared with the align keyword:

```
__declspec (align(16)) float a1[8];
 __declspec (align(16)) float b1[8];
 __declspec (align(16)) float c1[8];
```

Data alignment can increase the performance of an application significantly. Development of applications that use advanced assembly commands of the latest processor generations requires that the data are aligned on 16-byte boundary. Also, alignment of frequently used data on the string length in the cache is a very effective technique for increasing application performance. For example, if a structure whose size is less than 32 bytes is declared in a program, it should be aligned on 32-byte boundary for effective caching.

In this program, we use variables of both `float` and `_m128` types, so that you gain a better understanding of the interrelation between the classic types of variables such as `float` and 128-bit variables in the SSE extension. Like SSE extension intrinsics, variables of the `_m128` type are declared in the `xmmintrin.h` header file, so it is included in the project.

To move aligned data, the application uses the `movaps` command. To work with unaligned data, you can use the `movups` command instead of `movaps`. Such a substitution will not cause errors, but the performance of the application will be lower, and it will be pointless to use the `align` keyword.

The window of the application is shown in Fig. 10.19.

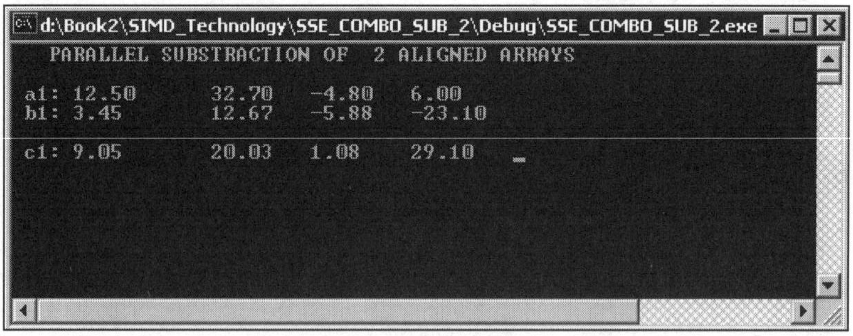

Fig. 10.19. Window of an application that demonstrates subtraction of floating-point array elements aligned on 16-byte boundary with the SSE extension assembler

This example can be modified so that no variables of the `_m128` are used. In this case, the `xmmintrin.h` header file and a few assembly commands can be removed. The source code of the application will appear as shown in Listing 10.31.

Listing 10.31. A modified version of the application that subtracts the elements of arrays

```
// SSE_COMBO_SUB_2_MOD.cpp : Defines the entry point for the console
// application

#include "stdafx.h"

int _tmain(int argc, _TCHAR* argv[])
{
    __declspec(align(16)) float a1[4] = {34.5, -12.44, 7.53, -7.4};
```

```
    __declspec(align(16)) float b1[4] = {3.54, 1.23, -3.56, 7.55};
    __declspec(align(16)) float c1[4];
    printf(" PARALLEL SUBSTRACTION OF  2 ALIGNED ARRAYS WITH ASM INSTRUCTIONS
ONLY\n");
    _asm {
            movaps xmm0, XMMWORD PTR a1
            subps  xmm0, XMMWORD PTR b1
            movaps XMMWORD PTR c1, xmm0
            };
printf("\n a1: ");
for (int cnt = 0; cnt < 4; cnt++)
        printf("%.2f\t", a1[cnt]);
printf("\n b1: ");
for (int cnt = 0; cnt < 4; cnt++)
        printf("%.2f\t", b1[cnt]);
printf("\n\n c1: ");
for (int cnt = 0; cnt < 4; cnt++)
        printf("%.2f\t", c1[cnt]);
getchar();
return 0;
};
```

The window of the application is shown in Fig. 10.20.

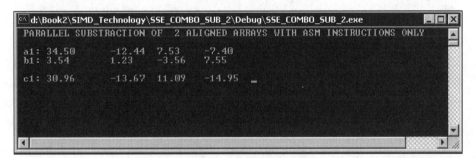

Fig. 10.20. Window of the modified application that demonstrates parallel subtraction of array elements

For multiplication and division operations on 128-bit data, you can use the following SSE extension assembly commands:

❏ `mulps` — parallel multiplication of 128-bit operands. The result is put into one of the registers `xmm0`, ..., `xmm7`.

❑ divps — parallel division of 128-bit operands. The result is put into one of the registers xmm0, ..., xmm7.

❑ mulss — scalar multiplication of the low order double words of two operands. The result (a 32-bit value) is put into one of the registers xmm0, ..., xmm7. One of the operands can be a 32-bit memory variable.

❑ divss — scalar division of 32-bit operands. The syntax of this command is the same as mulss.

Below is the source code of an application that demonstrates parallel multiplication and division (Listing 10.32).

Listing 10.32. Parallel multiplication and division of SSE data

```
// SSE_MUL_DIV_ALIGN_2_ARRAYS.cpp : Defines the entry point for the
// console application

#include "stdafx.h"

int _tmain(int argc, _TCHAR* argv[])
{
  __declspec(align(16)) float a1[4] = {34.5, -12.44, 7.53, -7.4};
  __declspec(align(16)) float b1[4] = {3.54, 1.23, -3.56, 7.55};
  __declspec(align(16)) float c1[4] = {1.5, 2.5, 3.5, 4.5};
  __declspec(align(16)) float d1[4];
printf(" PAR. MUL/DIV OF  2 ALIGNED ARRAYS WITH ASM INSTRUCTIONS ONLY\n");
_asm {
        movaps xmm0, XMMWORD PTR a1
        mulps  xmm0, XMMWORD PTR b1
        divps  xmm0, XMMWORD PTR c1
        movaps XMMWORD PTR d1, xmm0
      };
printf("\n a1: ");
for (int cnt = 0; cnt < 4; cnt++)
    printf("%.2f\t", a1[cnt]);
printf("\n b1: ");
for (int cnt = 0; cnt < 4; cnt++)
    printf("%.2f\t", b1[cnt]);
printf("\n c1: ");
for (int cnt = 0; cnt < 4; cnt++)
    printf("%.2f\t", c1[cnt]);
```

```
printf("\n\n d1: ");
for (int cnt = 0; cnt < 4; cnt++)
    printf("%.2f\t", d1[cnt]);
getchar();
return 0;
};
```

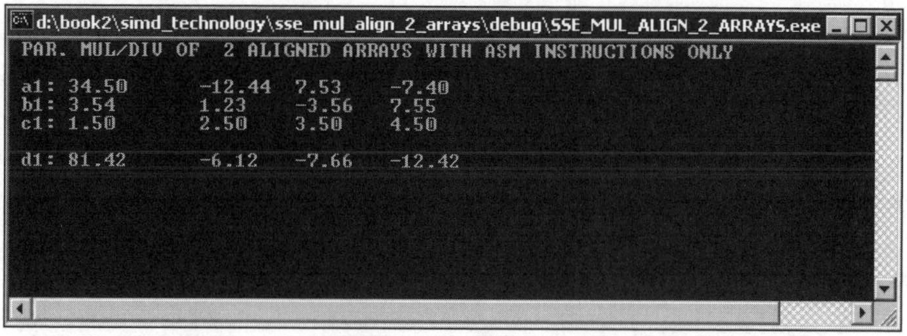

Fig. 10.21. Window of an application that demonstrates parallel multiplication and division of the elements of floating-point arrays with the SSE extension assembler

This listing is straightforward. The window of the application is shown in Fig. 10.21.

Multiplication and division of scalar values is demonstrated in the next example (Listing 10.33).

Listing 10.33. Scalar multiplication and division with SSE extension assembly commands

```
// SCALAR_SSE_MUL_DIV_WITH_ASM.cpp : Defines the entry point for the
// console application

#include "stdafx.h"

int _tmain(int argc, _TCHAR* argv[])
{
float a1[4] = {4.98, 1.44, 3.16, -0.42};
float b1[4] = {-3.54, 1.23, -9.56, 5.09};
float c1[4] = {1.5, 2.5, 3.5, 4.5};
float d1[4];

printf(" SCALAR MUL/DIV OF  2 ARRAYS WITH ASM \n");
```

```
int    asize = sizeof(a1)/4;
_asm {
       lea    EAX, a1
       lea    EDX, b1
       lea    ESI, c1
       lea    EDI, d1

       mov    ECX, asize
       sub    EAX, 4
       sub    EDX, 4
       sub    ESI, 4
       sub    EDI, 4
next_4:
       add    EAX, 4
       add    EDX, 4
       add    ESI, 4
       add    EDI, 4
       movss  xmm0, DWORD PTR [EAX]
       mulss  xmm0, DWORD PTR [EDX]
       divss  xmm0, DWORD PTR [ESI]
       movss  DWORD PTR [EDI], xmm0
       loop   next_4
       };
printf("\n a1: ");
for (int cnt = 0; cnt < 4; cnt++)
     printf("%.2f\t", a1[cnt]);
printf("\n b1: ");
for (int cnt = 0; cnt < 4; cnt++)
     printf("%.2f\t", b1[cnt]);
printf("\n c1: ");
for (int cnt = 0; cnt < 4; cnt++)
     printf("%.2f\t", c1[cnt]);
printf("\n\n d1: ");
for (int cnt = 0; cnt < 4; cnt++)
     printf("%.2f\t", d1[cnt]);
getchar();
return 0;
};
```

Since we deal with 32-bit values, the registers EAX, EDX, ESI, and EDI are used to access them. The addresses of the arrays are loaded to these registers. The ECX register is used as an array element counter. To access the next elements of the arrays, the values in the registers EAX, EDX, ESI, and EDI are increased by four after each iteration.

For multiplication and division, the mulss and divss SSE commands are used.

The window of the application is shown in Fig. 10.22.

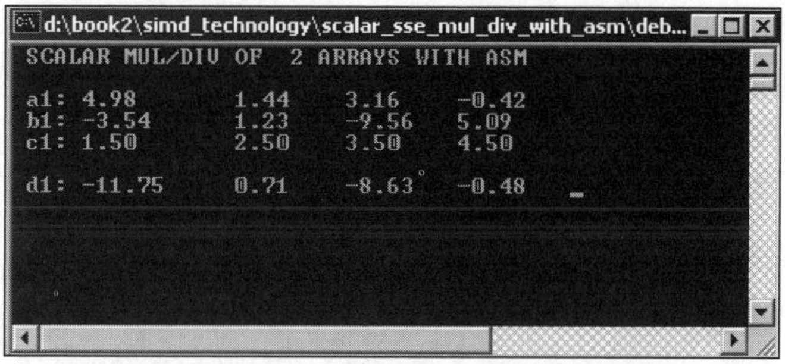

Fig. 10.22. Window of an application that demonstrates scalar multiplication and division of the elements of floating-point arrays

The next group of assembly commands we will describe includes comparison commands. It is best to illustrate their work with examples.

For the first example, we will consider one method of comparing two packed 128-bit values for equality. The result of such an operation is a 128-bit floating-point mask. If all the bits of the mask are equal to 1, two 128-bit numbers are equal.

In this example, this method is used for checking the elements of floating-point arrays for equality. For simplicity's sake, let the size of the arrays be equal to four. To make it easier to understand the algorithm, consider a variant that uses C++ .NET 2003 SSE intrinsics first. The source code of the console application is shown in Listing 10.34.

Listing 10.34. Using SSE extension intrinsics to compare array elements

---

```
// SSE_CMPEQPS_INTR_EXAMPLE.cpp : Defines the entry point for the console
// application

#include "stdafx.h"
#include <xmmintrin.h>

int _tmain(int argc, _TCHAR* argv[])
{
    __m128 a1 = {12.4, 19.1, -4.68, 3.12};
```

```
  __m128 a2 = {12.4, 19.1, -4.68, 3.12};
  __m128 ares;
 float res[4];

ares = _mm_cmpeq_ps(a1, a2);
_mm_storeu_ps(res, ares);

printf("Result of comparison 2 packed elements\n\n");
for (int cnt = 0; cnt < 4; cnt++)
    printf("res[%d] = %f\n", cnt, res[cnt]);
for (int cnt = 0; cnt < 4; cnt++)
   {
    if (res[cnt] == 0)
    {

       printf("\nSSE-operands are not equals!\n");
       getchar();
       return 0;

    }

 }
printf("\nSSE-operands are equals!\n");
getchar();
return 0;
};
```

Here, we will analyze the source code. As always, if an application uses intrinsics and variables of the __m128 type, the xmmintrin.h header file should be included (the corresponding line is in bold).

The a1 and a2 variables of the __m128 type are assigned four floating-point values each. In fact, the elements in braces make up a floating-point array. It is not declared explicitly, but it is very convenient to manipulate with such a "virtual" array using 128-bit variables. Such manipulations are valid in C++ .NET.

A pairwise comparison of the arrays a1 and a2 is implemented with the following functions:

```
ares = _mm_cmpeq_ps(a1, a2)
_mm_storeu_ps(res, ares)
```

The result of comparison is written to the res array. For the given values of a1 and a2, the comparison operation returns their equality, as is seen in Fig. 10.23.

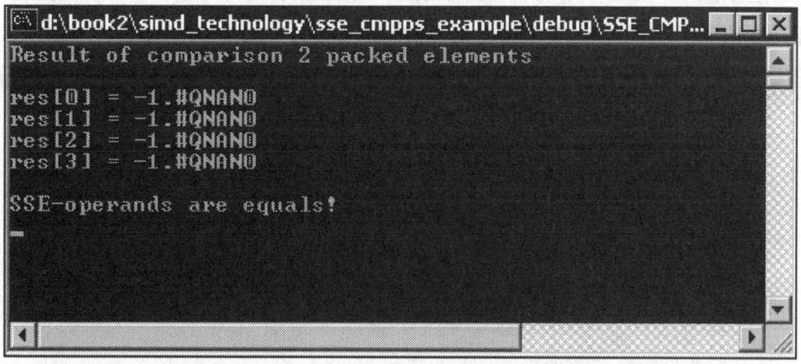

Fig. 10.23. Result of comparing array elements with the application
in Listing 10.34 that uses intrinsics

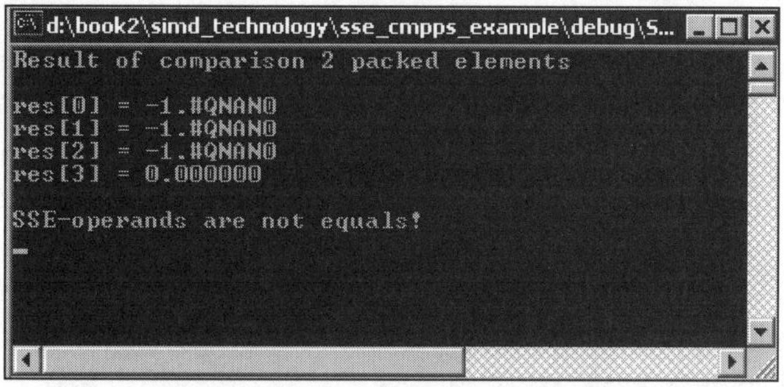

Fig. 10.24. Result of comparison of arrays when
the third elements are unequal

You can tell from Fig. 10.23 that all elements of the res array took the value of –1, which corresponds to one in all bits. In this case, this means the arrays a1 and a2 are equal.

If you change the source data, for example, give the third element of the a1 array a value of 3.13 instead of 3.12, the result of comparison will change. This is shown in Fig. 10.24.

Since the third elements of the arrays are unequal, the third element of the res array is zero, which means a1 and a2 are unequal.

Like with the MMX extension, using intrinsics for programming SSE leads to code redundancy. For example, the statements

```
ares = _mm_cmpeq_ps(a1, a2)
 _mm_storeu_ps(res, ares)
```

from Listing 10.34 appear as shown in Listing 10.35 when disassembled.

Listing 10.35. The disassembled code of SSE extension intrinsics

---

```
        ares = _mm_cmpeq_ps(a1, a2);

00411C78  movaps      xmm0, xmmword ptr [a2]
00411C7C  movaps      xmm1, xmmword ptr [a1]
00411C80  cmpeqps     xmm1, xmm0
00411C84  movaps      xmmword ptr [ebp-150h], xmm1
00411C8B  movaps      xmm0, xmmword ptr [ebp-150h]
00411C92  movaps      xmmword ptr [ares], xmm0

        _mm_storeu_ps(res, ares);

00411C96  movaps      xmm0, xmmword ptr [ares]
00411C9A  lea         eax, [res]
00411C9D  movups      xmmword ptr [eax], xmm0
```

The code is redundant because developers at Microsoft wanted to avoid manipulations with the registers xmm0, ..., xmm7 in C++ .NET programs and to store the result in a 128-bit memory variable. The commands

```
00411C84  movaps      xmmword ptr [ebp-150h], xmm1
00411C8B  movaps      xmm0, xmmword ptr [ebp-150h]
```

can be advantageously replaced with

```
movaps xmm0, xmm1
```

The command

```
00411C80  cmpeqps     xmm1, xmm0
```

can be replaced with a command whose one operand is in the memory.

Modify this example so that the inline assembler can be used. The source code of the application is shown in Listing 10.36.

**Listing 10.36. A modified version of the application that compares
array elements with SSE extension assembly commands**

```
// SSE_CMPEQPS_ASM_EXAMPLE.cpp : Defines the entry point for the console
// application

#include "stdafx.h"

int _tmain(int argc, _TCHAR* argv[])
```

```
{
  float a1[4] = {12.4, 19.17, -4.68, 3.12};
  float a2[4] = {12.4, 19.1, -4.68, 3.12};
  float res[4];

  printf("Comparison 2 packed elements with SSE assembler\n\n");
  printf("a1: ");
  for (int cnt = 0; cnt < 4; cnt++)
      printf("%.2f\t", a1[cnt]);
  printf("\na2: ");
  for (int cnt = 0; cnt < 4; cnt++)
      printf("%.2f\t", a2[cnt]);

  _asm {
        movups  xmm0, XMMWORD PTR a1
        cmpeqps xmm0, XMMWORD PTR a2
        movups  XMMWORD PTR res, xmm0
       };

  printf("\nResult of comparison:\n\n");
  for (int cnt = 0; cnt < 4; cnt++)
      printf("res[%d] = %f\n", cnt, res[cnt]);
  for (int cnt = 0; cnt < 4; cnt++)
    {
      if (res[cnt] == 0)
        {
          printf("\nSSE-operands are not equals!\n");
          getchar();
          return 0;
        }

        }
printf("\nSSE-operands are equals!\n");
getchar();
return 0;
};
```

Comparison is done in the assembly block and requires only three assembly commands! We also changed the type of the variables a1, a2, and ares from __m128 to float to illustrate the use of floating-point numbers in the SSE extension. Comparison of 128-bit values is done with the cmpeqps command. It compares four 32-bit packed numbers in pairs and sets the bits in corresponding positions of a 128-bit result mask if the numbers are equal. Otherwise, the corresponding bits are reset to zeroes.

The window of the application is shown in Fig. 10.25.

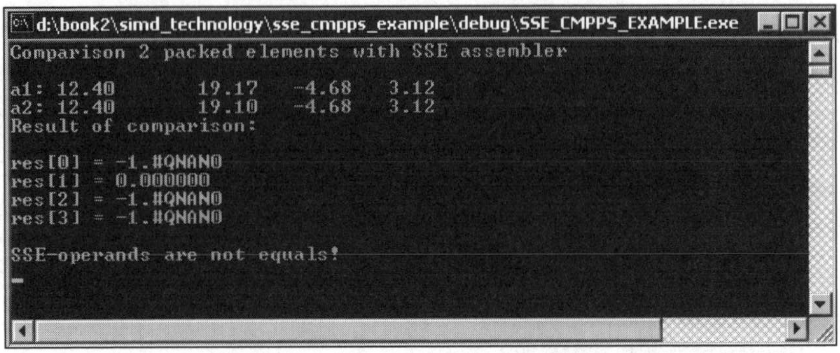

Fig. 10.25. Window of an application that compares floating-point arrays with the cmpeqps SSE command

In addition to checking numbers for equality, it is often required to compare the values of two numbers. The next example demonstrates how the elements of two floating-point arrays can be compared according to the "greater than"/"less than" principle with the cmpleps SSE command. The source code of the C++ .NET console application is shown in Listing 10.37.

Listing 10.37. Comparing two floating-point arrays for "greater than"/"less than"

```
// SSE_CMPLEPS_ASM.cpp : Defines the entry point for the console
// application

#include "stdafx.h"

int _tmain(int argc, _TCHAR* argv[])
{
 float a1[4] = {3.4, 9.17, -4.39, 3.12};
 float a2[4] = {12.7, 19.1, -4.68, 3.52};
 float res[4];

 printf("LT-EQ comparison 2 packed elements with SSE-ext. assembler\n\n");
 printf("a1: ");
 for (int cnt = 0; cnt < 4; cnt++)
       printf("%.2f\t", a1[cnt]);
 printf("\na2: ");
 for (int cnt = 0; cnt < 4; cnt++)
```

```
        printf("%.2f\t", a2[cnt]);

_asm {
        movups   xmm0, XMMWORD PTR a1
        cmpleps  xmm0, XMMWORD PTR a2
        movups  XMMWORD PTR res, xmm0
        };

printf("\n\nResult of comparison:\n\n");
for (int cnt = 0; cnt < 4; cnt++)
  {
    if (res[cnt] != 0)
        printf("\na1[%d] <= a2[%d], mask = %.2f\n", cnt, cnt, res[cnt]);
    else
        printf("\na1[%d] > a2[%d], mask = %.2f\n", cnt, cnt, res[cnt]);
  }
getchar();
return 0;
};
```

Like in the previous example, comparing array elements is a matter of comparing two 128-bit numbers. One of four 32-bit masks sets or resets the bits depending on the result of comparing pairs of 32-bit packed numbers located at the corresponding positions in the source and target arrays. For example, if one of the 32-bit elements of the a1 array is less than or equal to the number at the corresponding position in the 128-bit variable that represents the a2 array, ones are written to the corresponding bits of the result mask. Otherwise, i.e., if the element of a1 is greater than that of a2, zeroes are written to the corresponding positions.

The window of the application is shown in Fig. 10.26.

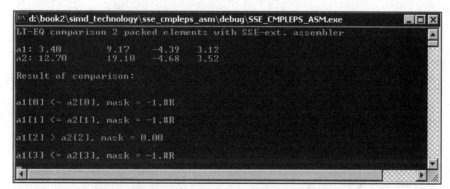

Fig. 10.26. Window of an application that compares two floating-point arrays for "greater than"/"less than" with SSE extension assembly commands

The examples above demonstrate parallel comparison of packed elements. There are a few more SSE extension assembly commands that perform scalar comparison of pairs of the low-order double words. The result is defined by setting the corresponding bits in the flag register. One of these commands is comiss.

The next example demonstrates the use of this command for pairwise comparison of the elements of two floating-point arrays. The source code of the application is shown in Listing 10.38.

Listing 10.38. Comparing floating-point arrays with the comiss command

```
// SSE_COMISS_ASM.cpp : Defines the entry point for the console
// application

#include "stdafx.h"

int _tmain(int argc, _TCHAR* argv[])
{
 float a1[4] = {12.7, 19.17, -4.68, 3.52};
 float a2[4] = {12.7, 19.17, -4.68, 3.52};
 bool cres = true;

printf("EQ comparison 2 arrays with COMISS \n\n");
printf("a1: ");
for (int cnt = 0; cnt < 4; cnt++)
        printf("%.2f\t", a1[cnt]);
printf("\na2: ");
for (int cnt = 0; cnt < 4; cnt++)
        printf("%.2f\t", a2[cnt]);

_asm {
        lea     EAX, a1
        lea     EDX, a2
        mov     EBX, 0
        mov     ECX, 4
next:
        movss   xmm0, DWORD PTR [EAX]
        comiss  xmm0, DWORD PTR [EDX]

        jne     no_eq
        add     EAX, 4
        add     EDX, 4
        loop    next
        mov     EBX, 1
```

```
no_eq:
      mov        DWORD PTR cres, EBX
      }
if (cres)printf("\nEquals!\n");
else
  printf("\nUnequals!\n");

getchar();
return 0;
}
```

Comparison is done in the assembly block. To perform the operations in a loop, the pointer should be moved to the next element in each iteration. Note the following fragments of code:

```
    lea        EAX, a1
    lea        EDX, a2
```

and

```
    add        EAX, 4
    add        EDX, 4
```

Comparison proper is done with the following command:

```
comiss   xmm0, DWORD PTR [EDX]
```

The low order part of the xmm0 register contains an element of a1 that is compared to the element of a2. The current address of the element of a2 is in the EDX register. The ECX register is iteration counter that is equal to the size of the arrays. Depending on the result of array comparison, the EBX registers contain either one or zero. One means the arrays are equal while zero means the opposite.

The window of the application is shown in Figs. 10.27 and 10.28.

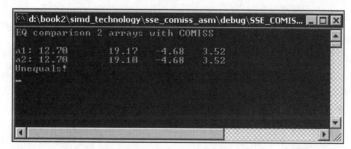

Fig. 10.27. Window of an application that demonstrates scalar comparison with the comiss command. The arrays are equal

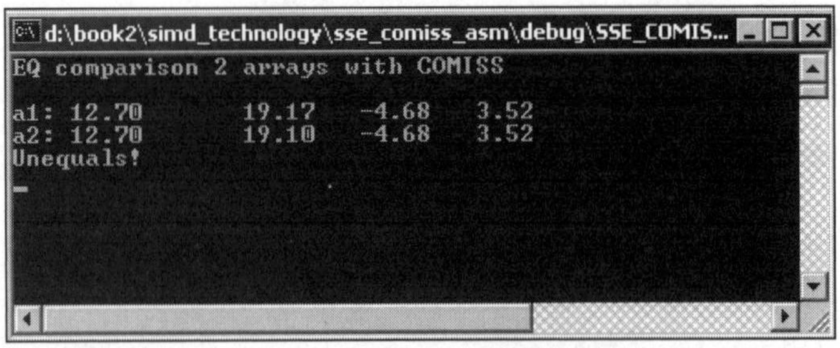

Fig. 10.28. Window of an application that demonstrates scalar comparison
with the `comiss` command. The arrays are unequal

The SSE extension includes a number of commands that make it possible to convert formats between SSE, MMX, and the common integer format. The commands of this group can perform both scalar and parallel operations. We will illustrate the use of these commands with examples.

The first example relates to parallel conversion of two 32-bit integers stored in the mm0 MMX register to two 32-bit floating-point numbers that are written to two low order words of the xmm0 SSE register. The source code of the application is shown in Listing 10.39.

Listing 10.39. Converting MMX integers to SSE floating-point numbers

```
// MMX_INT_INTO_SSE_FLOAT.cpp : Defines the entry point for the console
// application

#include "stdafx.h"

int _tmain(int argc, _TCHAR* argv[])
{
 int i1[2];
 float f1[2];

 printf("PARALLEL CONV. 2 INTS TO 2 FLOAT WITH SSE-EXT.ASM\n\n");
 while (true)
  {
   printf("\nEnter first integer i1[0]: ");
   scanf("%d", i1);
   printf("\nEnter second integer i1[1]: ");
```

```
    scanf("%d", &i1[1]);
    printf("\n");


    _asm {
            movq        mm0, MMWORD PTR i1
            cvtpi2ps    xmm0, mm0
            movlps      DWORD PTR f1, xmm0
            emms
        };
    for (int cnt = 0; cnt < 2; cnt++)
        printf("f1[%d] = %.3f\n", cnt, f1[cnt]);
    printf("f1[0] / f1[1] = %.3f\n", f1[0]/f1[1]);
    };
    return 0;
}
```

Parallel conversion of two 32-bit integers to two 32-bit floating-point numbers is done with the cvtpi2ps command. The assembly block that performs the conversion contains both SSE and MMX commands. The command

```
    movq    mm0, MMWORD PTR i1
```

moves a 64-bit number (two integers) to the mm0 register. The command

```
    cvtpi2ps    xmm0, mm0
```

converts two 32-bit packed numbers stored in the mm0 register to two floating-point numbers and puts the result to the xmm0 SSE register. Two high order double words of the xmm0 register do not change. The precision of the result of conversion depends on which bits of the status/control SSE register are set. Storing the result of conversion as a floating-point array of two 32-bit numbers is done with the command

```
        movlps      DWORD PTR f1, xmm0
```

that moves two low order double words from the xmm0 register to the f1 array. To illustrate the correctness of the integer-to-floating-point conversion, the statement

```
    printf("f1[0] / f1[1] = %.3f\n", f1[0]/f1[1])
```

displays the result of division of two floating-point numbers.

The window of the application is shown in Fig. 10.29.

The next example demonstrates the reverse conversion of a 32-bit floating-point number to the integer type. The source code is shown in Listing 10.40.

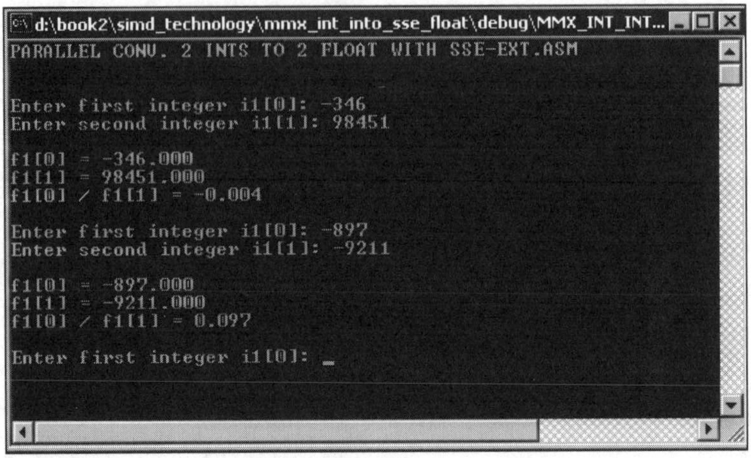

Fig. 10.29. Window of an application that demonstrates parallel conversion
of two 32-bit integers to floating-point numbers with SSE extension assembly commands

Listing 10.40. Converting SSE floating-point numbers to MMX integers

```
// SSE_INTO_MMX_CONV.cpp : Defines the entry point for the console
// application

#include "stdafx.h"

int _tmain(int argc, _TCHAR* argv[])
{
 int i1[2];
 float f1[2] = {0,0};

 printf("PARALLEL CONV. OF 2 FLOATS TO 2 INTS WITH SSE-EXT.ASM\n\n");

 printf("Enter real f1: ");
 scanf("%f", &f1[0]);
 printf("Enter real f2: ");
 scanf("%f", &f1[1]);
 _asm {
        movlps      xmm0, QWORD PTR f1
        cvtps2pi    mm0, xmm0
        movq        QWORD PTR i1, mm0
        emms
```

```
    };
printf("\nAfter conversion f1 --> i1, f2 --> i2\n\n");
printf("i1 = %d\n", i1[0]);
printf("i2 = %d\n", i1[1]);

printf("i1 / i2 = %d\n", i1[0]/i1[1]);
getchar();
getchar();
return 0;
}
```

Parallel conversion of two floating-point numbers to two integers is done in the assembly block with the command

```
cvtps2pi  mm0, xmm0
```

The floating-point numbers stored in the xmm0 SSE register are converted to integers and stored in the mm0 MMX register. The commands movlps and movq move the data. When using MMX extension assembly commands, make sure that the last command is emms!

To illustrate correctness of the conversion, the statement

```
printf("i1 / i2 = %d\n", i1[0]/i1[1])
```

displays the result of division of two integers.

The window of the application is shown in Fig. 10.30.

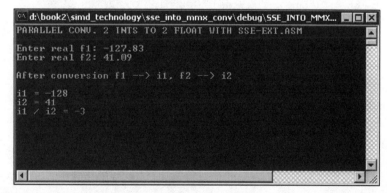

Fig. 10.30. Window of an application that demonstrates parallel conversion of 32-bit floating-point numbers to integers with the assembler

In addition to these commands of parallel conversion, the SSE extension includes scalar conversion commands. By using them, you can convert 32-bit numbers. We will not provide examples of how to use these commands, but you can do this as an exercise.

To complete the review of SSE extension commands and examples of their use in practice, we will concentrate on a few specific but very useful instructions. These are extraction of the square root and finding the maximum/minimum value of a pair of numbers. SSE extension includes both parallel and scalar commands.

We will look at an example that extracts the square root from floating-point packed numbers. For this operation, the `sqrtps` command is used. The source code of the application is shown in Listing 10.41.

Listing 10.41. Parallel extraction of the square root from floating-point packed numbers

```
// PARALLEL_SQRT.cpp : Defines the entry point for the console
// application

#include "stdafx.h"

int _tmain(int argc, _TCHAR* argv[])
{
__declspec (align(16)) float f1[4] = {34.78, 23.56, 876.98, 9423.678};
float fsqrt[4];

printf("PARALLEL SQRT CALCULATION WITH SSE-EXT.ASSEMBLER\n\n");
printf("f1: ");
for (int cnt = 0; cnt < 4; cnt++)
    printf("%.3f\t", f1[cnt]);
printf("\n\n");

_asm {
    movaps xmm0, XMMWORD PTR f1
    sqrtps xmm0, xmm0
    movups XMMWORD PTR fsqrt, xmm0
    };
for (int cnt = 0; cnt < 4; cnt++)
    printf("SQRT(%.3f)= %.3f\n", f1[cnt], fsqrt[cnt]);
getchar();
return 0;
}
```

The square root is extracted with the command

```
sqrtps xmm0, xmm0
```

The source and destination of this command is the same SSE register xmm0. The destination of the result is always one of the registers xmm0, ..., xmm7. For the second operand, a 128-bit memory variable can be used. To improve performance, the address of the 128-bit variable should be aligned on 16-bit boundary. This is done in the line

```
__declspec (align(16)) float f1[4] = {34.78, 23.56, 876.98, 9423.678}
```

The window of the application is shown in Fig. 10.31.

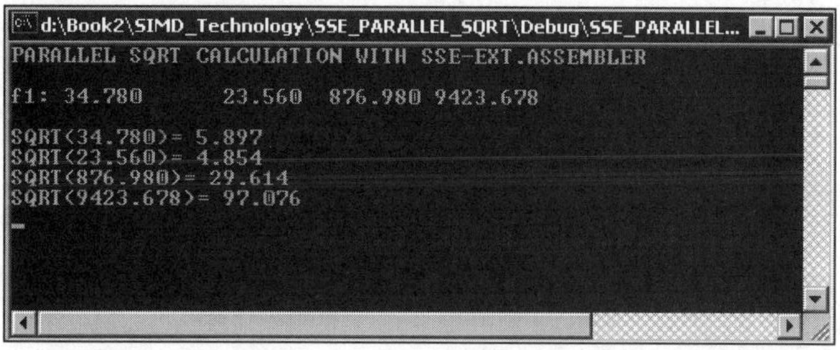

Fig. 10.31. Window of an application that demonstrates parallel extraction of the square root from floating-point packed numbers with the SSE extension assembler

The final example demonstrating the features of the SSE extension searches for the maximum and minimum element among pairs of floating-point packed numbers. For this purpose, the maxps and minps SSE extension commands are used. Both commands operate on 128-bit packed operands, and the destination for the result can be only one of the SSE registers. The source code of the application is shown in Listing 10.42.

Listing 10.42. A search for the maximum and minimum element among pairs of floating-point packed numbers

```
// SSE_PARALEL_MIN_MAX.cpp : Defines the entry point for the console
// application

#include "stdafx.h"

int _tmain(int argc, _TCHAR* argv[])
{
    __declspec (align(16)) float f1[4] = {34.78, 23.56, 876.98, 9423.678};
    __declspec (align(16)) float f2[4] = {34.98, 21.37, 980.43, 1755.786};

    float fmin[4];
    float fmax[4];
```

```
int    choice;

printf("PARALLEL MINIMAX CALCULATION WITH SSE-EXT.ASSEMBLER\n\n");
printf("f1: ");
for (int cnt = 0; cnt < 4; cnt++)
printf("%.3f\t", f1[cnt]);
printf("\n");
printf("f2: ");
for (int cnt = 0; cnt < 4; cnt++)
    printf("%.3f\t", f2[cnt]);
while (true)
 {
  printf("\n\n");
  printf("Enter 0 - get MAX elements, 1 - get MIN elements: ");
  scanf("%d", &choice);
  printf("\n");
  switch(choice)
        {
          case 0:
              _asm {
                    movaps xmm0, XMMWORD PTR f1
                    maxps  xmm0, XMMWORD PTR f2
                    movups XMMWORD PTR fmax, xmm0
                    };
              printf("\n\nMAX: ");
              for (int cnt = 0; cnt < 4; cnt++)
                printf("%.3f\t", fmax[cnt]);
              break;
          case 1:
              _asm {
                    movaps xmm0, XMMWORD PTR f1
                    minps  xmm0, XMMWORD PTR f2
                    movups XMMWORD PTR fmin, xmm0
                    };
              printf("\n\nMIN: ");
              for (int cnt = 0; cnt < 4; cnt++)
                printf("%.3f\t", fmin[cnt]);
              break;
          default:
```

```
                break;
        };
    };
  return 0;
};
```

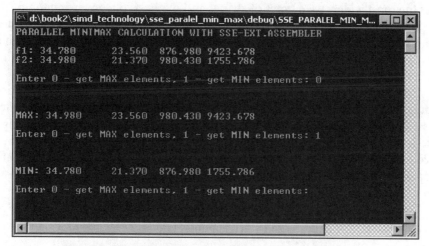

Fig. 10.32. Window of an application that demonstrates
a parallel search for the maximum and minimum elements
in two floating-point arrays with the assembler

The window of the application is shown in Fig. 10.32.

Here are a few conclusions regarding the use of the MMX and SSE extensions of SIMD technology. The use of these extensions significantly speeds up applications that process large amounts of data when the time is limited, because the data can be processed in parallel in one loop. Although Visual C++ .NET 2003 has intrinsics for work with the SIMD technologies, the inline assembler provides a higher performance than they do because it has one fundamental advantage: It lacks redundancy. Moreover, the intrinsics are written in the assembler.

Operations on packed numbers in the MMX and SSE extensions have increased precision, so they should be preferred, all things being equal.

Before you use the numerous possibilities provided by the SIMD technologies, thoroughly think about the algorithm of your task and estimate the logic of using them. Because of the limited scope of this book, not all of SIMD features are discussed. However, we hope you derive benefit from this section and will be able to effectively use these technologies in your programs.

Processing Strings with the Inline Assembler

The inline assembler can be used for processing strings. Despite the fact that the C++ .NET development environment has powerful string processing procedures, the use of the inline assembler appears to be effective in this case as well. It is often required that string variables be processed in a specific manner, and implementation of such processing with standard procedures is cumbersome and slow. First, we will discuss the most widely used types of strings and methods of converting them.

Like all high-level programming languages, C++ .NET widely uses null-terminated strings. Many various functions were developed for manipulations with such strings in this development environment. Optimization of processing such strings with assembly procedures was discussed in *Chapters 2* and *3*.

However, other string types are also used in C++ .NET. The complication of manipulations with null-terminated strings led Microsoft developers to create the CString class. This class became very popular among programmers. A CString string is a variable-length sequence of characters. The characters can be either 16-bit (the UNICODE encoding) or 8-bit (the ANSI encoding). For string manipulations, the methods and properties of the CString class are used. This class has powerful functions whose features exceed some standard functions of C++ such as strcat or strcopy.

To initialize a CString object, use the CString statement:

```
CString s = "This is a CString string";
```

You can assign the value of one CString object to another object:

```
CString s1 = "This is a test string";
CString s2 = s1;
```

In this piece of code, the contents of s1 are copied to s2. For concatenation of two or more strings, you can use the "+" or "+=" operators:

```
CString s1 = "String 1";
CString s2 = "String 2";
s1 += " is concatenated ";
CString sres = s1 + "with " + s2;
```

The result of this piece of code is the following string:

```
String 1 is concatenated with String 2
```

To manipulate with individual elements of a CString string, use the GetAt and SetAt functions of this class. The first element of a string always has a zero index. For example, to get the character that has index 3 in the s1 string that has the value "STRING 1", execute the following statement:

```
s1.GetAt(3)
```

The same result could be achieved with the "[]" operator. In that case, the string element would be accessed like an array element:

```
s1[3]
```

The result of this operation is an 'I' character. To put the 'g' character to the position with index 5 (the sixth element) in the same string, use the statement

```
s1.SetAt(5, 'g')
```

The most powerful function of the CString class is Format. It allows you to convert data of other types to text and is similar to the standard functions sprintf and wsprintf. In the previous examples, we used this function to output the elements of an array to an edit control. Here is a small piece of code:

```
for (int cnt = 0; cnt < size_i1; cnt++)
{
  s1.Format("%d", i1[cnt]);
  s_Src = s_Src + " " + s1;
};
```

This code outputs the elements of an integer array i1 to an edit control. The control has the CString type because it is associated with the s_Src variable of the CString type. An auxiliary variable s1 has the same type and is used to convert an integer element of the array to the string type. The operator

```
s_Src = s_Src + " " + s1;
```

is familiar to you. It is used to display the converted elements of the array.

As you see, the CString class significantly simplifies the work with strings (although we looked at only a few of its features!) How can you manipulate with CString objects with the inline assembler?

It is best to illustrate this with an example. We will consider the following task: Suppose you need to substitute all spaces in a CString string with "+" characters and display the result.

To implement the task, develop a dialog-based application and place three edit controls, three static text labels, and a button on its main form. Associate the s1 variable of the CString type to the Edit1 control, the s2 variable of the CString type to the Edit2 control, and the length_s1 integer variable to the Edit3 control.

The original string with spaces will be entered into the Edit1 control, the Edit2 control will display the result of substitution of spaces with "+" characters, and the Edit3 control will display the string length.

Now, look at a fragment of the C++ .NET code that processes the string (Listing 10.43).

Listing 10.43. An OnBnClicked handler that processes a CString string with C++ .NET statements

```
void CReplacecharinStringDlg::OnBnClickedButton1()
{
  // TODO: Add your control notification handler code here

  UpdateData(TRUE);
  LPSTR lps2;

  s_Len = strlen((LPCTSTR)s1);
  s2 = s1;
  lps2 = s2.GetBuffer(128);
  for (int cnt = 0; cnt < s_Len; cnt++)
  {
    if (*lps2 == ' ') *lps2 = '+';
    lps2++;
  }
  UpdateData(FALSE);
  s2.ReleaseBuffer;
}
```

As you know, to access a random element of a string or array, you have to know the address and the size of this array and the type of its elements. For null-terminated strings, the address of a string is the address of its first element. The string elements are accessed by indexing the string address.

To access the elements of a CString string, use the GetBuffer function and pass it the buffer size as a parameter. In this case, 128 bytes will be enough. This function returns a pointer to the buffer, allowing you to work with individual elements in the same fashion as in common string processing functions. If you use the following statements:

```
    ...
LPSTR lps2;
    ...
lps2 = s2.GetBuffer(128);
    ...
```

you will get the address of the string buffer. Now, you have to determine the string length. This is simple: Use the strlen classical function and store the result in the s_Len variable:

```
s_Len = strlen((LPCTSTR)s1);
```

Now, search for spaces in the string buffer and substitute them with '+' characters. This can be done with the for loop. After you finish all manipulations, release the buffer:

```
s2.ReleaseBuffer;
```

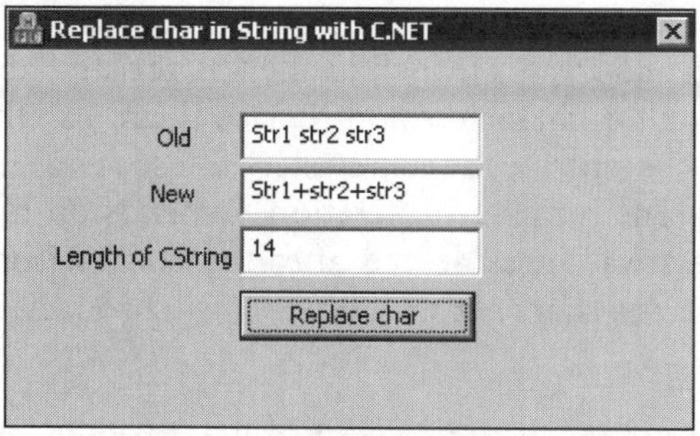

Fig. 10.33. Window of an application that substitutes spaces with "plus" characters in a `CString` string

The window of the application is shown in Fig. 10.33.

You can optimize the previous program by replacing the `for` loop with an assembly procedure. The source code of the procedure (we will name it `replaceChar`) is shown in Listing 10.44.

Listing 10.44. An assembly function that looks for and replaces characters in a `CString` string

---

```
void CReplaceCharinCStringwithBASMDlg::replaceChar(char* ps1, int ls1)
{
  _asm {
        mov     EDI, ps1
        mov     ECX, ls1
        cld
        mov     AL, ' '
    next:
        scasb
        je      change
    cont:
        loop    next
        jmp     ex
    change:
        mov     [EDI-1], '+'
        jmp     cont
    ex:
  };
}
```

This procedure takes the address of a string buffer and the string length as parameters. The buffer address is loaded to the EDI register, and the string length to the ECX register. To look for characters and replace them, use the scasb string command that compares the contents of the AL register (the space character) to the current element of the string. The number of iterations depends on the string length. Since the value of the address was incremented after the comparison, the space (if found) is substituted with the '+' character with the following command:

```
mov     [EDI-1], '+'
```

The source code of the OnBnClicked handler after the changes are made is shown in Listing 10.45.

Listing 10.45. The use of an assembly procedure for searching for and replacing characters in a CString string

---

```
void CReplaceCharinCStringwithBASMDlg::OnBnClickedButton1()
{
  // TODO: Add your control notification handler code here

  UpdateData(TRUE);
  LPSTR lps2;
  length_s1 = strlen((LPCTSTR)s1);
  s2 = s1;
  lps2 = s2.GetBuffer(128);
  replaceChar(lps2, length_s1);
  UpdateData(FALSE);
  s2.ReleaseBuffer;
};
```

Processing strings with the inline assembler is especially advantageous when specific manipulations with string elements are required, or when the string processing algorithm is complicated. For such tasks, if the code is developed only in C++, the program usually becomes excessively complicated and slow. A wise combination of C++ and the assembler is the best solution in this case.

We looked at the features of the Visual C++ .NET 2003 inline assembler that assist you in developing effective applications. Attention was given to techniques of using the inline assembler in practice when working with various data types. We emphasize that the material presented here does not exhaust the possibilities of modern data processing technologies such as MMX and SSE, but it creates a good basis for future work in this direction.

Chapter 11: Optimizing Multimedia Applications with Assembly Language

Multimedia applications are the most performance-dependent. They work in real time and have strict requirements regarding hardware and software. This chapter will focus on a few methods for optimizing multimedia applications using the assembler. First, we will review a few notes concerning performance improvement, regardless of which language is used for programming.

Multimedia applications' code must be as simple as possible. The same is true for the data structures used in these applications. Avoid data type conversion if possible. Converting integers to floating-point numbers and vice versa decreases performance because additional commands are required.

Use 32-bit data for operations on variables. 8-bit or 16-bit data require less memory, but operations on 32-bit data are the best for Pentium processors.

In your multimedia applications, avoid floating-point operations because integer operations are faster.

Pass parameters to your functions by reference, rather than by value. Also, align your data on a double-word boundary. Prefer global variables to local.

The performance of multimedia applications can be improved by optimizing the vector conversion algorithms and by using multithreading.

The concept of multithreading is a very important aspect of writing multimedia applications. No serious multimedia applications can do without threads. Threads are usually used to implement the following tasks:

☐ Creating controls and menus
☐ Creating sound effects
☐ Updating data structures
☐ Updating animation frames

The use of threads is not confined to these tasks; there are other ways of using them. Multithread applications are discussed in more detail in *Chapter 12*. For now, we will consider an example of a program with two threads (main and auxiliary), in which a 3D vector is scaled. The vector's coordinates are stored in the a1 array, and the scale factor is 4. Additionally, the vector's length is computed. First, we will consider a variant of the application with common C++ .NET statements (Listing 11.1).

Listing 11.1. Using multithreading for scaling a vector and computing its length (in C++)

```cpp
// MHTHREAD_GRAPHICS.cpp : Defines the entry point for the console.
// application

#include "stdafx.h"
#include <windows.h>
#include <math.h>

int i1;

// The vector's coordinates (x, y, z)

int a1[4] = {4, 7, -3};

void myFunc(LPVOID k1)
{
  for(i1 = 0; i1 < 4; i1++)
   a1[i1] = (int)k1*a1[i1];
}

int _tmain(int argc, _TCHAR* argv[])
{
  HANDLE mythread;
```

```
    DWORD mythread_id;
    double vec_len;

    printf("CHANGING THE LENGTH OF VECTOR a = (a0, a1, a2) (DirectX
Optimizing Tips)\n");
    printf("\nBefore scaling vector a = (%d, %d, %d)\n", a1[0], a1[1],
a1[2]);
    vec_len = sqrt((double)(a1[0]*a1[0]+a1[1]*a1[1]+a1[2]*a1[2]));
    printf("\Length of a1 = %.2f\n", vec_len);

    printf("\n\n          Starting thread...\n\n");

    mythread = CreateThread(NULL,0, (PTHREAD_START_ROUTINE)myFunc,
                         (LPVOID)(4), 0, &mythread_id);
    while(true)
    {
     if (WaitForSingleObject(mythread, 0) == WAIT_OBJECT_0)
     {
      vec_len = sqrt((double)(a1[0]*a1[0]+a1[1]*a1[1]+a1[2]*a1[2]));
      break;
     }

// Any useful operations

     }
    CloseHandle(mythread);

    printf("After scaling vector a1 = (%d, %d, %d)", a1[0], a1[1], a1[2]);
    printf("\nLength of a1 = %.2f\n", vec_len);
    printf("\n          Thread terminated...\n");
    getchar();
    return 0;
}
```

In this program, the main process uses the auxiliary thread `mythread`. This thread computes the new coordinates of the 3D vector. The main thread waits for `mythread` to complete computation and then computes the length of the vector with the statement

```
    vec_len = sqrt((double)(a1[0]*a1[0]+a1[1]*a1[1]+a1[2]*a1[2]))
```

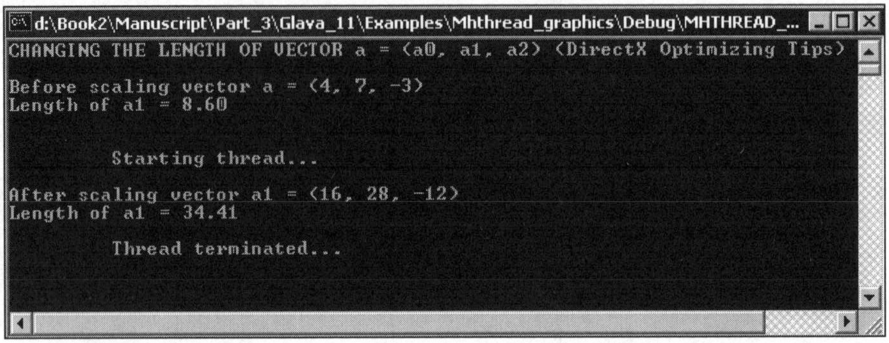

Fig. 11.1. Window of a program demonstrating operations on vectors

The window of the program is shown in Fig. 11.1.

The program can be improved by optimizing a few fragments of the code that are related to mathematical calculations. First, the computation in the thread function can be simplified if the assembler is used. The function

```
void myFunc(LPVOID k1)
{
 for(i1 = 0;i1 < 4; i1++)
  a1[i1] = (int)k1*a1[i1];
}
```

can be rewritten in the assembler as follows:

```
void myFunc(LPVOID*)
{
_asm {
      lea    ESI, a1
      lea    EDI, c1
      mov    ECX, 3
      sub    ESI, 4
   next:
      add    ESI, 4
      fild   DWORD PTR [ESI]
      fimul  DWORD PTR c1
      fistp  DWORD PTR [ESI]
      dec    ECX
      jnz    next
    }
}
```

For optimization, it is best to use a mathematical coprocessor or one of the extensions (MMX or SSE). The source code of the modified program is shown in Listing 11.2.

Listing 11.2. A modified variant of the vector operations

```cpp
// OPTIMIZING_VECTOR_OPERATIONS.cpp : Defines the entry point for the
// console application.

#include "stdafx.h"
#include <windows.h>
#include <math.h>

int i1;
int a1[4] = {4, 7, -3}; // Size of vector = sqrt((a1-a0)*(a1-a0)+....)
const int c1 = 4;

void myFunc(LPVOID k1)
{
_asm {
      lea    ESI, a1
      lea    EDI, c1
      mov    ECX, 3
      sub    ESI, 4
   next:
      add    ESI, 4
      fild   DWORD PTR [ESI]
      fimul  DWORD PTR c1
      fistp  DWORD PTR [ESI]
      dec    ECX
      jnz    next
   }
}

int _tmain(int argc, _TCHAR* argv[])
{
 HANDLE mythread;
 DWORD mythread_id;
 double vec_len;

printf("MOD. VARIANT VECTOR OPERATIONS with a = (a0, a1, a2) (DirectX ⤵
Tips)\n");
printf("\nBefore scaling vector a = (%d, %d, %d)\n", a1[0], a1[1], ⤵
a1[2]);
```

```
vec_len = sqrt((double)(a1[0]*a1[0]+a1[1]*a1[1]+a1[2]*a1[2]));
printf("\Length of a1 = %.2f\n", vec_len);

printf("\n\n          Starting thread...\n\n");

mythread = CreateThread(NULL,0, (PTHREAD_START_ROUTINE)myFunc,
                        (LPVOID)(4), 0, &mythread_id);
while(true)
{
 if (WaitForSingleObject(mythread, 0) == WAIT_OBJECT_0)
  {
   vec_len = sqrt((double)(a1[0]*a1[0]+a1[1]*a1[1]+a1[2]*a1[2]));
   break;
  }

// any useful operations

 }
CloseHandle(mythread);
printf("After scaling vector a1 = (%d, %d, %d)", a1[0], a1[1], a1[2]);
printf("\nLength of a1 = %.2f\n", vec_len);
printf("\n          Thread terminated...\n");
getchar();
return 0;
}
```

Further improvement of the program code can be done using the MMX extension assembly commands. They can be used to optimize the vector scaling code. The source code of the program is shown in Listing 11.3.

Listing 11.3. Using the MMX extension for vector operations

```
// OPTIMIZING_VECTOR_OPERATIONS.cpp : Defines the entry point for the
// console application.

#include "stdafx.h"
#include <windows.h>
#include <math.h>

int i1;

int a1[4] = {4, 7, -3, 0};
int c1[4] = {4,4,4,4};

void myFunc(LPVOID*)
```

```
{
 _asm {
        mov         ECX, 3
        lea         ESI, a1
        sub         ESI, 4
next:
        add         ESI, 4
        pxor        mm0, mm0
        movd        mm0, DWORD PTR [ESI]
        packssdw    mm0, mm0
        pxor        mm1, mm1
        movd        mm1, DWORD PTR c1
        packssdw    mm1, mm1

        pmaddwd     mm0, mm1
        movd        DWORD PTR [ESI], mm0
        dec         ECX
        jnz         next
        emms
      };

}

int _tmain(int argc, _TCHAR* argv[])
{
 HANDLE mythread;
 DWORD mythread_id;
 double vec_len;

 printf("MOD. VARIANT VECTOR OPERATIONS with a = (a0, a1, a2) (DirectX ⏎
Tips)\n");
 printf("\nBefore scaling vector a = (%d, %d, %d)\n", a1[0], a1[1], ⏎
a1[2]);
 vec_len = sqrt((double)(a1[0]*a1[0]+a1[1]*a1[1]+a1[2]*a1[2]));
 printf("\Length of a1 = %.2f\n", vec_len);

 printf("\n\n        Starting thread...\n\n");
 mythread = CreateThread(NULL, 0, (PTHREAD_START_ROUTINE)myFunc,
                         (LPVOID)(4), 0, &mythread_id);
 while(true)
 {
  if (WaitForSingleObject(mythread, 0) == WAIT_OBJECT_0)
  {
    vec_len = sqrt((double)(a1[0]*a1[0]+ a1[1]*a1[1]+ a1[2]*a1[2]));
    break;
```

```
    }

// Any useful operations

    }
    CloseHandle(mythread);

    printf("After scaling vector a1 = (%d, %d, %d)", a1[0], a1[1], a1[2]);
    printf("\nLength of a1 = %.2f\n", vec_len);
    printf("\n        Thread terminated...\n");
    getchar();
    return 0;
}
```

In the examples above, the statement

```
    if (WaitForSingleObject(mythread, 0) == WAIT_OBJECT_0)
```

is used, in which a WIN API function, WaitForSingleObject, plays an important role. This function waits for setting a signal by the mythread thread. If the signal is not set, the function immediately passes control to the next program statement. Such a design makes it possible to run several threads without decreasing performance.

The window of the program is shown in Fig. 11.2.

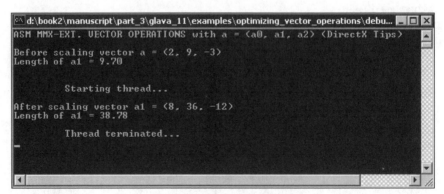

Fig. 11.2. Window of the program demonstrating the use of the MMX extension for operations on vectors

When developing multimedia applications, special DirectX function libraries are widely used. Combining the assembler with DirectX functions makes it possible to develop high-performance applications. Although the assembler interface to DirectX functions has a few distinct features, it is quite similar to common function calls.

Chapter 12: Optimizing Multithread Applications with Assembly Language

In Win32, a thread is the main executed element. An application (a process) can contain several independent threads, which share its address space and other resources. A thread is an independent unit inside a process. Using threads allows you to simplify your application and enjoy the advantages of parallel processing. Ordinary applications are executed as a single thread, but this slows down the work of applications that require simultaneous data processing (such as file search, sorting several arrays, etc.). It should be noted that arranging a thread also requires certain processor resources. Therefore, it is logical to use multithreading when the thread is executed long enough.

Programming multithread applications is described in special literature quite comprehensively, so we will not focus on their design. Rather, we will demonstrate how the C++ .NET 2003 inline assembler can be used to improve the performance of multithread applications. The main advantages of the assembler — a high speed of data processing and a small size of the code — can be successfully used for the optimization of multithread applications.

We will illustrate this with a specific example. Consider a task of simultaneously searching for and counting the number of particular characters in a text file.

Suppose you need to find the number of the characters 'r', 't', and 'f' in the testchar text file and display the result. It would be convenient to implement this task as three independent threads. One of the threads could look for the 'r' characters and count their number, and the second and third threads could do the same for the 't' and 'f' characters.

The source code of the program is shown in Listing 12.1.

Listing 12.1. A three-thread application for counting the number of characters

---

```cpp
// THREAD_EXAMPLE_FPU.cpp : Defines the entry point for the console
// application.

#include <stdio.h>
#include <windows.h>
#include <process.h>

FILE *fp;
char buf[128];
int  i, numread;
int num_t, num_f, num_r;

HANDLE tTimer = NULL;
HANDLE rTimer = NULL;
HANDLE fTimer = NULL;
LARGE_INTEGER liDueTime;

void char_t(void*)
{
_asm  {
    mov   EDX, 0
    lea   ESI, buf
    mov   ECX, 70
    mov   AL, 't'
next_char:
    cmp   AL, BYTE PTR [ESI]
    jne   inc_address
    inc   EDX
inc_address:
    inc   ESI
    dec   ECX
    jnz   next_char
    lea   EAX, num_t
    mov   DWORD PTR [EAX], EDX
    }
    tTimer = CreateWaitableTimer(NULL, TRUE, "tTimer");
    SetWaitableTimer(tTimer, &liDueTime, 0, NULL, NULL, 0);
```

```
}
void char_f(void*)
{
_asm {
     mov   EDX, 0
     lea   ESI, buf
     mov   ECX, 70
     mov   AL, 'f'
next_char:
     cmp   AL, BYTE PTR [ESI]
     jne   inc_address
     inc   EDX
inc_address:
     inc   ESI
     dec   ECX
     jnz   next_char
     lea   EAX, num_f
     mov   DWORD PTR [EAX], EDX
     }
   fTimer = CreateWaitableTimer(NULL, TRUE, "fTimer");
   SetWaitableTimer(fTimer, &liDueTime, 0, NULL, NULL, 0);
   }

void char_r(void*)
{
_asm {
   mov   EDX, 0
   lea   ESI, buf
   mov   ECX, 70
   mov   AL, 'r'
next_char:
   cmp   AL, BYTE PTR [ESI]
   jne   inc_address
   inc   EDX
inc_address:
   inc   ESI
   dec   ECX
   jnz   next_char
   lea   EAX, num_r
   mov   DWORD PTR [EAX], EDX
   }
  rTimer = CreateWaitableTimer(NULL, TRUE, "rTimer");
```

```
    SetWaitableTimer(rTimer, &liDueTime, 0, NULL, NULL, 0);
}

int _tmain(int argc, _TCHAR* argv[])
 {
   printf("OPTIMIZING OF MULTITHREADING APPLICATION WITH ASM DEMO\n\n");
   if ( (fp = fopen( "d:\\testchar", "r" )) == NULL )
   {
    printf( "The file 'testchar' was not opened\n" );
    exit(1);
   };
   numread = fread(buf, sizeof(char), 70, fp);

   fclose(fp);
   printf( "            First 70 chars :\n\n");
   printf("%.70s\n", buf);

   liDueTime.QuadPart=-10;

   _beginthread(char_f, 0, NULL);
   _beginthread(char_t, 0, NULL);
   _beginthread(char_r, 0, NULL);

   while (WaitForSingleObject(fTimer, INFINITE) != WAIT_OBJECT_0);
   CancelWaitableTimer(fTimer);

   while (WaitForSingleObject(tTimer, INFINITE) != WAIT_OBJECT_0);
   CancelWaitableTimer(tTimer);

   while (WaitForSingleObject(rTimer, INFINITE) != WAIT_OBJECT_0);
   CancelWaitableTimer(rTimer);

   printf("\nNumber of 'f' characters = %d\n", num_f);
   printf("\nNumber of 't' characters = %d\n", num_t);
   printf("\nNumber of 'r' characters = %d\n", num_r);
   MessageBox(NULL, "Searching completed!", " FIND CHARS", MB_OK);
   return (0);
 };
```

Each of the three threads is started with the _beginthread function. The uniform functions char_f, char_t, and char_r written almost entirely in the assembler are passed to this function in turn as the first parameter. Waitable timer objects are used to synchronize the threads. Why?

When a few threads are started in an application, it is likely that a thread does not process data on time, and the application cannot run correctly. To synchronize data processing by the application and individual threads, it is necessary to inform the application that a particular thread has completed data processing, and the data are ready.

This and other issues of synchronizing applications and threads are related to system programming and are rather complicated. We will not focus on these issues in too much detail; however, we will concentrate on one of the possible solutions to the synchronization problem using the waitable timer, specifically on its practical implementation.

First, a waitable timer object is created with the CreateWaitableTimer function. The function returns the descriptor of the waitable timer object. This descriptor can be used by so-called wait functions for locking or terminating processes and threads. Although this might be a simplified explanation, it will help you to understand the key concepts. A wait function does not pass control to other pieces of code until a certain condition is satisfied. Setting the signal by the synchronized object is most often used for such a condition. It is often said that the object is in the signal state. In our case, the synchronized object is the waitable timer.

Now, we will look at how the main process interacts with one of its threads in our example:

1. A waitable timer object is created with the CreateWaitableTimer function in the thread. In a certain time interval (for example, when the thread completes data processing), the waitable timer object enters the signal state.

2. The waiting function of the main thread or process (WaitForSingleObject in our example) checks the synchronized object (the waitable timer). If the object entered the signal state, the wait function returns the WAIT_OBJECT_0 value. After receiving this value, the main process can consider the called thread complete and start processing the received data. The synchronized object that is not needed any longer should be deleted with the CancelWaitableTimer function.

In practice, this procedure is the following. A new waitable timer object is created with the CreateWaitableTimer function in each of the threads. The function returns the object descriptor that is used later to access the waitable timer object. After that, the timer is activated with the SetWaitableTimer function. One of this function's parameters is a pointer to a variable that contains the time interval, after which the timer object will enter the signal state. In our case, this interval (measured in units equal to 0.1 microsecond) is written to the liDueTime variable. The length of the interval is chosen at will and is equal to 10 milliseconds.

The code fragments for each of the threads are almost the same:

```
. . .
jnz   next
fwait
};
  yTimer = CreateWaitableTimer(NULL, TRUE, "yTimer");
  SetWaitableTimer(yTimer, &liDueTime, 0, NULL, NULL, 0);
}
  . . .
```

In our program, the time interval that defines the termination of the character search function in the auxiliary thread is set to 10 milliseconds. Although this value was chosen at will, remember that setting this parameter when developing such applications should depend on the performance of the thread. It is likely that required operations will not all finish before the signal is set. It is not by chance that the assembler is used intensively in such applications. Since it is very fast, the assembly code makes it possible for several threads to work with a minimum synchronization time!

The character search algorithm implemented in the assembly block is rather simple, and you will easily make sense of it.

When the WaitForSingleObject wait function is called by the main thread or process, it checks the signal condition. If the condition is not satisfied, the calling thread or process enters the waiting state. In this state, the processor resources are used little or not used at all. When the condition is satisfied, the application resumes its work. As soon as the wait function completes, the waitable timer object is canceled with the CancelWaitableTimer function that takes the waitable timer object descriptor as a parameter. Here is a piece of code of the main program:

```
  . . .
  while (WaitForSingleObject(tTimer, INFINITE) != WAIT_OBJECT_0);
  CancelWaitableTimer(tTimer);
  . . .
```

This program requires the multithreading library. For example, if you compile the program in the mythreads.cpp file from the command line, type

```
cl /MT /D "_X86_" mythreads.cpp
```

If you compile in the Visual C++ .NET 2003 environment, set the /MT option manually using the following procedure:

1. Select **Properties** in the **Project** menu.
2. Select the Configuration Properties / C/C++ / Code Generation / Runtime Library page.
3. Set the /MT compiler option.

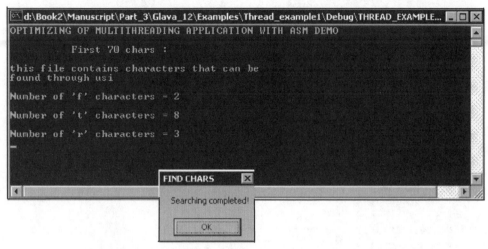

Fig. 12.1. Window of a program demonstrating three threads

The window of the program is shown in Fig. 12.1.

Here is another example of a multithread application. The application computes the quotient of division of the square root of one variable by the square root of another. Both variables are stored at the same position in two equal-length arrays of floating-point numbers.

The computation is implemented as follows:

❑ One thread computes the square root of the variable from the first array (f1).
❑ The other thread computes the square root of the variable from the second array (f2).
❑ After the threads complete computation, the main program uses the obtained data for future computation (division).

This example is similar to the previous one, but it demonstrates how the floating-point variables can be processed. Since floating-point operations require much more intensive computation than operations over characters, be sure to carefully select the time interval for synchronizing waitable time objects with the main process. The source code of the console application is shown in Listing 12.2.

Listing 12.2. Performing mathematical operations in a two-thread application

---

```
// THREAD_EXAMPLE_FPU.cpp : Defines the entry point for the console
// application.
// SQRT(f1)/SQRT(f2);

#include "stdafx.h"
#include <windows.h>
```

```
#include <process.h>

FILE *fp;
float f1[7] = {34.13, 96.03, 234.1, 954.25, 54.103, 3.14, 8.33};
float f2[7] = {67.11, 23.12, 5.87, 76.32, 19.43, 67.11, 5.09};
float fdv[7];

HANDLE xTimer = NULL;
HANDLE yTimer = NULL;
LARGE_INTEGER liDueTime;

void sqrt_x(void*)
{
_asm {
     lea  ESI, f1
     mov  ECX, 7
     finit
     fldz
next:
     fld  DWORD PTR [ESI]
     fsqrt
     fstp DWORD PTR [ESI]
     add  ESI, 4
     dec  ECX
     jnz  next
     fwait
     };
   xTimer = CreateWaitableTimer(NULL, TRUE, "xTimer");
   SetWaitableTimer(xTimer, &liDueTime, 0, NULL, NULL, 0);
 }

void sqrt_y(void*)
{
_asm {
     lea  EDI, f2
     mov  ECX, 7
     finit
     fldz
next:
     fld  DWORD PTR [EDI]
     fsqrt
     fstp DWORD PTR [EDI]
     add  EDI, 4
```

```
        dec  ECX
        jnz  next
        fwait
      };

   yTimer = CreateWaitableTimer(NULL, TRUE, "yTimer");
   SetWaitableTimer(yTimer, &liDueTime, 0, NULL, NULL, 0);
 }

int _tmain(int argc, _TCHAR* argv[])
{

 printf("OPTIMIZING OF MULTITHREADING APPLICATION WITH ASM FPU \n\n");

 printf("\nf1  : ");
 for (int cnt = 0; cnt < 7; cnt++)
      printf("%.3f  ", f1[cnt]);

 printf("\nf2  : ");
 for (int cnt = 0; cnt < 7; cnt++)
      printf("%.3f  ", f2[cnt]);

  liDueTime.QuadPart=-10;
 _beginthread(sqrt_x, 0, NULL);
 _beginthread(sqrt_y, 0, NULL);

while (WaitForSingleObject(xTimer, INFINITE) != WAIT_OBJECT_0);
CancelWaitableTimer(xTimer);

while (WaitForSingleObject(yTimer, INFINITE) != WAIT_OBJECT_0);
CancelWaitableTimer(yTimer);

_asm {
        lea  ESI, DWORD PTR f1
        lea  EDI, DWORD PTR f2
        lea  EDX, DWORD PTR fdv
        mov  ECX, 7
        finit
        fldz
next:
        fld  DWORD PTR [ESI]
        fld  DWORD PTR [EDI]
        fdiv
```

```
        fstp DWORD PTR [EDX]
        add  ESI, 4
        add  EDI, 4
        add  EDX, 4
        dec  ECX
        jnz  next
        fwait
  };
 printf("\n\nSQRT(f1)  : ");
 for (int cnt = 0; cnt <  7; cnt++)
        printf("%.3f  ", f1[cnt]);

 printf("\nSQRT(f2)  : ");
 for (int cnt = 0; cnt <  7; cnt++)
        printf("%.3f  ", f2[cnt]);

 printf("\n\nSQRT{f1) / SQRT(f2) : ");
for (int cnt = 0; cnt <  7; cnt++)
    printf("%.3f  ", fdv[cnt]);

MessageBox(NULL, "Calculations completed!", " FIND SQRT", MB_OK);
return 0;
}
```

Computation is done by the main process and two auxiliary threads. The threads compute the square roots of the elements of two arrays, and the main process finds the quotient of division of one value by the other. The threads are started with the following statements.

```
_beginthread(sqrt_x, 0, NULL)
_beginthread(sqrt_y, 0, NULL)
```

One of the threads executes the sqrt_x function, while the other executes the sqrt_y function. These functions create waitable timer objects and set the signal states for the WaitForSingleObject functions of the main thread. The WaitForSingleObject functions wait for the threads to terminate and bring the waitable timers to inactive states:

```
while (WaitForSingleObject(xTimer, INFINITE) != WAIT_OBJECT_0)
CancelWaitableTimer(xTimer)


while (WaitForSingleObject(yTimer, INFINITE) != WAIT_OBJECT_0)
CancelWaitableTimer(yTimer)
```

The results of the auxiliary threads' work are used by the main process for further computation in the assembly block.

The window of the program is shown in Fig. 12.2.

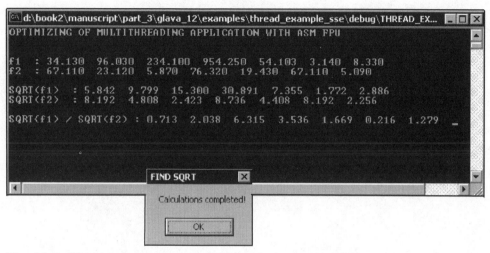

Fig. 12.2. Window of a program demonstrating mathematical operations in two threads

Multithreading is a complex topic, and it can be implemented in various ways. In this chapter, we described one of the most frequently used ways: with waitable timers. Using the assembler in such programs significantly improves the performance and quality of a program as a whole.

These examples of simple programs demonstrate the use of the assembler and can help programmers when writing applications with intensive computation requiring parallel execution of operations.

Chapter 13: C++ Inline Assembler and Windows Time Functions

A significant part of applications that work in the Windows family of operating systems use time functions and timers. Such functions are necessary for real-time operations, work with device drivers, and multimedia applications. Note that Windows operating systems are not real-time ones. This means that it is very difficult to execute operations that depend on precise time intervals or relate to them. Those programmers who have to write applications that work with very short time intervals encounter many problems. With regard to operations with relatively long intervals (a few seconds or a few minutes), there are usually no problems. Things are much more complicated for applications operating with milliseconds or tens of milliseconds. Delays, which appear during processing audio and video data, and inaccurate sampling when working with physical devices lead to losses and distortions of data, thus making the applications inoperable.

All problems related to time dependencies can be divided into two categories: the difficulty of executing a particular algorithm within a particular time and the impossibility of measuring a time interval with the required precision while the algorithm is quite operable.

In the first case, the best option is to use assembly language. Implementing such a task in "pure" C++ is not always possible. A well-designed algorithm written in the assembler will always be faster than its analog coded in C++. Therefore, using the assembler often makes it possible to fit both crucial pieces of code and a whole application to reasonable time limits.

Setting a time interval precisely is a more complicated task. As developers at Microsoft say, it is almost impossible to obtain a time interval shorter than 50 microseconds in the Windows operating system. This is because of the structure of the operating system and time dependencies among its subsystems.

Nevertheless, there are solutions that allow a programmer to obtain rather short intervals. Assembly code is also useful in this case.

To work precisely with short time intervals, the GetTickCount WIN API function is often used. It returns the number of milliseconds elapsed since the Windows startup. Generally, one could say that this function computes the time between its subsequent calls. Using GetTickCount is very useful in the following situations:

❑ When you need to compute the interval between two events. These could be the beginning and end of execution of a particular code fragment or, for example, the beginning and end of receiving data in a data processing system.

❑ When you need to specify a certain time interval for execution of a program.

The effectiveness of this function significantly increases when the assembler is used for implementing such tasks. We will illustrate this with examples.

The first example demonstrates the use of the GetTickCount function to determine the time of execution of a for loop that computes the sine of monotonically increasing floating-point numbers. The for loop is implemented in C++. The source code of the application is shown in Listing 13.1.

Listing 13.1. Computing the time of execution of a `for` loop with C++ .NET statements

```cpp
// GetTickCount_plus_ASM.cpp : Defines the entry point for the console
// application

#include "stdafx.h"
#include <windows.h>
#include <math.h>

int _tmain(int argc, _TCHAR* argv[])
{
 float i1 = 0.0;
 float ires = 0.0;
 const float one = 1.0;

printf("Comparison ASM and C++ speed of execution (pure C++) \n");
DWORD dwStart = GetTickCount();
for (int cnt = 0; cnt < 1000000; cnt++)
```

```
    ires = sin(++i1);

DWORD dwInterval = GetTickCount() - dwStart;
printf("\nSine = %.3f \n", ires);
printf("Operation is completed through %d ms!\n", (int)dwInterval);
getchar();
return 0;
}
```

To compute the time interval in milliseconds, a simple expression is used that evaluates the difference between the readings of the counter after the `for` loop completes and at the start of the application:

```
DWORD dwInterval = GetTickCount() - dwStart
```

The window of the application is shown in Fig. 13.1.

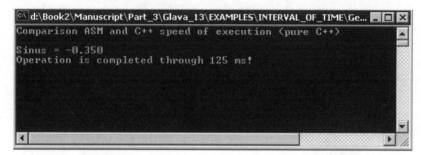

Fig. 13.1. Window of an application that displays
the time of execution of a `for` loop

Note the time of execution of the loop; we will need it later to compare it with the result of a modified version of this application.

Rewrite the `for` loop in the assembler. The source code of the modified application appears as shown in Listing 13.2.

Listing 13.2. Replacing the `for` loop with an assembly block

```
// Time of calculating with ASM.cpp : Defines the entry point for the
// console application

#include "stdafx.h"
#include <windows.h>
#include <math.h>
```

```
int _tmain(int argc, _TCHAR* argv[])
{
 float i1 = 0.0;
 float ires = 0.0;

printf("Comparison ASM and C++ speed of execution (ASM block) \n");
    DWORD dwStart = GetTickCount();

_asm {
      mov   ECX, 1000000
      finit
  next:
      fld1
      fadd  DWORD PTR i1
      fstp  DWORD PTR i1

      fld   DWORD PTR i1
      fsin
      fstp  DWORD PTR ires
      dec   ECX
      jnz   next
      fwait
      };
DWORD dwInterval = GetTickCount() - dwStart;
printf("\nSine = %.3f \n", ires);
printf("Operation is completed through %d ms!\n", (int)dwInterval);
getchar();
return 0;
}
```

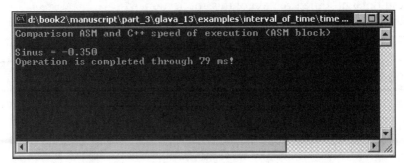

Fig. 13.2. Window of an application that demonstrates the performance of a loop implemented with assembly commands

The window of the application is shown in Fig. 13.2.

Compare the time of execution with that from the previous example. The assembly block is executed much faster. Both results were obtained on a computer with Pentium IV 2.4 GHz. On computers with other processors and other system parameters, the results will look different, but the relationship will be the same: The assembler version of the for loop is executed faster!

The GetTickCount function can be used for repeatedly executing a program with certain time intervals. Usually, such programs are generators of signals of a particular shape or electronic circuit simulators in modeling applications.

The next example demonstrates computing ten values of sine of a floating-point number with time intervals of 5 msec. The source code of the application is shown in Listing 13.3.

Listing 13.3. Computing ten values of the sine with time intervals of 5 msec

```cpp
// SINE_X_5MS_ASM.cpp : Defines the entry point for the console
// application

#include "stdafx.h"
#include <windows.h>
#include <math.h>

int _tmain(int argc, _TCHAR* argv[])
{
  float f1[10] = {1.5, 4.1, 0.7, 2, 45.12, 21.7, 9.65, 11.3, 0.7, 77};
  float fsin[10];
  DWORD dwStart;

printf("Calculation SIN(x) each 5 milliseconds with ASM\n\n");

for (int cnt = 0; cnt < 10; cnt++)
{
  dwStart = GetTickCount();
  while ((GetTickCount() - dwStart)<=5);

  _asm {
        mov    ECX, 10
        lea    ESI, DWORD PTR f1
        lea    EDI, DWORD PTR fsin
```

```
        finit
   next:
        fld1
        fadd   DWORD PTR [ESI]
        fstp   DWORD PTR [ESI]

        fld    DWORD PTR [ESI]
        fsin
        fstp   DWORD PTR [EDI]
        dec    ECX
        jz     ex
        add    ESI, 4
        add    EDI, 4
        jmp    next
   ex:
        fwait
        };
   }
   printf("\nf1:        ");

   for (int cnt = 0; cnt < 10; cnt++)
     printf("%.2f ", f1[cnt]);

   printf("\n\nSIN(f1): ");

   for (int cnt = 0; cnt < 10; cnt++)
     printf("%.2f ", fsin[cnt]);

   getchar();
   return 0;
   }
```

Note this very important point. When computing time intervals, the precision of computation also depends on the time of execution of the statements that compute (this is true not only for the GetTickCount function). For relatively long intervals (compared to the time of execution of commands), the time of execution of statements does not influence precision significantly because it is a hundred times less than those intervals.

The window of the application is shown in Fig. 13.3.

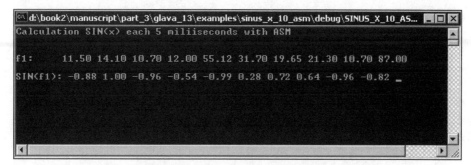

Fig. 13.3. Window of an application that computes
the sine of a number every 5 milliseconds

To work with very short time intervals (hundreds of milliseconds or shorter), use special techniques and WIN API functions such as QueryPerformanceCounter and QueryPerformanceFrequency. These are beyond the scope of this book.

Operations that should be performed with certain fixed time intervals can be implemented with a timer. The timer is a scheduled event created by the operating system with specified intervals. The precision of the system timer is a little less than that computed with the GetTickCount function, but it is satisfactory for many applications. The timer can be used in either of these two ways:

❏ Create the WM_TIMER message and write a handler for this event.
❏ Write a callback function for handling the timer event.

You can create or change the system timer with the SetTimer function. Having used the timer, delete it with the KillTimer function. The parameters of these functions are thoroughly covered in special literature, so we will not concentrate on them. Rather, we will proceed with an example that handles the timer event with a WM_TIMER handler. In this example, the Windows system timer is used for performing a mathematical operation: more precisely, for extracting the square root from a floating-point number.

To generate the application frame, use the C++ .NET 2003 Application Wizard and generate a 32-bit procedure-oriented application. Modify the template to use the system timer function (the changes are in bold in the listing below).

The square root is computed in the assembly block. The source code of the application is shown in Listing 13.4.

Listing 13.4. Using Windows system timers

```
// GL13_TEST_TIMER.cpp : Defines the entry point for the application

#include "stdafx.h"
```

```c
#include <stdio.h>

#include "GL13_TEST_TIMER.h"
#define MAX_LOADSTRING 100

char buf[32];
float f1 = 0;
float fres = 0;
int nTimer;
int written = 0;

// Global Variables:
HINSTANCE hInst;                        // Current instance
TCHAR szTitle[MAX_LOADSTRING];          // The title bar text
TCHAR szWindowClass[MAX_LOADSTRING];    // The main window class name

// Forward declarations of functions included in this code module:
ATOM              MyRegisterClass(HINSTANCE hInstance);
BOOL              InitInstance(HINSTANCE, int);
LRESULT CALLBACK  WndProc(HWND, UINT, WPARAM, LPARAM);
LRESULT CALLBACK  About(HWND, UINT, WPARAM, LPARAM);

int APIENTRY _tWinMain(HINSTANCE hInstance,
                       HINSTANCE hPrevInstance,
                       LPTSTR    lpCmdLine,
                       int       nCmdShow)
{

// TODO: Place code here.
MSG msg;
HACCEL hAccelTable;

// Initialize global strings
LoadString(hInstance, IDS_APP_TITLE, szTitle, MAX_LOADSTRING);
LoadString(hInstance, IDC_GL13_TEST_TIMER, szWindowClass, MAX_LOADSTRING);
MyRegisterClass(hInstance);

// Perform application initialization:
if (!InitInstance (hInstance, nCmdShow))
  {
```

```
    return FALSE;
  }
hAccelTable = LoadAccelerators(hInstance, (LPCTSTR)IDC_GL13_TEST_TIMER);

// Main message loop:
while (GetMessage(&msg, NULL, 0, 0))
 {
  if (!TranslateAccelerator(msg.hwnd, hAccelTable, &msg))
   {
    TranslateMessage(&msg);
    DispatchMessage(&msg);
   }
}
  return (int) msg.wParam;
}


//  FUNCTION: MyRegisterClass()
//  PURPOSE: Registers the window class.
//  COMMENTS:
//  This function and its usage are only necessary if you want this code
//  to be compatible with Win32 systems prior to the 'RegisterClassEx'
//  function that was added to Windows 95. It is important to call this
//  function so that the application will get 'well formed' small icons
//  associated with it.

ATOM MyRegisterClass(HINSTANCE hInstance)
 {
  WNDCLASSEX wcex;
  wcex.cbSize = sizeof(WNDCLASSEX);

  wcex.style          = CS_HREDRAW | CS_VREDRAW;
  wcex.lpfnWndProc    = (WNDPROC)WndProc;
  wcex.cbClsExtra     = 0;
  wcex.cbWndExtra     = 0;
  wcex.hInstance      = hInstance;
  wcex.hIcon          = LoadIcon(hInstance, (LPCTSTR)IDI_GL13_TEST_TIMER);
  wcex.hCursor        = LoadCursor(NULL, IDC_ARROW);
  wcex.hbrBackground  = (HBRUSH)(COLOR_WINDOW-2);
  wcex.lpszMenuName   = (LPCTSTR)IDC_GL13_TEST_TIMER;
  wcex.lpszClassName  = szWindowClass;
```

```
    wcex.hIconSm        = LoadIcon(wcex.hInstance, (LPCTSTR)IDI_SMALL);

   return RegisterClassEx(&wcex);
  }


// FUNCTION: InitInstance(HANDLE, int)
// PURPOSE: Saves instance handle and creates main window
// COMMENTS:
// In this function, we save the instance handle in a global variable and
// create and display the main program window.

BOOL InitInstance(HINSTANCE hInstance, int nCmdShow)
 {
   HWND hWnd;
   hInst = hInstance; // Store instance handle in our global variable

   hWnd = CreateWindow(szWindowClass, szTitle, WS_OVERLAPPEDWINDOW,
                                       CW_USEDEFAULT, 0,
                                       CW_USEDEFAULT, 0,
                                       NULL, NULL, hInstance,
                                       NULL);
   if (!hWnd)
   {
      return FALSE;
   }

   ShowWindow(hWnd, nCmdShow);
   UpdateWindow(hWnd);

   return TRUE;
}

//  FUNCTION: WndProc(HWND, unsigned, WORD, LONG)
//  PURPOSE:  Processing messages for the main window
//  WM_COMMAND  - Process the application menu.
//  WM_PAINT    - Paint the main window.
//  WM_DESTROY  - Post a quit message and return.

LRESULT CALLBACK WndProc(HWND hWnd, UINT message, WPARAM wParam, LPARAM lParam)
  {
```

```
    int wmId, wmEvent;
    PAINTSTRUCT ps;
    HDC hdc;
    RECT rc;

    #define TIMER1 1

    switch (message)
      {
        case WM_COMMAND:
            wmId    = LOWORD(wParam);
            wmEvent = HIWORD(wParam);

// Parse the menu selections:
          switch (wmId)
            {
              case IDM_ABOUT:
                DialogBox(hInst, (LPCTSTR)IDD_ABOUTBOX, hWnd, (DLGPROC)About);
                break;
              case IDM_EXIT:
                DestroyWindow(hWnd);
                break;
              default:
                return DefWindowProc(hWnd, message, wParam, lParam);
            }
          break;
        case WM_PAINT:
          hdc = BeginPaint(hWnd, &ps);
          GetClientRect(hWnd, &rc);

// TODO: Add any drawing code here...

      TextOut(hdc, (rc.right-rc.left)/4, (rc.bottom-rc.top)/2, buf, written);
      EndPaint(hWnd, &ps);
      break;
    case WM_CREATE:
      nTimer = SetTimer(hWnd, TIMER1, 5000, NULL);
      break;
    case WM_TIMER:
      switch(wParam)
```

```
        case TIMER1:
          {
          _asm {
                finit
                fld1
                fadd   DWORD PTR f1
                fstp   DWORD PTR f1
                fld    DWORD PTR f1
                fsqrt
                fstp   DWORd PTR fres
                fwait
              };
          written = sprintf(buf, " Value = %.3f, SQRT = %.3f", f1, fres);
          hdc = GetDC(hWnd);
          GetClientRect(hWnd, &rc);
          InvalidateRect(hWnd, &rc, FALSE);
          ReleaseDC(hWnd, hdc);
          break;
        }
      break;
    case WM_DESTROY:
      KillTimer(hWnd, nTimer);
      PostQuitMessage(0);
      break;
    default:
      return DefWindowProc(hWnd, message, wParam, lParam);
    }
  return 0;
}

// Message handler for about box.
LRESULT CALLBACK About(HWND hDlg, UINT message, WPARAM wParam, LPARAM lParam)
{
    switch (message)
      {
      case WM_INITDIALOG:
          return TRUE;
      case WM_COMMAND:
          if (LOWORD(wParam) == IDOK || LOWORD(wParam) == IDCANCEL)
            {
```

```
        EndDialog(hDlg, LOWORD(wParam));
        return TRUE;
      }
    break;
    }
  return FALSE;
}
```

We will explain this listing with the declarations of variables. The following variables are declared at the beginning of the code:

- `char buf[32]` — a character buffer for storage of a floating-point number converted to a string which will be subsequently displayed with the `TextOut` function
- `float f1` — a positive floating-point number, from which the square root is extracted
- `float fres` — the result of square root extraction
- `int nTimer` — the handle of a new timer
- `int written` — the number of characters written to the buffer during conversion of the number to a string

To create a system timer, the `SetTimer` function is used:

```
nTimer = SetTimer(hWnd, TIMER1, 5000, NULL)
```

This statement creates a system timer with the `TIMER1` identifier that triggers an event every 5 seconds. The `nTimer` handle is used by the `KillTimer` function to destroy the timer after the application terminates. The `NULL` parameter indicates the absence of a callback function for handling the event (in this case, the `WM_TIMER` handler is used).

The window of the application is shown in Fig. 13.4.

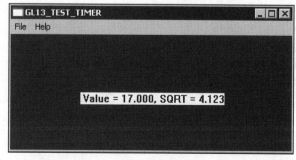

Fig. 13.4. Window of an application that demonstrates computing a square root in a `WM_TIMER` handler

Note that the code of the WM_TIMER should be as short as possible. The smaller the interval between triggering events, the stricter this limitation will be. In the preceding example, this interval is equal to 5 seconds, which is sufficient both for fast mathematical computation and for processing the data before displaying them. However, if the interval between triggering the timer is short (for example, 10 milliseconds), the hardware performance and the quality of the code affect the situation.

With short intervals, it is not advisable to write a handler that displays or saves the processed data in a file. These operations take too much time that is comparable to the interval of triggering timer events. It is likely that the next event occurs while the data is still being processed. In such a case, the application will behave unpredictably, and the data might be lost.

Be sure to take into account another factor. The system triggers the WM_TIMER message only when there are no unprocessed messages in the queue. You could describe this by saying that all other messages (except WM_PAINT) have priorities higher than that of the timer messages.

You can optimize the last application if you try to move a few or all data displaying operations from the WM_TIMER handler to, for example, the WM_PAINT handler. After analysis of the source code, it turns out that the

```
written = sprintf(buf, " Value = %.3f, SQRT = %.3f", f1, fres)
```

statement can be moved from the WM_TIMER handler to the WM_PAINT handler:

```
. . .
case WM_PAINT:
 hdc = BeginPaint(hWnd, &ps);
 GetClientRect(hWnd, &rc);

// TODO: Add any drawing code here...
 written = sprintf(buf, " Value = %.3f, SQRT = %.3f", f1, fres);
 TextOut(hdc, (rc.right-rc.left)/4, (rc.bottom-rc.top)/2, buf, written);
 EndPaint(hWnd, &ps);
 break;
. . .
```

The next example is similar to the previous, but it has one important feature: It uses a callback function for handling the timer event. The source code of the application is shown in Listing 13.5.

Listing 13.5. Using a callback function for handling a timer event

```
// MyTimer_with_ASM.cpp : Defines the entry point for the application

#include "stdafx.h"
#include "MyTimer_with_ASM.h"
```

```
#include <stdio.h>

#define MAX_LOADSTRING 100

char buf[64];
float f1 = 0;
float fres = 0;
int nTimer;
int written = 0;

// Global Variables:
HINSTANCE hInst;                            // Current instance
TCHAR    szTitle[MAX_LOADSTRING];          // The title bar text
TCHAR szWindowClass[MAX_LOADSTRING]; // The main window class name

// Forward declarations of functions included in this code module:
ATOM               MyRegisterClass(HINSTANCE hInstance);
BOOL               InitInstance(HINSTANCE, int);
LRESULT CALLBACK   WndProc(HWND, UINT, WPARAM, LPARAM);
LRESULT CALLBACK   About(HWND, UINT, WPARAM, LPARAM);

int APIENTRY _tWinMain(HINSTANCE hInstance,
                       HINSTANCE hPrevInstance,
                       LPTSTR    lpCmdLine,
                       int       nCmdShow)
{
// TODO: Place code here.
MSG msg;
HACCEL hAccelTable;

// Initialize global strings
LoadString(hInstance, IDS_APP_TITLE, szTitle, MAX_LOADSTRING);
LoadString(hInstance, IDC_MYTIMER_WITH_ASM, szWindowClass, MAX_LOADSTRING);
MyRegisterClass(hInstance);

// Perform application initialization:
if (!InitInstance (hInstance, nCmdShow))
 {
  return FALSE;
 }
```

```
hAccelTable = LoadAccelerators(hInstance, (LPCTSTR)IDC_MYTIMER_WITH_ASM);

// Main message loop:
while (GetMessage(&msg, NULL, 0, 0))
  {
    if (!TranslateAccelerator(msg.hwnd, hAccelTable, &msg))
      {
        TranslateMessage(&msg);
        DispatchMessage(&msg);
      }
  }

return (int) msg.wParam;
}


//  FUNCTION: MyRegisterClass()
//  PURPOSE: Registers the window class.
//  COMMENTS:
// This function and its usage are only necessary if you want this code
// to be compatible with Win32 systems prior to the 'RegisterClassEx'
// function that was added to Windows 95. It is important to call this
// function so that the application will get 'well formed' small icons
// associated with it.

ATOM MyRegisterClass(HINSTANCE hInstance)
{
 WNDCLASSEX wcex;

 wcex.cbSize = sizeof(WNDCLASSEX);

 wcex.style          = CS_HREDRAW | CS_VREDRAW;
 wcex.lpfnWndProc    = (WNDPROC)WndProc;
 wcex.cbClsExtra     = 0;
 wcex.cbWndExtra     = 0;
 wcex.hInstance      = hInstance;
 wcex.hIcon          = LoadIcon(hInstance, (LPCTSTR)IDI_MYTIMER_WITH_ASM);
 wcex.hCursor        = LoadCursor(NULL, IDC_ARROW);
 wcex.hbrBackground  = (HBRUSH)(COLOR_WINDOW-1);
 wcex.lpszMenuName   = (LPCTSTR)IDC_MYTIMER_WITH_ASM;
 wcex.lpszClassName  = szWindowClass;
```

```
   wcex.hIconSm        = LoadIcon(wcex.hInstance, (LPCTSTR)IDI_SMALL);

   return RegisterClassEx(&wcex);
}

// FUNCTION: InitInstance(HANDLE, int)
// PURPOSE: Saves instance handle and creates main window
// COMMENTS:
// In this function, we save the instance handle in a global variable and
// create and display the main program window.

BOOL InitInstance(HINSTANCE hInstance, int nCmdShow)
{
   HWND hWnd;

   hInst = hInstance; // Store instance handle in our global variable
   hWnd = CreateWindow(szWindowClass, szTitle, WS_OVERLAPPEDWINDOW,
                                      CW_USEDEFAULT, 0,
                                      CW_USEDEFAULT, 0, NULL,
                                      NULL, hInstance, NULL);

   if (!hWnd)
   {
      return FALSE;
   }

   ShowWindow(hWnd, nCmdShow);
   UpdateWindow(hWnd);

   return TRUE;
}

//   FUNCTION: WndProc(HWND, unsigned, WORD, LONG)
//   PURPOSE:  processes messages for the main window
//   WM_COMMAND - process the application menu
//   WM_PAINT   - paint the main window
//   WM_DESTROY - post a quit message and return

VOID CALLBACK MyTimerProc(HWND hWnd,      // Handle to window
                          UINT message,    // WM_TIMER message
```

```
                                UINT idTimer,      // Timer identifier
                                DWORD dwTime)      // Current system time
{
 HDC hdc;
 RECT rc;
 _asm {
        finit
        fld1
        fadd   DWORD PTR f1
        fstp   DWORD PTR f1

        fld    DWORD PTR f1
        fsqrt
        fstp   DWORd PTR fres
        fwait
         };

hdc = GetDC(hWnd);
GetClientRect(hWnd, &rc);
InvalidateRect(hWnd, &rc, FALSE);
ReleaseDC(hWnd, hdc);
}


LRESULT CALLBACK WndProc(HWND hWnd, UINT message, WPARAM wParam, LPARAM lParam)
{
 int wmId, wmEvent;
 PAINTSTRUCT ps;
 HDC hdc;
 RECT rc;

 #define TIMER1 1

switch (message)
{
  case WM_COMMAND:
      wmId = LOWORD(wParam);
      wmEvent = HIWORD(wParam);

// Parse the menu selections:
   switch (wmId)
```

```
                {
        case IDM_ABOUT:
            DialogBox(hInst, (LPCTSTR)IDD_ABOUTBOX, hWnd, (DLGPROC)About);
            break;
        case IDM_EXIT:
            DestroyWindow(hWnd);
            break;
        default:
            return DefWindowProc(hWnd, message, wParam, lParam);
            }
            break;
    case WM_PAINT:
        hdc = BeginPaint(hWnd, &ps);
        GetClientRect(hWnd, &rc);

// TODO: Add any drawing code here...
        written = sprintf(buf, "Value f1 = %.3f,
                        SQRT(f1) = %.3f", f1, fres);
        TextOut(hdc, (rc.right-rc.left)/4,
            (rc.bottom-rc.top)/2 , buf, written);
        EndPaint(hWnd, &ps);
        break;
    case WM_CREATE:
        nTimer = SetTimer(hWnd, TIMER1, 5000, (TIMERPROC) MyTimerProc);
        break;
    case WM_DESTROY:
        KillTimer(hWnd, nTimer);
        PostQuitMessage(0);
        break;
    default:
        return DefWindowProc(hWnd, message, wParam, lParam);
        }
    return 0;
}


// Message handler for about box
LRESULT CALLBACK About(HWND hDlg, UINT message, WPARAM wParam, LPARAM lParam)
{
  switch (message)
    {
```

```
case WM_INITDIALOG:
    return TRUE;
case WM_COMMAND:
    if (LOWORD(wParam) == IDOK || LOWORD(wParam) == IDCANCEL)
     {
      EndDialog(hDlg, LOWORD(wParam));
      return TRUE;
     }
    break;
    }
  return FALSE;
}
```

In this listing, note significant modifications. The system timer setting function

```
nTimer = SetTimer(hWnd, TIMER1, 5000, (TIMERPROC) MyTimerProc)
```

defines the MyTimerProc callback function. It performs the same actions as the WM_TIMER handler does in the previous listing. Regarding the WM_TIMER handler, it is removed from the code of the application because it is not needed any longer. The WM_TIMER message is handled with the MyTimerProc callback function rather than by using the application's message queue. This allows you to speed up handling the timer event.

The window of the application is shown in Fig. 13.5.

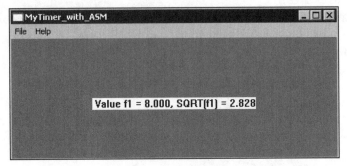

Fig. 13.5. Window of an application that handles
a timer event with a callback function

Very often, a waitable timer is used for synchronized operations. A waitable timer is an object of Windows operating system, which periodically triggers signals indicating that a certain time interval has elapsed. These signals can be used by processes or threads to control operations in real time. Waitable timers are used in most Windows system processes. They are very important for normal work of user applications that utilize synchronization. A waitable timer provides high accuracy of time measurement and a variety of methods for using it in user applications.

To use a waitable timer, a programmer must understand how is works. Since it is a fairly complicated object, it needs a detailed explanation.

The first thing you should do when using a waitable timer object is to create it with the CreateWaitableTimer WIN API function. The newly-created timer object returns a handle that can be used in later operations with the timer. The syntax of the function is as follows:

```
HANDLE CreateWaitableTimer(LPSECURITY_ATTRIBUTES lpTimerAttributes,
                    BOOL bManualReset,
                    LPCTSTR lpTimerName)
```

where

☐ lptimerAttributes — a pointer to a structure that defines a security handle. It defines whether the newly-created process can inherit the security attributes of its parent process. The default value of the handle is NULL.

☐ bManualReset — defines the timer type. If the bManualReset flag is TRUE, the timer is controlled manually. This means the application should reset the timer in a special manner. If bManualReset is FALSE, the timer is reset automatically.

☐ lpTimerName — a pointer to a null-terminated string that defines the name of the timer object. The name is case-sensitive, and its length is limited to the MAX_PATH value.

Then set the required parameters of the object and start it. This is done with the SetWaitableTimer function. Its syntax is as follows:

```
BOOL SetWaitableTimer( HANDLE hTimer,
                    Const LARGE_INTEGER *pDueTime,
                    LONG lPeriod,
                    PTIMERAPCROUTINE pfnCompletionRoutine,
                    LPVOID lpArgToCompletionRoutine,
                    BOOL fResume)
```

where

☐ hTimer — a handle to the waitable timer.

☐ pDueTime — defines a moment when the timer trigger. This is defined in intervals of 100 nanoseconds (0.1 microsecond). For example, setting liDueTime.QuadPart = –100000000 defines triggering 10 seconds after the timer start. A positive value defines an absolute time interval, i.e., the time elapsed from the start of the operating system. Though the accuracy of triggering is high, it depends on hardware.

☐ lPeriod defines the triggering period in milliseconds. If it is equal to zero, the timer triggers once. When it is greater than zero, the timer triggers repeatedly.

❏ `pfnCompletionRoutine` and `lpArgToCompletionRoutine` define a user function that will be called when the timer signal is set. An example of using these parameters is shown in Listing 13.7.

❏ `fResume` defines a power-saving mode and depends on the platform, on which the application runs. Let it be equal to zero.

Another WIN API function cancels the timer object. It is the `CancelWaitableTimer` function that takes the timer handle as a parameter.

How can a process or thread know that the timer has triggered and certain actions can be performed? So-called *wait functions* are used for this purpose. One of the most important and frequently used wait functions is the `WaitForSingleObject` WIN API function. The `WaitForSingleObject` function returns control to the application in one of these two cases:

❏ The synchronized object (such as a waitable timer) entered the signal state.

❏ The timeout for a signal from the object has expired (a timeout exit).

The syntax of this function is as follows:

```
DWORD WaitForSingleObject(HANDLE hHandle,
                          DWORD dwMilliseconds)
```

where

❏ `hHandle` — the handle to the synchronized object.

❏ `dwMilliseconds` — the timeout in milliseconds. When the `dwMilliseconds` intervals expire, the function immediately returns control to the application even if the synchronized object did not set a signal. If `dwMilliseconds` is equal to zero, the function checks the state of the synchronized object and returns control. If `dwMilliseconds` is equal to `INFINITE`, the timeout of the function is unlimited.

When developing an application that uses a waitable timer, it is very important to define crucial (for the execution time) pieces of code and to try to optimize their performance. The shorter time interval is allocated for a particular computation, the stricter performance requirements are laid on this piece of code. Implementation of high-performance algorithms or their fragments in the assembler under strict time limitations is often the only optimization method, and high-level software methods of optimization often do not work in such a situation.

Here is an example that illustrates this. Develop an application that finds the maximum element of an array of seven integers. To fill the array with random integers, use a random number generator implemented with the `rand` library function. To generate time intervals 0.5 seconds long, use a waitable timer. Let the timer synchronization time be equal to 10 seconds. This will be used only to illustrate the timer object's features.

The source code of the application is shown in Listing 13.6.

Listing 13.6. Using a waitable timer for computing the maximum every 0.5 seconds

```cpp
// WAITABLE_TIMER_USE_WITH_ASM.cpp : Defines the entry point for the
// console application

#include "stdafx.h"
#include <windows.h>
#include <stdio.h>
#include <stdlib.h>
#include <time.h>

int _tmain(int argc, _TCHAR* argv[])
{

  HANDLE hTimer = NULL;
  LARGE_INTEGER liDueTime;
  liDueTime.QuadPart = -100000000;

  int i1[10];
  int imax;

  // Seed the random-number generator with current time so that
  // the numbers will be different every time we run.

  srand( (unsigned)time( NULL ) );

 // Create a waitable timer.

  hTimer = CreateWaitableTimer(NULL, FALSE, "WaitableTimer");
  if (!hTimer)
   {
     printf("CreateWaitableTimer failed (%d)\n", GetLastError());
     exit(1);
   }
  printf("USING WAITABLE TIMER IN CALCULATION MAXIMUM INT\n\n");
  printf("Waiting for 10 seconds...\n");

// Set a timer to wait for 10 seconds.

 if (!SetWaitableTimer(hTimer, &liDueTime, 500, NULL, NULL, 0))
```

```
    {
      printf("SetWaitableTimer failed (%d)\n", GetLastError());
      exit(1);
    }

    // Wait for the timer.

while (true)
 {
   while (WaitForSingleObject(hTimer, INFINITE) != WAIT_OBJECT_0);
   printf("\n\ni1: ");
   for(int cnt = 0; cnt < 10; cnt++ )
     {
       i1[cnt] = rand();
       printf("%6d ", i1[cnt]);
     }
   _asm {
         lea  ESI, i1
         mov  ECX, 10
         mov  EAX, DWORD PTR [ESI]
         sub  ESI, 4
     next:
         add  ESI, 4
         cmp  EAX, [ESI+4]
         jl   change
         dec  ECX
         jnz  next
         jmp  ex
     change:
         xchg EAX, [ESI+4]
         dec  ECX
         jnz  next
       ex:
         mov  imax, EAX
       };
   printf("\nimax:  %6d\n", imax);
 };
   CancelWaitableTimer(hTimer);
   return 0;
}
```

Now, we will analyze the source code in more detail. A sequence of random numbers is generated with the statements:

```
srand( (unsigned)time( NULL ) )
```

and

```
. . .
for(int cnt = 0; cnt < 10; cnt++ )
  {
   i1[cnt] = rand();
   printf("%6d ", i1[cnt]);
  }
. . .
```

Filling the `i1` array with random numbers and displaying a generated sequence is done in the `for` loop.

The waitable timer is created with the function:

```
hTimer = CreateWaitableTimer(NULL, FALSE, "WaitableTimer");
```

Note the second parameter of the function. It is `FALSE`, indicating that the timer will be reset automatically. The timer object is started with the function:

```
SetWaitableTimer(hTimer, &liDueTime, 500, NULL, NULL, 0)
```

This function uses the `hTimer` handle returned by the `CreateWaitableTimer` function. The `liDueTime` variable sets the timer triggering time to 10 seconds:

```
liDueTime.QuadPart = -100000000;
```

The data are processed in the `while` loop that contains the `WaitForSingleObject` function with the `INFINITE` parameter:

```
. . .
while (true)
  {
    while (WaitForSingleObject(hTimer, INFINITE) != WAIT_OBJECT_0);
. . .
```

The maximum is computed in the assembly block. First, the ESI and ECX registers are initialized to the address of the `i1` array and its size, respectively. Then, the maximum is assumed to be equal to the first element of the array, and this value is stored in the EAX register:

```
lea   ESI, i1
mov   ECX, 10
mov   EAX, DWORD PTR [ESI]
```

The maximum is computed with the following algorithm. The contents of the EAX register are compared to the next array element whose address is [ESI+4]. If the value in the EAX register is greater than or equal to the element at this address, the iteration is repeated. If the contents of EAX are less than the value in the [ESI+4] address, the values in the EAX register and in the memory are swapped, and the next iteration begins. This is illustrated with the following code fragment:

```
        . . .
next:
        add    ESI, 4
        cmp    EAX, [ESI+4]
        jl     change
        dec    ECX
        jnz    next
        jmp    ex
  change:
        xchg   EAX, [ESI+4]
        dec    ECX
        jnz    next

        . . .
```

After all iterations are completed, the maximum value is stored in the imax variable with the mov imax, EAX command.

When the work is over, the waitable timer must be canceled with the CancelWaitableTimer(hTimer) function, where hTimer is the handle of the waitable timer.

Note that the interval of data processing is set to 0.5 seconds only for demonstration purposes. The assembly code is executed so quickly that this interval can be safely decreased hundreds or thousands of times!

Also note that if, for example, you need to perform more complex computation with large floating-point arrays in a relatively short time, the load on the processor will increase. Most likely, a correct execution of code written only in a high-level language will be problematic with such time requirements. By contrast, the assembly code will be fast, and no problems will arise.

The window of the application is shown in Fig. 13.6.

You can simplify the application in the previous example (Listing 13.6) if you replace the WaitForSingleObject wait function with a timeout function. The latter can be specified as the fourth parameter of the SetWaitableTimer function. As the fifth parameter, you can specify the address of a structure or variable used by this function (this parameter is optional). Name the timeout function findmax. It will look for the maximum with an assembly block. The parameter of this function is an integer variable (name it Cnt) that is a loop counter.

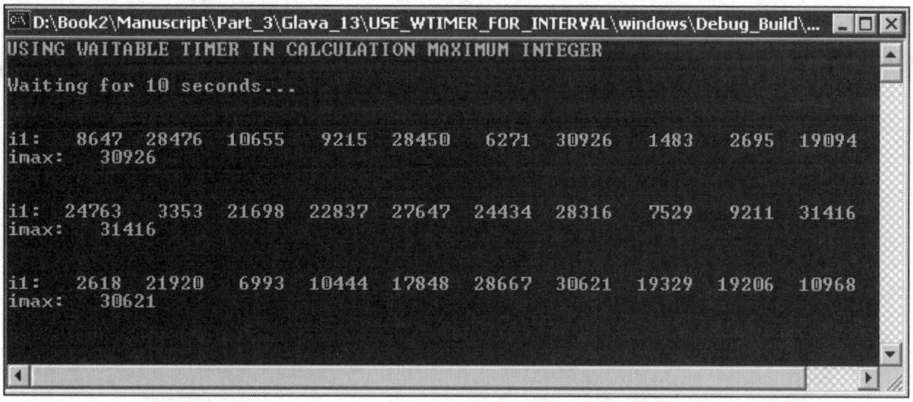

Fig. 13.6. Window of an application that demonstrates the use
of a waitable timer when finding the maximum in the integer array

To demonstrate this version of the application, we will assume that five iterations
(Cnt=5) are executed with a 0.5-second interval (like in the previous example).
The source code of the application is shown in Listing 13.7.

**Listing 13.7. A modified variant of the application that finds the maximum with
a timeout function in the waitable timer**

```cpp
// WTIMER_CALC_MAX_VAR_2.cpp : Defines the entry point for the console
// application

#include "stdafx.h"
#include <windows.h>
#include <stdio.h>
#include <stdlib.h>
#include <time.h>

HANDLE hTimer = NULL;
LARGE_INTEGER liDueTime;

int i1[10];
int imax;
int Cnt;

void findmax(void)
{
  int cnt;
```

```
if (Cnt!= 0)
{
 printf("\n\ni1: ");
 for(cnt = 0; cnt < 10; cnt++ )
 {
  i1[cnt] = rand();
  printf("%6d ", i1[cnt]);
 }
 _asm {
      lea  ESI, i1
      mov  ECX, 10
      mov  EAX, DWORD PTR [ESI]
      sub  ESI, 4
   next:
      add  ESI, 4
      cmp  EAX, [ESI+4]
      jl   change
      dec  ECX
      jnz  next
      jmp  ex
   change:
      xchg EAX, [ESI+4]
      dec  ECX
      jnz  next
    ex:
      mov  imax, EAX
  };
 printf("\nimax:  %6d\n", imax);
 Cnt--;
 }
 else
 {
  CancelWaitableTimer(hTimer);
  CloseHandle(hTimer);
 };
}

int _tmain(int argc, _TCHAR* argv[])
{
```

```
// Seed the random-number generator with current time so that
// the numbers will be different every time we run.

  srand( (unsigned)time( NULL ) );
  Cnt = 5;

// Display 5 numbers.

  liDueTime.QuadPart=-100000000;

// Create a waitable timer.

  hTimer = CreateWaitableTimer(NULL, FALSE, "WaitableTimer");
  if (!hTimer)
    {
      printf("CreateWaitableTimer failed (%d)\n", GetLastError());
      exit(1);
    }
  printf("WAITABLE TIMER IN CALCULATION MAXIMUM INT (VAR 2)\n\n");
  printf("Waiting for 10 seconds...\n");

 // Set a timer to wait for 10 seconds.

  if (!SetWaitableTimer(hTimer, &liDueTime, 500,
                     (PTIMERAPCROUTINE)findmax, &Cnt, TRUE))
    {
      printf("SetWaitableTimer failed (%d)\n", GetLastError());
      exit(1);
    }
  while (Cnt != 0)
    SleepEx(INFINITE, TRUE);
  return 0;
}
```

We will analyze this listing briefly. The findmax function is specified as a parameter of the SetWaitableTimer function:

```
SetWaitableTimer(hTimer, &liDueTime, 500,
            (PTIMERAPCROUTINE)findmax, &Cnt, TRUE)
```

Another parameter points to the address of the Cnt counter that defines the number of iterations when finding the maximum. The findmax function decrements the Cnt iteration counter and cancels the waitable timer when the counter value reaches zero.

The source code now contains the SleepEx(INFINITE, TRUE) WIN API function. It suspends the current process so that the findmax timeout function can be executed. This explains how the

```
while (Cnt != 0)
    SleepEx(INFINITE, TRUE)
```

loop works. The rest of the source code is simple and does not need further explanation.

The window of the application is shown in Fig. 13.7.

```
D:\Book2\Manuscript\Part_3\USE_WTIMER_INTERVAL_2\windows\Debug_Build\USE_WTIMER_I...
WAITABLE TIMER IN CALCULATION MAXIMUM INT (VAR 2)

Waiting for 10 seconds...

i1:  27835    3419  24925  19227  19103  22756  14472   4498  16465  28357
imax:   28357

i1:  11013    7983  20833  15110   2488    160  28372  23209  22277  20082
imax:   28372

i1:   8405    9288   5925  29908  10395   5619   5800  30347   9877   9284
imax:   30347

i1:  21323   18224   4317   9924  29437   6321   1500  23939  29996  14344
imax:   30347
```

Fig. 13.7. Window of a modified version of the application that finds
the maximum and uses a timeout function

The principles of using the inline assembler for time-dependent computation discussed in this chapter are not exhausted in the examples given here. However, these examples will help you understand more complicated uses of the assembler to work in real time.

Chapter 14: Using Assembly Language for System Programming in Windows

In this chapter, we will focus on issues related to the optimization of system programming tasks in Windows operating systems. System programming is a very complicated area that requires a strong knowledge of how the operating system works. Improvement of application quality is possible only when a programmer thoroughly understands those features of the operating system that are related to software optimization.

System programming deals with tasks such as managing the file system, memory and processes, inter-process communication, networking, and other tasks that use Application Programming Interface, specifically, WIN API functions of 32-bit operating systems of Windows family. In this chapter, we will demonstrate a few aspects of optimizing such tasks with a low level language such as the assembler. Traditional advantages of the assembler such as compactness and speed of code execution can be useful when implementing system-programming tasks as well.

Some issues related to optimizing tasks with the assembler (such as multithreading, timers, and system services) are discussed in other chapters. This chapter will focus on optimization of file operations and memory management. These operations are decisive for performance of most applications, so increasing the effectiveness of their execution is important.

We will begin with file operations. Copying, moving, searching, and deleting files and directories can be done with both C++ .NET library functions and the operating system's WIN API functions. The performance of execution depends heavily on the algorithm used in the file operations. Now, we will look at file copying.

The performance of this file operation strongly depends on the size of the read/write buffer, the way in which the data are arranged in the memory, and the number of bytes being copied or moved.

When copying one file to another, data conversion is often required. Software implementation of such a conversion significantly affects application performance. The inline assembler allows you to implement effective data conversion with minimum loss of performance. Also, the assembler allows you to write specific algorithms for data processing and conversion that would be difficult to implement in C++ with only library functions.

Here is an example. Suppose you want to substitute spaces in a file with "plus" characters and save a copy of the file with another name. Suppose also that the source file is a text file named `readfile`, and the destination file is named `writefile`. Character substitution will be done with an assembly block. The source code of the console application is shown in Listing 14.1.

Listing 14.1. Copying files with character substitution

```cpp
// COPY_F_C_ASM.cpp : Defines the entry point for the console
// application

#include "stdafx.h"
#include <stdio.h>

int _tmain(int argc, _TCHAR* argv[])
{
  FILE *fin, *fout;
  char buf[256];
  int bRead, bWritten;

  if ( (fin = fopen( "d:\\readfile", "r" )) == NULL )
  {
   printf( "The file 'readf' was not opened\n" );
   exit(1);
  }

// Open for write

  if ( (fout = fopen( "d:\\writefile", "w+" )) == NULL )
   {
     printf( "The file 'writefile' was not opened\n" );
```

```
    exit(1);
}
while ((bRead = fread(buf, sizeof(char), sizeof(buf), fin)) > 0)
{
  _asm {
        mov   ECX, bRead
        lea   ESI, buf
        mov   AL, ' '
  next_ch:
        cmp   BYTE PTR [ESI], AL
        je    repl
        inc   ESI
        dec   ECX
        jnz   next_ch
        jmp   ex
    repl:
        mov   [ESI], '+'
        inc   ESI
        dec   ECX
        jnz   next_ch
    ex:
      };

  bWritten = fwrite(buf, sizeof(char),  bRead, fout);
};
  fclose(fin);
  fclose(fout);
  return 0;
}
```

The assembly block does the conversion. The address of the memory buffer that stores the read data is loaded in the ESI register. The ECX register contains the number of bytes to process. The character being substituted, i.e., a space, is in the AL register. Each iteration compares a character in the memory to the character in the AL register. If they are equal, a "plus" character is written to the memory address, at which the space is stored, and the program jumps to the next iteration. The address of the item in the memory buffer is incremented, and the character counter is decremented:

```
cmp   BYTE PTR [ESI], AL
je    repl
inc   ESI
dec   ECX
jnz   next_ch
```

When the characters are not equal, the program jumps to the next iteration and simultaneously increments the address in the ESI register.

After conversion, the contents of the buffer are saved in a new file with the fout handle:

```
bWritten = fwrite(buf, sizeof(char), bRead, fout)
```

Using the assembler, you can create rather complicated algorithms for processing data in files, and the possibilities are unlimited.

None of these applications can do without memory operations. C++ includes the malloc function and the new operator. In most cases, programmers get along with these tools. However, some tasks require more flexible control over memory. In such cases, a WIN API function VirtualAlloc is very useful.

This function is widely used and has several important advantages in comparison with the malloc library function.

Unlike malloc, the VirtualAlloc function allows you to allocate a block of memory aligned on the page boundary and assign access attributes to it (such as read, read/write, executable, etc.). This makes it possible to process data appropriately and with maximum speed. Also, the VirtualAlloc function can reserve memory without physically allocating it, which decreases the load on the operating system as a whole.

The next example relates to the use of the VirtualAlloc memory allocation function when copying. Copying is done in an assembly block, in which string primitive commands with the rep repetition prefix are used. This makes it possible to perform the operation with high speed. The source code of the application that uses the advantages of both the VirtualAlloc function and string primitive assembly commands is shown in Listing 14.2.

Listing 14.2. Copying characters with the VirtualAlloc function

```
// VA_EXAMPLE.cpp : Defines the entry point for the console application

#include "stdafx.h"
#include <windows.h>
#include <time.h>

int _tmain(int argc, _TCHAR* argv[])
{
  int* src = NULL;
  int* dst = NULL;

  printf(" VirtualAlloc copying with ASM EXAMPLE\n\n");

  srand( (unsigned)time( NULL ) );
```

```
src = (int*)VirtualAlloc(NULL, 10, MEM_COMMIT, PAGE_READWRITE);
int* bsrc = src;

dst = (int*)VirtualAlloc(NULL, 10, MEM_COMMIT, PAGE_READWRITE);
printf("\nsrc : ");
for(int cnt = 0; cnt < 10; cnt++)
  {
    *src = rand();
    printf("%d ", *src);
    src++;
  }

_asm {
      mov   ESI, bsrc
      mov   EDI, dst
      mov   ECX, 10
      cld
      rep   movsd
    }
printf("\n\ndst : ");
for(int cnt = 0; cnt < 10; cnt++)
  {
    printf("%d ", *dst);
    dst++;
  }
VirtualFree(bsrc, 0, MEM_RELEASE);
VirtualFree(dst, 0, MEM_RELEASE);

getchar();
return 0;
}
```

Note the following statement:

```
int* bsrc = src
```

It is necessary for correctly setting the address of the array in the `bsrc` pointer.

The memory for a ten-element array of random numbers `src` is allocated with the command:

```
src = (int*)VirtualAlloc(NULL, 10, MEM_COMMIT, PAGE_READWRITE)
```

The memory for a destination array `dst` is allocated in a similar fashion:

```
dst = (int*)VirtualAlloc(NULL, 10, MEM_COMMIT, PAGE_READWRITE)
```

High-speed copying is done with the following assembly commands:

```
mov  ESI, bsrc
mov  EDI, dst
mov  ECX, 10
cld
rep  movsd
```

When you do not need the allocated memory any longer, you should free it. This is done with the functions:

```
VirtualFree(bsrc, 0, MEM_RELEASE)
VirtualFree(dst, 0, MEM_RELEASE)
```

The window of the application is shown in Fig. 14.1.

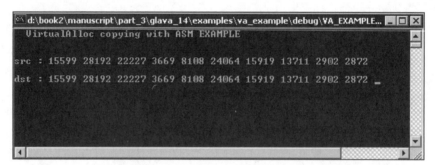

Fig. 14.1. Window of an application that copies integers with the `VirtualAlloc` function

Windows operating systems support another very useful technology for working with files. File mapping to the memory is done. This is very convenient for processing files with several processes simultaneously, and this technology is widely used. The virtual memory manager of the operating system allows an application to work with a file as if it is loaded in the computer's memory. To work with a file mapped to the memory, proceed as follows:

1. Open the file with the `CreateFile` function.
2. Pass the file handle to the `CreateFileMapping` WIN API function.
3. Get a pointer to the memory buffer containing the file with the `MapViewOfFile` function. This is a common pointer, i.e., you can perform on it any operations valid for pointers.

4. After you complete the work with the file, call the `UnmapViewOfFile` function.
5. Delete the handle to the file-mapping object and close the file handle with the `CloseHandle` function.

The next example demonstrates the use of file mapping to memory. Depending on which option is selected (one or zero), alphanumeric characters in the `testmap` text file are converted to the upper or lower case. Like in the previous listing, the conversion is done with the inline assembler, which provides good performance. The source code of the application is shown in Listing 14.3.

Listing 14.3. Converting a file mapped to the memory with the assembler

---

```cpp
// FILE_MAPPING_EXAMPLE.cpp : Defines the entry point for the console
// application

#include "stdafx.h"
#include <windows.h>

int _tmain(int argc, _TCHAR* argv[])
{
 HANDLE fin;
 HANDLE map_fin;
 char* mapBase = NULL;
 int fSize;
 int choice = 0;

 printf("   USING FILE MAPPING WITH ASM OPTIMIZING\n\n");

 printf("Enter 1 - convert to upper, 0 - convert to lower:");
 scanf("%d", &choice);

 fin = CreateFile("d:\\testmap", GENERIC_WRITE|GENERIC_READ,
                  0, NULL, OPEN_EXISTING,
                  0, NULL);
 if (fin == INVALID_HANDLE_VALUE)
  {
   printf("Cannot open file\n");
   exit(1);
  }
```

```c
fSize = GetFileSize(fin, NULL);

map_fin = CreateFileMapping(fin, NULL,
                              PAGE_READWRITE, 0,
                              0, NULL);
if (!map_fin)
{
printf("Cannot open mapping\n");
getchar();
exit(2);
 }


mapBase = (char*)MapViewOfFile(map_fin,
                              FILE_MAP_WRITE,
                              0, 0, 0);
if (!mapBase)
 {
  printf("Cannot get the map pointer\n");
  getchar();
  exit(1);
 }
char* dmapBase = mapBase;
switch(choice){
      case 1:
        _asm {
                mov  ECX, fSize
                mov  EDI, dmapBase
    next_char:
                mov  AL, BYTE PTR [EDI]
                cmp  AL, 96
                jg   high_check
                jmp  next
    high_check:
                cmp  AL, 122
                jg   next
                sub  AL, 32
                mov  BYTE PTR [EDI], AL
         next:
                add  EDI,1
                dec  ECX
```

```
                jnz   next_char
                }
          break;
      case 0:
          _asm {
                mov   ECX, fSize
                mov   EDI, dmapBase
      next1_char:
                mov   AL, BYTE PTR [EDI]
                cmp   AL, 64
                jg    high1_check
                jmp   next1
      high1_check:
                cmp   AL, 90
                jg    next
                add   AL, 32
                mov   BYTE PTR [EDI], AL
          next1:
                add   EDI, 1
                dec   ECX
                jnz   next1_char
                };
        break;
      default:
        break;
    };
printf("\n       NEW CONTENT OF FILE: \n\n");
for (int cnt = 0; cnt < fSize; cnt++)
      printf("%c", *mapBase++);
UnmapViewOfFile(mapBase);
CloseHandle(map_fin);
CloseHandle(fin);
getchar();
return 0;
}
```

The window, in which characters are converted to the upper case, is shown in Fig. 14.2, and the window with the conversion to the lower case is in Fig. 14.3.

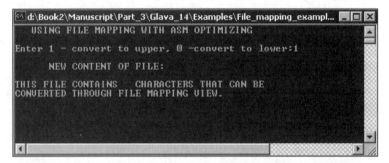

Fig. 14.2. Converting characters in a text file to the upper case

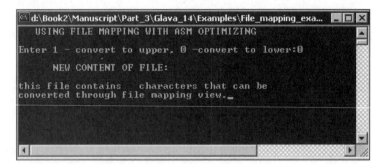

Fig. 14.3. Converting characters in a text file to the lower case

This completes the discussion of using the assembler for optimization of system programming tasks. This chapter addressed the most important system programming tasks and their optimization with the assembler.

Chapter 15: Optimizing Procedure-Oriented Applications and System Services

This chapter will focus on principles of using the C++ .NET 2003 inline assembler in procedure-oriented Windows applications and system services. Using the assembler for each of these task types has distinct features, which will be discussed here.

We will begin with a classical procedure-oriented Windows application.

Suppose an application should display the difference between two integers in the application's work area. The frame of such an application can be easily obtained with the Visual C++ .NET Application Wizard. Suppose the difference should be displayed by left clicking on the application window.

The source code of the application is shown in Listing 15.1.

Listing 15.1. A procedure-oriented Windows application that computes the difference between two integers

```
// WIN_CLASSIC.cpp : Defines the entry point for the application

#include "stdafx.h"
#include "WIN_CLASSIC.h"
#include <stdio.h>
#define MAX_LOADSTRING 100
```

```
// Global Variables:

HINSTANCE hInst;                       // Current instance
TCHAR szTitle[MAX_LOADSTRING];         // The title bar text
TCHAR szWindowClass[MAX_LOADSTRING];   // The main window class name

// Forward declarations of functions included in this code module:

ATOM                    MyRegisterClass(HINSTANCE hInstance);
BOOL                    InitInstance(HINSTANCE, int);
LRESULT CALLBACK        WndProc(HWND, UINT, WPARAM, LPARAM);
LRESULT CALLBACK        About(HWND, UINT, WPARAM, LPARAM);

int APIENTRY _tWinMain(HINSTANCE hInstance,
                       HINSTANCE hPrevInstance,
                       LPTSTR    lpCmdLine,
                       int       nCmdShow)
{
// TODO: Place code here.

 MSG msg;
 HACCEL hAccelTable;

// Initialize global strings

LoadString(hInstance, IDS_APP_TITLE, szTitle, MAX_LOADSTRING);
LoadString(hInstance, IDC_WIN_CLASSIC, szWindowClass, MAX_LOADSTRING);
MyRegisterClass(hInstance);

// Perform application initialization:

if (!InitInstance (hInstance, nCmdShow))
 {
  return FALSE;
 }

hAccelTable = LoadAccelerators(hInstance, (LPCTSTR)IDC_WIN_CLASSIC);

// Main message loop:

while (GetMessage(&msg, NULL, 0, 0))
 {
  if (!TranslateAccelerator(msg.hwnd, hAccelTable, &msg))
   {
```

```
      TranslateMessage(&msg);
      DispatchMessage(&msg);
    }
  }

  return (int) msg.wParam;
}

//  FUNCTION: MyRegisterClass()

//  PURPOSE: Registers the window class.

//  COMMENTS:

// This function and its usage are only necessary if you want this code
// to be compatible with Win32 systems prior to the 'RegisterClassEx'
// function that was added to Windows 95. It is important to call this
// function so that the application will get 'well formed' small icons
// associated with it.

ATOM MyRegisterClass(HINSTANCE hInstance)
{
  WNDCLASSEX wcex;

  wcex.cbSize = sizeof(WNDCLASSEX);

  wcex.style = CS_HREDRAW | CS_VREDRAW;
  wcex.lpfnWndProc = (WNDPROC)WndProc;
  wcex.cbClsExtra = 0;
  wcex.cbWndExtra = 0;
  wcex.hInstance = hInstance;
  wcex.hIcon = LoadIcon(hInstance, (LPCTSTR)IDI_WIN_CLASSIC);
  wcex.hCursor = LoadCursor(NULL, IDC_ARROW);
  wcex.hbrBackground = (HBRUSH)(COLOR_WINDOW-1);
  wcex.lpszMenuName = (LPCTSTR)IDC_WIN_CLASSIC;
  wcex.lpszClassName = szWindowClass;
  wcex.hIconSm = LoadIcon(wcex.hInstance, (LPCTSTR)IDI_SMALL);

  return RegisterClassEx(&wcex);
}

//  FUNCTION: InitInstance(HANDLE, int)

//  PURPOSE: Saves instance handle and creates main window
```

```
//  COMMENTS:

// In this function, we save the instance handle in a global variable and
// create and display the main program window.

BOOL InitInstance(HINSTANCE hInstance, int nCmdShow)
{
  HWND hWnd;
  hInst = hInstance; // Store instance handle in our global variable

  hWnd = CreateWindow(szWindowClass, szTitle, WS_OVERLAPPEDWINDOW,
                                      CW_USEDEFAULT, 0,
                                      CW_USEDEFAULT, 0,
                                      NULL, NULL, hInstance,
                                      NULL);
 if (!hWnd)
 {
  return FALSE;
 }

ShowWindow(hWnd, nCmdShow);
UpdateWindow(hWnd);

return TRUE;
}

//  FUNCTION: WndProc(HWND, unsigned, WORD, LONG)

//  PURPOSE:  Processing messages for the main window

//  WM_COMMAND - Process the application menu.
//  WM_PAINT - Paint the main window.
//  WM_DESTROY - Post a quit message and return.

LRESULT CALLBACK WndProc(HWND hWnd, UINT message,
                         WPARAM wParam, LPARAM lParam)
{
 int wmId, wmEvent;
 PAINTSTRUCT ps;
 HDC hdc;
 RECT rc;
 int i1, i2, ires;
```

```
char buf[32] = "i1 - i2 = ";

switch (message)
{
 case WM_COMMAND:
       wmId    = LOWORD(wParam);
       wmEvent = HIWORD(wParam);

// Parse the menu selections:

       switch (wmId)
         {
           case IDM_ABOUT:
              DialogBox(hInst, (LPCTSTR)IDD_ABOUTBOX,
                               hWnd, (DLGPROC)About);
              break;
           case IDM_EXIT:
              DestroyWindow(hWnd);
              break;
           default:
              return DefWindowProc(hWnd, message, wParam, lParam);
         }
       break;
 case WM_PAINT:
    hdc = BeginPaint(hWnd, &ps);

// TODO: Add any drawing code here...

    EndPaint(hWnd, &ps);
    break;

// Added code

 case WM_LBUTTONDOWN:
    i1 = 45;
    i2 = 98;
    hdc = GetDC(hWnd);
    GetClientRect(hWnd, &rc);
    _asm {
         mov EAX, i1
         sub EAX, i2
         mov ires, EAX
         }
```

```
      sprintf(&buf[9], "%d", ires);
      TextOut(hdc, (rc.right-rc.left)/3, (rc.bottom-rc.top)/2, buf, 12);
      InvalidateRect(hWnd, &rc, FALSE);
      ReleaseDC(hWnd, hdc);
      break;
  case WM_DESTROY:
      PostQuitMessage(0);
      break;
  default:
      return DefWindowProc(hWnd, message, wParam, lParam);
   }
  return 0;
  }


// Message handler for about box.

LRESULT CALLBACK About(HWND hDlg, UINT message, WPARAM wParam, LPARAM
lParam)
{
  switch (message)
    {
    case WM_INITDIALOG:
      return TRUE;
    case WM_COMMAND:
      if (LOWORD(wParam) == IDOK || LOWORD(wParam) == IDCANCEL)
          {
              EndDialog(hDlg, LOWORD(wParam));
              return TRUE;
          }
      break;
     }
   return FALSE;
}
```

Since we deal with a classical procedure-oriented Windows application, the WM_LBUTTONDOWN message handler is used for displaying the result:

```
  case WM_LBUTTONDOWN:
        i1 = 45;
        i2 = 98;
        hdc = GetDC(hWnd);
        GetClientRect(hWnd, &rc);
        _asm {
            mov EAX, i1
```

```
        sub EAX, i2
        mov ires, EAX
        }
    sprintf(&buf[9], "%d", ires);
    TextOut(hdc, (rc.right-rc.left)/3, (rc.bottom-rc.top)/2, buf, 12);
    InvalidateRect(hWnd, &rc, FALSE);
    ReleaseDC(hWnd, hdc);
    break;
```

Put the code of the `onBnClicked` handler, for example, after the `WM_PAINT` handler in the callback function. We will look at this code more closely.

The first two statements assign values to variables (`i1` и `i2`). In our case, these are `i1 = 45` and `i2 = 98`.

The variables are declared in the `WndProc` callback function. This function also declares auxiliary variables `rc`, `ires`, and `buf`.

To display the result in the application window, you should first access the display device context. This is done with the following statement:

```
hdc = GetDC(hWnd)
```

To get the coordinates of the client rectangle of the application window, use the following statement:

```
GetClientRect(hWnd, &rc)
```

You will need these coordinates to position and display the text.

The assembly block does the main job in this handler: It computes the difference between two numbers. The result is stored in the `ires` variable.

To display the value of the `ires` integer variable, convert it to a text string. The `sprintf` function is suitable for this purpose. The function is defined in the `stdio.h` header file; therefore, this file must be included in the source code. The `sprintf` function has the following form:

```
sprintf(&buf[9], "%d", ires)
```

After the `ires` integer variable is converted to a character string (the `buf` variable), the result can be output to the client rectangle. This is done with the function:

```
TextOut(hdc, (rc.right-rc.left)/3, (rc.bottom-rc.top)/2, buf, 12)
```

Finally, tell the operating system to redraw the client rectangle of the application window. This is done with the function:

```
InvalidateRect(hWnd, &rc, FALSE);
```

Before you exit the handler, release the device context:

```
ReleaseDC(hWnd, hdc);
```

Using assembly blocks and commands in a procedure-oriented application is simple. Simply put the code into the handler of an event. Keep in mind that the results of mathematical calculations should be converted to the character type before displaying or printing them. Functions such as TextOut operate with character data; therefore, such a conversion is required.

The window of the application is shown in Fig. 15.1.

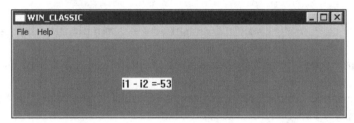

Fig. 15.1. Window of a procedure-oriented Windows application
that displays the difference between two integers

Assembly language is an effective tool for optimization when developing Windows system services. These are the most mysterious part of the operating system, and at the same time the most important. You could roughly define a system service as a program that runs outside the user's context.

System services are supported only in Windows NT/2000/XP/2003 operating systems. In Windows, the services are used for implementing the most important tasks related to operating system management and monitoring. They provide access to drivers of the file and disk system of a computer and are an intermediate link for accessing the computer's hardware.

Most of the services are exact to the time of execution, especially when they work with the computer's hardware. Using the assembler for writing crucial pieces of code for such services is often the only way of providing their correct work within strict time limitations.

Suppose an application receives a data stream from the USB or COM port of a PC and writes it to a file for future processing. With particular time intervals, a system service reads the data from this file and processes it in background. Suppose that the data stream written to the file from the USB port is a sequence of integers (which often is the case). Processing such data by a system service can involve looking for the maximum value in the data received and written to the file at this moment.

Such a software configuration is typical for data measurement and processing systems in industry and scientific research. A driver reads data from a physical device and performs some preliminary processing. After this processing, the data are usually saved in a file. The subsequent manipulations with data are done by another program that is often implemented as a system service.

A device driver works in real time, and it can make a few thousands or even tens of thousands data samples per second. For storing and preliminarily processing the data, a large amount of memory and a lot of processor time might be required. If the number of received bytes is not large, or time limitations are strict, the use of the computer memory is reasonable. However, this is true only in this case. It is very convenient to save data in a file (the space on hard disks makes it possible to do this), but this creates a problem: A high-level application slowly processes data in a file. Even if the driver writes the data on the disk very fast (which is quite achievable), high-level processing, analysis, and displaying of the results in real time may be a very difficult task. Redundancy of the code of the system service at the data processing stage will make the whole data collecting and analysis system completely inoperable.

In such cases, the code of the Windows service should be as compact and fast as possible. Also keep in mind that Windows NT/2000/XP/2003 operating systems are not real-time systems, and data processing can take much more time than planned. The assembler is useful in this case. A well-designed code fragment or function can provide required performance in crucial parts.

We will look at two examples of developing Windows system services that use the assembler to improve performance. Taking into account the complexity and importance of the topic, we will begin with some theoretical information on the basic principles of system service development. We will focus on just the main issues, so that you can understand the examples in this chapter and write your own.

From a software developer's point of view, system services are programs, usually console ones, that are related to the operating system's Service Control Manager (SCM) in a special manner. SCM is an internal component of Windows that controls system services and device drivers. SCM interacts with the user via Services Control Panel (Windows NT 4.0) or one of Microsoft Management Console (MMC) modules in Windows 2000/XP/2003.

Like any other console application, the system service has the `main` function that can support the work of several services. In the following examples, applications for one service are considered. The console application of a service must contain the entry point of the service that is usually named `ServiceStart` or `ServiceMain`. This entry point is associated with the text identifier of the service.

For interaction between a service and the system, a service control handler should be registered. The service usually runs in background and requires a separate thread. You can develop code of a system service either manually or with Visual C++ .NET 2003 Application Wizard.

Regardless of which tools you are using, you should stick to the following procedure:

1. Define the `main()` entry point that will register the service in SCM. Tell the Service Control Dispatcher the entry point (`ServiceStart`) and name of the service. This is done with the `StartServiceCtrlDispatcher` function.

2. Pass control to the ServiceStart function to register the service control handler. This is done with the RegisterServiceCtrlHandler function. In addition, the ServiceStart function usually starts the main thread of the service with one of the following functions: _beginthread, _beginthreadex, or CreateThread.

3. Create the service control handler.

Now, we will continue with practical examples. The first one models a small data collecting and processing system. Unfortunately, we cannot illustrate its work in real time in this example. The goal of this demonstration is to show you how assembly language can be used in a Windows system service that processes data from a file. The task of the system service is simple: It looks for the maximum value among integers saved in a file named test.

Instead of a driver, we will use a test program that will write five random integers in the test file and display the contents of the file every time you hit the <Enter> key. Also, the maximum read from the testmax file will be displayed.

This "virtual" data processing system starts a system service (we will name it FileWriter) that reads the contents of the test file every 30 seconds, finds the maximum, and writes it in the testmax file.

Now, we will examine how the maximum is looked for with an assembly block in the FileWriter system service. To develop the service, create a project of a console application without source files (i.e., an empty project) and add the filewriter.cpp source file to it (Listing 15.2).

Listing 15.2. The FileWriter system service that looks for the maximum element in a binary file

---

```
#include <windows.h>
#include <stdio.h>
#include <string.h>
#include <time.h>
#include <process.h>

SERVICE_STATUS          Service1Status;
SERVICE_STATUS_HANDLE   Service1StatusHandle;
int modtime=30;         // Interval = 30 seconds

HANDLE thread;
BOOL manual=FALSE;
int rx[256];
int imax;
FILE* fp;
```

```c
void findmax(void *)
{
 time_t timeval;
 while (Service1Status.dwCurrentState != SERVICE_STOPPED)
 {
  if (Service1Status.dwCurrentState != SERVICE_PAUSED)
   {
     time(&timeval);
     if ((timeval%modtime)==0|| manual)
      {
       if (!(fp = fopen("d:\\test", "a+b")))
             exit(1);
       int fres = fseek(fp, 0, SEEK_END);
       int fsize = ftell(fp);
       fres = fseek(fp, 0, SEEK_SET);
       fread(&rx, sizeof(int), fsize, fp);
       fclose(fp);
       _asm {
               mov   ECX, fsize
               shr   ECX, 2
               lea   ESI, rx
               mov   EAX, DWORD PTR [ESI]
           again:
               add   ESI, 4
               cmp   EAX, DWORD PTR [ESI]
               jge   next_int
               xchg  EAX, DWORD PTR [ESI]
         next_int:
               dec   ECX
               jnz   again
               mov   imax, EAX
             };
       if (!(fp = fopen("d:\\testmax", "w+b")))
             exit(1);
       fwrite(&imax, sizeof(int), 1, fp);
       fclose(fp);
       }
     manual=FALSE;
     }
 Sleep(500);
  }
```

```
}

VOID __stdcall CtrlHandler (DWORD Opcode)
{
  DWORD status;
  switch(Opcode)
    {
     case SERVICE_CONTROL_PAUSE:

// Do whatever it takes to pause here.

       Service1Status.dwCurrentState = SERVICE_PAUSED;
       break;
     case SERVICE_CONTROL_CONTINUE:

// Do whatever it takes to continue here.

       Service1Status.dwCurrentState = SERVICE_RUNNING;
       manual=TRUE;
       break;
     case SERVICE_CONTROL_STOP:

// Do whatever it takes to stop here.

       Service1Status.dwWin32ExitCode = 0;
       Service1Status.dwCurrentState = SERVICE_STOPPED;
       Service1Status.dwCheckPoint = 0;
       Service1Status.dwWaitHint = 0;
       if (!SetServiceStatus (Service1StatusHandle, &Service1Status))
           status = GetLastError();

       return;
     case SERVICE_CONTROL_INTERROGATE:
       break;
     default:
     }

// Send current status.

  if (!SetServiceStatus (Service1StatusHandle,  &Service1Status))
     status = GetLastError();
  return;
}
```

```
void __stdcall Service1Start (DWORD argc, LPTSTR *argv)
{
 DWORD status;
 DWORD specificError;
 if (argc > 1) modtime = atoi(argv[1]);
 if (modtime == 0) modtime = 1;

 Service1Status.dwServiceType          = SERVICE_WIN32;
 Service1Status.dwCurrentState         = SERVICE_START_PENDING;
 Service1Status.dwControlsAccepted     = SERVICE_ACCEPT_STOP |
                                         SERVICE_ACCEPT_PAUSE_CONTINUE;
 Service1Status.dwWin32ExitCode        = 0;
 Service1Status.dwServiceSpecificExitCode = 0;
 Service1Status.dwCheckPoint           = 0;
 Service1Status.dwWaitHint             = 0;
 Service1StatusHandle = RegisterServiceCtrlHandler(TEXT("FileWriter"),
                                          CtrlHandler);
 if (Service1StatusHandle == (SERVICE_STATUS_HANDLE)0)
    return;

// Initialization code goes here.

 status=NO_ERROR;

// Handle error condition

 if (status != NO_ERROR)
 {
   Service1Status.dwCurrentState         = SERVICE_STOPPED;
   Service1Status.dwCheckPoint           = 0;
   Service1Status.dwWaitHint             = 0;
   Service1Status.dwWin32ExitCode        = status;
   Service1Status.dwServiceSpecificExitCode = specificError;
   SetServiceStatus (Service1StatusHandle, &Service1Status);
   return;
 }

// Initialization complete - report running status.

   Service1Status.dwCurrentState         = SERVICE_RUNNING;
   Service1Status.dwCheckPoint           = 0;
   Service1Status.dwWaitHint             = 0;
   if (!SetServiceStatus (Service1StatusHandle, &Service1Status))
```

```
       status = GetLastError();
// This is where the service does its work.

   thread= (HANDLE)_beginthread(findmax, 0, NULL);
   return;
}
void main(int argc, char *argv[])
{
 SERVICE_TABLE_ENTRY   DispatchTable[] =
  {
   { TEXT("FileWriter"), Service1Start        },
   { NULL,                NULL                 }
  };
 if (argc>1 && !stricmp(argv[1], "delete"))
  {
   SC_HANDLE scm = OpenSCManager(NULL, NULL, SC_MANAGER_CREATE_SERVICE);
   if (!scm)
    {
       printf("Can't open SCM\n");
       exit(1);
    }
   SC_HANDLE svc = OpenService(scm, "FileWriter", DELETE);
   if (!svc)
    {
       printf("Can't open service\n");
       exit(2);
    }
   if (!DeleteService(svc))
    {
       printf("Can't delete service\n");
       exit(3);
    }
   printf("Service deleted\n");
   CloseServiceHandle(svc);
   CloseServiceHandle(scm);

   exit(0);
  }
  if (argc>1 && !stricmp(argv[1], "setup"))
   {
    char pname[1024];
    pname[0] = '"';
    GetModuleFileName(NULL, pname+1, 1023);
```

```
    strcat(pname, "\"");
    SC_HANDLE scm = OpenSCManager(NULL, NULL, SC_MANAGER_CREATE_SERVICE, svc);
    if (!scm)
        {
          printf("Can't open SCM\n");
          exit(1);
        }
    if (!(svc=CreateService(scm,"FileWriter","FileWriter",
                      SERVICE_ALL_ACCESS,
                      SERVICE_WIN32_OWN_PROCESS,
                      SERVICE_DEMAND_START,
                      SERVICE_ERROR_NORMAL,
                      pname, NULL, NULL,
                      NULL, NULL, NULL)))
        {
         printf("Registration error!\n");
         exit(2);
        }
  printf("Successfully registered\n");
  CloseServiceHandle(svc);
  CloseServiceHandle(scm);
  exit(0);
}

if (!StartServiceCtrlDispatcher( DispatchTable))

}
```

How does the `FileWriter` system service work? When the `ServiceStart` function is called (which is the entry point to the service), the main thread containing the `findmax` function is started, which does the service's job:

```
thread= (HANDLE)_beginthread(findmax, 0, NULL)
```

In accordance with the value of the `modtime` variable, the assembly block of the `findmax` function is called every 30 seconds:

```
_asm {
        mov   ECX, fsize
        shr   ECX, 2
        lea   ESI, rx
        mov   EAX, DWORD PTR [ESI]
    again:
        add   ESI, 4
        cmp   EAX, DWORD PTR [ESI]
        jge   next_int
```

```
        xchg EAX, DWORD PTR [ESI]
next_int:
        dec  ECX
        jnz  again
        mov  imax, EAX
    };
```

This fragment of code implements the search for the maximum element in the memory buffer whose address is in the ESI register. ESI contains the address of the rx buffer that contains integers read from the test file. The found maximum value is stored in the imax variable. Then the

```
if (!(fp = fopen("d:\\testmax", "w+b")))
        exit(1);
fwrite(&imax, sizeof(int), 1, fp);
fclose(fp);
```

statements write the maximum value from the imax variable to the testmax file.

This operation repeats every 30 seconds. However, another interval can be specified in the modtime variable.

Now, we will provide a few words about starting the FileWriter system service. The first thing you should complete is the installation of the service in the operating system. For this purpose, execute the

```
FileWriter setup
```

command from the command line.

To delete the system service, execute the following command:

```
FileWriter delete
```

Installation of the system service is shown in Fig. 15.2.

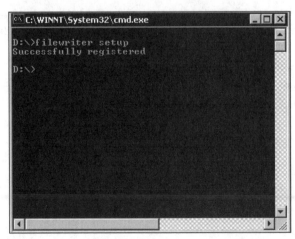

Fig. 15.2. Installation of the FileWriter system service in Windows

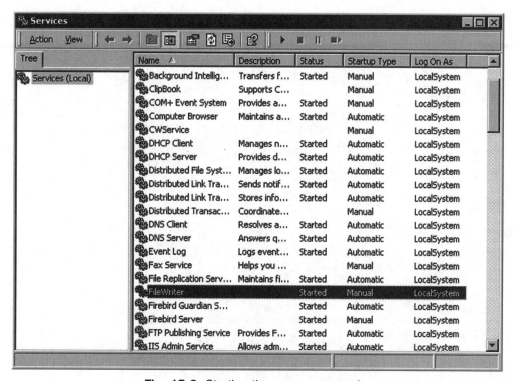

Fig. 15.3. Starting the FileWriter service

The installed FileWriter service can be started from the service control window (Fig. 15.3).

The program that tests the FileWriter system service writes five random values in the test binary file. The same program finds the maximum of the elements in the file. This program also opens the testmax file created by the FileWriter system service and checks the maximum value written to it. The testmax file will contain the maximum obtained with the system service before the next start of the test program. The source code of the test console program is shown in Listing 15.3.

Listing 15.3. A program that tests a system service

```cpp
// FILE_WRITE_ADD_EXM.cpp : Defines the entry point for the console
// application

#include "stdafx.h"
#include <stdlib.h>
#include <time.h>
```

```
int _tmain(int argc, _TCHAR* argv[])
{
FILE* fp;
int ix[25];
int rx[256];
int imax;
int imax1 = 0;

printf("SYSTEM SERVICE FILEWRITERS' TEST APPLICATION\n\n");
srand( (unsigned)time( NULL ) );
for (int cnt = 0; cnt < 5; cnt++)
    ix[cnt] = rand();

if (!(fp = fopen("d:\\test", "a+b")))
  {
   printf("Cannot open file!\n");
    exit(1);
}
fwrite(&ix, sizeof(int), 5, fp);
int fres = fseek(fp, 0, SEEK_END);
int fsize = ftell(fp);

printf("Size of file TEST = %d Bytes\n\n", fsize);
fres = fseek(fp, 0, SEEK_SET);
fread(&rx, sizeof(int), fsize, fp);
for (int cnt = 0; cnt < fsize/4; cnt++)
printf("%d ", rx[cnt]);

fclose(fp);
_asm {
      mov  ECX, fsize
      shr  ECX, 2
      lea  ESI, rx
      mov  EAX, DWORD PTR [ESI]
again:
      add  ESI, 4
      cmp  EAX, DWORD PTR [ESI]
      jge  next_int
      xchg EAX, DWORD PTR [ESI]
next_int:
      dec  ECX
      jnz  again
      mov  imax, EAX
      };
printf("\nMaximum = %d\n", imax);

if (!(fp = fopen("d:\\testmax", "a+b")))
  {
```

```
  printf("Cannot open file!\n");
  exit(1);
}
fread(&imax1, sizeof(int), 1, fp);
printf("\nFile TESTMAX contains = %d ", imax1);
getchar();
return 0;
}
```

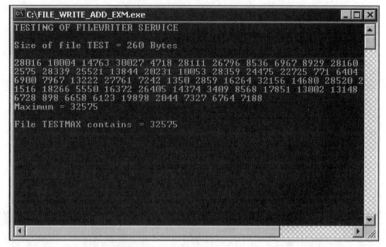

Fig. 15.4. Window of a program that tests a system service

The window of the application is shown in Fig. 15.4.

The second example of using the assembler in a system service is more complicated. Suppose you want to count words in a text file periodically and display this number. Text information is written to or deleted from the file at random moments. Like in the previous example, a real-time data processing system is modeled here. Implementation of the program as a system service is best suited for monitoring changes in a file.

This time, use the Visual C++ .NET Application Wizard to create the frame of the service. Be very careful when making the following steps.

Select the Windows Service application type (Fig. 15.5).

We will name the project CWService. After the sample system service is created, change the CWServiceWinService name given by the Wizard to CWService and leave the other options unchanged (Fig. 15.6).

Add the installer for the service to your project. This is required for installation/deinstallation and for setting the start options of the service. You can add the installer in the project constructor area by clicking the right mouse button and selecting the **Add Installer** option (Fig. 15.7).

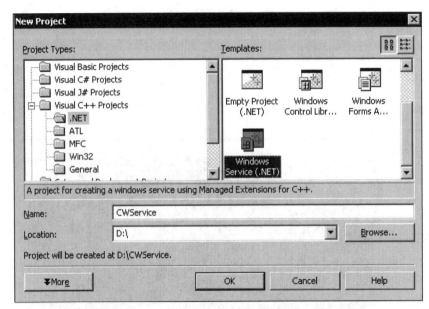

Fig. 15.5. Selecting the Windows Service application type

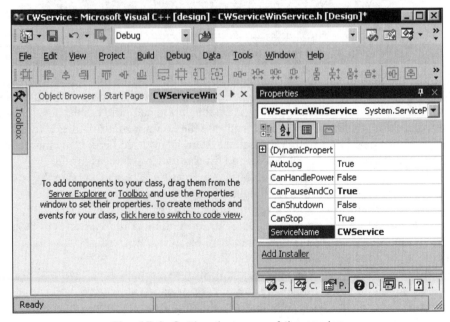

Fig. 15.6. Setting the name of the service

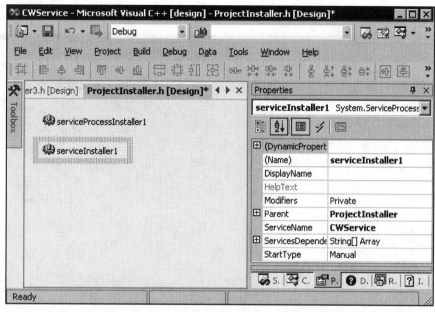

Fig. 15.7. Adding the installer to the project

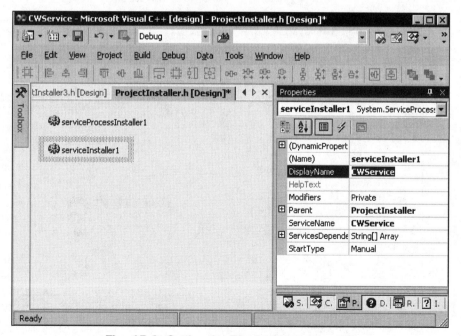

Fig. 15.8. Setting the **DisplayName** property

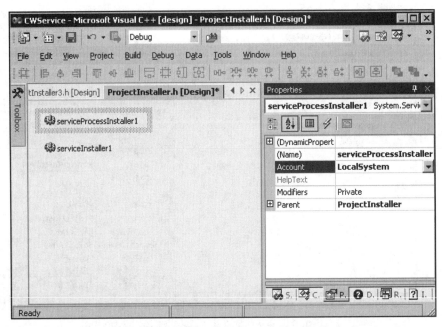

Fig. 15.9. Setting the **Account** property

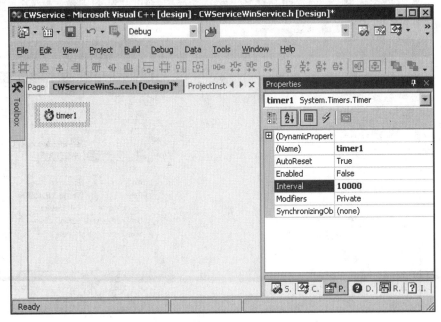

Fig. 15.10. Setting the timer properties

Then, assign the CWService name to the **DisplayName** field of the service installer (Fig. 15.8).

Note that generally, the names assigned to the **DisplayName** and **ServiceName** fields can be different. Leave the **StartType** field unchanged (the service is started manually).

The **Account** field of the process installer should contain the LocalSystem record (Fig. 15.9).

The subsequent steps involve modulation of the code of the service. Recall that your service should periodically count words in a text file. To perform periodical operations, use the Timer component on the Toolbox panel. Put the component on the design work area. Set the timer properties as shown in Fig. 15.10.

As you can see from Fig. 15.10, the timer-triggering interval is set to 10 seconds, and the initial state of the timer is "off." In addition, put the EventLog component on the work area. We will need it to display the number of words in the file. This component connects your service to the Windows event log. Set the properties of the EventLog component as shown in Fig. 15.11.

We will continue with a few explanations concerning setting the properties of the EventLog component. The source of events to log is the CWService service, and the events will be recorded in the event log file.

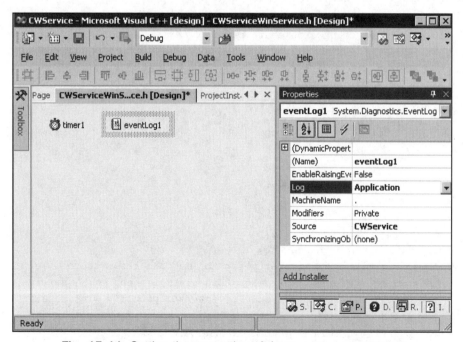

Fig. 15.11. Setting the properties of the EventLog component

For the CWService system service to do some useful work, the timer should be started in the OnStart event handler. After that, the OnTimer event handler will be able to perform required actions.

When the service stops, the timer should be stopped as well. This is done in the OnStop event handler. Below is the source code of the CWServiceWinService class that defines the behavior of your service (Listing 15.4).

Listing 15.4. The source code of the CWServiceWinService class

```
#pragma once

using namespace System;
using namespace System::Collections;
using namespace System::ServiceProcess;
using namespace System::ComponentModel;

#include <windows.h>
#include <stdio.h>

using namespace System::Runtime::InteropServices;
[DllImport("cw.dll")]
 extern "C" int countwords(char* path);

int cntWords;
char buf[64];
int ibuf;

namespace CWService
{
// <summary>
// Summary for CWServiceWinService
// </summary>
//
// WARNING: If you change the name of this class,
// you will need to change the
// 'Resource File Name' property for the managed resource compiler tool
// associated with all .resx files this class depends on. Otherwise,
// the designers will not be able to interact properly with localized
// resources associated with this form.
        public __gc class CWServiceWinService : ↵
public System::ServiceProcess::ServiceBase
```

```
        {
public:
        CWServiceWinService()
        {
                InitializeComponent();
        }
        // <summary>
        // Clean up any resources being used.
        // </summary>
        void Dispose(bool disposing)
        {
                if (disposing && components)
                {
                        components->Dispose();
                }
                   super::Dispose(disposing);
        }


protected:
        // <summary>
        // Set things in motion so your service can do its work.
        // </summary>
        void OnStart(String* args[])
        {
        // TODO: Add code here to start your service.

         timer1->Enabled = true;
        }

        // <summary>
        // Stop this service.
        // </summary>
        void OnStop()
        {
// TODO: Add code here to perform any tear-down necessary
// to stop your service.
                timer1->Enabled = false;
        }
        private: System::Diagnostics::EventLog *  eventLog1;
        private: System::Timers::Timer *  timer1;

        private:
        // <summary>
```

```
              // Required designer variable.
              // </summary>
              System::ComponentModel::Container *components;

              // <summary>
              // Required method for Designer support - do not modify
              // the contents of this method with the code editor.
              // </summary>
       void InitializeComponent(void)
       {
          this->eventLog1 = new System::Diagnostics::EventLog();
          this->timer1 = new System::Timers::Timer();
          (__try_cast<System::ComponentModel::ISupportInitialize * >↵
(this->eventLog1))->BeginInit();
          (__try_cast<System::ComponentModel::ISupportInitialize * >↵
(this->timer1))->BeginInit();
                      //
                      // eventLog1
                      //
          this->eventLog1->Source = S"CWService";
                      //
                      // timer1
                      //
          this->timer1->Interval = 10000;
          this->timer1->Elapsed += new ↵
System::Timers::ElapsedEventHandler(this, timer1_Elapsed);
                      //
                      // CWServiceWinService
                      //
          this->CanPauseAndContinue = true;
          this->ServiceName = S"CWService";
          (__try_cast<System::ComponentModel::ISupportInitialize * >↵
(this->eventLog1))->EndInit();
          (__try_cast<System::ComponentModel::ISupportInitialize * >↵
(this->timer1))->EndInit();

          }

       private: System::Void timer1_Elapsed(System::Object * sender, ↵
 System::Timers::ElapsedEventArgs * e)
             {
                ibuf = sprintf(buf, "%s", "Number of words in file = ");
                cntWords = countwords("d:\\testfile");
```

```
        sprintf(buf + ibuf, "%d", cntWords);
        eventLog1->WriteEntry("CWService", (LPSTR)buf);
    }


    };
}
```

If you only glance at the listing, you will wonder where the function that processes the file is. We put this function in the cw.dll dynamic link library and named it countwords. The function is written in the assembler and counts words in a file. The DLL is linked to the service with these lines:

```
using namespace System::Runtime::InteropServices;
[DllImport("cw.dll")]
 extern "C" int countwords(char* path)
```

Counting words and writing the result to the log are done in the timer handler:

```
ibuf = sprintf(buf, "%s", "Number of words in file = ");
cntWords = countwords("d:\\testfile");
sprintf(buf + ibuf, "%d", cntWords);
eventLog1->WriteEntry("CWService", (LPSTR)buf);
```

For word count, a small text file named testfile is used. As noted earlier, the words are counted with the countwords function from the cw.dll library, and the result is stored in the cntWords variable. A formatted string with the result is written to the application log.

The source code of the cw.dll dynamic link library is shown in Listing 15.5.

Listing 15.5. The source code of cw.dll

```
// cw.cpp : Defines the entry point for the DLL application

#include "stdafx.h"
#include <windows.h>

BOOL APIENTRY DllMain( HANDLE hModule,
                       DWORD  ul_reason_for_call,
                       LPVOID lpReserved
                                          )
{
    return TRUE;
```

```
}

extern "C" __declspec(dllexport) int countwords(char* path)
  {
    HANDLE hIn;
    DWORD bytesRead, lenFile;
    int cntWords = 0;
    char buf[2048];

    hIn = CreateFile(path, GENERIC_READ, 0,
    NULL, OPEN_EXISTING, 0, NULL);
    lenFile = GetFileSize (hIn, NULL);

    ReadFile(hIn, buf, lenFile, &bytesRead, NULL);
    CloseHandle(hIn);
    _asm {
         lea  ESI, buf
         mov  EDX, bytesRead
         dec  ESI
         inc  EDX
         //
check_space:
         inc  ESI
         dec  EDX
         jz   ex
         cmp  BYTE PTR [ESI], ' '
         je   check_space
         cmp  BYTE PTR [ESI], 0xd
         je   check_space
         cmp  BYTE PTR [ESI], 0xa
         je   check_space
         jmp  next_char
next_char:
         inc  ESI
         dec  EDX
```

```
            jz    ex
            cmp   BYTE PTR [ESI], ' '
            je    inc_cntWords
            cmp   BYTE PTR [ESI], 0xd
            je    inc_cntWords
            cmp   BYTE PTR [ESI], 0xa
            je    inc_cntWords
            jmp   next_char
inc_cntWords:
            inc   cntWords
            jmp   check_space
ex:
            mov   EAX, cntWords
        }
    }
```

The parameter of the `countwords` function is a pointer to a character string containing the name of the text file. The contents of the file are written to a memory buffer with the size of 2K. Keep in mind that the size of the file must not be greater than the size of the buffer, and the latter can be chosen at will.

Then, the words in the buffer are looked for. The search algorithm assumes that the words are separated with spaces or carriage-return characters, which is the most frequent case. The source code of DLL is straightforward.

Note the following information about starting the `CWService` system service. It is installed from the command line:

```
cwservice.exe –install
```

and deinstalled with the command:

```
cwservice.exe –install /u
```

After installation, the service is started or stopped as always, i.e., with MMC. You can monitor the work of the `CWService` service by looking through the event log (Fig. 5.12).

The contents of the `testfile` text file are shown in Fig. 15.13.

In this chapter, we provided specific examples regarding use of the assembler for programming procedure-oriented applications and Windows system services. Despite their complexity, we believe they will be useful to you.

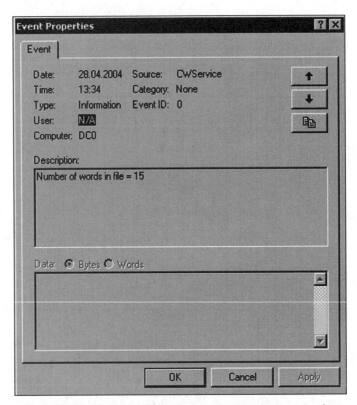

Fig. 15.12. Message from the CWService system service

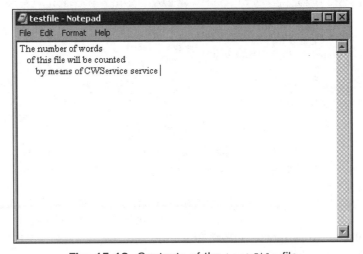

Fig. 15.13. Contents of the testfile file

Conclusion

In this book, I tried to present much information on using assembly language for programming applications in the Microsoft Visual C++ .NET 2003 development environment. In conclusion, I would like to make a few additional notes concerning the material of this book. Despite the broad range of issues covered in this book, a few topics remain untouched. Nevertheless, I hope the book will be useful to readers.

In fact, most of the assembly applications are written in Microsoft MASM. Considering that the same macro assembler is used in the C++ .NET development environment, the examples in this book use the syntax of MASM. This does not mean that you cannot use other stand-alone assembly compilers. I recommend that you try other tools for programming in assembly language, such as NASM, which is a very good assembler.

By using assembly language, you can significantly improve the performance of your C++ .NET applications, and the cost will be much less than for other optimization methods. You can also write full-featured graphics applications in assembly language, with the help of such powerful development tools as MASM32 or AsmStudio available now.

They make it possible to create applications in assembly language quickly and with good quality. Although stand-alone packages for programming in assembly language have certain advantages, the development of large applications with these packages requires much more time than with high level languages.

Stand-alone assembly compilers are very effective when writing individual modules and linking them to applications written in high-level languages such as C++ .NET. Unfortunately, Microsoft and other major manufacturers of development tools for Windows do not develop stand-alone assembly compilers any longer. A good alternative is third-party products such as NASM. One of the reasons for abandoning assembly compilers by major companies is that assembly language has become a part of high-level language development environments.

Although the inline assembler of high-level languages is not an independent development tool, it is very effective for creating fast programs. I hope the examples of using the Visual C++ .NET inline assembler convinced you to use this language in your programs.

I also hope this book will become a handbook for many programmers, both novice and experienced.

On the CD-ROM

The accompanying CD-ROM contains the source code of all the projects described in this book. These projects were compiled and built using the Microsoft Visual C++ .NET 2003 integrated development environment and a free assembly compiler MASM version 8 that includes Microsoft ML 6.14 compiler and LINK 5.12 linker.

All the programs on the CD-ROM were tested in the Windows 2000/XP/2003 operating systems and are fully operable. Most of the programs will work in Windows 98/ME without any limitations and changes. It is desirable that the latest package updates for the Windows 2000/XP operating system are installed on your computer.

To debug the programs, install the Visual C++ .NET 2003 package and its updates on your computer.

All the examples are located in the folders corresponding to the chapters of this book.

The DivX511Bundle.exe file shows video about the A-List Publsihing books. To watch this file, install Standard DivX Codec(FREE) available for free download from **http://www.divx.com/divx/**.

Index